Jesus said, "If you hold to my teaching,
you are really my disciples.
Then you will know the truth,
and the truth will set you free."
JOHN 8:31-32

It gave me great joy
to have some brothers come and tell
about your faithfulness to the truth
and how you continue to walk in the truth.
3 JOHN 3

KNOW the TRUTh

REVISED EDITION

A HANDBOOK OF CHRISTIAN BELIEF

FOREWORD BY
J. I. PACKER

BRUCE MILNE

InterVarsity Press
Downers Grove, Illinois

InterVarsity Press
P.O. Box 1400, Downers Grove, IL 60515
World Wide Web: www.ivpress.com
E-mail: mail@ivpress.com

InterVarsity Press® is the book-publishing division of InterVarsity Christian Fellowship/USA®, a student
movement active on campus at hundreds of universities, colleges and schools of nursing in the United States
of America, and a member movement of the International Fellowship of Evangelical Students. For
information about local and regional activities, write Public Relations Dept., InterVarsity Christian
Fellowship/USA, 6400 Schroeder Rd., P.O. Box 7895, Madison, WI 53707-7895.

Cover illustration: Roberta Polfus

ISBN 0-8308-1793-X

Printed in the United States of America ♻

Library of Congress Cataloging-in-Publication Data

Milne, Bruce.
    Know the truth : a handbook of Christian belief / Bruce Milne;
foreword by J.I. Packer. — 2nd ed.
        p. cm.
    Includes bibliographical references and index.
    ISBN 0-8308-1793-X (pbk. : alk. paper)
    1. Theology, Doctrinal. I. Title.
BT75.2.M49 1999
230—dc21   99-10869
                                                                            CIP

20	19	18	17	16	15	14	13	12	11	10	9	8	7	6	5	4	3	2
15	14	13	12	11	10	09	08	07	06	05	04	03	02	01	00	99		

Contents

Foreword

The chaplain used to take chapel-going undergraduates for pastoral walks, which is how I came to be shambling along beside him that raw afternoon in my first term. He was urging me to read theology, the subject which he himself taught, as a sequel to the classics degree on which I had embarked. I explained to him that I would rather not, since theology was so bad for one's soul. 'Nonsense!' exploded he, with what may have been the loudest snort in history; 'theology's the queen of the sciences!' Then he fell silent, and so did I, and thus we finished our walk. I thought him unenlightened. What he thought about me is not on record. But he had every reason to feel miffed. He was right, and knew enough to know that he was right, and I was as wrong as an opinionated ignoramus of eighteen could possibly be. In my time I have dropped clangers in abundance, but none so daft or discourteous as what I said that afternoon.

Why did I talk such twaddle? The awful truth is that, as a Christian of about six weeks' standing, I was regurgitating what I had heard in the Christian Union that was nurturing me. No doubt there was some excuse for dark suspicions. In the war years Oxbridge theology was not at its best, and, as sad experience shows, bad theology infects the heart with misbelief and unbelief, the spiritual equivalents of multiple sclerosis. Many who ran well have been progressively paralysed through ingesting bad theology, and the danger remains. Also, theological expertise can feed intellectual pride, turning one into a person who cares more for knowing true notions than for knowing the true God, and that is disastrous too. But this only shows how a good thing can be spoiled. *Corruptio optimi pessima* (corruption of what is best is the worst corruption); nevertheless, *abusus non tollit usum* (misuse does not take away right use). Thankfully I record that by God's mercy I saw in due course that I had been talking through my hat, and I followed classics with theology, after all – a move that I never regretted, and would not hesitate to recommend to anyone else.

It has been said that a habit of personal Bible study makes the study of theology unnecessary. But in fact you penalize yourself as a Bible student by not studying theology, for theology (that is, an overall grasp of Bible teaching) enriches Bible study enormously. How? By enabling you to see more of what is there in each passage. As the effect of knowing botany is that you notice more flora and fauna on a country walk, and the effect of knowing electronics is that you see more of what you are looking at when you take apart your TV, so the effect of knowing theology is that, other things being equal, you see further into the meaning and implications of Bible passages than you would do otherwise. The ultimate context of each scriptural sentence is the whole Bible, by which I mean not only sixty-six books but also biblical teaching; and the better one knows one's Bible in this double sense, the deeper one will see into what particular texts involve. That good theology grows by induction out of Bible study, and must always be taught with reference to its biblical base, is familiar truth. Less familiar, but not less true, is the converse, that Bible study is informed by theology.

This is the case also with Christian witness, which in Scripture means not just relating experience, excellent as that practice is, but primarily proclaiming the Creator as Redeemer, and Jesus Christ as risen Saviour. What has to be said about God and the Son comes from Scripture, but theological study will enable us to see it, and therefore say it, more clearly than would otherwise be possible.

Historical theology too is important here, for learning with and from saints of past days is one dimension of fellowship in the body of Christ, and the great Bible students of yesterday

(Augustine, Luther, Calvin, Owen, Edwards and the rest) often have richer insight into key themes than do their current counterparts. And since, as has been truly said, it is beyond the wit of man to invent a new heresy, it is a great help to know the old ones, so that one can spot them when they reappear in modern make-up.

Which books of theology will help us most at these points? For years I have been getting help from Calvin's 1559 *Institutes of the Christian Religion* (1300 pages), which from its second edition on was explicitly tailored to help Bible students and teachers in living and witnessing for God. It still does the job marvellously for those who can take it, but there is no denying that not all Christian stomachs can digest so mountainous a meal. Dr Milne's book, however, on its smaller scale, could hardly be bettered for our purpose. I wish it long life and big sales; it merits both. The words *Tolle; lege* ('Take and read'), which Augustine heard over the garden wall and which led him to a saving encounter with the Bible, are my words to thoughtful Bible students regarding *Know the Truth*. Try it; you'll like it, and you'll get great benefit too. It is a privilege to commend so sensible, clear and fruitful an overview of basic Christian belief.

J. I. PACKER

Preface to the first edition

It would be quite impossible to list all those who have had some part in the shaping of this book: my parents who by precept and example first pointed me to the truth of God; the members of my former congregation in Scotland and the churches where I have had opportunities to minister in this country and overseas; the many students I have been privileged to teach in this College over the years, as well as members of my evening classes in the University of London Extra-Mural Department; my friends and colleagues on the staff of Spurgeon's College; and, in particular, all those who read the manuscript at some stage of its production and offered valuable comments and criticisms. None of these, of course, bears any responsibility for the views expressed in the book, which are in the end my own, though I dare hope not only mine. My thanks are also due to Kingsway Publications for permission to include some material in Part 7 which appears in fuller form in *What the Bible Says about the End of the World*, my contribution to their Bible Teaching Series. Finally I would like to pay special tribute to my wife, who, as well as giving encouragement throughout the various stages of production, typed two entire drafts of the manuscript, one of which was considerably longer than its final form.

It is my earnest prayer that Almighty God may be pleased to use these pages to reveal more of the greatness and power of his truth as it is made known in Holy Scripture, and hence that he, our blessed and glorious Lord, may be magnified. To him be the glory for ever.

Spurgeon's College   BRUCE MILNE

Preface to the new edition

It is a delight to write a few lines as this revised edition of *Know the Truth* goes into circulation. During the years since its first appearance in 1982, as I have travelled to many parts of the world, it has been immensely gratifying to be approached by Christian leaders and former students who have testified to finding help in its pages. These years have seen significant changes in the Christian community, and brought the world at large to the brink of a new millennium. This revision is an attempt to reflect a little of that changed context. For me the period since its first publication has been largely spent giving leadership and expounding Scripture to a wonderfully warm and hugely diverse Christian community at the heart of a beautiful, but deeply secularized, North American city. The experiences of these years have served only to deepen my convictions regarding the truth and relevance of the things *Know the Truth* seeks to express. May the Holy Spirit be pleased to use this new edition to God's further praise.

Vancouver   BRUCE MILNE

Introduction

'Of course, I'm no theologian.' How often have I heard that comment over the years, not infrequently from those who ought to know better! It usually implies that serious thinking about Christian beliefs and the attempt to express them in an ordered form are altogether distinct from real Christianity, which is about practical concerns: our personal walk with the Lord, sharing the gospel, and so on. While the theologians may have their place, the serious study of doctrine is seen as something which need not bother ordinary Christians, and indeed may even hinder their Christian life if they go into it too deeply.

This prevalent anti-doctrine spirit is a major departure from the Christian instincts of earlier ages and its roots go deep into contemporary western culture. In face of the tremendous challenges and opportunities facing the church today this dismissal of doctrine is, in my judgment, nothing short of a recipe for disaster.

Why then is the study of doctrine so vital?

First, as a matter of plain fact every Christian *is* a theologian! Theology literally means 'the science of God', or more fully, 'thought and speech which issue from a knowledge of God' (*cf.* 1 Cor. 1:5). By virtue of being born again we have all begun to know God and therefore have a certain understanding of his nature and actions. That is, we all have a theology of sorts, whether or not we have ever sat down and pieced it together. So, properly understood, theology is *not* for a few religious eggheads with a flair for abstract debate – it is everybody's business. Once we have grasped this, our duty is to become the best theologians we can to the glory of God, as our understanding of God and his ways is clarified and deepened through studying the book he has given for that very purpose, the Bible (2 Tim. 3:16). This handbook is written with the simple aim of helping you do that.

Secondly, getting doctrine right is the key to getting everything else right. If we are to know who God is, who we are, and what God wants of us, we need to study Scripture. That means its teaching as a whole, and that means doctrine. This holds true for every single area of the Christian life, worship (Jn. 4:23), witnessing (Acts 17:11), discipleship (Jn. 8:31f.), Christian relationships (1 Cor. 12:12), daily work (Eph. 6:5–9); at every point right living begins with right thinking. The NT writers exemplify this principle. Faced with practical problems in the churches, they always sought first to clarify the theological issues underlying the problem, then to apply the practical remedy. In this profound sense doctrine is the key to life; the Holy Spirit uses God's truth in his work in and through us.

Of course correct doctrine in itself is not enough; it is tragically possible to fail to work God's truth out in practical obedience. That is one reason why doctrine often gets a bad press. If correct doctrine does not lead to holy, loving, mature lives, something has gone terribly wrong. But that is no reason for neglecting or discounting it. In an effort to drive this point home, I have concluded each Part of the handbook with a section of application. These are by no means exhaustive; their significance lies in what they attempt to demonstrate, that correct doctrine is the basis for correct living.

Thirdly, the study of doctrine is an expression of loving the Lord with our minds (Mt. 22:37). True thinking and understanding are as valid an expression of our response to God as true actions and true speech, and as significant in bringing glory to the God of truth. At a time when for many practice is the test of truth, there is need to stress that the pursuit of truth itself is God-honouring.

Fourthly, doctrine is vital because it is impossible finally to separate Christ from the truths which Scripture reveals concerning him. There is no other Christ than the Christ who is known through the truths and doctrines of the whole Bible. He comes to us, as Calvin used to say, 'clothed in his gospel'. Hence loyalty to his person inevitably involves commitment to the truths about him. And conversely, carelessness or indifference concerning these biblical doctrines is a form of disloyalty to his name and unconcern for his honour.

These four arguments are not alternatives but complements. Their combined message is simple and inescapable: *doctrine matters.* 'Do your best to present yourself to God as one approved, a workman . . . who correctly handles the word of truth' (2 Tim. 2:15).

This handbook is concerned with the major areas of Christian doctrine as they have been formulated over the centuries. It is aimed primarily at the thoughtful Christian who wants to know more of what the Bible teaches and a little of how the doctrines in question have been stated over the centuries, as well as something of current trends. The dominant concern has been to expound the Bible's teaching. The principal passages of Scripture dealing with each theme are listed after each block of teaching; some readers may prefer to begin with the Scripture passages and work back to the doctrine. Questions are also set after each section to stimulate reflection and aid revision. An introductory reading list covering each area has also been added to direct and encourage further study.

General bibliography

Doctrinal

L. Berkhof, *Systematic Theology* (Banner of Truth, 1959).
J. M. Boice, *Foundations of the Christian Faith* (IVP, 1986).
G. Bray (ed.), Contours of Christian Theology series (IVP, 1993–).
J. Calvin, *Institutes of the Christian Religion*.
S. B. Ferguson *et al.* (eds.), *New Dictionary of Theology* (IVP, 1988).
S. J. Grenz, *Created for Community* (Victor/BridgePoint, 1996).
W. Grudem, *Systematic Theology* (IVP, 1994).
T. C. Hammond, *In Understanding Be Men* (IVP, 6th edn, 1968).
C. Hodge, *Systematic Theology* (James Clarke, 1960).
J. I. Packer, *God's Words* (IVP, 1981).
G. Vos, *Biblical Theology* (Banner of Truth, 1976).

Historical

L. Berkhof, *The History of Christian Doctrines* (Banner of Truth, 1969).
G. C. Berkouwer, *A Half Century of Theology* (Eerdmans, 1977).
G. W. Bromiley, *Historical Theology: an Introduction* (T. & T. Clark, 1978).
S. J. Grenz and R. E. Olson, *20-Century Theology* (Blackwells, 1992).
J. N. D. Kelly, *Early Christian Doctrines* (A. & C. Black, 5th edn, 1977).
J. G. Machen, *Christianity and Liberalism* (Eerdmans, 1946).
J. Orr, *The Progress of Dogma* (Eerdmans, 1962).

Abbreviations

Books of the Old Testament: Gn., Ex., Lv., Nu., Dt., Jos., Jdg., Ru., 1, 2 Sa., 1, 2 Ki., 1, 2 Ch., Ezr., Ne., Est., Jb., Ps. (Pss.), Pr., Ec., Song, Is., Je., La., Ezk., Dn., Ho., Joel, Am., Ob., Jon., Mi., Na., Hab., Zp., Hg., Zc., Mal.

Books of the New Testament: Mt., Mk., Lk., Jn., Acts, Rom., 1, 2 Cor., Gal., Eph., Phil., Col., 1, 2 Thes., 1, 2 Tim., Tit., Phm., Heb., Jas., 1, 2 Pet., 1 2, 3 Jn., Jude, Rev.

AV	Authorized, or King James, Version (1611)
cf.	Compare
Gk.	Greek
Heb.	Hebrew
IBD	*The Illustrated Bible Dictionary* (IVP, 1980)
Lat.	Latin
NDT	*New Dictionary of Theology* (IVP, 1988).
NEB	New English Bible, 1970
NIV	New International Version, 1984
NT	New Testament
OT	Old Testament
PRPC	Presbyterian and Reformed Publishing Company
RSV	Revised Standard Version, 1952, 1971
RV	Revised Version, 1885

PART 1
The final authority in matters of faith

1. Authority

'If people don't know Jesus they simply don't know God at all, and that's that. There's no way to experience peace with God except by Jesus.'

'I'm sorry, but with the greatest respect I have to disagree with you. Jesus is the centre of it, for sure, but God has revealed himself in lots of other ways. I have a friend who is into New Age and she says she really feels God within her.'

Issues like these are discussed constantly among Christians today. But in the heat of such exchanges we may fail to notice a more basic disagreement, about religious authority. Should we appeal simply to what we feel personally, or what people claim to experience? Would the findings of students of comparative religion or psychologists of religion have any light to shed on this issue? And what about the teaching of the Bible?

Similar questions could be asked about many of the issues constantly debated; the existence of God, reincarnation, tongue-speaking, the resurrection, the Christian and political activism, religious pluralism *etc.* At root the diverse viewpoints adopted are often largely determined by a prior decision, taken consciously or unconsciously, about the seat of religious authority. To raise the question of authority may not resolve the disagreements; but it may clarify the real points of difference and so prevent unnecessary misunderstanding.

Any exposition of basic Christian doctrine needs to begin at this point. How do we decide what *is* correct Christian teaching?

To what can we appeal to resolve differences and conflicts? What is our criterion of truth? These are the questions which must first claim our attention.

THE MEANING OF AUTHORITY

Authority is the right or power to require obedience. There is a widespread crisis of authority in contemporary society where the only authority acceptable to many is one consciously self-imposed.

From the perspective of Christian faith, God has the supreme right and power to require obedience because he is the Creator and Lord of everyone. 'I know God's view of this, but I feel no obligation whatever to conform to it' is a sentiment which true Christians can never share. They may disobey God's will, even deliberately, but always against their better judgment. Their subsequent bad conscience will witness that God's authority remains in operation and continues to be recognized. Authority lies in God.

Once Christians grasp this fundamental principle, the question of authority becomes the practical one of finding God's will and mind on any issue. But how do we encounter God and discover his mind and will? More particularly, has God provided a source from which we may arrive at his truth and thus bring ourselves under his authority?

THE SOURCE OF AUTHORITY

Over the centuries Christians have appealed to a variety of voices as the source of final authority.

The creeds

These summaries of Christian truth were produced in the early centuries to state the essence of the faith in a time of theological confusion. The Apostles' Creed[1] is the oldest and best known, and therefore has a strong claim to authority. It certainly provides a useful series of pegs on which to hang expositions of the Christian faith, but it will not serve as the final source and standard of Christian truth. First, it is too general. It has value in checking extreme viewpoints, but does not provide a full enough

---

1. The title is somewhat misleading. This creed probably dates from the third century and was a summary of the faith learned by baptismal candidates.

statement of the doctrines in question. Secondly, its claim to authority rests on something earlier and more primitive, the teaching of Jesus Christ and his apostles.

The historic confessions
These statements of the Christian faith belong to the Reformation and post-Reformation period, *e.g.* the 39 Articles (1571) and the Westminster Confession (1647). These are much fuller than the creeds but again will not do as final authorities. First, they are 'party' statements reflecting views of one branch of the universal church, and therefore contain elements which could not command the support of other branches. Further, they too are 'secondary' statements. A cursory glance shows that they consciously justify their assertions by appeal to biblical teaching.

The mind of the church
According to this approach, God's presence in the church implies that his mind can be discovered by consulting the main trend of Christian opinion, the 'mind of the church'. While we should not dismiss out of hand fellow Christians' beliefs and convictions, there are major difficulties in adopting this as our ultimate norm. The 'Christian consensus' is extraordinarily difficult to nail. Whom do we listen to: theologians, clergy, church commissions, average lay opinion, or what? Further, if this 'mind' is our ultimate authority, any conflict of opinion brings us to an impasse since there is no authority beyond it. Again, what do we make of the fact that over the centuries the 'consensus' of opinion in the church has been neither invariably faithful to 'the faith that was entrusted to the saints' (Jude 3) nor consistent with the consensus in other ages?[2]

Christian experience
This approach begins with actual human experience of God and tries to identify the doctrines expressed by that experience. Many influential nineteenth-century theologians followed this path. It suffers from two crucial difficulties. Within our experience of

---

2. Roman Catholicism claims that Christ established a teaching office in the person of Peter and his successors as bishop of Rome; hence the papacy represents the voice of God. Some of the above-mentioned difficulties apply to this claim; objections to the Roman view will be examined more closely in Part 6.

God, we somehow have to distinguish between objective truth about God and our own subjective opinions, limited and biased; this difficulty is seriously compounded by our being fallen creatures with fallen minds. It also limits Christian truth, ruling out anything beyond our immediate experience, *e.g.* the doctrine of the Trinity.

Christian reason

This approach claims that Christian truth consists in what we can demonstrate about God by logical reasoning, and has had its advocates since the third century. Few would entirely exclude rational considerations in formulating Christian truth; but it will not serve as our ultimate authority. Fallen humanity's perception of truth, particularly in the moral and spiritual sphere, is severely limited; the mind of the creature cannot measure the Creator; and this approach always fails to capture the vitality of authentic biblical religion.

The 'inner voice'

Some claim that God speaks directly in the depths of our consciousness and that this 'voice within' is the ultimate source of authority. This view is common today, being frequently interpreted as the prompting of the Holy Spirit. Of course, it includes an element of truth; the Holy Spirit does fulfil a crucial role in the Christian understanding of authority, but he works essentially in and through the Scriptures. Any specific claim to his prompting should be treated with instinctive scepticism if it makes no reference to the written Word of God or receives no confirmation through the experience of one's own church or group. The sincerity of many making such claims must not obscure the immense dangers of self-delusion here. The records of many Christian counsellors provide ample evidence of the spiritual shipwreck repeatedly made on this reef.

The ultimate source

None of these is adequate to bring us God's mind and hence be the authoritative source of Christian truth, but each makes a contribution. The creeds, confessions and the 'mind of the church' stress our place in the worldwide, centuries-old church of Jesus Christ; we would obviously be wise to weigh its testimonies with care. Christian experience reminds us that doctrine is never merely intellectual, while Christian reason insists we state our doctrines in accordance with our creaturely ways of communicating. *The ultimate source of authority, however, is the triune God himself, as he is made known to us through the words of the Bible.* This combines three truths.

1. God has taken the initiative. We learn of him and come under his direct authority because of his decision to make himself and his will known to us. This process is called 'revelation'.

2. God has come to us himself in Jesus Christ, the God-man. As the eternal Word and Wisdom of God, Jesus Christ is the mediator of all our knowledge of God (*cf.* Jn. 1:1f.; 14:6–9; 1 Cor. 1:30; Col. 2:3, Rev. 19:13).

3. Our knowledge of God comes through the Bible. He has caused it to be written and through it speaks to us today as he spoke to his people when those words were first given. The Bible is to be received as God's words to us and revered and obeyed as such. As we submit to its authority we place ourselves under the authority of the living God who is made known to us supremely in Jesus Christ. This terse statement of the ultimate source of authority will be amplified below.

Scriptures
Gn. 1:1; Jb. 40:1–5; 42:1–6; Ps. 95:6; Is. 40:21–23; 45:9; Rom. 9:19f.; 11:33–36; Eph. 1:11; Rev. 4:9–11.

Questions
1. State the Christian view of authority.
2. Explore the implications of this view for (a) Christians working at all levels of education, (b) questions of law and order, (c) a Christian approach to the arts.
3. Summarize the strengths and weaknesses of the various claimants to final authority in the sphere of Christian truth.
4. Outline the advice you would give a Christian seeking to know God's will in a specific matter.

Bibliography
Arts. 'Authority' in *IBD* and *NDT*.
D. A. Carson and J. D. Woodbridge (eds.), *Scripture and Truth* (IVP, 1983).
C. F. H. Henry, *God, Revelation and Authority* 1 and 2 (Word Books, 1976).
H. Heppe, *Reformed Dogmatics* (Baker, 1978).
B. Ramm, *The Pattern of Religious Authority* (Eerdmans, 1957).
P. Schaff, *The Creeds of Christendom* (Baker, 1977).

2. Revelation

THE SIGNIFICANCE OF REVELATION

Revelation means unveiling something hidden, so that it may be seen and known for what it is. The principal OT word, *gala*, comes from a root meaning 'nakedness' (*cf.* Ex. 20:26), but is frequently used metaphorically: in Isaiah 53:1 God's arm is literally 'made naked' in his work of salvation (*cf.* Is. 52:10); 2 Samuel 7:27, 'you have revealed this to your servant', is literally 'you have made naked your servant's ear'. The Greek equivalent, *apokalyptō*, is used in the NT only in the developed theological sense of making known religious realities (*cf.* Lk. 10:21; Eph. 3:5).

These terms spell out what is implied every time the Bible refers to God's speaking to and relating himself to men and women; biblical religion is a religion of revelation, a faith based on the claim that God has come to us and disclosed himself. If we are to know God, revelation is indispensable for two complementary reasons.

We are creatures

'In the beginning God created . . . man' (Gn. 1:1, 27). These first words of the Bible express the distinction between God and humankind. God as the Creator exists freely apart from ourselves; the creature depends utterly on God for existence (*cf.* man and woman as 'dust' in Gn. 2:7; 3:19; Ps. 103:14). God and humankind therefore belong to different orders of being.[1]

This distinction is not absolute. We are made 'in the image of God'; God communicates with us (Gn. 1:28; *etc.*); God became a human being in the Lord Jesus Christ (Jn. 1:1, 14); God the Spirit indwells Christians and brings them into a personal relationship to God (Rom. 8:9–17). All these factors confirm a degree of correspondence between God and humanity. Yet a profound, irreducible distinction remains.

This distinction in *being* involves a distinction in *knowing*: 'who among men knows the thoughts of a man except the man's spirit within him? In the same way no-one knows the thoughts

---

1. The technical term for this kind of distinction is *ontological*; it is a distinction in *being*.

of God except the Spirit of God' (1 Cor. 2:11). Only God truly knows God. Since God is Creator and Lord of humankind, his knowledge includes our self-knowledge (Ps. 139:2f.); *but* our knowledge does not include God's self-knowledge.[2] Our creaturehood, therefore, requires God to reveal himself if we are to have adequate knowledge of him. Even unfallen Adam needed to be personally addressed by God before he could know God's will (Gn. 1:28ff.; 2:16f.).

We are sinners
Our need of revelation is immeasurably increased by our sinfulness. The fall has affected every aspect of our being, not least our perception of moral and spiritual reality. Sin renders us spiritually blind and ignorant of God (Rom. 1:18; 1 Cor. 1:21; 2 Cor. 4:4; Eph. 2:1f.; 4:18).

There is therefore no road from our intellectual and moral perception to a genuine knowledge of God. The only way to knowledge of God is for God freely to place himself within range of our perception, and renew our fallen understanding. Hence, if we are to know God and have any adequate basis for our Christian understanding and experience, revelation is indispensable.

THE LIKELIHOOD OF REVELATION
If God is our Creator, revelation in some form is overwhelmingly probable since we may presume that God made us for a purpose; and since his creatures are obviously responsive beings with inherent tendencies for relationship, we may also presume that God's purpose in creating us involved some kind of relationship and response to himself. Such a relationship and response require revelation in some form; creation itself, therefore, appears to imply revelation. Indeed, would a patently wise, intelligent Creator leave his creatures to grope in the dark for some clue to his existence without making himself known? The thought is palpably absurd.

If we suppose further, as many do vaguely, that the Creator God is loving, the likelihood of revelation becomes overwhelming; no loving parent would deliberately keep out of a

---

2. The technical term for this kind of distinction is *epistemological*; it is a distinction in *knowing*.

child's sight and range of reference so that it grew up ignorant of its parent's existence. Although we cannot equate human loving with God's love, we can presume a sufficient degree of identity to render a deliberate, total self-effacement on God's part a denial of love. Owing to the fall our capacity to perceive and profit fully from such revelation is sharply qualified, however, as we shall see below.

GENERAL REVELATION

Theologians usually distinguish two main branches of revelation: 'general' and 'special'. *General* revelation is a revelation of God made to all people everywhere. It has a number of forms and features.

Creation

In Romans 1:18–32 Paul explains God's judgment on the Gentile (non-Jewish) world of his day. God has 'given them over' (1:24, 26, 28) to the self-destructive tendencies of their fallen natures because 'although they knew God, they neither glorified him as God nor gave thanks to him' (1:21). But they 'exchanged the glory of the immortal God ... exchanged the truth of God for a lie ... did not think it worth while to retain the knowledge of God' (1:23, 25, 28). This lost knowledge of God consisted of their recognizing 'God's invisible qualities – his eternal power and divine nature [which] have been clearly seen, being understood from what has been made' (1:20). Accordingly they are 'without any excuse' (1:20). This revelation of God dates from 'creation of the world' (1:20); it seems, therefore, that Paul sees the created order as God's revelation to all people of his eternal power and deity, which obliges them to acknowledge God and give glory and thanks to him (1:20f.). In Acts 14:17 Paul informs the pagans in Lystra that God 'has not left himself without testimony'; this is confirmed by his kindness in 'giving you rain from heaven and crops in their seasons; he provides plenty of food and fills your hearts with joy'. Acts 17:26f. refers to the Creator's ordering of the affairs of individuals and of nations 'so that men would seek him and perhaps reach out for him and find him'.

Moral experience

Romans 2:14f. states that 'when Gentiles, who do not have the

[OT] law, do by nature things required by the law ... they show that the requirements of the law are written on their hearts, their consciences also bearing witness, and their thoughts now accusing, now even defending them'. Thus the conflicts of the human conscience are relevant to the issues of God's final judgment (Rom. 2:16, *cf.* 1:32). The OT prophets frequently speak of God's just judgments on the Gentile nations, although these nations had not been taught the OT law (*e.g.* Je. 46–51; Am. 1:6 – 2:3). The NT recognizes that the non-Christian conscience is qualified to judge Christians' general behaviour (*e.g.* 1 Tim. 3:7; 1 Pet. 2:12). Indeed the moral appeal of the gospel, its assertion that all have sinned (Rom. 3:9–23), its call to repentance (Acts 17:30), its interpretation of the work of Christ in moral terms (Rom. 3:21–26; 1 Cor. 15:3) all imply a genuine continuity between universal moral experience and that of the believer; this in turn implies some awareness of God's will on the part of non-Christians.

These biblical references confirm the fact that God has revealed himself to all in the conflicts of our moral experience. This is not invalidated by discrepancies between human moral codes. While God reveals himself in the conscience of the non-Christian, owing to the fall the non-Christian's knowledge of God's will is by no means perfect. Sin causes a moral obtuseness which distorts all our consciousness of God and his will. The dictates of the non-Christian conscience are not therefore 'God's voice within' in an unambiguous sense. Our point is the limited but crucial one, that 'God has not left himself without testimony'; under all the conflicts of human moral experience, we all have some awareness that the sense of obligation to do good and to spurn evil reflects the will of an ultimate Lord to whom we are finally responsible.

This does not 'prove' God's existence, any more than general revelation from creation does. Rather, Scripture claims that *in fact* God gives some witness to himself to all people in these dimensions of their experience, whether or not this can be verified by rational deduction.

We can briefly mention one other aspect of general revelation which is sometimes referred to, though its biblical basis is less certain.

Universal religious sense

The instinct for worship appears to be a universal human phenomenon. Anthropologists have yet to uncover any people, no matter how primitive, who lack a sense of awe before the supernatural. Calvin referred to a 'sense of deity' which is implanted in the human heart, and Luther asserted that 'Human beings must have God or an idol'. John 1:9 is referred to in support of this form of general revelation; *cf.* also Psalm 139:1–18.

The dynamic factor

God's revelation, however, is not detached and objective like a museum exhibit. Rather it is a dynamic ongoing reality; God repeatedly reveals himself, humankind repeatedly resists, obscuring and misusing the revelation (Rom. 1:21–28). Hence only in an attitude of utter submission and obedience can God's revelation be truly encountered. When people refuse to adopt that attitude they may close the door to further revelation (*e.g.* Mt. 25:29; Lk. 8:18; *cf.* Herod in Mk. 6:21–28 and Lk. 23:9).

A person who repeatedly resists God's revelation may eventually become incapable of recognizing or responding to it. The Bible is not unacquainted with the 'secular person' who shows no sense of the reality of God. What the Bible *does* assert is that God is just. He reveals himself to all people at some point or points in their total life pilgrimage. When that light is resisted and the heart hardened against it, the light may be removed.

Since as sinners we all in practice constantly react against God's revelation in just this way, despite the evidence it offers of God's goodness and love for us, one of the profoundest comments to be made about us is simply that we are fools (Ps. 14:1; Rom. 1:22).

Its effects

If general revelation suffers from all these limitations, what significance does it have?

First, it reflects the goodness of God. The stabilizing of human society due to the sanction of the moral law is a fruit of general revelation. Our sense of moral obligation, whereby good and evil are distinguished, evil held in check, and human life in general enabled to function tolerably without being submerged in uninhibited outbursts of wickedness, is due finally to this revelation of God, however little it may be acknowledged.

Second, due to human fallenness, in practice it renders us guilty before God. God has not left himself without testimony. In the totality of their life experience God addresses all people. If the light he gives is extinguished, the responsibility for the subsequent darkness remains theirs. 'Let God be true though every man be false' (Rom. 3:4, RSV). Thus the people of Lystra are challenged with making the 'kindness of God' an occasion for idolatry (Acts 14:11–18).

This truth is particularly important for Christian evangelism. Everyone is confronted by God and therefore carries responsibility for the lack of a true relationship to him. This universal human guilt is presupposed by the gospel. Of course, people will be judged at the end by the light and opportunity which they had; clearly that is not the same for everyone (Mt. 13:11; Lk. 10:13f.; *cf.* 'Judgment' in Part 7). The Bible, however, teaches clearly that light *is* brought in some measure to all, and all therefore incur guilt for their ignorance of God.

Its limitations

General revelation was insufficient even for unfallen Adam; meaningful relationship with, and knowledge of, God came only when God addressed him directly (Gn. 1:28f.; 2:17f.). Sin ruined this relationship and knowledge, opening up a chasm between our thinking and experience and God's being and nature. General revelation is unable to bridge the chasm. As Paul puts it (1 Cor. 1:21), for all its wisdom the world left to itself does not know God.

Accordingly, since general revelation will not suffice a further and fuller revelation is necessary; if we are to know God 'it remains for God to give witness of himself from heaven' (Calvin).

To summarize, the Bible teaches clearly that 'God has not left himself without a testimony'. We live in God's world as God's creatures; we exist at every moment 'before the eye of God' (Luther). Despite the blinding effects of sin, we cannot plead entire ignorance of God. Through general revelation God has disclosed something of his nature and purposes to humankind.

SPECIAL REVELATION

Special revelation denotes the ways God makes himself known with a clarity and fullness which far surpass general revelation. It is centred in the miracle of the incarnation and mediated through the God-inspired words of the Bible. Special revelation thus assumes more than one form.

Jesus Christ

The supreme form of God's self-disclosure was his becoming incarnate in the person of Jesus Christ (Jn. 1:1f., 14). In this 'grand miracle' (C. S. Lewis) God bridged the gulf separating Creator from creature by himself 'taking the very nature of a servant . . . being found in appearance as a man' (Phil. 2:7, 8). In Jesus Christ God is present in person, and his character and essential nature are revealed to us. 'He who has seen me has seen the Father' (Jn. 14:10). This identity of Father and Son is critical for our knowledge of God. Jesus is not a partial or temporary image of God which needs to be complemented by other images and other pictures from other places and from other times. He is 'the exact representation of God's being' (Heb. 1:3). In Jesus Christ we confront the eternal heart of God. Jesus Christ is therefore the centre and summit of all divine revelation.

Holy Scripture

The Bible will be considered in the sections which follow. Here we simply assert its claim to record God's words to his creatures (Jn. 10:35; Rom. 3:2; 2 Tim. 3:16). These words were originally written and spoken to particular generations, but by his providence they address every generation (Acts 7:38; Rom. 15:4; 1 Cor. 10:11).

The relationship of these forms

These forms cannot be separated. Christ, the incarnate Word, is known through the written Word of God, the Bible. Knowing Christ is, of course, a richer reality than mere acquaintance with Bible teaching about him. But the Christ we know in personal experience is the Christ of the scriptural witness; there is no other Christ. Saving response to Christ means commitment to him in terms of Scripture's testimony to him.

Conversely the written Word cannot be separated from the incarnate Word. The Bible can be properly interpreted only from the perspective of a living faith in Christ who is its central theme, the climax and focus of the entire biblical revelation of God's person and purposes.

A third form?

Some writers refer to a third form of special revelation, the witness borne to the gospel by Christians. This would encompass formal preaching and all kinds of informal Christian witness or teaching. While it cannot be on the same level as Jesus Christ and Scripture, Christian witness does link these primary forms of special revelation with our experience today, as it did in the days of the apostles (Acts 2:37f.; 8:4f., 26ff.; 11:20). Christian preaching and witness, however, can serve God's revelation only when they faithfully express God's Word, incarnate and written.

Redemptive revelation

Special revelation is a tremendous advance upon general revelation; how much more of God is disclosed by the cross of Jesus than by a star-lit sky. However, even special revelation in Christ and Scripture is not sufficient to bring us a full and satisfactory knowledge of God, because of the nature of humankind. Had Adam remained 'upright', special revelation would have been wholly sufficient as it was before the fall (Gn. 2:16). Fallen creatures, however, have an inherent tendency to resist *every* form of God's revelation and turn away from knowing him. Many Jews of Jesus' day rejected both the teaching of Scripture (Mt. 15:6; 22:29) and Christ himself (Jn. 19:15; Acts 7), and every Christian witness has grieved over people's mysterious capacity to resist not only God's general revelation in nature and conscience, but also the word of God, written, incarnate, and preached. We 'suppress' or stifle the truth about God (Rom. 1:18; 2 Cor. 4:4). If one is truly to know God, then, revelation must redeem as well as inform, transform as well as teach.

In the wonder of God's grace that is precisely the character of his special revelation in Christ and Scripture. It records both God's progressive self-revelation and his plan of salvation for us. Its centre lies in the cross where Christ died for our sins (1 Cor. 15:3) to overcome the barrier to our knowing God truly. The Holy Spirit makes Christ's redemption effective, subduing our rebellious wills and opening our blinded eyes to believe the gospel, thus enabling us to enter God's kingdom and truly know him (Jn. 3:1ff.; 15:26; 1 Thes. 1:5; Tit. 3:5).

To summarize, God's revelation has two major parts, a general revelation to all, chiefly through nature and conscience, and special revelation in Jesus Christ and Scripture. Special revelation, however, needs a further subdivision; by some it is rejected, while others receive it through the ministry of the Holy Spirit enabling them to believe in Christ. In this final case we may speak of a true revelation leading to a true knowledge of God.

Scriptures

Revelation in general: Dt. 29:29; Is. 55:8f.; Dn. 2:22; Rom. 1:18; 1 Cor. 1:21; 2:6–14.

Our need for revelation (a) as creatures: Gn. 2:7; Jb. 12:13–25; 42:1–6; Ps. 103:14; *(b) as sinners:* Jb. 37:19; Pss. 73:22; 82:5; Je. 17:9; Acts 17:23, 30; Rom. 1:18–32; 1 Cor. 1:21; 2 Cor. 4:4; Eph. 2:1f.; 4:18.

General revelation: Ps. 19:1f.; Jn. 1:9; Je. 46–51; Am. 1:2–2:5; Rom. 1:19–32; 2:14f.; Acts 14:17; 17:26f.; 2 Cor. 4:2.

Special revelation: Ex. 31:18; 2 Ki. 22; Ps. 19:7–11; Is. 55:11; Je. 20:9; Mk. 7:13; Jn. 1:1–18; 10:35; 14:6; 1 Cor. 1:21, 30; 2 Cor. 4:6; Gal. 1:12; Col. 2.2f.; 2 Tim. 3:16; Heb. 4:12; 2 Pet. 1:21.

The work of the Spirit: Jn. 3:1–16; 14:25; 15:26; 16:13f.; 1 Cor. 2:4–16; Eph. 1:17; 1 Thes. 1:5; 1 Jn. 2:20, 27; 3:24; 5:7f.

Questions

1. 'Only God can be a fit witness concerning himself.' 'We can know God only as he places himself within the reach of our knowledge.' Can these maxims be supported from Scripture? Investigate the implications for the way in which God can be known by us.
2. Distinguish between general and special revelation. Is this a necessary distinction? Can you suggest an alternative terminology?
3. What are the implications of general revelation for (a) evangelism, (b) a Christian view of culture, (c) Christian apologetics, (d) the Christian view of the state?
4. Is there any sense in which God is known in other world religions?
5. In what sense may conscience be a guide to our knowledge of God?
6. Explore the relationship between Christ and Scripture in Christian revelation.
7. What is the function of the Holy Spirit in our coming to know God truly?

Bibliography

Arts. 'Revelation' in *IBD* and *NDT*.

G. C. Berkouwer, *General Revelation* (Eerdmans, 1955).

John Calvin, *Institutes of the Christian Religion*, 1–3.

C. F. H. Henry (ed.), *Revelation and the Bible* (Tyndale Press, 1959).

C. F. H. Henry, *God, Revelation and Authority* 1 and 2 (Word Books, 1976).

L. Morris, *I Believe in Revelation* (Hodder, 1976).

J. I. Packer, *God Has Spoken* (Hodder, 2nd edn, 1979).

B. Ramm, *Special Revelation and the Word of God* (Eerdmans, 1961).

3. Scripture

THE BIBLE: THE MATERIAL FORM OF SPECIAL REVELATION

The special revelation of God comes to us in and through the Bible. There we learn about and meet Jesus Christ. It is the basis and norm for all Christian preaching and teaching, and can therefore be described as the material form of special divine revelation. Several implications follow from this.

God's condescension

Our knowledge of God arises from his condescension in communicating with us. Like an adult talking to a tiny child, he adjusts his language and expression to our capacity. 'As nurses do with infants God is wont in a measure to "lisp" in speaking to us' (Calvin, *cf.* 1 Thes. 2:7, RSV). We ought not to be offended therefore by the Bible's plain language or by its frequently mundane contents.

The possibility of verbal revelation

The claim that God has spoken through the words of the Bible fits the Christian presupposition of an uncreated personal God. He is well able to communicate with his own rational, verbal-izing creatures on their own level, *i.e.* by language. To dismiss verbal revelation in principle, as some do, is in effect to deny the reality of the Creator God. Does he who formed the mouth not speak? (*cf.* Ps. 94:9).

Analogical truth

In making himself known to humankind, God uses the principle of *analogy*, whereby something in one area of experience and language is used to explain something in another area. In special revelation we are concerned with the area of God's experience of himself and his eternal self-expression of it on the one hand, and the area of human experience and our expression of it on the other. God chooses those elements within our area of experience and language which can serve as relevant analogies of the truth of his own area of experience and self-expression. He alone knows himself, but as Creator and Redeemer he also knows us, and can, therefore, sovereignly establish points of contact where his area of experience is truly reflected within ours. The material expression of this analogical self-disclosure of God is the Scriptures.

Obviously the analogue does not *exhaustively* reflect the truth of which it is an analogy. We retain our human limitations; the language of the Bible remains human. Not all God's truth can be conveyed by it. Scripture itself distinguishes the 'secret things' which belong to God, from 'the things which are revealed' which 'belong to us and to our children for ever' (Dt. 29:29; Is. 55:8–11). This in no way qualifies its being a fully true statement throughout. 'Is there any reason why the non-created Personal (God) could not tell us truly about himself, though not exhaustively?' (Schaeffer). Human language is a fully adequate medium for communicating God's truth to us. The assertions of special revelation in Scripture, when received as God's trustworthy words to us, convey a true and reliable account of God and his purposes.

God's purpose

God provides us with a written record of his revelation in his great wisdom. The Dutch theologian Abraham Kuyper notes four advantages of a written record. 1. It achieves durability. Errors of memory, deliberate or accidental corruptions over a long period are minimized. 2. It can be universally disseminated through translation and reproduction. 3. It has the attributes of fixedness and purity. 4. It is given a finality and normativeness which other forms of communication cannot attain.

GROUNDS FOR RECEIVING THE BIBLE AS GOD'S WRITTEN WORD

One way of expressing the conviction that in the Bible God himself speaks his words directly to us is to call it 'God's Word'. This is a biblical concept. It appears in the OT in the notion of God's creative word (Gn. 1:11; Ps. 33:6), the personalized 'wisdom' of God (Pr. 8), the vehicle of God's activity (Is. 55:11). It is used of OT Scripture by Jesus (Mk. 7:13; Jn. 10:35) and the apostles (*e.g.* Acts 6:4; Rom. 9:6; Heb. 4:12). It is sometimes used of the gospel (*e.g.* Acts 11:1; 13:46). It is also used of Jesus himself (Jn. 1:1, 14; 1 Jn. 1:1; Rev. 19:13).

In classical culture the Greek term translated 'word', *logos*, meant the rational principle of coherence in the universe. Fundamentally, *logos* conveys the thought of God's act in which he makes himself known. Our application of the term to Scripture as a whole simply attempts to reflect Jesus' attitude to the OT.

Jesus' view of the Old Testament

Jesus accorded divine authority to the OT Scriptures. He quoted the OT in a manner which revealed his personal respect for its divine status (Mt. 4:4; Mk. 14:27), referred to it as 'the word of God' (Mt. 19:4f.; Mk. 7:11–13; Jn. 10:34f.), and spoke of its divine inspiration (Mk. 12:36). Luke 24:25–27 and 44 indicate his accordance with the entire canonical OT, and elsewhere he is cited as appealing to each of its main divisions, the law (Mt. 4:10), the poetic/'Wisdom' books (Mk. 12:10f.), and the prophets (Mk. 7:6).

Jesus accepted OT history as true (Mt. 22:29, 32; Jn. 8:56; Mk. 12:26; Lk. 11:30–31; Mt. 25:35; Mt. 12:3;, Lk. 17:26–28; Jn. 3:14). He affirmed OT prophecy (Mt. 11:10, Mk. 7:6), and asserted the normative character of OT ethics (Mt. 5:27f.; 19:3–6; Mk. 10:9). Crucially, Jesus saw the OT Scriptures as previsioning his own unique mission (Lk. 24:46f.; Jn. 5:30, 45f.). He was prepared to rebuke those who did not believe them (Mt. 22:29f.; Lk. 24:25), or robbed them of their divine authority (Mt. 15:3).

Significantly, although as incarnate deity he exercised the very authority of God, Jesus at no point opposed his personal authority to that of Scripture.[1] He deferred to its authority on two central issues: his teaching and actions (Mt. 12:3–5; 19:4f.; Jn. 10:35) and his messianic ministry (Mt. 26:24; 53f.; Lk. 24:46).

This latter is particularly significant. Being persuaded that he was the long-awaited Messiah through whom God's kingdom was to come, he modelled his messianic role in terms of OT teaching on it. It was the Scriptures that persuaded him of the inevitability of his rejection and coming suffering, and that took him on his last journey to Jerusalem, finally to submit to the horror of the cross (Mt. 26:24; Mk. 8:31; Lk. 22:37).

---

1. The 'but I tell you . . .' sayings in the Sermon on the Mount (Mt. 5:21–48) are no exception. They are concerned to vindicate the true intent of the OT passages in question against the current interpretations of the scribes and Pharisees. 'I have not come to abolish the law and the prophets but to fulfil them . . . whoever then relaxes one of the least of these commandments . . . shall be called least in the kingdom' (Mt. 5:17, 19, RSV). *Cf.* D. M. Lloyd-Jones, *Studies in the Sermon on the Mount* 1 (IVP, 1959), pp. 180–320.

Obviously his unique communion with the Father provided guidance at every stage; but this intuitive direction was clearly supported and filled out by the divine blueprint for Messiah's ministry found in the Scriptures.

This is important in meeting a common objection to our claims for Jesus' attitude to Scripture. Some hold that he appealed to Scripture, the current religious authority, only because it would carry weight with his contemporaries. This suggestion is refuted by the way he permitted the written Word to direct his mission; by his use of Scripture in resisting Satan in the desert (Mt. 4:1–11; Lk. 4:1–13); and by his citing Scripture during his last agony on the cross (Mt. 27:46; Lk. 23:46). At no point was Jesus an accommodator. He submitted to OT Scripture because that was, to his mind, the proper attitude to adopt to it, whether or not it went against the grain of the traditionalist or radical theologies of his day (or, for that matter, of ours).

Others argue that Jesus' convictions in this matter were conditioned by the thought-patterns of his society and culture; indeed, that was involved in his being truly incarnate and hence his attitude has no particular authority today. This position, however, makes a wholly gratuitous assumption: because *we* are conditioned by the axioms and norms of society, the same must have been true of Jesus. It is doubtful whether we would say this without qualification about any of the truly great figures of history, whose genius lay precisely in challenging the assumptions of their generation. Was Jesus inferior to these, bound to conform to the outlook of his society on the fundamental issue of religious authority?

This view also fails to reckon with the Bible's witness to what was involved in Jesus' case: not, as in ours, the emergence of a time-bound human consciousness, but rather the assuming of a human nature by one who was the eternal Word and Wisdom of God (Jn. 1:1–14; 8:58; 17:5; Phil. 2:5–11; Col. 1:15–20). It also ignores his unfallen human nature (Jn. 8:46; Heb. 4:15; 1 Pet. 1:19). It is therefore a fundamental error of method to use our experience of humanity to measure Jesus. He can be understood only as we lay aside the norms of our fallen, fragmentary insights and allow our thinking to be moulded by God's testimony to Jesus in the gospels. We therefore have no grounds for dismissing his attitude to anything, least of all something so close to the centre of his thought and activity.

This position further involves the difficulty of pronouncing Jesus mistaken, not on some peripheral issue, but at the very centre, in his understanding of authority, which in turn represented the basis of his understanding both of himself and of his entire mission. Kuyper put the issue thus:

> Can he have been mistaken, mistaken with respect to holiest things, in what must be to us the ground and source of our faith! Mistaken also therefore in assigning on the basis of Scripture a high Messianic character to Himself. But the very idea is incompatible with the confession of Jesus' divine nature. Erring in what is holy is no mere failure in intellect, but betrays a state of ruin of one's whole inner being. In the sinner therefore a mistake is natural but not in one who is holy ... The conflict which is begun in order to rob us of the Scripture as Holy Scripture can have no other tendency than to rob us of the Christ.[2]

In the final analysis the question we face is moral rather than academic. If we adopt a lower view of the divine character of the OT than Jesus did, in what sense – indeed, by what right – can we acknowledge him as teacher and lord (Jn. 13:13)?

The apostles' view of the Old Testament

The apostles also appealed directly to the letter of the OT to authorize their teaching and consistently presented the Christian faith as the fulfilment of the Scriptures (Acts 2:16–35; 3:22–25; 4:11; 7:2–53; 13:29–37; Rom. 1:2; Gal. 3:16–18; *etc.*). Indeed it was for this very fulfilment that the Scriptures had been written (Rom. 15:4; 1 Pet. 1:12). The apostles are particularly concerned to show the ways in which the life and mission of Jesus fulfils the OT hope of salvation. Thus his birth (Gal. 4:4; 2 Tim. 2:8), the circumstances and style of his ministry (Acts 3:22–26; Heb. 7:1–22), and supremely his death, resurrection and exaltation (1 Pet. 2:6–8, 22; Heb. 8:8–13; 10:5–22; Acts 2:25–36; 4:11, 25–27; 10:37–43; 13:26–37) were all anticipated in the prophetic Scriptures.

Conscious of their special authority as the appointed founders

---

2. A. Kuyper, *Principles of Sacred Theology* (Eerdmans, 1954), p. 430.

of the new movement (*cf.* 2 Cor. 10:8; Gal. 1:1) and of being the special objects of God's self-revelation (1 Cor. 2:13; 1 Thes. 2:13; 1 Jn. 1:1–3), they nevertheless related their teaching constantly to the OT. Paul, for example, is deeply concerned to show that his teaching on justification is rooted in Scripture (*cf.* Rom. 4). For the apostles, as for their master, the OT was the Word of God in written form (Acts 4:25; 2 Tim. 3:16f.; Heb. 4:3; 10:15–17; 2 Pet. 1:21). They taught their converts not to 'go beyond what is written' (1 Cor. 4:6). Their consistent attitude to the OT is aptly summarized by Paul's phrase, 'the oracles of God' (Rom. 3:2, RSV).

Jesus' words and teaching
Jesus clearly believed in the unique power and authority of his words (Jn. 6:63; 15:3). They will not pass away (Mk. 13:31) and must be heard and obeyed (Mt. 5:21f.; 7:24; Jn. 8:31f.).

The apostles recognized their divine authority (Acts 20:35; 1 Cor. 7:10; 11:23f.). 1 Timothy 5:18 is particularly significant, combining an OT verse (Dt. 25:4) with a NT verse from Jesus' teaching (Lk. 10:7). Set together as authoritative Scripture, they are equally invested with divine authority and equally express the mind and will of God. Apostolic reverence for Jesus' words is also demonstrated by the existence of four gospels.

The special authority of the apostles
Jesus deliberately chose certain men to be his immediate disciples (Lk. 5:27; 6:12–16; Jn. 17:6) and gave them a special endowment of the Holy Spirit (Jn. 20:22, *cf.* Acts 1:5). He commanded them to go and teach in his name (Mt. 28:18–20; Jn. 20:21; Acts 1:8), promising the Holy Spirit to guide their teaching and witness (Jn. 14:26; 15:26f.; 16:13f.).

The apostles claimed direct experience of this unique authority and insight (1 Cor. 2:9f.). Along with their fellow preachers, they proclaimed the gospel in the confidence that they spoke 'by the Holy Spirit' (1 Pet. 1:12), to whom they were prepared to attribute both the content and form of their message (1 Cor. 2:13). We can also note the special concern in Acts for the apostles' role as specially appointed witnesses (Acts 1:21–26, 2:32; 4:26, 33; 5:32; 10:41–42; 13:31) and hence as authoritative proclaimers (with the corroborative witness of the Spirit, Acts 5:32) of the gospel of Jesus. They spoke with complete assurance

(Gal. 1:7f.) and issued commands with authority (2 Thes. 3:6, 12). Indeed, a person's claim to have the Holy Spirit was measured by whether he or she recognized the divine authority of the apostles' teaching (1 Cor. 14:37).

This high view of their teaching and preaching applied as fully to their written as to their spoken statements. The test of truth is 'what I am writing' or 'our instruction in this letter' (1 Cor. 14:37; 2 Thes. 3:14). Peter actually classes Paul's letters as 'scriptures' (2 Pet. 3:16); and Paul commands that the letter to Colossae be 'read in the church' (Col. 4:16).

It is sometimes alleged that the argument used up to this point is dangerously circular, establishing the authority of Scripture by appeal to biblical texts. Part of the response to this challenge is met in our final reason for the authority of Scripture below. Here we note the difficulty of establishing a claim to ultimate authority except by reference to itself; any other authority summoned to support our final authority would itself become the ultimate authority. This principle applies equally to other areas of human investigation. What we *can* show is the self-consistency of the Christian doctrine of authority from the biblical writers' constant appeal to Scripture. Thus God speaking in Scripture is consistently the final authority.

God himself addresses us in its words

For many Christians the supreme reason for according the Bible the status of God's Word written is simply the fact that *God himself* addresses us in it. God speaks in the words of the Bible in such a manner as to remove all doubt as to its divine origin, character and authority. In the final analysis only God can be an adequate witness to himself. All other testimony such as historical evidence or philosophical deduction can at best possess only secondary value.

Multitudes of Christians in every generation have testified that, as they read the Bible and hear it expounded, they are moved to recognize its inherent authority. This was focused by Augustine when he put into God's mouth the words, 'Indeed, O man, what my Scripture says, I say.' Calvin saw this as the work of God the Holy Spirit bearing divine testimony to Scripture; he called it the 'inward witness of the Holy Spirit' which is 'stronger than all proof'.

Christians who know the reality of this 'inward witness' can, in the last resort, simply bear testimony that it is so. The Bible comes to them with the authority and conviction of God's Word searching them to the depths; there they encounter a majesty, an ultimate and unconditional summons which they can only describe as the voice and Word of God, their Creator and Redeemer. Against the charge of dangerous subjectivism they reply:

1. While a subjective element is inevitably present if the authority in question is to be fully personal (God addressing *me*), the Spirit's testimony directs us away from ourselves to the objective authority of written Scripture. Hence in defending this reality Christians do not speak about their own inward experience but cite Scripture.

2. This reality is not a private matter, but is common to God's people. The Christian community represents a check against over-subjective implications drawn from the experience of the Spirit's testimony.

3. This testimony has been common to Christians in every age and culture and at every level of understanding. God has not suspended the authority of his Word on the findings of scholars; rather it is universal, compassionate and gracious, as we would expect from the God disclosed in Jesus Christ.

4. This doctrine of authority is quite simply the orthodox Christian position. It is supported implicitly and explicitly in the writing of the church's leading theologians in almost every age.

5. Objective checks on this claim exist in the form of historical and other evidence. Some allege that it is inconsistent, even irrelevant, to adduce evidence to confirm the authority of the Holy Spirit's witness. The NT itself, however, gives rational, historical evidence to support the Christian claim (Acts 1:3, 2:32; 4:20; 1 Cor. 15:3–11; *cf.* 1 Pet. 3:15). Such evidence counters objections that the witness of the Spirit, being finally subjective, is valueless. Christians who cannot master this kind of evidence are not deprived of an adequate basis for their faith; but those able to appropriate it can show how their faith relates to the human historical process and is therefore rooted in a God whose self-witness is universal (Acts 17:31).

6. The charge of subjectivism pales before the sheer depth and persuasiveness of the Spirit's testimony. God has spoken and still speaks in the words of Scripture. No-one who has first-hand experience of Christian evangelism and the nurture of new believers can fail to notice their instinctive desire to study and

obey the Bible; *cf.* Peter's meaningful analogy of a newborn baby's milk (1 Pet. 2:2).

Critics of biblical authority can never come to terms with this. However cogent their case, however sophisticated their reasoning, all is overturned in a stroke by the sovereign ministry of the Spirit as he brings a new generation to life and implants in their hearts a sense of the divine authority of the Scriptures.

In the final analysis we recognize the authority of the Bible as God's Word written because we have no choice. The constraint comes from beyond ourselves: we are simply allowing God to be God.

INSPIRATION

'Inspiration' refers to the way in which God's self-revelation has come to be expressed in the words of the Bible. It is that activity of the Spirit of God whereby he superintended the human authors of Scripture so that their writings became a normative expression in human language of God's Word to humanity. To call the Bible 'inspired' is simply another way of saying that it is God's authoritative self-revelation. Indeed, its divine inspiration gives that very authority that the Spirit confirms. Accordingly all the arguments used above to establish the unique authority of the Bible as God's Word are also arguments which support its inspiration.

Every true Christian accepts the inspiration of the Bible in some sense. The controversies centre on *how* this inspiration occurred and on the implications of this for the authority and reliability of the actual words of Scripture as we now have them.

The method of inspiration
Inspiration implies that God was directly involved in the writing of the Bible. How pervasive was this divine influence?

Three important New Testament passages
2 Timothy 3:16 supplies the term 'inspiration': 'All scripture is given by inspiration of God' (AV); more literally, 'All Scripture is God-breathed' (NIV).[3] God's 'breath' is a familiar and graphic OT

---

3. The translation 'every inspired Scripture is profitable' is not a natural rendering of the Greek and takes little account of the object in question, the Jewish Scriptures (2 Tim. 3:15).

metaphor for the action of God, particularly through his Spirit (Gn. 2:7; Jb. 33:4; Ps. 33:6). The assertion that Scripture is inspired affirms its divine origin and character and implies something rather stronger than the English word *in*spiration. More accurately, the Scriptures are *ex*pired (forgive the word's funerary associations!), *i.e. breathed out* by God. Note that the object of God's action is the written Scriptures; the actual human writers are not mentioned. They were involved, of course, but here the forming of Scripture is referred wholly to *God's* activity. Note, too, the extent of inspiration. 'All' the Scriptures are the product of God's 'out-breathing'; in this context that means the whole of the OT.

2 Peter 1:19–21 confirms and extends these claims. The testimony of eye-witnesses confirms 'the word of the prophets', a reference to the OT in general. It did not emerge from the writers' private reflections, but 'men spoke from God as they were carried along by the Holy Spirit'. In Acts 27:15 the word 'carried along' describes the motion of a ship *driven along* by a storm. We must not read too much into this imagery, but it is clearly a strong assertion of the divine activity in the production of Scripture, again extending to the whole body of writings mentioned.

John 10:34–36 records discussion on the usage of the word 'god' in the law, in this case Psalm 82. Jesus argues that the authority of the law cannot be annulled because 'Scripture cannot be broken'. He expresses the same conviction when he equates words of the OT with God's words: 'He said' (Mt. 19:5).

Jesus' recognition of the divine authority and inspiration of the whole body of the OT writings has been documented earlier, together with the case for extending this claim for divine inspiration to the NT. Jesus' own sense of sovereign authority and his claim to speak God's very words, his promise of the Spirit to enlighten the apostles, the coming of the Spirit upon them, their own claims for the Spirit's special enlightenment in their teaching, their recognition of special divine authority in the apostolic writings, all point to the same inspiring activity of God in the case of the NT. Thus the entire Bible comes to us with the claim to divine inspiration, a document breathed out by God.

The Old Testament prophets
Insight into how this divine inspiring activity came to bear upon

the biblical authors may be gleaned from a study of the OT prophets.

The essence of the prophetic inspiration is expressed in Jeremiah 1:5–9: 'I appointed you as a prophet to the nations ... I have put my words in your mouth' (*cf.* Is. 6:8ff.; Ezk. 2). Hence the prophets' habit of prefacing their message with 'Thus says the LORD'. Constantly 'the word of the LORD came' to them, and their oracles are commonly cast in the form of God's direct address to his people. The prophets (which include Moses the law-giver and the psalmists, Lk. 24:25–27) were so grasped and taken up by God and his Word that under the inspiration of the Spirit their message was effectively identifiable as God's own utterance.

The reference to the prophetic writings helpfully reminds us to recognize God's condescension in the production of Scripture. God's truth comes to us, by his overruling, in our human language (1 Thes. 2:7, RSV). On examination we need to expand that to our human languages. At the first level this recognizes not only the use of Hebrew and Greek, but also the occasional loan word from other languages such as Aramaic (*cf.* Mk. 5:41; Mt. 27:46; 1 Cor. 16:22). At a further level, however, it recognizes that the Bible consists of a variety of literary genres. Thus, for example, there is historical narrative, poetry, prophetic oracle, parable, *etc.* God's inspiration of the text of the Bible means that these diversities of literary form were not overridden in the process of the composition of Scripture. Hence while all of Scripture is equally the result of the inspiring ministry of the Spirit, the way in which each sentence, section, passage, or word relates to us and carries implications for our understanding and action is bound up with its literary form. This takes us to the verge of questions of hermeneutics, to which we shall turn shortly.

Theories of inspiration
A number of theories have been formulated in an attempt to describe how God worked in the production of Scripture.

Dictation
This theory in its strongest form asserts that the human authors were in effect bypassed in the production of Scripture. They were simply the human keyboards or dictaphones through

whom the Word of God passed on its way to eventual incorporation in the sacred canon.

The prophetic 'model' referred to above, with its emphasis on the action of God ('grasped and taken up', we wrote), might suggest the dictation theory. It is not fully adequate, however, because it cannot accommodate biblical references which assert the human factor: 'men spoke . . .' (2 Pet. 1:21, *cf.* Mk. 7:6; 12:19; *etc.*). Hence, while such phenomena as visions, trances and heavenly voices certainly happened, they were not necessary for the inspiration of Scripture. An adequate theory needs to take account of this.

A less direct mode of inspiration is instanced in Luke's gospel, which was written because 'it seemed good to me' (Lk. 1:3). There is no indication of a manifest supernatural stimulus behind other scriptural passages such as the Song of Solomon, Paul's letter to Philemon or Agur's testament (Pr. 30). Further, the route by which the biblical documents arrived at their final literary form is also, in many cases, a relatively 'human' story, involving first-hand historical research (Lk. 1:3), direct dependence on earlier sources (1 and 2 Ch.), borrowing from another book (2 Pet. and Jude), or passing through several editions (Pr. 10:1; 24:23; 25:1). The language also in places bears clear evidence of the author's style, or even his lack of it.

Thus the common mode of inspiration did not bypass the human writers' intentions or personalities; they did not become human keyboards. This requires to be spelled out forcibly as evangelical Christians are frequently, and quite unjustly, accused of being wedded to the dictation view; in fact it has not been held by any responsible Protestant theologian from the Reformation to the present day.

Accommodation

This view expresses the thought that in the process of inspiration God accommodated himself to the limitations of the human authors. Scholars who hold that the Bible contains errors at numerous levels often champion this theory. Human blemishes in Scripture are inevitable, they assert, because God has chosen to accommodate himself to the writers' limitations. Just as light in passing through stained glass is coloured in the process, so the divine revelation appears in Scripture with the taint of its human contributors. This directly contradicts the Bible's own view as well as the Christian's Spirit-given assurance of its divine origin and reliability.

Supervision
This is a variant of accommodation which incorporates the valid insights of the above alternatives without their questionable accompaniments. To avoid confusion we prefer the distinctive term *supervision*, in the strong sense of 'exercising control over'. This theory asserts that in the process of inspiration God sovereignly supervised and ordered the background, heredity and circumstances of the individual writers; as a result, when they recorded events, meditations or sermons in writing, the words used were consciously the free composition of the authors and at the same time the very Word of God.

Their inspired words, therefore, are clearly stamped as 'theirs' and address their immediate situation, but are also in God's providence part of his eternal Word to his people in every age. So the illustration of the stained glass applies in another way. 'What if the colours of the stained glass window have been designed by the architect for the express purpose of giving to the light that floods the cathedral precisely the tone and quality it receives from them? What if the Word of God that comes to his people is framed by God into the Word of God it is, precisely by means of the qualities of the men formed by him for the purpose, through which it is given?' (Warfield).

It has been objected that this view fails to make due allowance for the fact of human sin. How can that great barrier between human beings and God be so surmounted that they may speak God's very words?

In reply we would make the following points: (a) We are not dealing here with 'natural' humanity; the people God used in conveying his truth had been renewed by his Spirit and drawn into relationship with himself. (b) To deny that mere humans can articulate the truth of God amounts to denying that human language can ever, in principle, be the vehicle of divine truth. (c) No doubt the human writers remained sinners to the end of their days, but this does not prevent their being the mouthpieces of God's truth; the biblical writers were uniquely superintended by the action of almighty God through his Spirit in all factors influencing their message.

Two related terms
Verbal

This adjective implies that the biblical authors were not merely inspired in their general ideas, but in the very words they used. This must be carefully distinguished from the 'dictation' view of inspiration. Strictly speaking this claim does not attach to our present copies of the OT and NT but to the original autographs from which our present versions have come by a process of transmission. In practice, however, the distinction between the originals and our present copies is largely academic (see below, 'As originally given', pp. 57–58).

Plenary

This adjective indicates that the inspiration claimed extends to the *whole* Bible. God has caused *all* Scripture to be written, not only the sections which carry the marks of inspiration most clearly. This is *not* the same as claiming that all parts are equally *significant* in the unfolding of the Bible's message. A tiny 'background' corner in a portrait is less important than the central figure, but it as surely a product of the artist's brush and makes its own contribution to the total picture.

Three final comments

1. The Bible teaches that it is directly and sovereignly inspired by God and is therefore to be submitted to as his living Word addressed directly to us. If we acknowledge its authority, we must bow to it at this point too: in its dual claim that it is God's inspired Word and that we should approach it with reverence and submission. To take another view is to stand in opposition to clear biblical teaching.

2. Obviously there will always be an element of mystery about the precise way in which the Bible has been produced. This ought not to surprise us, for mystery inevitably accompanies all God's dealings with his creatures. The incarnation is similarly a 'mystery' to us, for we can never state with final precision how the divine and human natures are united in the one person of Jesus Christ. In neither case, however, need the 'mystery' of God's activity inhibit us from believing it and rejoicing in its truth.

3. In the final analysis, the question of inspiration comes back to our doctrine of God. If we acknowledge God as the one 'who

works out everything in conformity with the purpose of his will' (Eph. 1:11), who 'does whatever pleases him' (Ps. 135:6), then we shall encounter no basic difficulty. There is nothing incongruous in his having produced a book which, while arising out of the experience of his creatures, is also through his sovereign ordering his very word to them.

CANONICITY

The word 'canonicity' comes from the Greek *kanōn*, meaning rule or standard of measurement. It occurs in the NT; for example: 'Peace and mercy to all who follow this rule' (Gal. 6:16), *i.e.* who live according to the apostolic gospel. Used in a general way of the Bible, the canon refers to its literary limits, and deals with such questions as why we regard these books alone as 'inspired' and why *all* of these books are included in 'inspired Scripture'.

Several general comments can be made. The very notion of Scripture commits us in principle to the idea of a canon, an authoritative body of writings with precise literary limits; indeed, Scripture contains scattered references to the idea (Lk. 11:51; Col. 4:16; Rev. 22:18). External historical factors were of major importance in deciding on canonicity, for example the apostolic authorship or supervision of certain books. The authentic biblical books carried an inherent authority, *i.e.* the people of God came to recognize his voice addressing them through these books.

The Old Testament canon

There are certain suggestions within the OT that its first five books, the Pentateuch, received official recognition at an early stage (*e.g.* Dt. 31:11; Jos. 1:7f.; 2 Ch. 23:18). The grounds for acceptance of the canon in Judaism are not known and hence our primary consideration must be that the Lord and his apostles acknowledged the OT canon. Jesus debated with the religious authorities of his time over various issues, but no disagreement is recorded over the canon. That the canon used in the synagogue in Jesus' day was equivalent to our present OT is implied in Lk. 11:51.

There appears to have been little dispute among the Jews at any period concerning the content of the canon. The Greek version of the OT included several apocryphal books, but none was apparently recognized in Palestine. Evidence that the Apocrypha was at any time recognized and accepted by official Judaism in either Palestine or Alexandria is lacking and Jews today still regard only our present OT books as Scripture.

The New Testament canon

A full canonical extension to the OT was not a pressing need in the apostolic period for at least two reasons. Firstly, the churches possessed a considerable body of oral tradition concerning the happenings and teaching of Jesus' ministry. Secondly, a more enduring form of the apostolic teaching was relatively unnecessary as long as the apostles and their immediate disciples were alive. Partly because of the scattering of the churches, the assembling and recognition of the NT books took considerable time.

Even in the apostolic period, however, certain factors pointed to the eventual emergence of a body of authoritative writings. The church's concern to preserve the traditions about Jesus shows they recognized the normative nature of Jesus' mission, and hence of the preserved record of it; this was precisely what underlay the writing of the four gospels. Further, the churches gave special respect to the letters of the apostles; Paul, for example, affixed his signature to confirm their apostolic authority (1 Cor. 16:21; Col. 4:18; 2 Thes. 3:17) and directed that his letters be read in the churches. 2 Peter 3:16 indicates that Paul's letters were regarded as 'scriptures' within the lifetime of both Peter and Paul. Revelation 22:18f. is further evidence of an early distinction between authorized and unauthorized writings.

Another significant pointer towards the emergence of the NT canon comes from the Christian writers of the immediate post-apostolic period (known as the apostolic Fathers). They distinguished any authority possessed by their writings from that primary authority residing in the writings of the apostles.

The earliest known attempt at a list of received books is the Muratorian Canon of around AD 175. The earliest complete list is that of Eusebius (died 340); he distinguished books universally received from those (six in number) accepted by the majority of churches. The grounds for doubting the six books are important: they could not be traced directly to an apostolic source. This shows that the church's concern was to ensure that the canonical books bore direct and authentic testimony to the great central realities of the faith. The book of Revelation understandably caused widespread hesitation; its message was rather veiled, and even then extremists made capital out of its symbolism. By the end of the fourth century unanimity had been attained by the churches.

A casual reading of the NT apocrypha is sufficient to show that in the main it is very different from the NT itself. It is important to understand that in the process of canonization the church did not aspire to impose its own authority on certain of the many documents circulating among the Christian groups. The church no more created the NT canon by recognizing and defining it than Isaac Newton created the law of gravity. In these writings and in these alone the church under the direction of the Holy Spirit heard, and continues to hear, the authentic tones of the Good Shepherd (Jn. 10:4f.).

OTHER ISSUES

The approach to authority, and to Scripture in particular, which we have outlined here needs to be filled out by reference to a number of other questions.

If the Bible is our supreme authority, inspired by God down to the words used by the original authors, what degree of truthfulness and reliability ought we to attribute to its statements?

Infallible

Applied to Scripture this word implies the quality of not misleading. This claim means that all the Bible's assertions are truthful and worthy of entire confidence, implying a contrast with human 'fallible' words and statements. It asserts that Scripture does not mislead because it is God's own self-testimony. The term 'infallibility' applied to Scripture needs to be precisely defined with reference to the actual phenomena of the biblical writings.

The infallibility of Scripture refers to its message viewed *as a whole*. This is not to imply that certain passages and texts are not infallible, but rather that each particular statement and section is infallible within the context of the whole of Scripture. If, for example, we quote in isolation James' question 'Can faith save him?' (Jas. 2:14, AV) with its implied answer 'No', we may miss the infallible truth of God in the letter of James. That is attained only when that is read within the total framework of the letter and set alongside the complementary teaching of other parts of

Scripture, notably Paul's letters to Romans and Galatians.[4]

The infallibility of Scripture is bound up with *the intention in the mind of the author*. The opening chapter of Genesis, for example, is infallible in teaching the construction of the physical universe in six 24-hour days only if that precise cosmological-scientific sense was intended by the writer. If that was not his intention, the infallibility of his account must not be pressed to the cosmological details (see further on this in Part 2, 'The question of origins'). Or a narrative may patently be just the literary vehicle for theological truths; an obvious example are Jesus' parables. Clearly we are not required to assert that the story of the good Samaritan was factual before we claim infallibility for these words of Jesus. The literary form of a passage will affect how we assert its infallibility.

These points in effect say Scripture is infallible only as correctly interpreted. It does *not* follow that any or every human interpretation of a passage of Scripture, or of the Bible as a whole, is infallible, nor do they foreclose questions of interpretation.

The fact that we need to qualify the term in this way has led some who hold a high view of the reliability of Scripture to question the wisdom of using it at all. By using it, however, we identify ourselves with the long historic stream of Christian orthodoxy and with many of the great historic statements of Christian truth over the centuries. Furthermore, it is difficult to see any other term which will do the job more effectively.

Infallibility is really the inevitable concomitant of the divine authority and inspiration which we have expounded above. It is simply the infallibility of God speaking. To assert with Jesus that 'Scripture cannot be broken' and 'Your word is truth', and to appeal to its very letter as he consistently did, is of the essence of what we seek to express by 'infallible'.

Inerrant

This word is frequently used in association with 'infallible', implying the absence of error. Like infallibility, inerrancy is a corollary of divine inspiration. If the Bible has been supervised down to its very words by the God of truth, we can be confident that it will be free from error. Thus whenever the Bible

4. On this see further Part 4, 'The penal metaphor: justification' (pp. 193–197).

prescribes the content of our belief (doctrine) or the pattern of our living (ethics) or records actual events (history), it speaks the truth. Again we must make clear that the degree of inerrancy claimed in any particular case is relative to what the text intends to teach. It is also relative to the kind of literature in which the text is expressed. Hence, for example, the inerrant truth of Jesus' parable of the prodigal son does not require us to hold that there has ever been exactly such a family in any particular society. When a passage of Scripture is interpreted in accord with the writer's intention and in harmony with other biblical passages, its inerrant truth will be plainly perceived.

A number of those who are committed to a high view of Scripture's inspiration and authority have shied away from the term 'inerrant', preferring to speak, for example, of the Bible as 'entirely trustworthy', or simply 'infallible'. Part of the reason for this is the way in which the term 'inerrancy' has tended to imply a foreclosure of important interpretive questions such as the specific literary genre of a passage, or the way in which the term can appear to underwrite unwarranted claims for finality for particular interpretations of Bible passages. However, provided it is seen as a corollary of the truthfulness of the God whose Word Scripture is, the assertion that Scripture is 'inerrant' is not without significance.

'As originally given'

This phrase is often used to acknowledge that we do not possess the *original* manuscripts of the Bible. The divine providence which sovereignly overruled and inspired inerrant, infallible of records God's very words to humankind did not operate with equal force in the production of the copies and translations which we have in our hands today.

Not that this undermines the entire doctrine as we have formulated it. Study of the very many manuscripts which have come down to us confirms that they vary little from the originals which underlie them. The copying was undertaken with a due sense of responsibility in the light of the divine character of the originals. One scholar who has investigated the biblical manuscripts and versions in considerable detail affirms: 'by the singular care and providence of God the Bible text has come down to us in such substantial purity that even the most uncritical edition of the Hebrew and Greek, or the most incompetent or even the most tendentious translation of such an edition, cannot effectively obscure the real message of the Bible or neutralize its saving power' (F. F. Bruce).

This gives further objective attestation to the fact that the Spirit does not mislead us when he bears witness in the church today to the divine authority of these copies. By using the phrase 'as originally given', however, we avoid claiming too much for any one current manuscript and thereby encourage the continuing search for an even purer and more reliable text in the future.

Difficulties

The view of Scripture outlined above could be shown without great difficulty to be the orthodox doctrine of biblical authority which the great majority of the people of God over the centuries have affirmed, whether implicitly by their practice or explicitly by their confessions and theological writings.

Over the last three centuries, however, this view has frequently been challenged and we can identify six areas of continuing discussion: historical reliability, the way in which NT writers cite OT passages, references to physical phenomena, moral questions, authorship and literary questions, the operation of the miraculous. Extended discussion of these and allied questions requires a book for each, and the reader is referred to the literature below.[5] The following general points may be made.

1. Many of the difficulties are resolved by simply clarifying the limits within which biblical infallibility and inerrancy operate.

2. A study of the literature concerned will show that there is no single issue raised by the critics of biblical infallibility which cannot receive, or has not received, an answer which is fully compatible with biblical infallibility.

---

5. J. Wenham, *The Goodness of God* (IVP, 1974); *Christ and the Bible* (IVP, 1972); C. Pinnock, *Biblical Revelation* (Moody, 1971); *A Defense of Biblical Infallibility* (PRPC, 1967); J. W. Montgomery, ed., *God's Inerrant Word* (Bethany, 1974); N. B. Stonehouse and P. Woolley, eds., *The Infallible Word* (PRPC, 1946); C. F. H. Henry, ed., *Revelation and the Bible* (Tyndale Press, 1959); R. Laird Harris, *Inspiration and Canonicity of the Bible* (Zondervan, 1975); N. Geisler, ed., *Inerrancy* (Zondervan, 1979); J. I. Packer, *Under God's Word* (Lakeland, 1980); D. A. Carson and J. D. Woodbridge, *Scripture and Truth* (IVP, 1983); (eds.), *Hermeneutics, Authority and Canon* (Zondervan, 1986).

3. It is a mistake to imagine that these difficulties were all thrown up by modern scholarship. Many were faced long ago by the early Fathers and later by the great Reformation and Puritan expositors, who frequently offered satisfactory solutions.

4. We should retain a proper reserve concerning scholarly claims to have 'disproved' biblical assertions. The history of biblical criticism is littered with such 'proofs' which fuller investigation has subsequently overturned. For example, the cavalier dismissal of the OT accounts of the patriarchs as ancient fable has today had to retreat in the face of hard evidence: Genesis has many historical allusions to, and affinities with, civilization in the ancient Near East in the second millennium BC.

5. Occasionally a problem still remains unresolved. Rarely, there may be no obvious solution on offer, or the solution proposed may not for the moment carry conviction. In such a case we need to live with the problem until a (more) satisfactory solution appears, as has frequently occurred in the past. It is important, in the meantime, neither to let the 'tail' of a particular unresolved problem 'wag the dog' of the biblical doctrine of Scripture, nor to let it cloud the witness of God himself to his Word through the Spirit.

6. We need to remember that this doctrine of biblical authority is one of the teachings of the Christian faith. As such it calls for faith, *i.e.* a believing commitment on our part, an attitude continuous with that of our Lord himself and his apostles, and with the historic view of the churches. This helps us to keep the doctrine of Scripture in perspective. We do not wait for a moment-by-moment account of our Lord's thoughts, words and actions before we trust ourselves to his sinlessness and hence his fitness to act as our Saviour, nor for signed statements of impartial eye-witnesses before believing and rejoicing in his resurrection; so we need not demand the resolution of every possible question before trusting ourselves to the infallible truth of Scripture and submitting to its authority.

HERMENEUTICS: THE SCIENCE OF INTERPRETING SCRIPTURE

We have sought to show how the question of infallibility cannot be isolated from that of our interpretation of Scripture. Great harm has been done by those who claim infallibility for dubious, even eccentric, interpretations of the Bible. The Bible is infallible *as correctly interpreted*. What principles ought to guide our attempts to interpret Scripture properly, or, to put it technically, to employ a correct *hermeneutic*? We can identify four major principles.

Scripture must be interpreted literally

This principle, technically known as the historico-grammatical method, takes the natural, straightforward sense of a text or passage as fundamental. This 'literal' approach must be carefully distinguished from the 'literalistic'. The latter interprets the words of Scripture in a wooden fashion without making allowance for imagery, metaphor, literary form, *etc.*; to take an extreme example, 'the eyes of the LORD range throughout the earth' (2 Ch. 16:9) teaches God's omniscience but does not teach that a pair of celestial eyes periodically sweeps over the globe. A 'literal' approach requires that we interpret Scripture:

1. According to the original meaning. God's Word is almost always immediately relevant to the situation to which it was addressed; we need, therefore, to uncover as fully as possible the original setting and meaning before attempting to relate it to ourselves.

2. According to literary form. The Bible is made up of all kinds of literature: poetry, prose, parables, allegory (Ezk. 16), apocalyptic (Revelation), fable (Jdg. 9:8–15), *etc.* This must always be taken into account. This is not to say that a poetic section, for example, cannot convey factual material, but it means one will not interpret poetic or visionary material in the same way as historical narrative or doctrinal passages. We must also be sensitive to the use of metaphor and other figures of speech.

3. According to context. The setting of a text or saying in the section and book of the Bible in which it occurs is fundamental to correct interpretation. It should be noted in this connection that the divisions into chapter and verse are not original.

Scripture must be interpreted by Scripture

'The infallible rule of interpretation of Scripture is the Scripture itself; therefore, when there is a question about the true and full sense of any Scripture, it must be searched and known by other places that speak more clearly' (The Westminster Confession of Faith). This principle, technically known as the principle of harmonization, recognizes the unity and self-consistency of Scripture, deriving from its single divine author. It may be amplified in a number of sub-headings.

1. Interpret according to the purpose of Scripture. This applies to the Bible as a whole (Jn. 20:31; 2 Tim. 3:15). It is given to make us 'wise for salvation'. Calvin once said, 'if you would learn astronomy, or any other recondite art, go elsewhere'.[6] This principle also applies to each part of the Bible; we must identify the situation being addressed. James, for example, writes to people who are careless about the moral and social expression of the faith; in Galatians Paul addresses the opposite situation: people were depending on their own moral and religious attainments to merit God's favour. Not surprisingly the two writers say different, though complementary, things.

2. Interpret in the light of other passages on the same theme. This principle we would apply when reading any textbook; we look to see if the writer explains a difficult point in another place. Thus, for example, certain of the obscurities of the book of Revelation give sense when related to other prophetic sections of the Bible.

3. Interpret the earlier in the light of the later and fuller. The biblical revelation develops as God reveals more of himself and his purposes to his people. In particular, the NT interprets the OT. 'Christ fulfils the law' and therefore the OT is to be interpreted in the light of this fulfilment. Also, the letters of the NT interpret the gospels, since it is from the perspective of the apostolic teaching that the whole sweep of God's purpose and its culmination in the death and resurrection of Christ can be seen. Calvin's comment on Romans is sound advice: 'If a man understands it, he has a sure road opened for him to the understanding of the whole Scripture.'

Scripture can be interpreted only by the Holy Spirit

True understanding is not natural to us; it is God's gift (Mt. 11:25; 16:17) through the Holy Spirit (Jn. 16:13f.). This neither absolves us from hard work, nor implies that we can isolate ourselves from other Christians in our understanding of the Bible. The Holy Spirit is a corporate Spirit, dwelling in all God's people (1 Cor. 12:12f.). It is folly to expect God to teach us

6. Commenting of Gn. 1:6. See John Calvin, *Genesis* (Banner of Truth, 1975), p. 79.

through his Word if we neglect his ordained means of bringing us his truth, including the gift exercised by his chosen teachers.

This third hermeneutical principle carries a profound spiritual challenge. God's Spirit is *holy*; therefore what we understand of his truth is related less to the capacity of our brains than to the extent of our obedience. How far one can see depends on how high one has climbed rather than on how elaborately one is equipped. 'Blessed are the pure in heart, for they will see God' (Mt. 5:8).

The habit of approaching Scripture in an attitude of prayer is entirely correct in this connection. 'Open my eyes that I may see wonderful things in your law' (Ps. 119:18) are appropriate words every time we hear or handle the Bible. In the end we are dealing not so much with a book as with a living God who meets us in and through its inspired words. We are concerned not so much with 'who God is (or was, or will be)', as if he were some third party external to our conversation or searching. Rather, we are concerned with 'who you are, O God'. We are concerned with the God who is now here, before whom we bow in worship, upon whose power and grace we utterly depend in every moment for life and existence. 'Come, Holy Spirit!'

Scripture must be interpreted dynamically

This final principle is really an extension of the third. God's Spirit is a living Spirit; he uses his Word in accordance with his great goals for God's people, their regeneration and sanctification. Biblical hermeneutics cannot confine itself to elucidating the true contextual meaning of the Bible. The Word which we have mined from the vein of God's eternal truth must be brought to the surface and put to work in the present. After asking, 'What did this mean in its own time and context, and what does it mean in the light of the whole of Scripture?' we must ask, 'What does this mean for today – here and now in the life of this congregation, that person, and in my own life?'

Scriptures

The Bible: Gn. 15:1, 4; Ex. 20:1; Nu. 22:38; Dt. 5:22; Jos. 3:9; 2 Sa. 7:28; Ne. 9:13f.; Pss. 12:6; 19:7–14; 119; Je. 1:9; 30:2; Dn. 7:1f.; 8:15–18; 10:1f.; Mt. 4:1–11; 5:17–19; 19:4f.; 22:31f., 43; 26:53f.; Mk. 7:6–13; Lk. 16:17; 11:49; Jn. 3:33f.; 10:34f.; 17:17; 19:35; 21:24; Rom. 3:2; 15:4; 1 Cor. 10:11; 2 Cor. 6:16f.; 2 Tim. 3:15f.; Tit. 1:9; Heb. 4:12f.; 10:15–17; 1 Pet. 1:12; 2 Pet. 1:12; Rev. 21:5; 22:6–8. *Jesus' words:* Mt. 5:21–24; 7:24; Mk. 13:31; Jn. 15:26; Acts 20:35; 1 Cor. 7:10, 25; 11:23f.; 1 Tim. 5:18.

The apostles' authority: Mt. 28:18–20; Jn. 14:26; 15:26f.; 16:13f.; 17:6, 8, 26; 20:21; Acts 1:8; 1 Cor. 2:9–13; Gal. 1:7f.; Col. 4:16; 2 Thes. 3:6, 12.

The inward witness of the Spirit: Jn. 14:25; 15:26; 16:13f.; Rom. 8:15f.; 2 Cor. 1:22; Gal. 4:6f.; Eph. 1:13f.; 2 Tim. 1:14; 1 Thes. 1:5; 1 Jn. 2:20, 27; 3:24, 5.7f., 20.

The canon: Ex. 24:4–7; 31:18; Dt. 31:9–26; Jos. 1:7f.; 24:26; Ezr. 7:6, 14; Ne. 8:1–3; Is. 8:16; Je. 36:32; Dn. 9:2; Mt. 21:42; Lk. 24:27, 44; Jn. 5:39–47; 1 Cor. 14:37f.; 2 Cor. 10:8f.; Col. 4:16; 2 Thes. 2:15; 3:17; 1 Tim. 5:18; 2 Pet. 3:16; Rev. 1:1–3; 22:8f.

Hermeneutics: Gn. 40:8; Ne. 8:8; Dn. 4:18; Mt. 5:17–48; 15:3–9; 22:29–32; Lk. 24:27–44; Jn. 1:45; 5:39, 46; 16:5–15; Acts 2:16–21; 17:2f.; Rom. 1:2f.; 3:21f.; 4:24; 10:4; 16:25; 1 Cor. 10:11; 2 Cor. 1:20; 2 Tim. 2:15; 1 Pet. 1:10–12; 2 Pet. 1:20.

Questions

1. Distinguish the various meanings of 'Word of God'. Outline the case for viewing the Scriptures as God's Word.
2. What was Jesus' view of the OT and what is the significance of that for our attitude to Scripture today? How would you answer the objection that his view was culturally conditioned and hence not relevant to us?
3. What is the 'inward witness of the Holy Spirit' and what is its significance for our understanding of the authority of Scripture?
4. What is meant by 'the inspiration of Scripture'? Outline the various approaches, assessing their strengths and weaknesses.
5. Why do we speak of (a) *verbal* inspiration and (b) *plenary* inspiration?
6. Explore the link between the authority of Scripture and its inspiration.
7. What is meant by the 'canon of Scripture'? Outline the process by which (a) the OT canon and (b) the NT canon were settled.
8. Examine the basis for the claim that the Bible is infallible and inerrant. How far does the infallibility and inerrancy of Scripture extend?
9. List the considerations that need to be weighed when facing an apparent contradiction or inaccuracy in Scripture. How would you answer the charge, 'The Bible is full of errors' and 'Intelligent people no longer believe the Bible is true'?
10. Identify the main hermeneutical principles. Illustrate their significance with examples of errors which arise from their neglect.
11. 'The Holy Spirit is all we need to understand the Bible.' Discuss.
12. What is the role of 'secondary helps', such as notes and commentaries, in understanding Scripture? What is the place of preaching in increasing understanding of Scripture and how do hermeneutical principles affect it?

Bibliography

Arts. 'Canon', 'Inspiration', 'Interpretation' in *IBD* and *NDT*.

F. F. Bruce, *The New Testament Documents* (IVP, rev. edn 1960).

D. A. Carson and J. D. Woodbridge (eds.), *Hermeneutics, Authority and Canon* (Zondervan, 1986).

D. A. Carson and J. D. Woodbridge (eds.), *Scripture and Truth* (IVP, 1983).

G. D. Fee and D. Stuart, *How to Read the Bible for all its Worth* (SU, 1982).

N. L. Geisler (ed.), *Inerrancy* (Zondervan, 1979).

C. F. H. Henry, *God, Revelation and Authority* 1 and 2 (Word Books, 1976).

C. F. H. Henry (ed.), *Revelation and the Bible* (Tyndale Press, 1959).

J. I. Packer, *God Has Spoken* (Hodder, 2nd edn. 1979).

M. Silva (ed.), *Foundations of Contemporary Interpretation* (Apollos, 1997).
J. R. W. Stott, *Understanding the Bible* (SU, 1984).
B. B. Warfield, *The Inspiration and Authority of the Bible* (PRPC, 1951).

Application

THE NEED TO BE BORN AGAIN

Since we are creatures and sinners, God's truth can be had only as a gift of his condescension which overcomes our instinctive resistance to God and illumines our darkened minds. In biblical terms, we cannot know God and his truth until we have been born again (Jn. 3:3).

This miracle of rebirth and illumination is always associated with a response to the gospel (or 'good news') which lies at the heart of the Christian faith. This wonderful message at first appears to be anything but 'good' news, for it confronts us with our sin, our moral helplessness, intellectual blindness and the sombre fact of God's wrath against us. But in the same breath it assures us of his almighty love for sinners expressed in the gift of his son Jesus Christ who died for sinful men and women on the cross. The gospel summons us to turn from our sin and to cast ourselves upon God's mercy held out to us in Christ.

In responding to that summons in simple trust we experience a new beginning in our lives, a new birth, and with it a new capacity to grasp and respond to God's revelation. If we are true Christians, this first implication will already be a reality for us, but we can never be too clear about this biblical axiom: 'Unless a man is born again, he cannot see the kingdom of God.' This principle operates throughout our Christian life. God makes his truth available only to the humble. As we come in utter dependence, acknowledging our sinful ignorance and blindness and our constant need of his divine illumination, he stoops to us in grace and grants us again and again the gift of his truth.

THE NEED TO WORK HARD AT THE BIBLE

Scripture has come to us out of a period of time spanning several millennia, from the experience of peoples whose culture is unfamiliar. It is written in languages which are not our own. To understand and interpret the Bible correctly therefore requires the demanding discipline of bridging these cultural and linguistic gulfs which separate us from the Bible's time and world.

Obviously the Holy Spirit is an indispensable guide, and we need to guard against the suggestion that untutored Christians with the Spirit cannot grasp the message of the Bible or use it to their profound spiritual profit. To deny this is to fly in the face of the clear evidence of history; it also comes perilously near to repeating the error of the pre-Reformation Catholic Church of interposing an intermediary between God and the individual soul (in the medieval case the church's teaching office, in the present case the biblical scholar). Nor do we deny that God can give immediate, particular and relevant applications of his Word in specific situations through his Spirit, though that is certainly not the norm, and does not even begin to exhaust what 'living according to the Scriptures' means.

Much of the truth of the Bible is uncovered only by hard and demanding study. Fresh and significant aspects of the cultures within which the Bible was written are constantly being discovered, throwing new light even on well-known passages; the vocation of biblical and theological study is therefore tremendously important. But even if that more specialist calling is for comparatively few, all Christians are called to use their minds to the full and to work at the Bible with such capacity and opportunity as they have. There is no substitute for hard work on the Word of God.

THE NEED TO PREACH AND EXPOUND THE BIBLE

The supreme means which God has instituted in the church to unveil and disseminate his truth among his people is preaching. All that we have argued in this chapter serves to underline how vital it is that preaching should be biblical in its appeal and character.

This does not mean, of course, merely stringing together a few Bible passages. In the context of a Christian congregation gathered for worship, preaching should surely aim to expound the Bible at depth and then apply it sensitively and directly to the life and situation of the hearers. All that has been said about the need for hard work on the Bible is especially applicable to preparation for this kind of preaching.

If we are not called to be preachers ourselves, we can play a highly significant role by our prayers for, and encouragement of, biblical preaching. Nothing is more calculated to bring renewal of the life, vigour and faith of the church in any generation than the unleashing of God's everlasting Word in the midst of his people through the ministry of expositor-preachers anointed by his Holy Spirit.

THE NEED TO BE OBEDIENT TO SCRIPTURE

If God has revealed himself and his purposes to us in Jesus Christ as he is known to us through all the Scriptures, then clearly we are under a total obligation to submit our lives to the teaching of the Bible. It is a particular temptation of student life to imagine that truth is for the mind alone; but for Scripture 'knowing the truth' implies living it out in particular situations. In the OT, truth is primarily a moral quality implying the characteristic of dependability or faithfulness in action (*e.g.* Ps. 51:6). This understanding is expressed also in John's concern for *doing* the truth (Jn. 3:21; 1 Jn. 1:6). So this final section is integral to the exposition of the Christian doctrine of authority, for Christian truth in the deepest sense exists only where there is a mind which is set both to understand it and to *obey* it. If our passion for truth does not imply a passion for obedience to truth, then we are not really serious about it.

In the end the doctrine of authority is eminently practical. It confronts us with a specific challenge: to obey all that the Bible teaches, all of the time. Nothing could be more searching or down to earth than that.

PART 2
The doctrine of God

4. The being of God

THE GROUNDS FOR CHRISTIAN THEISM

The basis of our belief in God has in principle been given in Part 1: God has revealed himself to us. The Bible offers no rational demonstration of God's existence, but rather points to his unquestionable reality: 'In the beginning God created the heavens and the earth' (Gn. 1:1); 'I am the LORD, and there is no other; apart from me there is no God' (Is. 45:5, *cf.* Rom. 11:36). His existence and self-disclosure are the ultimate presuppositions of biblical religion.

Humankind's intuitive awareness of God is broadly confirmed by social anthropology, which recognizes a virtually universal religious consciousness. In global terms atheists remain very much in the minority. Calvin described this elemental awareness of God as 'a sense of divinity'; the American theologian Charles Hodge (1797–1878) spoke of the universal human conviction 'that there is a Being on whom they are dependent and to whom they are responsible'. We must not overvalue this innate awareness of God, however, because:

1. The Bible does not view it as an adequate basis for a saving relationship with God.

2. We may thereby insensitively dismiss the difficulties which may be encountered by non-Christians in coming to faith.

3. The Bible says we must approach God by 'faith': 'anyone who comes to God must believe that he exists and that he rewards those who earnestly seek him' (Heb. 11:6). The innate

awareness of God does not remove the approach to God from the realm of faith, though faith, of course, has its own certainties. Hence, the historic creeds, 'I *believe* in God . . .'

THE RATIONAL 'PROOFS' OF GOD'S EXISTENCE

Over the centuries many Christian thinkers have tried to 'prove' the existence of God from factors within the world. This is known as 'natural theology'. Appealing to the laws of logic, the reality of the world, and certain current philosophical ideas, they have sought to show (a) (the stronger version) that the existence of God is logically necessary, or (b) (the weaker version) that it is relatively probable that God exists, *or* that the arguments for his non-existence are not compelling, *or* that to believe in the existence of God is certainly no act of intellectual suicide. Their main 'proofs' are the following:

Ontological

This is the most important philosophically. The classical statement, given by Anselm (1033–1109), has two steps. First: God is 'a being than which nothing greater can be conceived' ('greater' = 'more perfect'). Second: something which exists only in the mind is distinct from something which exists in the mind *and* in reality. Put the two steps together: if God does not exist (*i.e.* exists only in the mind but not in reality), it is possible to conceive of a more perfect being than the most perfect being; that is an impossible contradiction. Hence we must accept the alternative; the most perfect being exists in reality as well as in the mind.

The ontological argument suffered a severe mauling at the hands of the German philosopher Kant (1724–1804); he showed that the argument 'proved' only that *if* there is a supreme being, then he exists. Existence as such does not add anything to a concept. Thus, in Kant's illustration, a real £100 is not more in currency value than an imaginary £100 (though some of my fellow Scots might insist that the reality adds a great deal!). More recently Bertrand Russell (1872–1970), who at one time was attracted by the argument, reached a similar conclusion after analysing the function of the word 'exists'.

In recent years the ontological argument has experienced something of a revival in popularity. Several philosophers of religion believe today that if it once be conceded that a highest conceivable being is possible then he must exist in actuality (*cf.* A. Plantinga, *The Nature of Necessity*; C. S. Evans, *Philosophy of Religion*).

Cosmological

This argument, classically formulated by Thomas Aquinas (*c.* 1225–1274), asserts that the existence of the world requires a supreme being to account for it. Attention is directed to the fact of causality: every event has a cause, which in turn has a cause, and so on back to a first cause, God.

Critics claim that it does not face the alternative, that there may be no 'source' or ultimate origin; 'the universe just is and that's all' (Russell). Its defenders, however, do not believe the argument can be so easily side-stepped. It is more commonly formulated today in terms of proving God from 'contingency'. Things may be either 'contingent' (they exist but equally might not have existed), or 'necessary' (they must exist). While the existence of particular contingent realities can be explained at a certain level by reference to prior contingent causes, the coming into being and the continued existence of all contingent reality can be explained only in terms of a necessary being, God (*cf.* A. McGrath, *Bridge-Building*; E. L. Mascall, *He Who Is*; A. M. Farrer, *Finite and Infinite*).

Teleological

This ancient argument entered the West through Plato's dialogue, *Timaeus*. It argues that evidences of design and purpose in the universe require a universal Designer. The classical formulation of the argument was by William Paley (1743–1805). In his *Natural Theology* (1802), he used the analogy of a working, ticking watch which is chanced upon lying on the ground. Its existence could be explained by a fortuitous convergence of natural forces, wind, rain, heat, volcanic action, *etc.*, but this is plainly much less credible than the postulate of an intelligent watchmaker. By the same token a universe manifesting design implies a designer.

Major criticism was formulated by the Scottish philosopher David Hume (1711–76) in his *Dialogues Concerning Natural Religion*. Granted the vastness of the universe plus infinite time, probability alone could produce a universe such as the one we inhabit; it would inevitably show evidence of design, since a degree of mutual adaptation of its factors would be necessary for its existence and continuance. The argument has also to cope with the fact of dysteleology, *i.e.* processes in the universe which appear relatively purposeless as far as present knowledge is concerned.

An American lawyer, J. E. Horigan, has sought to rehabilitate this argument. He contends that narrowly anti-religious Darwinism ignores the way in which inanimate nature is in harmony with organic evolution; nor, he claims, can evolutionary theory possibly explain the rapid emergence of the large brain in the developing human species (*cf.* J. E. Horigan, *Chance or Design?*; J. P. Moreland, *The Creation Hypothesis*). Certainly many people, when meeting design in the universe at close quarters (say, in the wonder of a newborn baby, or in the staggering complexity of the rod and cone cells of the human eye), find Hume's objections somewhat academic; philosophically, however, they retain a certain cogency.

Moral
This approach asserts that our universal experience of moral obligation, the sense of 'ought', and our inability to fulfil the dictates of moral conscience cannot be adequately explained in terms either of disguised self-interest or of social conditioning. The existence of these objective moral values implies the existence of a transcendent Ground of values.

Kant is particularly linked with this argument. He claimed that God (and freedom and immortality) are 'postulates' of the moral life, presuppositional beliefs which account for our sense of unconditional moral obligation.

The argument has been charged with assuming the very truth it claims to demonstrate, that moral experience can be satisfactorily explained only in religious terms. It also has to face the evidence for the variety of moral codes (people have different notions of what 'good' means) and the presence of moral dilemmas. To be sustained it also has to show that alternative explanations (sociological, psychological) of the rise and continuance of moral feeling are inadequate. Some moral philosophers and Christian apologists think these difficulties can be overcome (H. P. Owen, *The Moral Argument for Christian Theism*; C. S. Lewis, *Mere Christianity*).

The mental proof

This argues that pure materialism is unable to explain the capacity of the mind to move logically from premises to conclusions; only the existence of a transcendent Mind explains the effective operation of our human intelligence, or indeed of other non-material qualities of the mind and imagination. If there is no divine intelligence, it asks, how can we trust our thinking to be true, and hence, what grounds can there be for trusting any argument advanced in support of atheism? C. S. Lewis championed this position (*cf. Miracles*) and more recently, though by a different route, the American philosopher of religion, A. Plantinga (*God and Other Minds*).

The prophetic proof

This is closely related to the previous proof, arguing that the way in which the circumstances of the life and mission of Jesus Christ fulfilled the OT prophecies, which were written many centuries before his coming, defies explanation other than God's action in the whole biblical process of messianic anticipation and fulfilment.

Christological

This approach appeals to the canons of historical probability to show that Jesus Christ can be satisfactorily accounted for only if we assume God's presence and activity in him. Its advocates cite his unimpeachable personal character, his astonishing claims for himself and his mission, and especially the evidence for his resurrection. In this latter case, attention is particularly drawn to the difficulty in giving any other more adequate explanation for the emergence of the Christian church so hard upon the heels of Jesus' ignominious death.

This argument has to face critical questions concerning the historical reliability of the NT text and also the philosophical difficulties raised by alleged miracles. There are scholars today, however, who stand with popular apologists in claiming that these objections can be answered and that purely historical considerations drive us to the brink of faith.

PRESUPPOSITIONAL APOLOGETICS

One area where evangelical thought has advanced in recent years is in the attempt to move the debate with non-Christian thinkers and truth systems away from questions about the validity of Christian claims, to the viability and consistency of non-Christian positions. In a whole series of writings Cornelius Van Til argued that non-Christian thought can give no answer to the fundamental problems of life and philosophy, and that all non-Christian philosophy is essentially a covert attempt to flee from the living God, the ontological Trinity who makes himself known to all people.

More recently Francis Schaeffer sought to demonstrate the necessity for the Christian presupposition of the existence and reality of the God of the Bible, since to deny his existence means denying all facticity and meaning. Schaeffer also argue that non-Christians do not, and indeed cannot, live in a manner that is wholly consistent with their God-denying presuppositions, which are in fact inadequate to justify human existence.

EVALUATING THE RATIONAL APPROACH

Arguments against the rational proofs

What are we to make of the claim that God can be known by rational argument quite apart from his special revelation in Scripture and in Jesus Christ? Over the centuries some Christian thinkers have expressed unhappiness with this whole approach. Quite apart from the recognition that the arguments often appear to fall short of 'proof', they ask:

1. Who is this God? At best, the traditional arguments give us an Almighty Power or First Cause, the Moral Guarantor, *etc.* He is not immediately recognizable as the God of the Bible, the object of Christian faith and worship. The historical and prophetic arguments are obviously less open to this particular objection.

2. How is God known? Scripture teaches that God is known truly by faith. The rational apologetic assumes that God may be known without special revelation. Further, as history clearly shows, when reason is given this degree of autonomy, sooner or later it outgrows its limits and usurps the role of faith; this in turn threatens the concept of redemptive grace and detracts from God's glory.[1]

---

1. *E.g.* Socinianism in the late 16th century, unitarianism in the 17th, deism in the 18th, classical liberalism in the 19th.

3. Where does humankind stand with respect to God? The rational approach assumes a continuity between humankind and God which the Bible denies. It obscures the fact that unbelief is a form of enmity against God, and does a major disservice to the unbeliever by hiding this from him. Further, if rational argument fails to convince non-Christians, they could well be confirmed in their unbelief and rendered less open to subsequent presentation of the moral challenge of the gospel.

4. What does the Bible teach? According to Scripture humankind is already aware of God but has rejected this witness. Our task as Christians is to confront non-Christians with the God of whom they are already aware, *not* to consider their (sinful) presupposition that God might not exist. Fallen men and women can attain a true knowledge of God only through being born again by the Holy Spirit in response to the gospel.

A few final comments are in order.

1. Our assessment of the value of the rational defence of Christian theism will reflect our assessment of how far the fall and sin have affected humankind's original awareness of, and capacity for, God. Here as elsewhere Christian doctrines overlap.

2. There might appear to be a place for apologetic argumentation to meet extreme anti-rational prejudice against Christianity. This is probably best done, however, by showing the overall coherence and superiority of the Christian view as an interpretation of existence, rather than in pursuing one or two specific arguments.

3. The rational approach, particularly in its appeal to the evidence for the divinity of Christ and the biblical witness to him, can help to counter the charge that the Christian faith depends on subjective factors.[2] We need to note in this connection that Jesus and Paul frequently debated with their audiences. Paul's witness in the centres of Greek culture involved defending the gospel against rational criticism (Acts 19:9). At Athens Paul reasoned with his hearers on the basis of their immediate experience (Acts 17:28), and appealed to their authorities in support of his position (Acts 17:28) as well as ultimately to the gospel and revelation (Acts 17:20f.). Further,

2. Something approximating to this appears to be Calvin's view; *cf. Institutes* 1, 8.

the early Christian preachers appealed to historical evidence in support of their claims for Jesus, and his resurrection in particular (Acts 3:15; 4:20; 5:31; 1 Cor. 15:3f.).

4. We must, however, avoid any approach to the non-Christian which diminishes the nature of God, or ignores or obscures the moral character of humankind's relationship to God, or the need for repentance, pardon and reconciliation.

5. The God of the Bible is undoubtedly a far greater concept than the God of natural theology. Since the way God is known can be properly discussed only in the light of who he is, Christians will best serve those they hope to see awakened to faith by setting forth, as adequately as possible, the God of the Bible, the ever-blessed Trinity, Father, Son and Spirit, in all his transcendent majesty and greatness, beauty and power, grace and holiness, and by demonstrating something of his reality in their personal lives and in their Christian community.

Scriptures
Gn. 1:1; Ex. 3:14f.; Jb. 23:1–17; 37:19; Is. 40:25–28; 42:8; 43:11–13; Acts 14:14–18; 17:16–34; Rom. 1:18–32; 11:33; 2 Cor. 4:4; 1 Thes. 1:9; 1 Tim. 6:16; Heb. 11:6.

Questions
1. Rehearse the various philosophical arguments for God's existence. Which do you find most persuasive?
2. Assess the role of these arguments in the light of (a) the Bible's teaching on the nature of God, (b) the Bible's teaching on the nature of humankind, (c) the witness of the apostles.
3. What are the function and limits of apologetics in (a) strengthening the faith of Christians, (b) defending the faith against critics, (c) presenting the gospel to non-Christians?
4. What is the Bible's view of the relationship between faith and human reason?

Bibliography
Art. 'God' in *NDT*.
G. Bray, *The Doctrine of God* (IVP, 1993).
C. Brown, *Philosophy and the Christian Faith* (Tyndale Press, 1969).
J. Calvin, *Institutes of the Christian Religion*, 1.
C. S. Evans, *Philosophy of Religion* (IVP, 1982).
C. F. H. Henry, *God, Revelation and Authority* 1 (Word Books, 1976).
C. S. Lewis, *Mere Christianity* (Fontana, 1952).
A. McGrath, *Bridge-Building* (IVP, 1992).
F. A. Schaeffer, *Francis A. Schaeffer Trilogy* (IVP, 1990).
J. Sire, *Why Should Anyone Believe Anything At All?* (IVP, 1994).

5. God the Holy Trinity

What is God like? A general provisional answer is 'God is a living personal Spirit'. The God of the Bible is emphatically a *living* God who does things (Pss. 97:7; 115:3f.). He is not an impersonal power or energy, but a *personal* God with a distinct character and nature. He is a *Spirit* who transcends the entire world-order, though that order depends totally on him.

THE BIBLICAL BASIS

The Bible presents God as three distinguishable persons, commonly referred to as Father, Son and Spirit. The technical term for this, Trinity, does not occur in the Bible, but belongs to that class of terms which are biblical in the sense of expressing clear biblical teaching.

Old Testament

For Israel the fundamental unity of God is an axiom: 'Hear O Israel: the LORD our God is one' (Dt. 6:4). This insistence on the divine unity was most important because of the idolatrous, depraved polytheism of the surrounding nations. The OT, however, contains intimations of a 'fullness' in the Godhead which foreshadow NT trinitarian teaching.

First, there are the occasions where God refers to himself in plural terms (Gn. 1:26; 3:22; 11:7; Is. 6:8); the evangelist John treats the Isaiah passage as a vision of Jesus (Jn. 12:41). Then, there are references to the Angel of the LORD who is identified with, yet distinct from, God (Ex. 3:2–6; Jdg. 13:2–22). The OT also refers to the Spirit of God as God's personal agent (Gn. 1:2; Ne. 9:20; Ps. 139:7; Is. 63:10–14). It speaks of the wisdom of God, particularly in Proverbs 8, as a personalized outgoing of God to the world, and of the Word of God, the creative utterance of God (Ps. 33:6, 9, *cf.* Gn. 1:26). There are also prophecies which identify the long-awaited Messiah with God (Ps. 2; Is. 9:6f.).

This clearly does not amount to the full doctrine of the Trinity, but in presenting plurality within God's unity these OT passages anticipate the fuller NT teaching.

New Testament

The teaching latent in the OT comes to the surface in the NT.

First, in coming to terms with the impact of Jesus' life and character, claims and miracles, and above all his resurrection and ascension, the apostles found themselves increasingly led to worship him as God. Secondly, the reality and activity of the Holy Spirit among them was clearly the presence of God himself. Hence the trinitarian mould given them by Jesus (Mt. 28:19) determined their own understanding. God the Lord was one, yet distinguishable as three: God the Father, God the Son, and God the Spirit.

Several NT passages presuppose, imply or state God's triunity (Mt. 3:13–17; 28:19; Jn. 14:15–23; Acts 2:32f.; 2 Cor. 13:14; Eph. 1:1–14; 3:16–19).

Each person of the Godhead is asserted to be divine.

The Father is God: Mt. 6:8f.; 7:21; Gal. 1:1.

The Son is God: Jn. 1:1–18; Rom. 9:5; Col. 2:9; Tit. 2:13; Heb. 1:8–10.

The Spirit is God: Mk. 3:29; Jn. 15:26; 1 Cor. 6:19f.; 2 Cor. 3:17f.

The Bible thus presents this unique and mysterious reality: one God, Father, Son and Spirit.

One way of understanding the distinctions between Father, Son and Spirit is to refer different functions to each. The most popular form of this attributes creation to the Father, redemption to the Son and sanctification to the Spirit. Paul gives a modified form in Ephesians 1:3–14, where election is referred to the Father (vv. 4, 5, 11), redemption to the Son (3, 7, 8) and 'sealing' to the Spirit (13, 14). Romans 11:36 has given rise to another understanding based on the prepositions used to refer to God's activity with respect to the universe: '*from* him [Father] and *through* him [Son] and *to* him [Spirit].' These distinctions, however, must not obscure the fundamental truth of the divine unity whereby all three are involved in the activity of any one, *e.g.* while creation may be particularly assigned to the Father (Gn. 1:1; Rev. 4:11), it can equally be associated with the Son (Jn. 1:3) and the Spirit (Is. 40:13).

UNDERSTANDING THE DOCTRINE

The biblical revelation of God's three-in-oneness was explored as the post-apostolic church attempted to expound its faith in the context of Graeco-Roman culture. The conclusions of these early debates are expressed in the Athanasian Creed (*c.* eighth century): 'We worship one God in Trinity, and Trinity in

Unity; neither confounding the Persons: nor dividing the Substance.'

It goes beyond the range of this handbook to explore the technical details of these controversies; suffice it to refer briefly to four important questions.

The limits of language

The inter-trinitarian life of God patently has no parallel in our experience. We can speak about this mystery only because God has spoken about it himself in Scripture. Language here is inevitably placed under strain. Augustine, for example, discussing the propriety of the term 'person' in the case of the Trinity, remarked: 'When the question is asked: three *what*? human language labours altogether under great poverty of speech. The answer however is given "three persons", not that it might be spoken but that it might not be left unspoken.' He made a similar point about the use of the numerical identity 'three' with reference to God's being: 'in this Trinity two or three Persons are not any greater than one of them'.

The way we use 'God'

Christian writers use the word 'God' in two ways; sometimes they mean the Father in particular, at other times the entire Godhead. If 'God' is thought to refer to the Father only, a subordination of Son and Spirit to the Father becomes inevitable. Many sects miss this important distinction and so fall into difficulties with the biblical teaching concerning the full Godhead of the Son and the Spirit. The Jehovah's Witnesses, for example, fail to recognize that in the OT God the LORD (Yahweh/Jehovah) = the triune God (*cf.* in Part 4, 'The Deity of Christ'). The 'Godhead' of the Father is not that which distinguishes him from the Son and Spirit. Godhead is possessed by all three Persons equally; it is by virtue of this that God is unity in Trinity.

Three what?

How may we refer to the 'three' in the Godhead without endangering God's unity? The classical formula, three 'Persons', has come under increasing strain, since contemporary usage rarely distinguishes 'person' from 'personality' with the latter's overtones of distinctiveness and independence. Hence 'three Persons' today comes close to denoting three separate Gods. No generally agreed alternative term has appeared, however, so the traditional formula is usually retained despite its limitations.

Has the Trinity any analogies in human experience?

The difficulty of conceiving of God as 'three-in-one' has encouraged Christian thinkers over the centuries to seek some illuminating analogy of the Trinity. In Augustine's classical exposition the Trinity was illustrated by reference to the unity and distinctions of the memory, understanding and will in the individual human soul. Such a tripartite view of the human being, however, is fairly arbitrary from the standpoint of modern psychology; more seriously, the analogy cannot parallel the unique unity in the Godhead whereby the three Persons coinhere and are all intrinsically involved in the activity of each.

Under the impulse of certain modern views of personality, a number of theologians have revived the ancient analogy of a group of three people. Just as human personality is capable of merging and uniting itself with other personalities, so the 'Persons' of the Godhead coinhere one with another and express themselves in the divine unity. This approach may claim some biblical anchorage. Jesus asserts that in the marriage union 'they are no longer two, but one' (Mt. 19:5f.). This 'social analogy' throws valuable light on the plurality of persons in the Godhead, but can seriously endanger the divine unity.

THE IMPORTANCE OF THE DOCTRINE

Such complexities may tempt us to question the value of raising these issues at all, especially in face of the sheer conundrum of 'one plus one plus one equals one'. In fact, however, just about everything that matters in Christianity hangs on the truth of God's three-in-oneness.

Take the supreme issue of our sin which separates us from God and renders us subject to his wrath. In the final analysis sin concerns two parties, the offending sinner and the offended God. Hence, if Jesus is not God, my sin really has nothing to do with him. Once when Jesus forgave a man's sins he was accused of blasphemy, for only God can forgive sins (Mk. 2:5-7). In one sense his critics were perfectly correct; their error lay in not seeing who Jesus was. Only if Jesus is God come to us in person can he deal with our sins; conversely, if he deals with our sins, he must be God. God is therefore not a simple undifferentiated unity of being.

Similarly with the Holy Spirit. Christians claim that God's regenerating power has come into their lives; now they know God and experience his presence, are persuaded of the authority of his Word, and receive strength to live for him and gifts with which to serve him. But if this is not God himself at work in us, Christian claims about the activity of the Holy Spirit are a delusion, unrelated to supernatural reality. Only if the Holy Spirit who acts upon us is God himself, can our experience make good its claim to be truly redemptive. On this basis, too, we must say that God is more than a simple unity of being.

Thus the entire fabric of Christian redemption and its application to human experience depend wholly on the three-in-oneness of God. The Trinity is as important as that.

The threeness of God is also the basis of the fundamental assertion that God is love. God is not a lonely God who needs the creation as an object for his love. As Trinity God is fulfilled in himself and does not *need* to create or redeem. Creation and redemption are acts of sheer grace, expressions of God as free eternal love.

The fact that in this doctrine there are difficulties which burst through the simple formulae constructed out of the raw materials of our human experience is in one sense entirely predictable, since God is the transcendent Lord of all being. Indeed if we did not encounter deep mystery in God's nature there would be every reason for suspicion concerning the Bible's claims. For all its difficulty, the Trinity is simply (!) the price to be paid for having a God who is great enough to command our worship and service.

One final related point. To reflect upon God in his three-in-oneness, Father, Son, Spirit, in their distinguishable persons and functions yet perfect unity and harmony in mutual, everlasting love, is to catch a vision of something so unspeakably glorious, even beautiful and attractive, that it has ever and again down the centuries moved men and women to the heights of adoring worship, love and praise.

Holy, holy, holy, merciful and mighty,
God in three persons, blessed Trinity!

Scriptures

Gn. 1:2, 26; 3:22; 11:7; Ex. 3:3–6; Jos. 5:13 – 6:2; 1 Ki. 22:19f.; Ne. 9:20; Ps. 33:6, 9; Pr. 8; Is. 6:2, 8; 9:6f.; 11:1f.; Ezk. 37:24f.; Zc. 9:9; Mt. 3:13–17; 28:19; Jn. 14:15–23; Acts 2:32ff.; 2 Cor. 13:14; Eph. 2:18; 4:4–6; Phil. 3:3; 1 Jn. 5:1–12.

Questions

1. What does the doctrine of the Trinity assert?
2. Show how this Christian truth is rooted in Scripture (a) in the OT, (b) in the NT.
3. Imagine yourself speaking to (a) a Jew (who accepts the OT), (b) a Muslim (who denies biblical authority but accepts the reality of one God). How would you expound God's three-in-oneness to each of them?
4. Respond to the comment, 'The Trinity is an unpractical doctrine of relative unimportance.'

Bibliography

Art. 'Trinity' in *NDT*.
Augustine, *On the Trinity*, Library of Christian Classics 8 (SCM, 1954).
G. Bray, *The Doctrine of God* (IVP, 1993).
G. A. F. Knight, *A Biblical Approach to the Doctrine of the Trinity* (Oliver and Boyd, 1953).
S. Olyott, *Three Are One* (Evangelical Press, 1990).
A. W. Wainwright, *The Trinity in the New Testament* (SPCK, 1962).

6. The attributes or perfections of God

The triune God has so revealed himself that it is possible to attribute certain qualities or characteristics to him. These are not mere superficial distinctions of little importance. Rather, 'his attributes coincide with his being' (Bavinck). Some believe that it is a help in this connection to speak of God's perfections rather than attributes.

They have been classified in a variety of ways. The most important historically distinguish God's *incommunicable* attributes (such as his self-existence, which have no analogy in human beings) from his *communicable* attributes (such as his love or justice, which may be reflected in other moral agents).

In expounding God's perfections, Calvin reminds us that 'God to keep us sober speaks sparingly of his essence'. Hence without omitting any feature of God's self-disclosure, we are wise to avoid overdetailed descriptions and distinctions. It is also important to remember that all these perfections exist in God in an indivisible unity.

THE GLORY OF GOD

Glory is a familiar biblical term, normally conveying the visible manifestation of God's being. His glory carries us to the heart of all that is essential to his being as God, his divine majesty, his sheer *God*ness. A parallel term is 'transcendence' which refers to God's 'going beyond' all finite reality.

In Scripture this perfection was expressed in the manifestation of God at Mount Sinai (Ex. 19–24): 'the glory of the LORD looked like a consuming fire on top of the mountain' (Ex. 24:17, *cf.* 19: 16–22), and in Ezekiel's overwhelming vision of God by the Kebar river (Ezk. 1). Something similar is reflected by the description of the exalted Christ: 'his eyes were like blazing fire ... his face was like the sun in all its brilliance' (Rev. 1:14–16). After the blinding revelation of Christ on the road to Damascus, Paul testified to having beheld 'the glory of God in the face of Christ' (2 Cor. 4:6, *cf.* Jn. 1:14). This divine glory is focused only as we fall before him in awe and adoration.

God's glory is manifest in all three persons of the Godhead:
- the glory of the Father: 'Christ was raised from the dead through the glory of the Father,' writes Paul (Rom. 6:4);
- the glory of the Son: 'We have seen his glory,' writes John, 'the glory of the One and Only, who came from the Father' (Jn. 1:14);
- the glory of the Spirit: 'The Spirit of glory ... rests on you,' writes Peter (1 Pet. 4:14).

The connection which we make between the glory of God and his triunity is, however, profounder than simply the listing of proof-texts such as these. For to speak of God's glory is, as we have seen, a way of indicating the uniqueness of God, that by virtue of which he distinguishes himself from all other being and reality. His glory refers to that by and in which he alone is God. But that is in the end nothing other than his triunity, his being as Father, Son and Spirit. In his existence as the triune One, God's glory is supremely revealed. No wonder the long centuries of Christian worship have echoed with the cry, 'Glory be to the Father, glory be to the Son, glory be to the Spirit.' Truly 'in his temple all cry, "Glory!"' (Ps. 29:9).

This perfection may serve as a summary term for several other aspects. God's glory implies:

1. The *infinity* of God: he is without limitation. He 'lives in unapproachable light' (1 Tim. 6:16), a God of 'unsearchable judgments' whose paths are 'beyond tracing out' (Rom. 11:33).

2. The *self-existence* of God: he depends on nothing else. 'In the beginning God . . .' (Gn. 1:1); 'as if he needed anything' (Acts 17:25, *cf.* Is. 40:13f.).

3. The *immutability* of God: he is always consistent. 'I the LORD do not change' (Mal. 3:6); 'the Father of the heavenly lights, who does not change like shifting shadows' (Jas. 1:17); 'Jesus Christ is the same yesterday and today and for ever' (Heb. 13:8). 'The fruit of the Spirit is . . . faithfulness' (Gal. 5:22), the quality reflecting the Spirit's inner nature. God's changelessness is expressed in his faithfulness and dependability in his relationships with his people. The whole idea of the covenant is based on this perfection.

The glory of God proclaims God's utter priority and self-sufficiency. The creation of the universe and of humankind are acts of free grace and not requirements of God's being. Our ultimate value and significance lie, accordingly, in his glory (*cf.* Eph. 1:12).

This view of God is anathema to modern people. It is also resisted by some who argue that a self-sufficient God whose action is directed towards his own glory is unworthy of worship. This forgets, however, that the God of glory is the God of grace who sacrificed himself on a cross to save us. Thus while God's purposes certainly aim at, and procure, his glory, they aim also at our eternal well-being. The underlying principle was expressed by Calvin: 'It is for God above all things that we are born, and not for ourselves.' Whether we agree with that is a dividing-line and touchstone for all human thought about God.

THE LORDSHIP OF GOD

'The LORD' is the most frequent title of God in the English translations of the OT; the Hebrew word is *Yahweh*, supremely associated with the covenant between God and Israel. It is God's self-designation given in response to Moses' request that God name himself (Ex. 3:13–15). Its meaning, 'I am who I am', which may also be translated 'I will be what I will be', represents God's promise to fulfil his declared purpose of rescuing Israel from Egypt to establish them in the land of promise. The name stands for God's loyalty to his people and the infallibility of his promises.

A similar conviction is expressed by referring to God's *sovereignty*. He rules in the world and his will is the final cause of all things, including specifically creation and preservation (Ps. 95:6; Rev. 4:11), human government (Pr. 21:1; Dn. 4:35), the salvation of God's people (Rom. 8:29f.; Eph. 1:4, 11), the sufferings of Christ (Lk. 22:42; Acts 2:23), the sufferings of Christians (Phil. 1:29; 1 Pet. 3:17), our life and destiny (Acts 18:21; Rom. 15:32) and even the smallest details of life (Mt. 10:29). God reigns in his universe, exalted over all other claimants to power and authority. He alone is God: 'I am the LORD, and there is no other' (Is. 45:6, *cf.* 43:11; 44:8; 45:21).

Once again it is crucial to understand this perfection of God's lordship in trinitarian terms. Thus

- the Father is Lord: 'we praise our Lord and Father,' writes James (Jas. 3:9);
- the Son is Lord: '[God] brought back from the dead our Lord Jesus Christ,' says the writer of Hebrews (Heb. 13:20);
- the Spirit is Lord: 'the Lord is the Spirit,' writes Paul (2 Cor. 3:17).

Understanding God's lordship in trinitarian terms prevents us from allowing this perfection of God to degenerate into the operation of an impersonal will, a sort of fate or karma which hangs over us and which unfeelingly and remorselessly grinds its way forward. The One who is the eternal Father who so loves the world, the risen Son in his feeling humanity, and the living Spirit who came as dove as well as wind and fire – this is the God who is Lord.

God's lordship is expressed in three related perfections:

1. The *omnipotence* of God: he is all-powerful (Gn. 17:1). This is vividly expressed in God's question, 'Is anything too hard for the LORD?', asked after God's promise to Abraham and Sarah of a son in their extreme age (Gn. 18:14), and repeated again with his promise to restore and liberate Jerusalem in face of its imminent destruction by the Babylonian army (Je. 32:27). In both cases God's promise was fulfilled to the letter.

There is similar testimony to God's omnipotence in the NT. He reveals himself as the God with whom 'nothing is impossible', whether the virgin birth (Lk. 1:37) or the regeneration of fallen humanity (Mk. 10:27).

Here is the heart of God's lordship and it calls for an attitude of utter confidence in the midst of all the 'impossibilities' of human history and personal circumstances. He is Lord: 'can anything be too hard for the Lord?'

2. The *omnipresence* of God: he is everywhere present. This is expounded in Psalm 139:7–12. Confronted with the disturbing and overwhelming reality of God's searching presence, the psalmist realizes he can evade such a God neither in space and time nor in eternity. David's adultery with Bathsheba and his 'management' of her husband's death might be hushed up in the Jerusalem court, but all was seen by God, who could uncover it any time (2 Sa. 12:11f.). The Bible is full of these divine exposures (Gn. 3:11; Jos. 7:10–26; 2 Ki. 5:26; Acts 5:1–11).

God's omnipresence can also be most reassuring. When wickedness triumphs and injustice and sheer might rule unchallenged, God knows and sees all (Ps. 66:12; Is. 43:2; Acts 23:11). He is not mocked (Gal. 6:7) and has appointed a day to judge the world (Acts 17:31). Similarly we are comforted in moments of personal trial or suffering for our faith: 'Record my lament; list my tears on your scroll – are they not in your record?' (Ps. 56:8, *cf*. Rev. 6:9; 18:24).

God's *eternity* is a related aspect. Omnipresence in space has its counterpart in time. 'From everlasting to everlasting you are God' (Ps. 90:2). There is no moment 'before' him or after him.

3. The *omniscience* of God: God is all-knowing. This perfection is closely linked to his omnipresence (Ps. 139:1–12). The practical implications are therefore similar, disturbing and yet reassuring: God sees and hence knows all. This is particularly pertinent to the theme of judgment and is symbolically expressed by the 'opening of the books' (Rev. 20:12). The past is not gone for ever; all time is present to God. At the final judgment the evidence will far exceed what any human judge or jury ever considered: the 'replay' of the accused's entire life, all outward acts, each barely conscious motive and attitude. God's final judgment will be *utterly* just. This sets in perspective the 'mysteries' of life, events which appear absurd or meaningless; since God knows all, these too are subject to his understanding and will. With God there may be mysteries but never mistakes.

This perfection must not be 'sacrificed' in order to secure human freedom, as some scholars have recently argued. This is too high a price to pay. God's omniscience is fundamental to the finality of his self-revelation. If God knew only in part, his truth would be only provisional and Jesus Christ, his only Son, would not be the ultimate revelation, *the truth*. The lordship of God in his omniscience means that we do not await further revelation which might supersede his self-disclosure in Jesus Christ. As the eternal Son of God, the reality of the eternal God himself, Jesus is the ultimate revelation, *the truth* in whom are hidden all the treasures of wisdom and knowledge (Jn. 14:6; Col. 2:3). God's omniscience is also the basis for the Holy Spirit's work of revealing the mind and truth of God in Scripture, thereby guaranteeing its reliability and finality (Jn. 16:13; 17:17).

THE HOLINESS OF GOD

The danger mentioned earlier of separating the perfections of God arises most frequently with reference to the holiness and the love of God. Many have an unresolved tension between the holy God of the law and the loving God of the gospel. Some resolve this by over-stressing God's holiness; he is seen as an austere rigorist compelling restless moral endeavour by the threat of future judgment. Others overstress God's love, turning him into an indulgent, sentimental figure, devoid of moral strength. The biblical God is *both* holy and loving, in inseparable unity in each person of the Trinity.

God's holiness is central to his being and is particularly prominent in the OT (Lv. 11:44; 19:2; *etc.*; Jos. 24:19; 1 Sa. 6:20; Ps. 22:3; Is. 57:15). Its comparative absence in the NT is more apparent than real, in face of the NT stress on the person and work of the *Holy* Spirit. The fundamental element in the Hebrew *qāḏôš*, translated 'holy' in the English Bible, is most probably 'separation', with the positive implication, 'dedication to the ownership of'. Referred to God it carries two implications.

1. God is separate from all other beings; he alone is God. In this sense God's holiness is akin to his glory. Something of this is conveyed in Isaiah's vision: 'Holy, holy, holy is the LORD Almighty; the whole earth is full of his glory' (Is. 6:3), echoed in John's vision nearly a millennium later: 'Holy, holy, holy is the Lord God Almighty, who was, and is, and is to come' (Rev. 4:8, *cf.* 1 Tim. 6:16). This divine holiness is also referred to the Son (Mk. 9:2f.; Lk. 1:35; Acts 9:3f.; Rev. 1:12f.) and the Spirit (Lk. 11:13; Acts 2:4; 4:31; Eph. 4:30; Heb. 9:8).

2. The holiness of God as an ethical notion refers to his separation of himself from all that resists and opposes him. 'Holiness is that attribute in virtue of which God makes himself the absolute standard of himself' (Godet). This is the basis of all moral distinctions. Good is what God wills; evil is what resists and contradicts his will, and hence his nature.

God's holiness means that he is utterly pure and perfect, without any sin or evil; his very being is the outshining and outpouring of purity, truth, righteousness, justice, goodness, and every moral perfection. The ethical challenge this brings is clear in both Testaments. One of God's most frequent designations in Isaiah is 'the Holy One of Israel' (5:19; 30:12; 43:3; 55:5) who requires Israel to conform in her behaviour to the character of the God 'in the midst' of the nation (12:6). In the NT the indwelling of the Holy Spirit carries searching ethical implications: Christians are to 'avoid immorality' and to live as those called to 'a holy life' (1 Cor. 6:18f.; 1 Thes. 4:3, 7f.).

Failure to ground God's holiness in his essential nature is a primary cause of people's mistaken severance of the holiness from the love of God. If holiness is God's will, his acts of love and pardon must also be *holy* acts.

Once more we need to underline the relationship of this perfection to the wholeness of God as trinity:

- the Father is holy: 'Holy Father, protect them,' prayed Jesus (Jn. 17:11);
- the Son is holy: 'you will not ... let your Holy One see decay,' proclaimed Peter of Jesus (Acts 2:27; Ps. 16:10);
- the Spirit is holy: 'God ... gives you his Holy Spirit,' writes Paul (1 Thes. 4:8).

Thus God's holiness can never be separated from all else that we know of him, and certainly not from his everlasting grace in the gift and presence of his Son and Spirit.

Four related terms should be noted.

1. God's *righteousness* is his 'holy' conformity with himself; in the OT it is interpreted by his relationship with his creation (Ps. 145:17) and with his people (Ps. 31:1; Je. 11:20). It includes action which delivers and vindicates his people (Je. 23:6); he can thus be described as 'a righteous God and a Saviour' (Is. 45:21). Lack of righteousness constitutes humankind's moral predicament before God, and it is God's provision of righteousness in Christ which constitutes the heart of the gospel of his grace

(Rom. 1:17; 3:21f.; 5:17–21).

2. God's *justice* is his holy will in operation (Dt. 32:4; 1 Jn. 1:9; Rev. 15:3). Some theologians have distinguished between God's *rectoral* justice in his rule in the world in general, and his *distributive* justice revealed in the distribution of rewards and punishments. This perfection relates to God's love and mercy, since his justice at times vindicates the needy and the penitent (Pss. 76:9; 146:7; Is. 30:18; 1 Jn. 1:9).

3. God's *wrath* arises from his eternal self-consistency. His revealed character is an unalterable expression of his nature. All that opposes him he resists with a total and final commitment. 'Wrath is the holy revulsion of God's being against that which is the contradiction of his holiness' (J. Murray). God's wrath is *not*, as is often alleged, a crude piece of anthropomorphism. It is rather the response of the normative Person in his personal quality of holiness towards the presence of sin in his universe. Without his wrath God would not be truly holy and his love would degenerate into sentimentality. Nor is his wrath arbitrary, fitful or subject to emotion as in human beings. God's wrath is working itself out in history as people reap the moral and spiritual harvest for rejecting God's revelation (Rom. 1:18f.); this is but a preliminary form of something which is to be revealed at the end of the age and of which the cross of Christ represents the clearest and most sobering preview (Ps. 78:31; Ho. 5:10; Jn. 3:36; Eph. 2:3; 1 Thes. 1:10; Rev. 6:16).

4. God's *goodness* is a perfection which can be classified equally under holiness or love, and as such underlines the impossibility of separating these two attributes (Ex. 33:19; 1 Ki. 8:66; Ps. 34:8; Rom. 2:4).

THE LOVE OF GOD

'God is love' (1 Jn. 4:8) is the best-known biblical definition of God. In human contexts, however, love covers a considerable variety of attitudes and actions. Referred to God, it is a quite specific idea. 'This is love . . . that God sent his Son as an atoning sacrifice for our sins' (1 Jn. 4:10); 'This is how God showed his love . . . He sent his one and only Son into the world' (1 Jn. 4:9).

But the love of the three persons is not simply expressed internally within their own mutual relations, but spills over into a trinitarian love for God's human creatures. Thus

- the Father is love: 'God so loved the world that he gave his one and only Son,' writes John (Jn. 3:16);
- the Son is love: 'the Son of God, who loved me and gave himself for me,' blurts out Paul (Gal. 2:20);
- the Spirit is love: 'I urge you by the love of the Spirit,' says Paul again (Rom. 15:30).

The word here, *agapē*, has comparatively little currency beyond the NT. The common Greek term, *erōs*, speaks of a love which relates to a *worthy* object, while *agapē* is a love for the *un*worthy, for one who has forfeited all right to the lover's devotion. The OT has witness to this in God's love for Israel (Dt. 7:7f.), and in Hosea's love for his faithless wife (Ho. 3:1f.; *etc.*).

This might seem to reopen the division we have sought to overcome between the holiness and love of God. How can this God who acts freely in love be reconciled with the holy God who is concerned for his glory? We must remember, however, that the holiness of God is the basis and source of all good; in this way it can be seen as the necessary presupposition of his love. Furthermore, only he who is fully and freely God can fully and freely condescend to another in *agapē*-love, which is rooted in the everlasting mutual love of the three Persons of the Holy Trinity.

Holiness and love conjoin perfectly in the person and work of Jesus Christ. As God, he embodies divine holiness that is separate from and resistant to all sin and evil, yet his very coming is God's loving, gracious response to human guilt and helplessness. They unite also in the ministry of God the *Holy* Spirit whose essential ministry is the renewal and sanctification of God's people in fulfilment of God's purpose of love.

The love of God is therefore always bound up with *grace*, a stooping to embrace the worthless. His love is his free, unconstrained decision to rescue sinful men and women in Jesus Christ, and to renew and sanctify them in the Holy Spirit; it is therefore a sheer and unqualified miracle.

Three further aspects should be noted.

1. The love of God, *agapē*, is expressed principally in the redemption of sinners and all that goes with that. But it is also expressed in his care for his creation. This is referred to frequently as his *goodness* or *kindness*, which is also evident in the natural world (Acts 14:17).

2. God's *mercy* is his love as it encounters specific human sin.

In mercy he pardons people's transgression; God's mercy is always costly for it involves his accepting the consequences of human sin in the cross (Eph. 2:4; Tit. 3:5).

3. The *covenant* is a key biblical notion around which much of the Bible's teaching on God's love is gathered. It refers to God's love expressed in his entering into relationship with people. The central OT covenant was with Abraham and it reaches its full development in the new covenant (lit. new testament) in Christ. By this God freely commits himself to deliver his people and to remain their God. The Hebrew words for grace, *ḥēn, ḥeseḏ*, are covenant terms implying *loyal* love, or 'steadfast love' (RSV).

This aspect of the love of God is the Christian's ultimate security: 'if we are faithless, he will remain faithful' (2 Tim. 2:13). Our standing with God does not depend on our grasp upon Christ and is not finally qualified by our disobedience and half-hearted responses. God's almighty heart beats for us, and in that fact we find our final security and peace.

Here then is the God of the Bible:

the glorious God in his unapproachable and exalted majesty,
the Lord, exalted over all things and bringing all things into
  the service of his purpose,
the Holy one, exalted and separate from sin and evil,
the God of love, everlasting, gracious and redeeming.

Scriptures

The glory of God: Ex. 19 – 24; Nu. 14:21; 16:19f.; 1 Ki. 8:11; Ps. 19:1; Is. 6:1–8; Ezk. 1:28; Lk. 9:32; Jn. 1:14; 1 Tim. 6:16; Rev. 1:8–17; 21:11.
The lordship of God: Gn. 12:8; 17:1; Ex. 3:14ff.; Ps. 135:6; 139:1–12; Pr. 21:1; Is. 43:11; 45:6; Je. 32:27; Dn. 2:20f.; Mt. 10:29; Mk. 10:27; Acts 17:31; Rom. 8:29; Gal. 6:7; Eph. 1:11; Rev. 1:7; 4:11.
The holiness of God: Ex. 3:5; 19:10–25; 28:36; Lv. 11:45; 1 Sa. 2:2; Is. 6:1–3; 57:15; Am. 4:2; Zc. 14:20; Mt. 3:7; Mk. 9:2; Lk. 5:8; Jn. 3:36; Acts 2:1f.; 4:27, 31f.; Rom. 1:18; 3:21–31; 1 Cor. 1:30; 6:19; Col. 3:6; 1 Thes. 4:8; 1 Jn. 1:5, 9; Rev. 4:8; 15:4.
The love of God: Nu. 14:18; Dt. 7:8; Ne. 9:17b; Pss. 86:5; 103; 118:29; Ho. 3:1; Lk. 11:42; Jn. 3:16; Rom. 5:8; 8:35f.; Gal. 2:20.

Questions

1. What is meant by (a) the glory of God, (b) the lordship of God, (c) the holiness of God, (d) the love of God? Establish the biblical basis of each.
2. Try and relate each perfection to the three persons of the Trinity.
3. How do these perfections affect (a) Christian evangelism, (b) the priorities of a local church, (c) our Christian character?

4. How would you try to relate these divine perfections to someone facing (a) severe illness, (b) personal moral failure, (c) bereavement, (d) temporary loss of faith, (e) acute disappointment, (f) a broken relationship?

Bibliography

Art. 'God' in *NDT*.
L. Berkhof, *Systematic Theology*, Part I (Banner of Truth, 1958).
G. Bray, *The Doctrine of God* (IVP, 1993).
S. Charnock, *The Attributes of God* (1682) (Evangelical Press, 1980).
J. I. Packer, *Knowing God* (Hodder, 1973).
S. J. Mikolaski, *The Grace of God* (Eerdmans, 1966).
A. W. Tozer, *The Knowledge of the Holy* (STL Books, 1976).

7. The work of creation

Creation is that work of the triune God by which he called all things that exist, both material and spiritual, into existence out of non-existence.

Quite apart from the first two chapters of Genesis, there are clear references to creation in every section of Scripture: Psalms (90:2; 102:25f.); prophets (Is. 40:26f.; Je. 10:12f.; Am. 4:13); gospels (Mt. 19:4; Jn. 1:3); epistles (Rom. 1:25; 1 Cor. 11:9; Col. 1:16); Revelation (4:11; 10:6). Nehemiah 9:6 expresses the unambiguous testimony of the Bible, 'You alone are the LORD. You made the heavens, even the highest heavens and all their starry host, the earth and all that is on it, the seas and all that is in them. You give life to everything and the multitudes of heaven worship you.' It is noteworthy that each person of the Godhead is seen as active in creation: Father (1 Cor. 8:6); Son (Jn. 1:3); Spirit (Gn. 1:2; Is. 40:12f.). Creation is, therefore, a divinely revealed truth and hence an article of faith (Heb. 11:3).

CREATION 'OUT OF NOTHING'

God created the physical and spiritual universe at the first 'out of nothing' (Lat.: *ex nihilo*). While the actual phrase 'out of nothing' does not appear, the idea is clearly taught in the Bible (Gn. 1:1f.; Ps. 33:6; Jn. 1:3; Rom. 4:17; 1 Cor. 1:28; Heb. 11:3). It was particularly significant in the struggle of the early church against gnosticism, which regarded matter as evil, having its origin in some inferior deity.

Our experience of creating is of the rearrangement of previously existing materials into new forms and patterns; so an 'action' which brings both space and time into being is strictly beyond our comprehension. However, recalling the basis of this truth, divine revelation, we can confidently affirm the fact of creation, although we may not be able to understand it fully.

There is an important analogy of creation *ex nihilo* in redemption (2 Cor. 4:6). New life in the Holy Spirit is not a repair job but the creation of a radically new being (2 Cor. 5:17).

Positively, this doctrine implies God's free and sovereign transcendence and also the utter dependence of all things upon him. Negatively, it implies:

1. God did not make the universe out of previously existing primary matter, though the contrary idea goes back in western thought as far as Plato's *Timaeus*. Plato's view distinguishes two principles which underlie the world, God *and* primary matter. Against all such dualism Scripture's doctrine of creation asserts the sole causality of God.

2. God did not make the world out of 'nothing'. Some scholars have interpreted the very formula 'creation out of nothing' to imply that 'nothing' was an entity, an original negative which God 'overcame' in his work of creation. This unwarranted speculation finds no support in the biblical texts on creation.

3. God did not make the world out of himself. The world is not an extension of God's being; it is given a true independence of being by God. Creation *ex nihilo*, therefore, stands against all forms of pantheism. This has profound repercussions for our interpretation of evil, for if the world is an extension of God then either (a) evil and good are equally ultimate, or (b) there is no final distinction between good and evil: whatever is, is good. The former is followed by Zoroastrianism, the latter by Hinduism. There are also implications for our investigation of the world, as will be seen below.

4. 'Creation out of nothing', which we may call primary creation, does not cover every occasion of creation. Scripture also uses the term 'creation' for what we may call secondary creation, where God uses previously created materials in his further creative work, as in the forming of humankind (Gn. 2:7) or the beasts and birds (Gn. 2:19).

CONTINUING CREATION

The biblical view of God as creator includes his continuous, unbroken sustenance and renewal of the world. This is expressed in the idea of *upholding* (Heb. 1:3, *pherōn*, lit. 'carrying along'; Col. 1:17, *synestēken*, lit. 'stand together' or 'cohere'; *cf.* Acts 17:25). It is implied in the Hebrew participles used for God's creative work, *cf.* Jb. 9:8f.; Ps. 104:2f.; Is. 42:5; 44:24; 45:18. 'The [Hebrew] participate active indicates a person or thing conceived as being in the continual uninterrupted exercize of an activity' (Gesenius-Kautzsch, *Hebrew Grammar*). The English translations conspicuously fail to reproduce this sense, 'an indication of the latent deism in modern western thinking which prefers to speak of a once-for-all creation in the past rather than of the continuous creative activity of God' (R. T. France).

This continuous creative activity can be illustrated by the way the Bible refers to what *we* call the 'natural' order. Stars and seasons (Jb. 38:31–33; Is. 40:26; Acts 14:17), changes in the weather (Jb. 38; Mt. 5:45), the life cycle of the meanest creature (Jb. 39; Mt. 6:28–30), the whole human life cycle (Ps. 104:27–29, 36) are all directly referred to the work of God; likewise human skills such as farming (Is. 28:24f.), metalwork (Is. 54:16) and other crafts (Ex. 31:2–5), not excluding warfare (Ps. 144:1).

To put the position more philosophically, God has called the universe into being out of nothing, and hence at every moment it 'hangs' suspended, as it were, over the abyss of non-existence. If God were to withdraw his upholding Word, then all being, spiritual and material, would instantly tumble back into nothing and cease to exist. The continuation of the universe from one moment to the next is therefore as great a miracle and as fully the work of God as is its coming into being at the beginning. In this profound sense we all live every instant only by the grace of God.

A QUESTION OF LANGUAGE

These two aspects of creation highlight one misleading aspect of the common distinction between 'nature' (where immanent realities operate in terms of immediate cause and effect) and 'supernature' (where God 'is' and operates).

Much of the science–religion debate has been conducted within this nature/supernature framework with prejudicial results for both parties. The religious person's God is seen to be active in the 'gaps' in scientific explanation, where the 'natural' gives place to the 'supernatural'. Miracles then clearly breach the scientific law that every event must have a cause; thus scientist and believer are set on a collision course. As the scientist amasses explanations and causal chains, the area of supernatural intervention shrinks virtually to zero; believers retain their faith at the cost of repudiating the scientific enterprise; scientists retain their scientific integrity at the cost of renouncing genuine biblical religion.

'The Hebrew vocabulary includes no equivalent to our term "Nature". This is not surprising if by "Nature" we mean "the creative and regulative *physical* power which is conceived of as operating in the physical world and as the immediate cause of all its phenomena", the only way to render this idea into Hebrew would be to say simply "God"' (H. Wheeler Robinson). In the biblical view 'natural event' such as rainfall, and 'supernatural event' such as 'quailfall' (Ex. 16) are *both* the action of God. For the Bible the very continuance of the world is miraculous, in the sense that it is utterly dependent upon God for its continued existence. Hence '... it is not necessary or even desirable to regard divine creative activity as more miraculous than divine sustenance of the regularities of nature, nor to consider scientific investigation of creative activities as less creditable than that of "sustaining" activities' (R. Hooykaas).

This biblical view can be traced back through the history of theology, and is reflected in many of the great Christians who were the fathers of the modern scientific revolution.[1] It is, therefore, better in most cases to replace the nature/supernature model by an alternative such as immanent/transcendent, which has a much longer history and better reflects God's *continuous* creative activity in the universe.

This biblical idea must be distinguished from an unbiblical philosophical view, also known as 'continuous creation', which teaches that God is actually himself developing and evolving with the world.

To summarize, the doctrine of creation asserts two things: the free and sovereign lordship of God with respect to his world, and

---

1. Galileo, Kepler, Newton, Asa Gray, to mention several of the most celebrated. *Cf.* R. Hooykaas, *Religion and the Rise of Modern Science* (Scottish Academic Press, 1972).

the utter and unqualifiable dependence of all things upon God.

THE SCIENTIFIC ENTERPRISE

God's creation *ex nihilo* has profound implications for our investigation of the world. While utterly dependent on God for its continued being, the world is distinct from God; he did not make it out of himself. It may therefore be investigated in its own immanent terms.

The Christian perspective on the scientific enterprise lies not in finding God in various gaps in explanation, but in the awe which arises as we see the 'whole thing' as his creation and gift. 'The hand of God is to be seen in gaps in scientific description neither more nor less than in scientifically explained events' (F. Rhodes). Thus Laplace's celebrated claim, 'I have no need for that [God] hypothesis', in his account of the universe is in one sense eminently biblical. Nature, the immanent creaturely order, can be interpreted by looking at nature; correspondingly, despite creation's witness to his power and majesty (Acts 14:17; Rom. 1:20), God can be truly understood only by looking at God, *i.e.* by focusing on his word written and incarnate. Francis Bacon, the great Christian father of modern science, said, 'Give to nature what is nature's and to God what is God's.' Thus the biblical doctrine of creation legitimizes scientific investigation.

This is true in a further and allied sense. Natural processes are not simply random or objective happenings, but represent the response of created reality to the ordering of a personal rational Creator. 'There are no laws of nature, only customs of God' (Kingsley). But for that precise reason nature is inherently reliable and predictable, accordant with the self-consistency and faithfulness of the Creator. The uniformity of natural causes on which scientific experiment depends is the immediate implication of biblical revelation. It is no accident that the scientific revolution was located in the Christianized West at the close of the Middle Ages, nor that so many of the leaders of the revolution were people of profound Christian and biblical faith (see R. Hookyaas, *Religion and the Rise of Modern Science*).

MIRACLE

Is Christianity then simply a special way of looking at nature? What of the idea of miracle and the traditional claims for God's acts in the world?

In terms of the Christian understanding of God and the world, God's universe is open before him; he is sovereignly free at any point to order his world in a different way. Will he so choose? The answer depends on a further question: why did God create the world? Part of the answer here involves God's creating humankind to whom he could manifest himself, with whom he could enter into relationship, and in whom he could be glorified.

Hence his acting at certain critical points in history to disclose himself clearly and to establish a satisfactory relationship with humankind is not only possible, but overwhelmingly probable. At these points, God acts differently, though even here the immanent process may be taken into his action (*e.g.* the reference to the wind at the parting of the Red Sea, Ex. 14:21). These events are entirely compatible with his overall purposes, and are therefore neither arbitrary nor excessively numerous, and centre in his supreme self-disclosure in Jesus Christ.

With this basic framework believers can pursue their life with secure faith in God's miraculous redemption in Christ in the past, and in God's personal care and sovereign freedom to answer prayer and fulfil his redemptive purposes in the present and future. At the same time Christians as scientists can pursue their investigations with faith in God's consistency as expressed in the observed regularities of the physical universe in the past and future.

The case against miracles on scientific grounds appeared stronger when the scientific view of the universe and its function was dominated by Newtonian mechanics. For Newton (1642–1727) and his successors the universe was like a great interlocking machine operating according to fixed laws. By this model miracles were seen as external interruptions of the regular law-abiding function of things.

Einstein's relativity theory (1905) threw a wrench into the machine and modern physics was born. While the universe clearly exhibits order, it is not the order of a well-oiled machine but that of part of an infinitely more complex constellation of factors and forces. Quantum theory, following on the heels of relativity, has drawn attention to the apparent randomness or uncertainty in the basic structure of material existence. All of this has helped produce a new openness to the universe and less dogmatism about what may or what may not happen. Today many appreciate the place of surprise and beauty alongside order in any picture of the world and its function. This is not to imply that scientists are only a short step away from becoming believers. The way people construct a 'worldview' and the conclusions they come to are impacted by all kinds of factors in their personal experience, only some of which are 'scientific' in the narrow sense. The specifically scientific factors, however, are today less often set in opposition to miracle.

As far as philosophical objections to miracle are concerned, the reader is referred to the bibliography for fuller discussion. The philosophical case against miracles is classically associated with David Hume and has been updated in recent times by sceptical thinkers such as A. N. Flew. None of the arguments presented by these writers, however, carries conviction; the attempt to deny miracles in principle can succeed only by assuming the conclusion as one of the premises. In the end the occurrence of miracles is a matter of investigating the claim in each case in its own terms and weighing the relevant evidence. On biblical-theistic presuppositions there can be no questioning their possibility.

THE QUESTION OF ORIGINS

What is the relation between the Bible's account of creation (Gn. 1–2) and the explanation given by natural science, which in some cases denies a 'beginning', or sets it at a point in the infinite past?

The Genesis account

The opening chapters of Genesis are as fully inspired by the Holy Spirit as any others in Scripture. Our Lord and the apostles clearly saw them in this way and it is instructive to note how many NT passages allude to them, *viz.* Mt. 19:4f.; Mk. 10:6f.; 13:19; Jn. 1:1; Acts 17:24; 1 Cor. 6:16; 11:7, 9; 15:45, 47; 2 Cor. 4:6; Eph. 5:31; Col. 3:10; Jas. 3:9; 2 Pet. 3:5; Rev. 2:7; 22:2, 14, 19. The divine origin of the universe is therefore not in question; the real issue is the correct interpretation of the biblical teaching.

One position is to take the language literally; the universe was formed by God out of nothing through six distinct decrees over six successive twenty-four-hour periods. A modification of this sees the 'days' as eras or successive 'stages' during which God formed the cosmos (*cf.* Ps. 90:4; 2 Pet. 3:8). Another refers the 'six days' to a six-day period in which creation was *revealed* to the biblical author or was subsequently expounded to the people of Israel. Others see the whole as pictorial, the details being unimportant beside the central claim of the passage, that God created everything in the universe.

In Part 1 we stressed that the Bible should be interpreted in terms of its literary form (poetry as poetry, history as history, *etc.*), and that the writer's intention must be taken into account. This means asking of these Genesis passages: what is the literary genre? What is the writer seeking to convey? Is this a poetic-religious passage, or is it an attempt to describe within the images of the day the cosmological origins of the world? Or is it a bit of both of these, an account of real events couched in poetic-religious form? The presence of something close to the 'poetic' in the Genesis creation accounts has been noted by a number of scholars. One refers to its 'exalted, semi-poetic language'; another notes the rhythmic counterpart in Genesis 1 between days one and four, two and five, and three and six, and describes the passage as 'a story, not only a statement'. Many speak of it as a 'hymn'. But does that exclude its conveying genuine information about events?

When trying to resolve such questions, it is helpful to examine other biblical references to natural things. The following conclusions arise.

1. Biblical language is in general popular. The Bible is concerned to convey a message of salvation to all peoples of all ages and therefore adopts popular, non-technical language. It is remarkable that Genesis 1 was read during the Apollo 8 moon flight without sounding incongruous.

2. Biblical language is 'phenomenal', *i.e.* it relates to what immediately appears and describes things from the viewpoint of the observer. Thus the sun 'rises and sets'; we meet with 'stars', not asteroids or nebulae.

3. Biblical language is non-theoretical. The Bible does not theorize about the actual nature of things; it does not champion Einstein against Newton, or Copernicus against Ptolemy. It excludes dualism and pantheism certainly, but it does not teach a specific cosmology.

4. Biblical language is cultural, communicating its divine revelation primarily through the culture of its time. All these factors need to be weighed carefully before dogmatizing about the correct interpretation of Genesis 1 – 2.

Further questions

1. The creation of time raises a special difficulty. Augustine focused this centuries ago by observing that God created not *in* time but *with* time. We cannot strictly conceive of such an 'event'; all our thinking arises from a timescale of past/present/future. Hence an inferred past belongs to every event and will always be part and parcel of any system the human mind can conceive. In this sense the act of creation is, in principle, not amenable to scientific investigation since an inferable past is part of what God brought into being in the creation of space and time.

2. The coming into being of space and time implies an 'event' of unique character. It represents a boundary category concerning which our conceptual apparatus, shaped, as it is, by our experience within space and time, finds itself 'out of its depth'. This alone ought to make us cautious before dogmatizing as to the precise implications of the Genesis passages for the physicist's account of the origin of the cosmos.[2]

The reader is referred to various discussions which take these questions to greater depth. In the end we speak of creation at the beginning of time because Scripture so speaks. We may permit some degree of liberty in interpreting the biblical account of cosmological beginnings, though we should not hesitate to speak of a genuine act at the 'beginning' of time by which God brought the universe into existence out of nothing.

CREATION OF THE SPIRITUAL WORLD

God's creative work is not limited to the physical, observable universe, but extends to the creation of a spiritual world (Ps. 148:2, 5; Col. 1:16). The time of its creation is not stated in Scripture, but Genesis 1 – 2 may imply that it came into being at the same time as the physical universe (Gn. 1:1; 2:1; though *cf*. Jb. 38:4–7).

The beings who inhabit this world are variously described: angels, spirits, demons, cherubim, seraphim, sons of God, principalities, powers, thrones, dominions (Is. 6:2f.; Rom. 8:38; Eph. 6:12f.). Two are identified, Gabriel and Michael (Dn. 12:1; Rev. 12:7). They do not have material bodies (Heb. 1:7) and are normally referred to as being very numerous (Dt. 33:2; Ps. 68:17; Mt. 26:53; Mk. 5:13; Rev. 5:11).

2. *Cf.* also discussion of the theory of evolution in Part 3.

Among their functions are the worship of God (Is. 6; Rev. 4), the execution of God's will (Ps. 103:20) and ministering to 'those who will inherit salvation' (Heb. 1:14). They are particularly connected with the ministry and mission of Jesus (Mt. 1:20; 4:11; 28:2; Jn. 20:12; Acts 1:10f.).

Two dangers arise. One may virtually ignore this teaching, as happens in much modern theological writing, or else over-emphasize it, particularly with reference to the demonic. To be a biblical Christian means not only believing all that Scripture teaches, but holding its various teachings in scriptural balance. We ought, therefore, to take the struggle with evil powers seriously, as did our Lord and his apostles; but this dimension is not *all*-pervasive in the NT, nor ought it to be in our thinking.

The balance of Scripture should again be determinative in our consideration of evil angels. These too are creatures of God, held in being by him, and finally servants to his purpose. It seems clear that they were not created evil (Gn. 1:31, *cf.* 2 Pet. 2:4). Like humankind, their fall may have been due to pride (Jude 6). We should certainly reject the older view (based on a mistaken reading of Gn. 6:2) that they fell through sexual lust. Speculation ought to be avoided in this whole area. Satan (= 'adversary') is frequently named as the head of the forces of evil (Mt. 25:41; Jn. 8:44; 2 Cor. 11:14f.; 1 Jn. 3:8; Rev. 12:9). He is seen in Scripture as the 'god of this world' (2 Cor. 4:4), actively resisting God and his rule. Christ conquered Satan and the demonic order by his work of atonement (Jn. 12:31; Col. 2:15; Heb. 2:14) and that victory will be actualized finally at his return (2 Thes. 2:8f.; Rev. 20:10).

In recent years there has been considerable interest in spiritual agencies, not only among Christians but also in the wider culture. Several factors have contributed to this. One is the rise of New Age ideas (*cf.* the next section), with their attempt to explore the psycho-spiritual dimensions of human personality and achieve a wholeness transcending the division between spirit and matter. Another has been the arrival of the space age which has fed popular speculation about extraterrestrial life and alien 'invasions' of the earth. Over against this, there has been a contrasting tendency in some NT interpretation to reduce the biblical reference to supernatural agencies and understand the 'principalities and powers' referred to in Scripture as straight-forward political forces. All of this simply underlines the point made above about the need to struggle for an appropriate biblical balance in this area.

That there are conscious, created beings which are different from so called 'natural' life is clear from the Bible. Their being both positive and negative is also established. Hence the attempt to eliminate their reality is mistaken. Jesus is clearly represented in the gospels as engaged in a genuine struggle against a real and impressive enemy (*cf.* Mt. 4:1–11; Mk. 1:21–27; Lk. 11:14–28; Jn. 12:31; 14:30), and was supported at points by corresponding friendly forces (Mt. 4:11; Lk. 22:43; Jn. 20:12). Paul has numerous references in his writings to 'Satan' and spiritual warfare (*e.g.* 2 Cor. 12:7; Act 29:18; Rom. 16:20; 1 Cor 5:7; 7:5; Eph. 6:10–20; 2 Cor. 10:3–5) as have other NT writers (Jas. 4:7; 1 Pet. 5:8f.; 1 Jn. 5:19). The books of Daniel and Revelation explore the ways in which demonic powers can insinuate themselves into political organizations and structures, but not in the sense that they are reduced to these political forces *per se* (Rev. 13:1–18; 20:7–10). Like our Master we are called into a conflict which is not simply 'against flesh and blood', but also 'against spiritual forces of evil in the heavenly realms' (Eph. 6:12).

There is a danger, however, of so stressing these spiritual powers that we cease to engage the realities of creaturely life in this world. Thus the 'real' world becomes the hidden spiritual order, and the 'real' issues are determined at that level. When this view is carried to extremes, people become detached from everyday life with its relationships and responsibilities and exist in a quasi-world of spiritual entities and encounters. We need constantly to keep before us that the centre of God's purposes is the incarnation of Jesus, his taking up our flesh and blood and living a life as a carpenter and preacher, ministering to real people in their real, everyday world amid their tangible, everyday needs. Although, of course, a spiritual order exists 'behind the scenes', the NT, in unveiling it, reflects no loss of focus on this present world; and even when it speaks of the glorious future hope beyond the limitations of life here, it does so in terms of a 'new earth' and 'resurrection bodies' (see Part 7).

Scriptures

Gn. 1:1f.; Jb. 26:13; 33:4; Pss. 90:2; 102:26f.; 148:2, 5; Is. 40:26f.; Je. 10:12f.; Am. 4:13; Mt. 19:4; Jn. 1:3; Rom. 1:25; 1 Cor. 8:6; Col. 1:16; Heb. 11:3; Rev. 4:11; 10:6.

Creation 'out of nothing': Gn. 1:1; 2:4; Ps. 33:6; Jn. 1:3; Rom. 4:17; 1 Cor. 1:28; 2 Cor. 5:17; Heb. 11:3.
Upholding: Ps. 104:27–30; Is. 42:5; Acts 17:26–28; Col. 1:17; Heb. 1:3.

Questions

1. State the Christian doctrine of creation and indicate its basis.
2. Explain why Christians over the centuries have understood creation as 'out of nothing'. Explore the implications of this position (a) negatively, *i.e.* what it denies, (b) positively, *i.e.* what it affirms.
3. What significance does God's 'upholding' of the universe have for the way we think of his relationship to the world?
4. In what respects may biblical teaching on creation contribute to scientific investigation?
5. List the considerations to be borne in mind in interpreting the account of creation in Genesis 1 and 2.
6. 'Miracles do not happen' (Matthew Arnold). 'A miracle must be experienced before it can be believed.' Discuss.
7. What does Scripture have to tell us about the angels of God? What profit can the Christian derive from this teaching?

Bibliography

Arts. 'Miracles' in *IBD* and 'Miracle', 'Creation', in *NDT.*
R. J. Berry, *God and the Biologist* (Apollos, 1996).
H. Blocher, *In the Beginning* (IVP, 1984).
R. Hooykaas, *Religion and the Rise of Modern Science* (Scottish Academic Press, 1972).
R. Hooykaas, *Natural Law and Divine Miracle* (Brill, Leiden, 1959).
M. A. Jeeves and R. J. Berry, *Science, Life and Christian Belief* (Apollos, 1998).
C. S. Lewis, *Miracles* (Fontana, 1960).
D. M. MacKay, *The Clockwork Image* (IVP, 1974).
L. Osborn, *Guardians of Creation* (Apollos, 1993).
V. S. Poythress, *Philosophy, Science, and the Sovereignty of God* (PRPC, 1976).
N. H. Ridderbos, *Is There a Conflict Between Genesis 1 and Natural Science?* (Eerdmans, 1957).
F. A. Schaeffer, *Genesis in Space and Time* (Hodder, 1972).

8. The work of providence

Providence is 'that continued exercise of the divine energy whereby the Creator preserves all His creatures, is operative in all that comes to pass in the world, and directs all things to their appointed end' (Berkhof). The biblical doctrine takes its name from Genesis 22:8, 'God himself will provide . . .' and is classically expressed in the story of Joseph whose abduction and deportation to Egypt were seen subsequently as the divinely intended provision for the needs of his famine-stricken family

(Gn. 45). The definition above explicitly mentions the work of providence as the work of the Creator. Calvin correctly speaks of the two doctrines as 'inseparably joined'. Providence asserts that God, having called the world into being, continually sustains, renews and orders it.

THE EXTENT OF PROVIDENCE

Scripture witnesses to the universal range of God's providence; God acts in *all* things (Ps. 115:3; Mt. 10:30; Eph. 1:11). Natural events such as winds and rain, even seeming disasters (Lk. 13:1–5), are part of his ordering. Even evil is under his hand and he uses it for his own ends (Gn. 50:20; Acts 2:23; Phil. 1:17f.).

In order to lessen the moral problems raised by this doctrine, some theologians have asserted that God operates in a general 'background' sense, providing the essential 'input' for life which then operates according to its own relatively independent principles. Against this understanding of providence we can set Calvin's: 'God is deemed omnipotent not because he can indeed act, yet sometimes ceases and sits in idleness, or continues by a general impulse that order of nature which he previously appointed; but because, governing heaven and earth by his providence, he so regulates all things that nothing takes place without his deliberation.'

The God who acts in his providence 'sustaining', 'operating' and 'directing' is the triune God. This is crucial in distinguishing the Christian view from blind, impersonal causality or fate, such as was taught by Stoicism and, in practice, in Islam. The 'appointed end', with a view to which God acts in the world, is his redemptive and sanctifying purpose centred in Jesus Christ. Thus the assertion that 'in all things God works for the good' of his people (Rom. 8:28) must be understood in terms of *this* good, the separating and transforming of the people of God into his likeness (v. 27).

NECESSARY DISTINCTIONS

A distinction is sometimes drawn between the primary and secondary causality of God. The former refers to events in which God acts directly without human means, as in the resurrection of Jesus; the latter refers to events in which God acts through the agency of creaturely factors, as in his determining the rise and fall of nations or ordering factors in the daily lives of his people.

A similar distinction is sometimes drawn between God's directive will and his permissive will. The former refers to events which God sovereignly directs in his purposes of grace and judgment, the latter to events which God sovereignly permits. Though not always easy to apply in practice, this distinction is necessary to refute any suggestion that God is the cause of evil. If, however, an event as terrible as the cross is to be attributed to God's directive will (Acts 2:23), much that appears to oppose God's purposes may, from the perspective of eternity, be seen to be directly ordered by him.

GOD'S PROVIDENCE AND EVIL

How do we reconcile this providential rule of God to the fact of evil and sin in the world? The attempt to respond to this problem is technically known as theodicy; philosophical and apologetic works listed below attempt on rational grounds to accommodate the fact of evil to the Christian conviction concerning a good and omnipotent God.

The Bible recognizes an ultimate mystery as far as evil and sin are concerned (2 Thes. 2:7). Its approach to the problem of evil is essentially practical, concerned less to explain the presence of evil than to witness to its conquest by Christ and to bring divine consolation and reassurance to the believing sufferer. Biblical religion is not an unreal idealism which represents the life of faith as free from perplexity, anguish or acute suffering; it sets evil and suffering firmly in the context of its revelation concerning *the nature and destiny of humankind*, and *the person and work of Christ*.

As far as *human nature* is concerned, the Bible speaks unambiguously of humankind's *fall* into sin (Gn. 3; Rom. 5:12f.). The world as we now experience it, including its evil and suffering, is not as God intended it or made it at the first. While the Bible does not reveal the ultimate origin of evil, it emphatically insists that humankind was made with the capacity to resist it and to affirm God alone as his Lord. Adam's open-eyed disobedience created the 'way in' for evil and suffering in human life (Gn. 3:14–19; Rom. 5:12–21). As an act of rebellion against the Creator, sin cannot but have the most serious and extensive implications in a moral universe which reflects the holy character of its Creator. This does not imply any necessarily direct correlation between specific personal suffering and personal sin. In the deepest sense, however, they are linked because all our sinning flows from Adam's primal act of folly which subjected the whole universe prospectively and retrospectively to the forces of decay and cosmic wickedness, and hence to the possibility of suffering and tragedy.

As for *the destiny of humankind*, Scripture sets evil and suffering in the context of the future triumph of God's purpose for humankind. Sin, evil and suffering were never part of God's original intention for us, nor are they to be a permanent feature of our experience. They are temporary intrusions which cannot inhibit the final realization of his purpose when 'God himself will be with them . . . He will wipe every tear from their eyes. There will be no more death or mourning or crying or pain' (Rev. 21:3f.).

In *the person of Christ* God took our flesh in its vulnerability and weakness, another important dimension of the Bible's response. This identity with us finds supreme expression in the *cross*, where God made our suffering his very own and plumbed the ultimate depths of human pain and questioning, turning the agony of Calvary into the means of pardon and joy to all who believe.

In the light of the *resurrection* we see the triumph of God over all the forces of evil and darkness. Further, through the new life in Christ brought by the Holy Spirit we enter the kingdom of God and experience in measure the powers of the coming age in which all the forces of destruction will be no more. The fact of the resurrection body of Jesus is important at this point, for it secures a God who continues to identify with us in our human suffering and vulnerability. In times of overwhelming grief and numbing tragedy he suffers *with* us; he is there; his tears mingle with our own. When we cannot give any sense or meaning to our pain, we can nevertheless meet him in the midst of it, our sympathizing, human God.

In the light of the *return of Christ* we recognize that the present order of sin and suffering is not the final reality. The world as immediately encountered cannot afford any fully adequate vantage point from which to judge its nature. Christian faith lives in the sure expectation of the return of Christ when the injustices and the sufferings of this present life will be removed and all things appear in the light of the revelation of God and the utter triumph of his purposes. G. C. Berkouwer, in a discussion of theodicy, suggests that the ultimate Christian perspective is doxological, the adoration of God for his triumph over all his enemies.

Scriptures
Gn. 22:8; 45; Dt. 8:18; 2 Ki. 19:28; Ne. 9:6; Pss. 76:10; 104:20f., 30; 115:3; 136:25; 145:15; Dn. 4:3; Am. 3:6; Mt. 5:45; 10:29f.; Lk. 13:1–5; Acts 14:17; 17:28; Rom. 8:28; Phil. 2:13; Col. 1:17; 1 Tim. 6:15.

Questions
1. What is meant by the providence of God? What biblical basis is there for this notion? Explore the implications of a belief in providence for daily living.
2. Discuss the propriety of the distinction between God's directive and permissive will.
3. What is the 'problem of evil' and what are the insights for responding to this problem which derive from (a) the fall of humankind, (b) the incarnation, (c) the cross, (d) the return of Christ?
4. What would you say in reply to someone who asks 'Why are my prayers for healing from cancer not answered?' or 'Why did God allow my mother to be killed in the road accident?'

Bibliography
Arts. 'Suffering', 'Evil', in *NDT*.
G. C. Berkouwer, *The Providence of God* (Eerdmans, 1952).
John Calvin, *Institutes of the Christian Religion*, 1.
H. Blocher, *Evil and the Cross* (Apollos, 1994).
D. A. Carson, *How Long, O Lord?* (IVP, 1990).
P. Helm, *The Providence of God* (IVP, 1993).
C. S. Lewis, *The Problem of Pain* (Fontana, 1957).
J. S. Whale, *The Problem of Evil* (SCM, 1936).

Application

THE BEING AND NATURE OF GOD

'What comes into our minds when we think about God is the most important thing about us.' So A. W. Tozer expresses the paramount significance of the doctrine of God. In one sense its application is both immediate and pervasive; the convictions we have about God will affect everything about us, if we have seen him in the fullness of his divine being, Father, Son and Spirit, perfect in glory, lordship, holiness and love.

He is to be worshipped

To believe in the existence of such a God is to be summoned to pour out our beings before him in worship, thanksgiving and praise, delighting in him, blessing him; rejoicing in his truth, beauty, purity and faithfulness; glorying in his grace, mercy, kindness and steadfast love; exulting in his sovereign freedom and boundless power; magnifying him for his majesty and glory; recognizing in him the ultimate reality, the truth of all truth, the joy of all joys, the love of all loves, Father, Son, Spirit, ever adorable Trinity.

To believe in such a God means to recognize and worship him as the triune God, Father, Son, Spirit, eternally and indivisibly united, perfectly related, each existing and operating in perfect unity with the other persons, ever one, ever three; it means recognizing and worshipping him in the indescribable richness and everlasting beauty of his Godhead, beside which all other truth systems are but pale ephemeral shadows, pathetic idols, utterly unable to stand before the Lord, the almighty Saviour, he who is God alone.

In our worship we need to meditate upon each of the divine perfections and worship him under each.

We adore him, Father, Son, Spirit, for the perfection of his *glory*. He is utterly exalted above all things, God alone in his unapproachable majesty. Glory to his name.

We adore him, Father, Son, Spirit, for the perfection of his *lordship*. He is the exalted one who distinguishes himself from all other gods and lords and asserts his rule over them. Glory to his name.

We adore him, Father, Son, Spirit, for the perfection of his *holiness*. He is the God of awesome majesty, exalted over all things, separating himself from all that challenges and opposes him. Glory to his name.

We adore him, Father, Son, Spirit, for the perfection of his *love*. He who has loved from before the foundation of the world stoops in his grace to embrace and redeem the sinful creature who denies and opposes him. Glory to his name.

Scripture sets this worship in both the corporate setting of the assembled people of God (Ex. 4:31; 2 Ch. 29:28; 1 Cor. 14:25; Rev. 7:11) and the private setting of personal communion with God (Gn. 24:26f.; Ex. 34:8; Jb. 1:20), and speaks of the gracious ministry of the Holy Spirit of God in inspiring and releasing the worship of his people (Rom. 8:26f.; Eph. 5:18f.; Phil. 3:3).

He is to be served

The only proper response to such a God is to serve him. Worship is part of this service, which extends to every area of life.

Negatively, service of God implies renouncing all right to ourselves and giving up our will entirely to his will (1 Cor. 6:19; 2 Cor. 5:15; Phil. 3:7f.; Jas. 4:8; 1 Pet. 2:1f.). Positively, it means recognizing that we exist by God's will for God's sake, and therefore deliberately setting ourselves to live to his glory and honour in every area of our lives. 'The great thing is this; we are consecrated and dedicated to God in order that we may thereafter think, speak, meditate, and do nothing except to his glory' (Calvin).

He is to be proclaimed

Part of our response to God as he reveals his being and nature to us is our making him known in a world in which he is widely ignored or rejected. The world is not neutral, but is filled with idols, *i.e.* false objects of worship. These may be human leaders, political ideologies, social classes or groups, human thought systems, even demonic agencies. We are called to challenge these usurpers and to confront these false gods in the name of the true and living God. This involves spreading the knowledge of God throughout the world, both geographically and culturally, by our prayers, the investment of our resources and our personal witness.

This proclamation of God is not only direct and verbal, it is also indirect and incarnational. It involves living in such a way that the God we proclaim in our speaking is manifested in every area of our living. Here again we need to refer to God's provision through his Son and Spirit to bring what is a human impossibility into the realm of the possible (Mt. 28:19f.; Jn. 14:15f.; Acts 1:8).

These three applications of God's being and nature are indissoluble. To worship God is to serve and proclaim him; to serve God is to proclaim and worship him; to proclaim God is to worship and serve him.

CREATION

The fact that God is Creator has practical implications.

1. The world is not to be denied. It is God's world, having come from him. It is deeply marred by sin, certainly, but sin has not wrenched it out of God's hands, nor rendered it utterly alien to him. Therefore, we ought to reject the idea that space-time existence is worthless, that there is no value from a Christian perspective in general human endeavour, cultural interests, artistic creativity, social or political work, sporting achievement, *etc.*, or that there is something inherently unworthy in human sexuality. Such denial of the world reflects a failure to recognize God as creator or, alternatively, a mistaken division between the God of creation and the God of redemption. 'God likes matter; he invented it' (C. S. Lewis).

2. The world is not to be idolized. It has come from God but it is not itself God. It has been involved in the effects of the fall and is therefore not to be over-valued. Our ultimate loyalty is reserved for God himself, whom we seek beyond creaturely realities, even though at times we may meet him in the creaturely. For this reason the world can never ultimately satisfy us. We were made by God for God and so, in Augustine's often cited words, 'our hearts are restless till they find their rest in you'. Hence, if our experience of life in the world is not finally satisfactory, if its successes elude us, if through some tragic circumstances we lose the capacity to appreciate it, or our life span within it is threatened, we are not to be utterly cast down. God himself is our goal and fulfilment; to know him here and hereafter is the ultimate realization of our existence.

3. The world is to be used. God created the world for his own purpose, as the 'theatre of his glory'. In this space-time world he has become incarnate and manifested his glory and we are likewise to use the world in this sense by worshipping, serving and proclaiming God throughout our earthly lives.

This Christian perspective is the basis for a proper appreciation of the world, a respectful stewardship of its resources, an open-eyed recognition of its limitations, and a cheerful, thankful and free life within it to the glory of God the Creator.

PROVIDENCE

1. God's providence implies that he has his hand in all our affairs. We are not at the mercy of arbitrary, impersonal forces, but in all of life we confront God himself, Father, Son and Spirit. There is need therefore explicitly to identify the many particular benefits and blessings which God extends to us, so that we may thank him.

The overall goal of God's providential activity, like that of his creative and redemptive activity, is his glory and our good. More particularly, God aims at our sanctification, both individually and corporately, in family, society and church, and also at the spread of the gospel and the extension of his kingdom. These aims explain his dealings with us. In them God commonly uses secondary causes such as our 'natural' cast of personality, the activities and interests of members of our family, neighbours and workmates, the physical, social and economic framework of our lives as well as more direct intervention.

Since God works in his providence through all these factors, we ought not to confine our recognition of his activity in our lives to the major critical moments of decision; neither, conversely, should we constantly refer these secondary everyday factors to God's *direct* intervention. Rather we accept life as from him, and with quiet confidence set about living it to his glory, believing that in all things we are in his hands and that he who created and redeemed us is, through the daily ordering of our lives, furthering his purpose through us.

2. God's providence should have a humbling effect as it teaches that our lives are utterly dependent; therefore, pride in our powers and achievements ought to recede as we acknowledge our total dependence upon his providential upholding and rule.

3. God's providence is a profound comfort in face of those difficulties and sorrows which are in no sense attributable to our folly or wickedness, for there is no trying or even tragic circumstance but God has sovereignly permitted it. He who is involved in the life cycle of the sparrow is profoundly involved in the life and circumstances of those whom he has made the special objects of his love. Hence we can live with confidence even in face of such difficulties, assured that as the fatherly providence of God has permitted these things for our good and his glory, so he will

sustain us and watch over us in the face of them. While these remarks will inevitably appear trite to someone experiencing particularly acute suffering, they are supported by the testimony of Scripture and repeatedly endorsed in the experience of the people of God over the centuries.

4. A belief in God's providence should help us to see our times of elation and success in perspective as God's gifts rather than as simply the products of our own powers or wisdom. This will also prepare us for the possibility that they may be withdrawn from us later, should he see fit in his loving wisdom.

5. God's providence gives us a security in this insecure, often violent world. The Lord sits enthroned over all the military, political, social and economic forces of our generation and his eternal predetermined purposes are ripening through it all. Nothing has got out of hand, nor will it. We can therefore live day by day knowing that the hands which hold our lives are the same hands which hold all things.

6. God's providence means that the ultimate triumph of his purposes is assured. All the forces of opposition to God, sin and evil, corruption and injustice, greed and exploitation and the rest are held by God, kept in check by his providential reign, and are in the last analysis of merely temporary significance, no matter how impressive they may appear at present. God has appointed a day in which the glory of his rule will be manifest throughout the universe and all that opposes him is destined for judgment and for everlasting exclusion from his presence.

7. The recognition of the providence of God does not relieve us of the need to accept personal responsibility for our lives. Scripture clearly teaches that while God is Lord in all things, we are responsible to him for all that we are and do. Therefore we are to take due care in all the decisions we make, and seek consciously to act and to order our way as nearly as we can to what we can discern as God's will for us.

The Christian response to God's providence, therefore, ought not to express itself in a quietist withdrawal from human responsibilities or from involvement in the problems facing our world and our immediate society. Rather, the Christian who accepts these responsibilities has the immense reassurance that the just, pure and godly values which he or she pursues in the everyday world are reflections of the essence of the Lord who rules and orders all things; and further, in spite of the vastness of many of the problems which confront us, these values are destined to flourish unopposed in the new age of God's rule which is to appear.

PART 3
Humankind and sin

9. Essential human nature

THE PERENNIAL QUESTION

'What is humanity?' asked the psalmist centuries ago (*cf.* Ps. 8:4). Today this question continues to haunt us, for despite the enormous technological advances of our period and our vastly enhanced knowledge of the human species at the biological, chemical, and psychological levels we are still apparently no nearer arriving at a definitive answer.

One thing we can assert with confidence: as never before, humankind is a threatened species. Although we have emerged from the Cold War world with its threat of nuclear holocaust, the long-term survival of our race remains problematic. The prospect of nuclear destruction has not gone away despite major reductions in nuclear weaponry on the part of the former super-powers. Population levels continue to rise alarmingly, to put even greater strains on limited food resources. New and deadly viruses have already taken a massive toll of human life in many parts of the world. The ecological crisis continues to deepen, despite international conferences to agree limits on the more threatening forms of pollution. And the older Cold War polarities are being replaced by new power blocs gathered around global civilizations, loyalties frequently driven by fanatical ties of ethnicity and religion. The 'brave new world' remains a haunting chimera.

In this time of uncertainty, the ultimate anthropological questions still await an answer: what are we? Where did we come from? What is the meaning of our life? Is there any final significance in the age-long human struggle? And what of the future: where are we going? Secular anthropologies have signally failed to come up with answers, and by their very bankruptcy have thrown into relief the relevance of the Christian answer. For 'humanity never achieves a clear knowledge of itself unless it has first looked upon God's face, and then descends from contemplating him to scrutinize itself' (Calvin). We can understand ourselves only in the light of God and his purpose for humankind, *i.e.* in the light of divine revelation.

For Scripture, humankind is inescapably the creature of God (*cf.* Gn. 1:26; 2:7f., 21f.; Ps. 8:2; Acts 17:26, 28; *etc.*). We are neither self-made nor the product of some chance cosmic process. Whatever else is true of us, however we describe the relationship between God's creative act and the causal processes of human birth, here is the bedrock for the Bible: every man and woman exists only because God made them. Scripture asserts this throughout (Gn. 5:1f.; Ps. 139:13f.; Ec. 12:1; Mal. 2:10; Mt. 19:4; Rom. 1:25; Jas. 3:9; 1 Pet. 4:19).

In Adam's case the process was a special creative act with two aspects: 'the LORD God formed man from the dust of the ground and breathed into his nostrils the breath of life; and man became a living being' (Gn. 2:7). God's two-fold action corresponds to the two aspects of human nature, physical and spiritual. It is wise, however, not to separate the two aspects too sharply. We are a unity of body and spirit; the two aspects interrelate in a profound manner (see below, 'The unity of the person'). Eve is made from Adam by a further special creative act (Gn. 2:21) which underlines the fundamental complementarity of man and woman. Although later generations obviously receive life differently from Adam, our case is finally no different from his (*cf.* Part 2, 'Continuing creation'), owing our existence utterly to God. Scripture preserves a proper sense of wonder and mystery when it contemplates the emergence of human life (Ps. 139:13ff., *cf.* Jb. 10:8–12).

At creation humankind was invested by God with a special dignity, appointed ruler of the world under God, summoned to possess and subject it and to rule the other creatures (Gn. 1:27–2:3, *cf.* Ps. 8:5f.). Our present fallenness must not blind us to our original exaltation and dignity.

HUMANKIND IN RELATION TO GOD

The origin of life

Those who reject a Creator account for the emergence of life on earth in terms of chance. In some primeval pool of water, over a vast period of time, a uniquely complex series of reactions and combinations eventually produced protoplasm with properties which permit its being defined as 'living'. Experiments to reproduce these conditions have raised the question whether life can be 'created' in a test-tube and what this would mean for the Christian doctrine of creation. However:

1. Scientists disagree on the likelihood of ever achieving this.

2. Even if it were achieved, no essential contradiction to biblical teaching would appear to be involved; God clearly allows us to think his thoughts after him through his self-revelation, and to imitate his creative handiwork in other respects, *e.g.* in producing new strains of plants and animals.

3. Much depends upon what is meant by 'life' here.

4. The odds involved in the production of life on this planet 'by chance' are staggering. A leading biochemist and past President of the Royal Society has expressed this unlikelihood by calling the origin of life on the earth 'the most improbable event in the history of the universe' (M. Dixon). In face of this, the Christian's belief in a purposeful creation by the will of an intelligent Creator clearly places less strain on our credulity.

The origin of humankind

The question of human origins has aroused lively and sometimes bitter controversy over the past two hundred years. The publication of Darwin's *Origin of Species* (1859) in particular brought to a head the simmering clash between biological and religious accounts. We begin by affirming the full inspiration and divine authority of the biblical passages concerned (Gn. 1:20 – 2:9), and in seeking to interpret them ask two questions: What form of literature is this? What was the intention of the human author?

The contentious issue has been the relationship between these passages of Scripture and the theory of evolution. Organic evolution may be generally defined as 'the derivation of species from different pre-existing species by a process of descent with modification'. One can distinguish four broad approaches to this theory.

1. *Evolutionism* concedes to evolutionary theory a comprehensive account of human origins and dismisses any reference to the activity of a Creator. To this expanded Darwinism not an inch of ground may be yielded.

2. *Direct creationism* believes that humankind originated as described in Genesis 2:7f.; Adam was made from dust and Eve from his rib by acts of special divine creation. The palaeontological evidence regarding development within species and humankind's relationship to this process is accounted for on various grounds: the 'flood theory' argues that the catastrophic repercussions of Noah's flood account for the fossil materials; the 'gap theory' argues from Genesis 1:2 that the initial act of creation was followed by a global catastrophe which accounts for the geological realities as presently observed, and this was followed in turn by a further act of re-creation which produced the Earth as we now know it.

3. *Progressive creationism* holds that Genesis 1 records in broad outline successive creative acts of God; the universe is brought through its various stages from the initial *ex nihilo* act (Gn. 1:1) to the appearance of humankind (Gn. 1:27), which is viewed as a distinct new stage of divine creation. This view recognizes certain evolutionary developments within each main species, the gaps between them indicating successive creative acts; these may not have occurred in the precise order of Genesis 1 which, in any case, differs from that of Genesis 2.

4. *Theistic evolution* accepts the theory of evolution as a general explanation of how God worked in creating the world and producing life within it. With reference to the emergence of humankind, however, some further factor is posited whereby a particular anthropoid was separated and raised to a new level of awareness and to a relationship with God.

In evaluating these approaches we must take account of the following points:

1. Nothing should call in question creation 'out of nothing'. Taking the third and fourth views, and even to some extent the second, we need to think in terms of an initial act of creation out of nothing whereby the raw material of the universe came to be. This was succeeded by a divinely governed process, possibly punctuated by further primary creative acts whereby the universe as we know it was formed. The culmination of this

process was the special creation of humankind, either as a brand new product or by the critical refashioning of an already existing creaturely form.

2. Dogmatism is inappropriate here unless we can show that Scripture necessarily requires a particular interpretation. Bible expositors of undoubted probity, intelligence and faith support the second, third and fourth views above; this argues for a proper charity among Christians of differing convictions. Dogmatism is also out of place on the part of science since evolution remains a theory, which in principle is capable of being replaced by a more adequate one.

3. Humans are distinguished from all other animals by their transcendent nature. Our rational powers, moral awareness, pursuit of beauty, use of language, fear of extinction and spiritual perception all support the Bible's assertion of our uniqueness within creation. Some younger Christian scholars within the scientific disciplines believe the scientific basis of evolution is genuinely suspect at a number of points and that direct creationism not only accords with Scripture, but need not conflict with the most rigorous scientific investigation of human origins.

4. The effect of the evolutionary interpretation for many people has been to reduce the sense of divine purpose in creation and replace it within an apparently arbitrary process driven by the inherent ability of particular species to adapt to and overcome the challenges of their environment. However, there are Christian thinkers who, while necessarily rejecting 'total view' evolutionism, do not find a modified form of evolutionary theory inimical in principle to the notion of divine purpose. For example, the so-called 'anthropic principle' recognizes the massive unlikeliness of human life having appeared on this planet on the basis of pure randomness. It argues that life emerged and humans appeared because of a purpose-driven series of physical and chemical events creating the conditions within which such a development became possible.

5. An allied question concerns the antiquity of humanity. This question is raised by the genealogies in Genesis which relate Adam to Abraham and Israel (Gn. 5:1–32; 11:10–27) and led Archbishop Ussher in the 17th century to date creation at 4004 BC. The genealogies of Genesis, however, have been shown not to be strict father–son relationships. They are compressions of

generations and may even at points refer to dynasties, which in turn may be a key to the extraordinary ages attributed to the antediluvians. This means that Adam and Eve can be placed either very early in the genealogical time-scale or comparatively late, depending on which is thought to fit the palaeontological and biblical evidence best.

On the other hand, of course, the palaeontological evidence as a whole may itself be questioned, as some scientists judge it should be. In that case there could be no essential tension between the biblical and scientific views.

6. Much depends in the end on how we interpret Genesis 1–3. Is this religious myth? Is this straightforward historical, even 'scientific' description? A 'religious', non-historical interpretation obviously eases the conflict with accepted evolutionary theories; such an approach does not lack sincere Christian advocates, but it has its difficulties. It underplays the space and time references in Genesis 1 – 3; *e.g.* Eden's fairly precise location (Gn. 2:8–14) and Adam's historical relationship to Abraham and Christ (Gn. 10:1–11, 32; Lk. 3:23–38; Acts 17:26). In other words, there is no perceptible break in the narrative form between Genesis 1 – 3 and 4f., or between Genesis 1 – 11 and 12f. Further, Genesis 1 – 2 depict a perfect world into which suffering, death and evil subsequently came as a result of Adam's disobedience. We need to notice, however, the presence of what we earlier noted as 'semi-poetic' elements in the language of the opening three chapters of the Bible. The four rivers in 2:10–14 represent for some a symbol of the fullness of life-giving water, and the barring of Eden to humans in 3:24 an enacted parable of the spiritual reality of human separation from God due to the fall.

In all this we must remember the special order of these events, hovering on the perimeter of history. Our experience is firmly limited by sin and fallenness, but these happenings lie outside that limit. Obviously there is a degree of continuity: Adam and Eve were the same individuals after the fall; but there is need for caution in asserting what Genesis 1 – 3 must or must not mean.

7. Finally, we must ensure that discussions of these issues do not rob us of the great central biblical realities, *i.e.* that humankind is the creature of God, set in God's world, uniquely related to him and holding special responsibility for the created order.

The image of God

Humankind is said to be created 'in the image of God' (Gn. 1:26). The NT uses the phrase of Jesus Christ (2 Cor. 4:4; Col. 1:15; *cf.* Heb. 1:3), and Christian believers are destined to share the divine image through their union with Christ (Rom. 8:29; 1 Cor. 15:49b; Col. 3:10).

Creation in the image of God distinguishes humankind from all other life-forms. Traditional interpretations of 'the image' refer to features such as human knowledge, moral awareness, original moral perfection and immortality. Some scholars argue for a physical meaning for the image (*cf.* its use in Gn. 5:3), but the fact that God is spirit tells against this interpretation. Other possibilities which have been argued for are humanity's alleged Trinitarian constitution (so Augustine, finding the vestige of the Trinity in the human memory, understanding and will), or the image as human dominion (Gn. 1:26–28) looking forward to the renewal of that dominion in the kingdom of God through Christ, the embodiment of the image (*cf.* Heb. 2:5–9). More recent interpretation has spoken of the social nature of the image, human experience as being-in-community reflecting the divine being-in-community of the Godhead. Barth extended this interpretation specifically to the man–woman relationship; *cf.* Gn. 1:27: 'So God created [humanity] in his own image . . . male and female he created them.'

There is a variety of views on how the image has been affected by the fall. Irenaeus (c. 130–200) distinguished between the 'image' (Heb. *ṣelem*), which he identified with human reason and moral freedom, and the 'likeness' (Heb. *dᵉmûṯ*), identified with original righteousness, and taught that only the 'likeness' was lost in the fall. This interpretation was followed through the medieval period and contributed to its essentially optimistic view of human nature.

Luther, however, recognized that Genesis 1:26 is a case of Hebrew parallelism, *i.e.* 'image' and 'likeness' were synonyms; what was true for one was true for the other. The image of God has therefore been totally lost and can be restored only through regeneration by the Holy Spirit.

The Bible, however, does not actually refer to a *total* loss of the image of God, and indeed at several points uses the phrase generally of fallen humanity (*cf.* Gn. 9:6; 1 Cor. 11:7; Jas. 3:9). Calvin, therefore, spoke of 'relics' of the image of God in fallen humanity, which, while affording no basis for humanity's justification, still distinguish them from the brute creation and account for the undoubted gifts and achievements of non-Christians. Dutch scholars in the Reformed tradition, such as A. Kuyper (1837–1920) and H. Bavinck (1854–1921), spoke in this connection of 'common (*i.e.* universal) grace' whereby God in his pity restrains the worst effects of the fall and renders social life tolerable for humankind.

The full biblical perspective, however, embraces also the joyous recognition of the grace of God in Christ through whom the image of God will be fully restored in all who believe.

HUMANKIND IN RELATION TO ITSELF: THE NATURE OF HUMANKIND

The Bible distinguishes several aspects in humankind's nature: spirit (Heb. *rûaḥ*, Gk. *pneuma*), soul (Heb. *nepeš*, Gk. *psychē*), body (only in the NT, Gk. *sōma*), flesh (Heb. *bāśār*, Gk. *sarx*). There are also references, especially in the OT, to organs of the body such as liver (Heb. *kābēd*) and bowels (Heb. *mē'îm*), which are particularly associated with certain human emotions. In Scripture, 'heart' (Heb. *lēb*, Gk. *kardia*) refers usually to the entire person understood from the point of his or her governing centre, the essential person, rather than the emotional nature as in current English usage. There are three theological issues to be noted.

Dichotomy or trichotomy?
There has been debate over whether the human person consists of body and soul (dichotomy) or body, soul and spirit (trichotomy). Dichotomists appeal to the interchangeability of the terms 'soul' and 'spirit' in Scripture (*cf.* Mt. 6:25; 10:28; Lk. 1:46 with Ec. 12:7; 1 Cor. 5:3, 5). Death is 'giving up the soul' (Gn. 35:18) and 'giving up the spirit' (Ps. 31:5; Lk. 23:46); the dead are designated both 'spirits' (Heb. 12:23) and 'souls' (Rev. 6:9). Trichotomists make particular appeal to Hebrews 4:12 and 1 Thessalonians 5:23; neither verse, however, is conclusive. Hebrews 4:12 should probably be translated 'the word of God ... penetrates even to divide the soul *and* the spirit ...', *i.e.* God's Word exposes the person from whatever angle he or she is considered (*cf.* v. 13); 1 Thessalonians 5:23 asserts God's power to sanctify the *whole* person.

Some, including John Wesley, have held that the human person is a dichotomy before regeneration but a trichotomy afterwards, but it is doubtful whether the new birth imparts an extra element to our persons. This position can encourage the corollary that the 'third element' in the believer's nature is God the Holy Spirit himself. Theologically, it is precarious since it involves the almost blasphemous claim that we 'possess God' as part of ourselves; pastorally, it is dangerous since the individual can on this basis claim that the emanations of his or her spirit are the emanations of God's Spirit, and thereby dispense with the necessary correctives of Scripture and church.

The unity of the person

Today the dichotomy/trichotomy issue has largely been super-seded by an emphasis on the *unity* of the person. According to Scripture I do not consist of composite 'parts', whether two or three; I am a psychosomatic unity. The terms the Bible uses, whether 'body', 'soul', 'spirit', 'heart' or 'mind', are simply different ways of looking at the one person. It is significant that the words translated 'soul' (Heb. *nepeš*, Gk. *psychē*), while certainly referred to in distinction to the body at points (1 Ki. 17:22f.; Lk. 16:22f.), commonly refer to the whole person (Jos. 10:28ff.; 1 Ki. 19:14; Mt. 6:26; Acts 27:37).

This biblical unity is seen at its clearest when contrasted with Greek thought. Plato saw the human person as two separable parts, body and soul; at death the soul was liberated, the divine spark in the person passing from its shadowy life in the prison-house of the body to the real world beyond physical dissolution. By contrast the Hebrew vision of life beyond death is the resur-rection of the body; we can enter into true life only as embodied beings.

Two other comments are in order, however:

1. While our proper existence is embodied, this does not imply that the body is absolutely essential to our self-expression. The NT, and Jesus in particular, envisage a human existence apart from the body (Mt. 10:28; Lk. 16:19–31; 23:43). This has important implications for the intermediate state of believers between their physical death and the return of Christ, when they will receive their resurrection body (*cf.* Part 7). This disembodied state, however, is *not* the ideal (2 Cor. 5:1–10). The full and proper goal for believers is reached at the return of Christ, 'who

will transform our lowly bodies so that they will be like his glorious body' (Phil. 3:20f.).

2. Our ultimate goal lies in our relationship with God on the spiritual and moral level. While this relationship carries implications for our life at every level, including the bodily and social, and also holds promise for the ultimate renewal of our whole existence, these dimensions are not of the essence of the relationship. Thus regeneration does not involve any necessary implications for our bodies in the present (*cf.* 2 Cor. 12:7f.; 2 Tim. 4:20; *etc.*), any more than for our social or political status (1 Cor. 7:17–24).

The origin of the soul

Traditional discussions have explored how and at what point in the birth process the soul comes into being. This issue has been raised again in the debate over abortion. Three positions have been advocated.

1. *Pre-existence.* A few writers have argued that the soul pre-exists the moment of physical conception. Origen (*c.* 185–*c.* 254) taught a form of this and it appears in Wordsworth's Ode on Immortality. This highly fanciful theory has no basis in Scripture.

2. *Creationism.* This argues that the soul of each individual is created directly by God at some stage in the birth process. The texts claimed in its support cannot be said to represent a clear case (Ec. 12:7; Zc. 12:1; Heb. 12:9; as well as Gn. 2:7).

3. *Traducianism.* This third view teaches that the soul is inherited from the human progenitors along with the body, there being no further act of soul-creation by God. Genesis 2:21; Acts 17:26; Hebrews 7:9–18 and the Bible's teaching on the solidarity of the human race in sin (*cf.* Rom. 5:12ff.) are all lined up in support of this view.

All three of these traditional positions are predicated on the assumption of the fundamental distinction between soul and body. Today, the greater awareness of the Bible's sense of the unity of the human person has reduced the intensity of the debate, as soul and body are seen more as differing ways of referring to the essential human person. However, some sense of distinction continues to be appropriate; *cf.* Jesus' reference to the slaying of the body as distinct from the soul (Mt. 10:28). It is also significant in giving meaning to the Christian's hope of life in the intermediate state (see Part 7), before the gift of the resurrection body at the return of the Lord.

PERSONS IN RELATION TO THEIR NEIGHBOURS

A social animal

Before the fall, God declared Adam's loneliness to be 'not good' (Gn. 2:18). Eve was brought to Adam as a human complement and partner; from the beginning, therefore, 'man was formed to be a social animal' (Calvin). This may well reflect God's own nature, the eternal divine society of the Trinity. This perspective is maintained throughout the Bible. The entire story of Scripture is gathered round a nation (Israel) and a community (the church). While the individual dimension is crucial throughout, the basic insight of Genesis 2:18 is sustained and reaches its climax in the holy city, new Jerusalem, at the return of Christ (Rev. 21). Cain's question, 'Am I my brother's keeper?' (Gn. 4:9), receives an emphatic 'yes' from Scripture. We are not alone, nor were we ever intended to be; we were made through and with and for our human neighbour.

Man and woman

In addition to affirming the essential corporateness of human life under God, Adam and Eve's relationship expresses the divine propriety of the gender distinction – humanity as the creature of God exists in the distinction and partnership of male and female. The recognition of this and the exploration of its implications bring us to what some observers believe is *the* anthropological issue of our time. After the many long centuries during which the assumption of male superiority had gone largely unchallenged, and male dominance and exploitation of the female had been the norm in virtually all known societies, our period has witnessed an unprecedented awakening of female self-consciousness with an accompanying unwillingness to let the old inequalities and exploitations continue. The rise of feminism has had many contributory impulses, but it has developed dramatically since the Second World War. Its impact is still patchy in the Third World, but in western society its effect has been revolutionary. Today, women, as never before in the long human story, are demanding their proper place as full, equal (and, in the case of radical feminism, in some senses 'superior') partners with men in the human community. Although the degree to which this goal has been achieved varies, feminism has impacted every sector of life, including the church.

Christians cannot but be thankful for the affirmation of true dignity and equality which the feminist movement has represented, as well as the call it issues to repentance from hierarchical and exploitive attitudes and practices. Some of its more radical expressions have clearly had less sanguine effects, however, as for example in some cases the weakening of commitment to marriage and family, the bolstering of the pro-choice position on abortion, and the espousing of ancient, pagan goddess worship.

Bible-loving Christians continue to debate the many issues which are raised by this movement. As ever, the critical question is: what does the Bible teach? Perhaps not surprisingly, assembling the biblical material does not bring the discussions to a simple conclusion; however, it is certainly where we need to begin.

We can broadly distinguish two foci in what Scripture says about the relationship between men and women.

1. *Woman and man are essentially and irreducibly equal in dignity, value and status.* Eve is 'bone of my bones and flesh of my flesh' to Adam (Gn. 2:23). This equality is not merely biological, for she is described by her Maker as 'a helper fit for him' (Gn. 2:18), which has the force of 'equal and adequate to'. 'She is a helping being, in whom, as soon as he sees her, the man recognizes himself' (Delitzsch). There is no hint of inferiority; woman is not man's slave or subordinate, but stands in her integrity by his side before God. Her intrinsic dignity is seen at its clearest in Scripture in the gospels. Jesus instinctively conferred equality on the women he met and ministered to, one of the most striking and revolutionary features of his ministry (Lk. 7:36–50; 8:1–3; Jn. 4:1–30; 8:1–11; 12:1–8). The clearest statement of this equality occurs in Galatians 3:28, in Christ 'there is neither male nor female'.[1]

2. *Man and woman are in some respects complementary to each other.* This is primarily expressed through the different though complementary roles played by the woman and man in the bringing forth of the child who embodies their unity

---

1. The sexual distinction is not abrogated, of course. Heterosexual marriage remains the fundamental, God-ordained form of social relationship.

(Gn. 3:16). In Ephesians Paul sees a complementarity expressed in Christian marriage, where the two partners are called to give a certain leadership in submission and love, though within the parameters of a mutual submission and a mutual loving, which is fundamental to their prior and continuing relationship as members together of Christ's body (Eph. 5:22–33, *cf.* 5:21; 4:2; 4:32 – 5:2). In a number of places there is reference to a 'headship' on the part of the male (1 Cor. 11:3–16; Eph. 5:23; *cf.* also 1 Tim. 2:11–14; 1 Pet 3:1–7). The precise meaning of 'head' here is disputed, the older sense of 'having authority over' being questioned on several grounds. 'Beginning' or 'source', or 'pre-eminence' in the sense of one to whom respect is due, are offered as alternative translations.

Much continuing debate swirls around the application of these passages to the life of the church where some other NT texts also come into the picture (see under Part 7). At this point we can note that by linking the loving complementarity of husband and wife to that of Christ and the church (Eph. 5:23f.), Paul lifts the whole male–female relationship in Christ on to a breathtaking plane. The properly ordered relationship of Christian husband and wife faintly but genuinely portrays God's eternal covenant with his people. No higher dignity for the relationship is conceivable.

Some even assert that the man–woman relationship is the normative form of human life, *i.e.* humankind = man plus woman. Here is a deep truth (Gn. 2:20–25) with important implications for our social fulfilment as well as for the fundamental propriety of heterosexual marriage. We may not, however, infer that the unmarried are shut out from true humanity; Jesus, the normative man, was not married, and the NT nowhere urges marriage as essential to a fulfilled Christian life.

HUMANKIND IN RELATION TO THE CREATED ORDER

Here we touch another of the major social and political concerns of our period. As at no point in previous history, humans today are conscious of their natural environment and committed to its protection and preservation. The reason is not hard to find; our continued life as a species is in question. Unless we are able to reverse the trends of environmental destruction which have held sway during previous centuries, this planet will simply cease to be a viable home for humanity. Three factors contribute principally to the present crisis: population growth, resource depletion and runaway technology.

At the very outset of its account of human life, the Bible draws attention to our relationship to the natural order (*cf.* Gn. 1:29; 2:19). Humanity is set in a garden and is surrounded by the other species (Gn. 2:7–20). God, however, remains Lord and the focus of humanity's primary responsibility. This is another way of saying that the environment and the other species, though important, are not on a level with God. In distinction from other creation accounts promulgated by neighbouring peoples and alternative ways of thinking about the relationship to nature, the OT worshipper is alerted to the error and sin of offering worship to other than God himself. 'You shall have no other gods before [or besides] me' (Ex. 20:3), which is unpacked as not making 'an idol in the form of anything in the heaven above or on the earth beneath or in the waters below' (20:2, *cf.* 2 Ki. 23:5).

Thus the Bible rules out all pantheism (the view that God is in all things, and so all things have to be reverenced to the point of worship). It also rules out the virtual deification of nature in some forms of naturalism, and the kind of 'worshipping God in the open air' which is occasionally mooted as an alternative to the Christian-community-based worship of the God revealed and met in Jesus Christ. Although not to be worshipped, however, nature needs to be respected. The simple, obvious point of the Genesis accounts is that we share a common Creator! The world of nature, no less than the world of humankind, is the product of the creating hand of God. It is this truth which should awaken in the Christian a true sense of wonder before nature. The Bible has many examples of it (Jb. 38 – 41; Ps. 19:1–6; 104:1–35; Mt. 6:25–30; Rev. 4:11).

Our God-given relation to the world is expressed in two words. The first is *dominion*. We are set over the world and its other life-forms (Gn. 1:28; 9:2f.; Heb. 2:8). Humankind is the apex of creation and intrinsic to the purpose of the whole cosmos, a conviction which is not invalidated by the vastness of the universe (no recent idea, Gn. 15:5; Jb. 22:12). Tragically, due to human fallenness, the dominion which God gave has been grossly misused, as many environmentalists today assert. Nature has been raped by humankind over the centuries. Our legitimate human needs for food and shelter have been left far behind in the selfish exploitation of the earth, and sadly the biblical mandate has at times been cited in explicit support.

The dominion, therefore, must never be mentioned in separation from the other equally biblical term, *stewardship*. God is the owner of all things, including the earth we inhabit and all its life forms, all of its fauna and flora. 'The earth is the LORD's, and everything in it' (Ps. 24:1, *cf.* 1 Ch. 29:11). 'Our possession is therefore leasehold not freehold' (D. Field). Hence our dominion is a responsible dominion, in the exercise of which we are totally accountable to God. And one day we shall be required to render our accounts to him (Mt. 25:26f.; Lk. 12:42).

HUMANKIND IN RELATION TO TIME

The world in which we live and exercise dominion and stewardship is temporal as well as spatial. We are 'given time' by God in which to fulfil this stewardship and to enjoy communion with our Maker (Gn. 3:8f.). There is discussion on whether the time given to Adam was endless. Was humankind immortal by nature, becoming mortal only as a result of sin, or was a limited life-span always God's intention?

Scripture clearly links death and sin together (Gn. 2:17; 3:19; Rom. 5:12ff.). 'Adam, if he had not sinned, would yet have lived a corporeal life, which would have needed meat, drink, and rest; and which would have grown, increased and generated until God would have translated him to that spiritual life in which he would have lived without natural animality, if I may so express it . . . And yet he would have been a man with body and bones and not a pure spirit as angels are' (Luther).

Scriptures

Humankind create by God: Gn. 1:26f.; 2:7, 21–23; 5:1; Jb. 33:4; Ps. 139:13f.; Mt. 19:4; Mk. 10:6; Rom. 1:25; Jas. 3:9.
Humankind in God's image: Gn. 1:26; 5:3; 9:5f.; 1 Cor. 11:7; 15:49; 2 Cor. 4:4; Col. 3:10.
Human nature: Ec. 7:29; 12:7; Mt. 10:28; 22:37; Mk. 8:35f.; Lk. 16:19–31; 1 Cor. 2:14; 5:5; 15:35–37; 2 Cor. 5:1–10; 12:2; Phil. 3:20f.; 1 Thes. 5:23; Heb. 4:12.

Questions

1. Discuss the relevance of the Christian view of humankind in face of (a) the contemporary threats to its survival, (b) the present confusion in anthropology.

2. Can biblical and scientific accounts of human origins be harmonized? Assess the strengths and weaknesses of the various solutions proposed.
3. What do you understand by the phrase 'the image of God'? Examine the implications of this view of humankind for (a) Christian evangelism, (b) Christian living, (c) Christian hope.
4. In your view, is the human person bipartite, tripartite or something else? Show how your answer finds support in Scripture.
5. 'Man is man-in-community.' Examine the biblical teaching relevant to this claim and explore its implications for (a) society, (b) marriage and family, (c) the church.
6. What do the terms 'dominion' and 'stewardship' mean with reference to a Christian response to the natural environment? Why, and to what extent, should a Bible-respecting Christian be a 'green'?

Bibliography

G. C. Berkouwer, *Man: the Image of God* (Eerdmans, 1962).
R. J. Berry, *God and the Biologist* (Apollos, 1996).
D. Cairns, *The Image of God in Man* (Fontana, 1973).
B. Davidheiser, *Evolution and the Christian Faith* (PRPC, 1969).
J. M. Houston, *I Believe in God the Creator* (Hodder, 1979).
P. E. Hughes, *The True Image* (IVP, 1989).
P. Johnson, *Darwin on Trial* (IVP USA, 1991).
D. Kidner, *Genesis* (IVP, 1967).
J. G. Machen, *The Christian View of Man* (Banner of Truth, 1965).
J. Orr, *God's Image in Man* (Eerdmans, 1948).
L. Osborn, *Guardians of Creation* (Apollos, 1993).
E. K. V. Pearce, *Who was Adam?* (Paternoster, 1976).
C. Sherlock, *The Doctrine of Humanity* (IVP, 1996).

10. Humanity in sin

Chapter 9 pictures what might have been if Adam had remained upright. In fact, he fell and so we need to deal with the human race in sin.

THE FALL OF HUMANKIND

Genesis 3:1–7 recounts the first sin of the human race, but that far from exhausts biblical references to the fall (see p. 129). Quite apart from the many explicit references, the fall is integral to the whole biblical message: 'The fall is the silent hypothesis of the whole biblical doctrine of sin and redemption' (Bavinck). How are we to interpret the Genesis account?

1. The *literal* view sees the Genesis record as a direct historical description. This is the most widely accepted position in the church over the centuries and continues to have many sincere

defenders. It is less frequently adopted today, even among those who unquestionably acknowledge the full inspiration of Scripture.

2. The *mythical* view rejects *any* historical element and treats the Genesis story as a religious picture which conveys important truths about humankind and its moral condition; it is not about the origin of sin, but about its essence. It would be wrong to discount this entirely as a *supplementary* use of the fall account. Indeed, Paul may use it in something of this way in Romans 1 when portraying the sin and rebellion of the Gentile world of his day. It will not do, however, as the *primary* meaning of Genesis 3, since rejection of any historical element is clearly out of step with the later biblical writers. It also undermines the biblical concept of redemption (see below) and leaves human sin totally unexplained.

3. The *'historical'* view asserts that while Genesis 2 – 3 are not to be interpreted in a literal sense at every point, space-time events are certainly being recounted. The Bible comments on the fall as an event (Rom. 5:12f.), locates Eden fairly precisely (Gn. 2:10–14) and sets Adam in historical continuity with Abraham and Israel (Gn. 4:1; 5:4; 11:27; Lk. 3:38). The fall was a real event in our moral history.

The following considerations bear on our interpretation of this crucial passage:

1. There is a problem in relating our everyday language to the pre-fall situation, since all *our language is shaped by fallen experience*. Similarly, when the effects of the fall will be banished at the return of Christ, Scripture has again to employ a degree of symbolism to express that future situation (Rev. 21 – 22).

2. G. C. Berkouwer has argued that the fall can never be properly grasped until we are prepared to confess *our personal involvement* in that sorry event. While this principle must not inhibit all discussion of the nature of the fall, it provides a salutary corrective to unduly theoretical approaches.

3. Thorough-going evolutionists often reject the notion of sin and allied Christian arguments. But the believer can at least observe that, once human moral failure is admitted (and the empirical evidence for that is impressive enough in all conscience!), then that tendency in humankind must have had a starting-point in time. There occurred *a first distinct act of rebellion* against known moral norms, in this case the will of

God. The origin of sin was, therefore, datable in relation to the whole sequence of human events.

4. In Romans 5:12ff. (*cf.* 1 Cor. 15:22) Paul uses the fall as the counterpoint for an exposition of Christ's work of redemption. The effects of the 'one' (*i.e.* 'first') sin of Adam (vv. 16, 18) are undone by the 'one act of righteousness' (v. 18) of Christ in his death for sinners (*cf.* 3:25; 4:25; 5:8f.). It is impossible to sustain this *parallel between the work of Adam and the work of Christ* if the fall as a space-time event is denied.

THE NATURE AND EXTENT OF SIN

The nature of sin

Scripture uses a wide variety of terms to refer to sin, which is not surprising since the dominant theme of the Bible is human rebellion against God and God's gracious response. The full range of the biblical terms and their respective shades of meaning can be studied in a Bible dictionary. Here we simply note the principal OT and NT words translated as 'sin' in our English versions.

The commonest OT term is *ḥaṭṭāṯ* (*e.g.* Ex. 32:30) and its cognate term *ḥēt* (Ps. 51:9). It occurs several hundred times in the OT and expresses the thought of missing the mark, or erring. *peša'* (Pr. 28:13) has the sense of active rebellion, a trespass or transgression of God's will. *šāgâh* (Lv. 4:13) expresses the thought of going astray. *'āwôn* (1 Ki. 17:18) is related to a verbal form meaning 'to twist' and refers to the guilt which sin produces. The major word for sin in the Greek NT, *hamartia* (Mt. 1:21), also has the force of missing the mark; it covers the thoughts of failure, fault and concrete wrongdoing. *Adikia* (1 Cor. 6:8) renders the ideas of unrighteousness or injustice. *Parabasis* (Rom. 4:15) refers to breach of the law. *Anomia* (1 Jn. 3:4) similarly expresses lawlessness. *Asebeia* (Tit. 2:12) reflects the strong sense of godlessness, while *ptaiō* is more the moral stumble (Jas. 2:10).

The most characteristic feature of sin is that it is directed *against God* (*cf.* Ps. 51:4; Rom. 8:7; Jas. 4:4). Any minimizing of this, such as the notion of sin as selfishness, seriously underestimates its gravity. Its clearest expression is Satan's suggestion that Adam and Eve could usurp the place of their Maker, 'you will be like God . . .' (Gn. 3:5). In the fall, humanity snatched at equality with God (*cf.* Phil. 2:6f.), attempted to assert its independence of him and questioned the Creator's integrity and loving provision for it. People also blasphemously withheld that worship and adoring love which is our proper response to God, and paid homage to the enemy of God as well as to their own evil ambitions.

The extent of sin

Sin is *universal*. 'There is no-one righteous, not even one' (Rom. 3:10; *cf.* Rom. 3:1–10, 23; Ps. 14:1ff.). Jesus Christ alone lived as a human being 'without sin' (Heb. 4:15). This biblical assessment is amply vindicated by social anthropology and common experience.

The extent of sin is total not merely in a geographical sense, but also in an individual's life. Sin affects the *whole* of a human being: the will (Jn. 8:34; Rom. 7:14–24; Eph. 2:1–3; 2 Pet. 2:19); the mind and understanding (Gn. 6:5; 1 Cor. 1:21; Eph. 4:17); the affections and emotions (Rom. 1:24–27; 1 Tim. 6:10; 2 Tim. 3:4); as well as one's outward speech and behaviour (Mk. 7:21f.; Gal. 5:19–21; Jas. 3:5–9); and also, very often, social conditions in the form of oppressive political and social systems as 'structural sin'. Sin also affects human relationships. As well as penetrating to the heart of the individual, it can insinuate itself into the social and political structures of a nation or community (Am. 2:4–8; 5:7–15; Rev. 13:1–17). Not surprisingly, theologians have expressed this catalogue of sin's affects as *total depravity*. The phrase does not imply that we are as evil as we possibly can be, which would make us indistinguishable from demons; rather, no area or aspect of our nature is left intact by sin; we can point to no single area of our personality in order to claim moral self-justification.

The fact that we do at times think, speak or act in a way which is relatively 'good' (Lk. 11:13; Rom. 2:14f.) does not disprove total depravity, since this 'good' can never approach that entire, lifelong righteousness by which alone we can stand before God. There is no 'nature reserve' in the human personality in which our 'original state' is preserved intact. We are wholly fallen and hence wholly in need of redemption.

The Bible also teaches our total depravity by saying that sin has affected the very core of the person. The *heart* (Heb. *lēb*), the essential person, has been perverted by sin. We recall Jesus' judgment: 'from within, out of men's hearts come evil thoughts, sexual immorality, theft, murder . . . all these evils come from inside and make a man "unclean"' (Mk. 7:21f., *cf.* Gn. 6:5; Je. 17:9; Rom. 3:10–18; 7:23).

Further, it is precisely because we are 'totally depraved' in this biblical sense that we are utterly unable to save ourselves. Total depravity implies 'total inability'.

The transmission of sin: original sin

The relationship between Adam's act of disobedience and subsequent human sinning is the question of original sin, a phrase which has two related meanings. First, it simply refers to Adam's sin in Eden, *the* original sin. Secondly, the Bible teaches that Adam's sin involved the entire human race. In Romans 5:12 Paul asserts that through Adam's disobedience sin and death became realities for all, 'because all men sinned', *i.e.* because they all sinned in Adam's sin (Rom. 5:14–19; 1 Cor. 15:22). There are two traditional explanations of this.

Realism interprets Paul's reference in Romans 5:12 in a literal manner. 'All sinned in Adam' means that all were present and involved when Adam sinned: universal generic human nature, which encompasses the individual, personal natures of everyone, was present in some way 'in Adam', so that when he sinned every man and woman sinned with him (*cf.* Heb. 7:4–10; Levi was present 'in the body' of his forefather Abraham). This tries to avoid the danger of arbitrariness in the interpretation of original sin; but, putting aside the problem of giving genuine cash value to this generic humanity, we face the difficulty of its implications for the humanity of Christ. If Christ's humanity was not part of this universal generic humanity in Adam, then his essential oneness with us is threatened; if he was included, then he must have shared in the fall.

Federalism argues that, in view of the parallel drawn between Adam and Christ (Rom. 5:12–19; 1 Cor. 15:22, 45–49), our universal solidarity with Adam is of the kind which Christ has with those he redeems, *i.e.* representative, or *federal*, headship. Commonly today federalism means a particular political system; theologically the term derives from the *covenant* that God made with the human race in Adam (Lat. *foedus* = covenant). This covenant (often called the 'covenant of works') Adam breached by his sin, with dire consequences for those he represented. In Christ the covenant was renewed, and under it his perfect righteousness becomes the means of blessing and salvation for all those he represents (Gn. 2:15–17; Je. 31:31f.; Rom. 3:21–31; 5:12–21; 1 Cor. 11:25). The operative principle is the same in both cases; by virtue of our union with Adam, he being our representative head, we are constituted sinners; by virtue of our union by faith with Christ we are constituted righteous. Lest this seem to imply an arbitrariness as far as our condemnation in Adam is concerned, it is significant that the justice of God in finding the whole world guilty before him (Rom. 3:19) is amply demonstrated from the specific, overt sins of Jews and Gentiles (Rom. 1:18 – 3:8) before any reference is made to original sin 'in Adam' (Rom. 5:12f.). Scripture universally relates our ultimate judgment to our own moral 'works', which fall short of God's standards, and not in the first instance to our union with Adam (*e.g.* Mt. 7:21–27; 13:41; 25:31–46; Lk. 3:9; Rom. 2:5–10; Rev. 20:11–14).

THE EFFECTS OF SIN

Our fall into sin had far-reaching significance for each of the divisions of our being, which we spelled out in the previous chapter.

In relation to God

This is the heart of all the implications of sin which will be expounded below. In relation to God, sin means:

1. *We are unfit for God's presence.* Adam's expulsion from the Garden of Eden gave geographical expression to our spiritual separation from God, our unfitness to stand before him and enjoy the intimacy of his presence (Gn. 3:23). God's presence becomes a place of dread; the fiery sword which barred the way back to Eden represents the terrible truth that in our sin we encounter God's resistance and opposition, *i.e.* his holy wrath (Gn. 3:24; Mt. 3:7; Rom. 1:18; 1 Thes. 1:10). Beside the wrath of God, all other human dreads and fears are mere bad dreams; all our other needs, however acute or extensive, pale into relative insignificance.

2. *We are unable to do God's will.* Although God remains our Lord, summoning and commanding us, setting before us the way of life and freedom, we are no longer able truly to respond to that summons. Our will has lost its freedom to conform to the divine purpose and has become enslaved to sin (Jn. 8:34; Rom. 7:21f.).

3. *We are unrighteous before God's law.* Our failure to conform to God's will or law has the further serious implication that we become subject to the law's curse, the guilt and condemnation, which accrues to the law-breaker (Dt. 27:26; 28; Rom. 3:19f.; 5:16ff.; Gal. 3:10).

4. *We are insensitive to God's word.* God speaks through creation, through the moral law within, through Israel in the OT and the church in the NT, and above all through his Word, incarnate and written. In our sin we hear only enough to be rendered inexcusable for our unbelief, but not enough truly to comprehend God's way and will. Our sin brings us finally to a state of ignorance of God, unable to understand the things of the Spirit.

These effects of sin are manifest in human *pride*. We resist God's rule and set ourselves up as our own lord; we make ourselves the standard of reality and our own reason and experience the measure of truth. We claim mastery of the world and assume responsibility for the destiny of the race. Its ultimate expression takes the form of a titanism in which we climb Babel-like towards heaven to thrust God down (*cf.* Gn. 11:1–9; 2 Thes. 2:4).

In the religious sphere, this pride is expressed as *self-justification*. We adopt our own standard of goodness and justify ourselves in the light of it, finding excuse for our sin and standing confidently before God on the basis of our moral and religious attainments.

But we cannot escape from God. The broken relationship is manifest as *fear* of God – not the godly, self-abasement of the person of faith (*cf.* Dt. 10:12), but the terror of the fugitive, fleeing the God who has been disobeyed. This fear may drive us to seek a substitute God who will not expose our guilt. Some embrace theoretical denials of God, such as atheism, and fulminate against the injustices of life; others throw themselves into some 'just' cause, or become involved in an endless round of activities and responsibilities; all in order to hide from God (like Adam and Eve in the garden) and avoid the terror of standing exposed in their guilt before him.

In relation to one's neighbour
The breach in relationship with God directly affects our relationship with our fellow human beings. Adam turned upon

Eve and blamed her for his folly (Gn. 3:12), and the account of the fall is closely followed by the story of the murder of Abel (Gn. 4:1–16). Humanity against God is also humanity against its fellows, the stranger and the enemy, a threat instead of a friend.

Sin brings *conflict* and produces the great divisions of humankind. It causes racial prejudice and antagonism. It builds the great international power blocs. It creates social divisions and so leads to group and class conflict; it separates the 'haves' from the 'have-nots'. It causes conflict within all human groups, whether educational, community, social, leisure or religious. It divides families and churches. Paradoxically, the threat posed by our neighbour makes us run for security into various, sometimes unlikely, alliances.

Sin also produces *exploitation*; we 'use' our neighbours. We exploit them to bolster our self-esteem, to justify our evil schemes and to support our weaknesses. We make them the scapegoat for our own frustrations and sense of guilt. This exploitation can even be expressed in open physical or psychological violence; in the male–female relationship it has been expressed historically in male domination, the use of women for men's selfish ends, denying their essential equality and dignity. Even in loving our neighbour we seek the benefits of love's response; our giving is a getting.

Our breach with our neighbours also expresses itself as a *fear* that we shall be seen as we really are, in our weakness, guilt and self-contempt. We therefore try to hide from them on the one hand by projecting an untrue image of ourselves, and on the other by seeking to extinguish their threat by labelling them, making them ciphers: a 'case', a 'student', a 'teacher', a 'director', a 'worker'.

One of the bitterest fruits of this separation from our neighbour is the habitual experience of *misunderstanding*, even when there is a genuine desire to know and to be known.

In relation to oneself

Sin sets us against ourselves; we exist in inner conflict and division, crying out, 'I see another law at war with the law of my mind ... O wretched man that I am, who shall deliver me ...?' (Rom. 7:23f.). We lose clear inward direction and become ambiguous to ourselves, a legion of conflicting drives. This effect of sin is manifest in *self-deception*. The loss of true self-knowledge leads either into the error of narcissistic self-idealization, or into that of neurotic self-condemnation by unreal standards. Incapable of correctly judging ourselves, we are unable to commit all things to God and let God be our judge (1 Cor. 4:3f.).

This inward conflict is also expressed as *shame*, discomfort with oneself (*cf.* Gn. 3:7–8). Sin has robbed us of self-confidence and self-acceptance as God's own creature; we are ashamed of ourselves.

All these expressions of our inward conflict produce within us an incurable *restlessness*: '. . . the wicked are like the tossing sea, which cannot rest . . . "There is no peace," says my God, "for the wicked"' (Is. 57:20f.).

In relation to the created order

Humanity loses its harmony with the natural order and our God-given stewardship of the environment gives place to sinful plundering. This is manifest as *exploitation*, the needless destruction of the world without thought for its created beauty or intrinsic worth. It is also manifest as *pollution*, the selfish and rapacious use of raw materials, contaminating the oceans and the very atmosphere, all too often in the interests of economic profit, luxury and self-indulgence.

In relation to time

Our lost lives are spent within lost time. Through sin we forfeit immortality (Gn. 2:17; 3:19); our days are numbered. God's future judgment is foreshadowed in the judgment of death. We are given time by God, but it moves inexorably to its close, when all our plans, purposes and dreams are finally bracketed by mortality.

This effect of sin is expressed in *materialism* and in the practical hedonism which is simply materialism in application. We grasp at the tangible world of the senses in an effort to cast an anchor into the relentless stream of life. It is also evident in the desire to leave behind memorials, some material means of prolonging our memory beyond the grave.

This time-limit also produces *anxiety*. Death confronts us, as nothing else does, with our insignificance and weakness, and exposes the folly of our pretensions to greatness. Even when we attempt to face death with courage, we never succeed in finally overcoming it; it dominates us until at last we too go to receive the wages of sin.

FURTHER ISSUES

The unpardonable sin

Several NT passages refer to a sin which is unforgivable, the sin or blasphemy against the Holy Spirit. Jesus speaks of it (Mt. 12:31–32; *cf.* also Heb. 6:4–6; 10:26–29; 1 Jn. 5:16). Some have seen this sin as an explicit act of blaspheming the Holy Spirit, usually in relation to the witness he bears to Christ.

Recent interpretation sees the sin as essentially Christological. Jesus distinguished between sin against the Spirit and sin 'against the Son of Man' (Mt. 12:32) *before* his death and resurrection and the outpouring of the Spirit at Pentecost. Prior to the first Easter the 'Son of Man' was an enigmatic, hidden revelation of God. Failure to recognize Jesus during his earthly mission (*e.g.* by his own family, Mk. 3:21) was less serious than deliberately attributing his entire mission, its good works in particular, to Satan – of which the Pharisees were guilty. With Pentecost, the distinction vanishes. Jesus is demonstrated as Son of God with power in resurrection and the gospel of the cross is preached in the power of the Spirit. Rejection of *this* message and of the Christ it enshrines is rejection of the Spirit who bears testimony to its truth (Heb. 10:29). *This* sin is unpardonable if continued in, for it places one beyond the only hope of redemption. John calls it a 'sin that leads to death' (1 Jn. 5:16).

Human freedom

The question of the meaning and limits of human freedom since the fall has been debated strenuously over the centuries. Often more heat has been generated than light, not least through the tendency to fuse the theological issues with the parallel but distinct philosophical question of determinism and indeterminism. Freedom can refer to at least three things:

1. There is the everyday psychological experience of freedom: we face alternatives and make choices. These range from the comparatively trivial ('Which newspaper will I buy this morning?') to the ultimately serious ('Will you marry me?'). This is the freedom that is basic to moral responsibility. Scripture assumes that the power of voluntary, responsible choice belongs

to all people, Christians and non-Christians alike.

2. A second level of meaning arises from the question whether our future actions are determined by present factors and so may in principle be predicted. The Bible appears neither to affirm nor to deny freedom in this sense. It certainly takes character determination seriously; past decisions and actions shape the kind of people we become: 'A man reaps what he sows' (Gal. 6:7). Yet Scripture does not teach the elimination of human responsibility on that account.

3. The strictly theological aspect of freedom arises with the issue of whether non-Christians are free to fulfil God's will, and in particular whether they are free to repent of their sins and trust in Christ as Saviour and Lord. The enslavement of the human will through the fall would appear to rule out any suggestion that we are genuinely free to obey God. This inability to turn to God without his aid is reflected in the fact that entry to God's kingdom is only by regeneration.[1]

Present debates

Anthropological issues are central to present debates between Christians and non-Christians, and it is not possible to predict the precise relationship which will eventually emerge between the Christian view of humanity and contemporary scientific, psychological, and sociological interpretations. Here we briefly explore several fairly current approaches. The reader is referred to the bibliography (p. 148) for fuller discussions.

New Age

The New Age movement (NAM) is a widely scattered, loosely structured network of organizations and individuals bound together by a set of common values and a common vision of a coming 'New Age' of worldwide peace and enlightenment, the 'Age of Aquarius'.

The NAM came into public prominence during the 1980s, but its roots go back to the counterculture movements of the 60s. In so far as its religious heritage lies in eastern thought, particularly Hinduism and Zen Buddhism, the historic sources go back very much further. Indeed, some argue that it is not misleading to understand New Age as the appearance of Hinduism in western

---

1. On this see also Part 5, 'Regeneration'.

cultural dress. Its fundamental conviction is its vision of ultimate reality, 'All is One'. The cosmos is pure, undifferentiated energy – a consciousness or life force, vast, interconnected and finally impersonal. Humans are simply congealed energy, the All in self-reflective mode; hence 'you create your own reality'. That reality is finally unlimited in its potential, since we are part of the limitless whole; and hence 'we are God'. Death is an illusion, since the impersonal ground of existence is deathless and unchanging. Morality is an illusion also, in the sense that all moral distinctions are relative and finally 'unreal'. Humanity's dilemma is a limited consciousness. Through social conditioning we have fractured our perception of reality. Reason and belief, in particular, are barriers to a true perception of the One. But New Agers are persuaded that a new order of things, the Age of Aquarius, is about to appear with its mystical way of knowing. We can enter this new order in the present by a paradigm shift in our way of perceiving reality, an awakening to the One; *i.e.* a vision that transcends all dualities and differentiations and introduces us to the divine as the unification and harmonization of all things.

The limitations of this way of interpreting the world and human experience ought to be readily apparent to students of this book. New Ageism has no doctrine of creation and so confuses the three basic realities in the Bible's revelation of creation – God, the order of nature, and human beings. Particularly tragic is the loss of God as the glorious, infinite, personal Trinity. The loss of God necessarily implies a misunderstanding of the human condition, particularly the seriousness of our sin before him. Not only does the NAM misrepresent our plight, it also has no solution to offer. There is no Saviour to cleanse our guilty hearts, no personal, loving God to share our tears, no glorious hope in face of death. Because of its all-embracing vision Jesus is afforded a genuine respect in New Age thinking, but only as a supreme spiritual master. In essence, since we ourselves are God we cannot attribute deity to another: 'The myth of the saviour "out there" is replaced with the myth of the hero "in here"' (M. Ferguson). In the end, New Ageism is a modern representation of the ancient idolatry of Eden which led to our expulsion from the Garden of God's presence (Gn. 3:5, 'you will be like God'). Only Jesus Christ can lead us back there; but he has! (Rev. 2:7; 22:1–5).

Humanist liberalism

This label can serve as a general title for the anthropology which holds sway among the majority of educated people in the western world at the present time. Its historic roots lie in the seventeenth- and early eighteenth-century Enlightenment, a many-sided but hugely influential period in the development of human understanding which formulated many of the dominant instincts of modern self-consciousness. In particular, we can note the theme of autonomy, the assertion of the independence of the human spirit from all constraints, whether of religion or tradition. This feature was given political expression in the Peace of Westphalia (1648), which effectively ended religious wars and introduced a separation of spiritual and secular spheres of influence. Another critical feature of Enlightenment experience was the application of physical laws in the interpretation of the universe, bringing about the birth of modern science. Still another was the emergence of historical criticism, the forging of the intellectual tools to enable the mind to distinguish the present from the past and to evaluate both in terms of their own inherent principles. Descartes, Newton, Hume, Voltaire, Rousseau, Gibbon, Lessing and Jefferson expressed, in a variety of fields, this remarkable mutation in human thought. From it emerged the post-Enlightenment 'modern' individual, curious about the world, confident in his own judgments, sceptical of orthodoxies, generally rebellious against authority, proud of his humanity, conscious of his distinctiveness from nature, assured of his own intellectual capacity to comprehend and harness nature, and altogether less dependent upon an omnipotent God. During the nineteenth century this autonomous mind-set found further expression in the exploration of the unconscious mind (Freud) and the awakening to the significance of social forces (Marx). Both of these in turn called into question the objectivity of values, fuelling an uncertainty deepened by Nietzsche's writings, and, from a different perspective, Darwin's researches into the origins of the human and other species.

Today's humanist-liberal instinct, which stands in clear continuity from these Enlightenment views, can be briefly characterized as follows:

It is *secular*. That means it approaches reality typically in terms of the immanent natural factors involved. Its primary frame of reference is this-worldly. While supernatural agencies are not in principle discounted, they are viewed as peripheral and hence as not contributing significantly to understanding or to action. Thus, however much their history may owe to the stimulus or support of Christianity, contemporary science, industry, education, medicine, commerce and art operate without major reference to Christian values or beliefs.

It is *rational*. While the high rationalism of the earlier centuries has had to recede before the overwhelming evidence of humanity's enslavement to subjective and emotional forces, the modernist instinct still regularly carries, at least at the popular level, a fundamental self-assurance about its capacity to comprehend and evaluate data. Reason, though wounded, has not died. This lingering affair with reason may perhaps be seen reflected in postmodernism (see below), which, while launching a major frontal attack on the misuse of reason, nevertheless employs a highly sophisticated rational argumentation to make its case.

It is *'scientific'*. The modern mind continues to be profoundly impressed by the ability of the scientific method to tell us how things really are and to produce answers. The fact that some have ceased to make these kinds of claim for science tends to be outweighed by the astonishing recent advances in technology and the projections of the even greater transformations which lie ahead.

It is *liberal*. The Enlightenment's instinct to remove all boundaries continues to impact modern consciousness deeply. There is today a principled openness to the new and the previously unexplored. Not only in the arts but in every sphere there is an unwillingness to accept constraints of any kind; all ways are to be tried and all perspectives embraced.

It is *individualistic*. We will expand on this trait below. Here we simply note that the gradual break-up of the old order's traditional institutions of family, church, and government has projected the modern person into new uncharted waters of extreme isolation. Whereas people in the classical, pre-Enlightenment worlds knew themselves to be part of larger configurations and solidarities, however much that might have reduced their freedom and inhibited their expression, today's typical urban dweller inhabits a world in which people are thrown back upon themselves, struggling to create their own identity, realize their own possibilities and shape their own value system without significant reference to others.

It is *relativistic*. This feature flows directly from the previous one; it is simply the radical individualism of our time applied to the sphere of values. Because all previous systems evaluating and directing human behaviour are to be rejected in principle in the interests of personal liberty, there are no general laws as far as the determination of conduct is concerned. Right becomes what I as an individual deem to be right at a particular moment. Values are therefore infinitely fluid and irreducibly relative.

It is *optimistic/pessimistic*. At the heart of the modern mind-set is a major unresolved tension. The temper of its Enlightenment heritage reflects unbounded optimism in the capacities of the human spirit, especially with respect to the technological revolutions in communication, advances in biology and medicine, emerging globalization, the dawn of a new political world order, and the increasing penetration of space. Over against that, however, are the sombre realities which we listed at the beginning of this section on anthropology (see p. 113). Life on this planet is a fragile plant, and any one of a series of crises may develop out of control within the foreseeable future and bring the age-long story of humanity to an inglorious conclusion. Our optimism is anxious.

In concluding this survey of modern anthropology, we note two specific strands which he broadly within the humanist liberalism of our time, the first in self-conscious antithesis, the second in continuity of several of its essential trends.

Postmodernism
This is the name given to a variety of views and expressions which have surfaced on the heels of the radicalisms of the 1960s. Its common element is, as the name implies, a partial rejection of, and attempt to move beyond the 'modern' liberal anthropology whose salient features we have noted above.

In one sense postmodernism has been a long time coming, in that the Enlightenment never was a total enterprise. Voices like Nietzsche's attacked modernism's self-confident rationalism. However, it has only been in the recent period that that criticism has gathered momentum. Modernity is criticized on a number of fronts: (a) the attempt to find a basis for morality and society in reason alone has failed; (b) the Enlightenment's belief in the inevitability of progress has proved false; (c) the belief that knowledge is inherently good cannot be sustained; (d) the idea that there is somewhere a grand overarching perspective which can act as a reference point for explaining 'universal' human history (a 'metanarrative') is to be rejected; (e) (perhaps more controversially) the modernist assumption that the idea of God is superfluous is at least open to question.

Postmodernism is much more than a set of theoretical positions; it is in many respects a way of responding to the world, and hence it is expressed in art and theatre and in popular culture as effectively as in theoretical propositions. In a sense it is as much a style as a statement. But we can note several features that are often, though not always, present:

1. It is a rejection of all universal worldviews. All theories that claim to put everything together in a coherent whole are rejected in principle.

2. It celebrates a diversity of styles thrown together without any overall pattern. For postmodernism each piece is distinct and of equal worth.

3. It focuses on the individual and the specific. All attempts to generalize and unite in larger wholes are to be rejected. Style rather than substance is critical.

4. It majors on personal, immediate experience. Because the Enlightenment endeavour to find true objectivity has failed, subjectivity is to be celebrated. What I feel and experience at this particular moment is primary; all else is secondary.

5. It is acutely aware of the dangers of rationalizing and of the manipulation of knowledge. It is alert to 'power games' played by privileged élites in the name of 'ideologies' and 'explanations'.

6. It elevates the sense of irony. Because we are trapped in ourselves and with others who, like ourselves, play power games at every level of life, any meaningful ideology is impossible, final meaning is dead and we are left only with irony as the basis of life.

Not all postmodernists would subscribe to all of these tenets. Many people live by these instincts who have never heard the term. It represents, however, a significant and growing anthropological expression.

As an account of reality, postmodernism's limitations are obvious from the perspective of Christian faith. However, there are also points of overlap with biblical instincts. The critique of reason in its pretentious claim to afford a totally objective vantage point accords with the Christian view that sin has affected every area of human existence, not excluding the reason. Life's ultimate truth is found, as the Bible makes clear, in a context of personal repentance, commitment and faith, not of detached reason. Further, this movement can serve to remind us that while our responsibility to clarify and defend the Christian faith continues, the final apologetic, as we noted earlier, lies not in the soundness of arguments or the marshalling of evidence, but in the integration of the truths of our faith in a lifestyle and community which embrace the whole of our human experience. Similarly, postmodernism's rejection of the modernist belief in inevitable progress resonates with the Bible's reminder that only in dependence on God and his grace can we progress towards true freedom and fulfilment.

In its way, postmodernism also represents an opportunity for the Christian gospel, and this at several points. The bleakness of its inescapable individualism creates an inevitable longing to experience life in community. In the church, as a loving community bound together in the living Christ and his Spirit, there is a wonderfully attractive alternative to that chilling isolation. Again, postmodernism's concern to embrace diversity and its commitment to global perspectives create a significant relevance for the international Christian community spread through the world and embracing every nation and culture. Local churches which courageously embrace diversity, not as a threat but as a gift, can discover significant responsiveness from people impacted by the postmodern spirit.

Finally, postmodernism's disavowal of the metanarrative challenges the Christian to present the Christian gospel in its comprehensiveness as *the* story, centred in Jesus Christ, in which our individual experience is validated, our loneliness overcome, our guilt assuaged, our environment affirmed, our social responsibilities asserted, our historical reality underwritten, our imagination liberated, and our lives set free for a new and eternal purpose.

Free-market individualism

As we have seen, one of the prime marks of the modern mind-set is its individualism. Ancient authorities are swept away; the individual makes up his or her own mind. Actions are right not simply because others have held them to be so but because we ourselves deem them to be. In postmodernism, as we saw, this individualism is carried to its limits; we are imprisoned within our own personal perspective and all our judgments are inevitably skewed. Reality is in the end *my* reality, the reality I create for myself.

This deep-seated individualism is also reflected today in the sphere of economics. The revolution in communications brought about by the invention of the personal computer and its technological accompaniments has transformed the shape of economic activity, initially in the West, but increasingly as a global phenomenon. 'The great unifying theme at the conclusion of the twentieth century is the triumph of the individual,' write Naisbitt and Aburdene, and they see this expressed particularly in the new technology which allows the individual to become a personal entrepreneur, able to participate in the global marketplace.

The new globalism which has been spawned by the internet has hugely significant possibilities at the level of the exchange of information and the developing of networks of friendship and mutual understanding across political and cultural divides. These networks may yet prove to be the harbingers of that global consciousness which alone can enable humankind to surmount the global crises of our time, and the times to come. There is, however, a possibility, which a number of observers have already noted, that the primary result of computer technology will be to establish economics as the fundamental lens through which reality is viewed. By this view, economic activity in the pursuit of personal wealth becomes the driving force in human behaviour, and the considerations of the marketplace override all others. This does not mean that less tangible values, such as beauty, justice or faith, are seen as unimportant. But, it is argued, economics as the more immediate and accessible reality is what makes these other pursuits possible. In the end we are economic beings, and our ultimate good is economic well-being. Without it every other good would cease to be attainable. Further, the form of economic life which promotes the maximization of this goal is the free-market economy which has been characteristic, with some modifications, of western nations for much of the last hundred years. It is imperative therefore that the restrictive barriers to free trade and the flow and interplay of economic activity be eliminated. Let them come down and let individuals be freed to make their play, develop their investment, market their product, and hopefully make their fortune!

Clearly, no Christian need be hesitant about commending the significant expansion of personal opportunity which all this represents. Further, if the development of the international economy leads to improved relationships between peoples, and in addition promotes the expansion of the total resource-pool of the international community, then we need not be grudging in our appreciation. There are, however, questions which need to be asked from the Christian perspective:

1. Economics is hugely important, but not all-important. To expect economics to meet and overcome the critical problems of our time is a road to disillusionment. It is not dissimilar to the fallacy of the Enlightenment in imagining that reason, or universal education, would have a similarly benign effect.

2. To assume that the free flow of economic activity across the global economy is the guarantor of prosperity shows an unfounded and naïve faith in the operation of economics. We are entering uncharted waters as far as these developments are concerned. Historically, financial markets and international trade have often performed in unpredictable and even disastrous ways.

3. Economic activity, like all human activity, is the function of human beings who make moral choices, and who have a proven liability, which the Bible identifies as the sinful heart, to act out of purely selfish motivations. One reply to this contends that the beauty of the free-market system lies precisely in its ability to muffle the effects of human selfishness in that what is motivated by self-interest also maximizes profit and hence promotes the good of all. To argue thus, however, is to fail to learn the fundamental lessons of history. Economic considerations in themselves will pay no heed, for example, to ecological concerns. Why limit profitability for the sake of some alleged chemical pollution? But environmental concerns are not peripheral and can only be overcome if market forces are controlled. Further, the accumulation of personal wealth *may* contribute to the resource base of the global community, but it would be exceedingly naïve to believe that that is likely to be the case in practice. To believe that the accumulated wealth would find itself directed into the hands of the world's poor and underprivileged is to

anticipate a miracle on a global scale. Economics pursued by fallen humans inevitably has fallen effects. True sharing of resources and the control of world economic activity in the interests of the world community will happen only when there exists a universal spirit of sacrifice. To date, the only historical force which has regularly promoted such a spirit of sacrifice has been the gospel of Jesus Christ. Putting this point in another way, unrestricted free-market economic activity pursued by individuals will inevitably reflect all the limitations of uninhibited individualism. But we are not independent individuals. We are members of the human family who need others to achieve our wholeness. We were made for love, and only in a love which transcends our selfish individualism can fulfilment be experienced.

4. Finally, *laissez-faire* economics has nothing to say to the great questions of human existence. Where did we come from? What or who are we? Where are we going? What is life for? On these, economics is silent. But these questions cannot be eradicated. No matter how deeply overlaid they may be at different periods in the lives of individuals and societies, sooner or later they force their way once more to the surface. The only fully satisfying answers lie in the revelation of the Creator-Redeemer God of the Bible.

Summary

Scripture teaches two fundamental things about humankind. First, we are creatures of God, made in his image; neither cosmic accident, nor bureaucratic cipher, humankind once stood resplendent before its Maker. Secondly, we are sinners, fallen away from God and his destiny for us, living in implicit and explicit rebellion against him. Pascal combined these truths when he spoke of humanity as a dethroned monarch, cast down from our former eminence, vanquished and depraved, yet never quite able to forget what we once were and hence ought to be.

This biblical account of humankind as creature and sinner vindicates its truth against all alternative anthropologies, ancient or modern.

Scriptures

The fall: Gn. 3:1–7; Dt. 32:8; Jb. 31:33; Ec. 7:29; Is. 43:27; Ho. 6:7; Lk. 3:38; Rom. 5:12ff.; 1 Cor. 15:22f.; 2 Cor. 11:3; 1 Thes. 2:13f.; 1 Tim. 2:13f.; Jude 14.

The nature and extent of sin: Gn. 3:6; Pss. 14:1–3; 51:4; Is. 64:6; Je. 17:9; Mk. 7:21f.; Jn. 8:34f.; Rom. 3:9–20; 5:10; 7:14–24; 8:7; Gal. 5:19–21; Eph. 4:17f.; Jas. 3:5–9; 2 Pet. 2:19.

The effects of sin: Gn. 3:17–24; 4:14; 19:1–12; 1 Sa. 31:1–6; Ps. 90:5–10; Ec. 1 – 2; Is. 5:8–23; Rom. 1:18–32; 8:19–23; Eph. 2:1–3; Jas. 5:1–6; 2 Pet. 3:5–10.

Questions

1. Which interpretation of the fall do you believe to be truest to Scripture? Why is the mythical view not adequate?
2. 'The fall is the silent hypothesis of the whole biblical doctrine of sin and redemption.' Discuss.
3. What does 'total depravity' mean? Consider the importance of this notion for the evangelist's message and methods.
4. What do you understand by Paul's statement that 'through the disobedience of the one man the many were made sinners' (Rom. 5:19)?
5. Identify the principal effects of sin on our relationship with (a) God, (b) our neighbour, (c) ourselves, (d) our environment, (e) time. Find examples of these effects from biblical biography and from your daily newspaper.
6. Consider sin's effects upon our relationship with our neighbour (a) in international relations, (b) in your own society, (c) in your immediate neighbourhood, (d) in your place of work or college, (e) in your church or Christian group, (f) in your own life.
7. Imagine yourself speaking to (a) a New Ager, (b) a postmodernist, (c) a believer in free-market economics; how would you present the gospel of Christ to each of them?

Bibliography

G. C. Berkouwer, *Sin* (Eerdmans, 1971).

H. Blocher, *Original Sin* (Apollos, 1997).

M. Luther, *The Bondage of the Will* (tr. J. I. Packer and O. R. Johnston) (James Clarke, 1957).

C. Plantinga, *Not the Way It's Supposed to Be* (Apollos, 1995).

C. Sherlock, *The Doctrine of Humanity* (IVP, 1996).

R. Venning, *The Plague of Plagues* (Banner of Truth, 1965).

Present debates:

G. Carey, *I Believe in Man* (Hodder, 1977).

D. Cook, *Blind Alley Beliefs* (IVP, 1996).

D. Groothuis, *Confronting the New Age* (IVP, 1993).

O. Guinness, *The Dust of Death* (IVP, 1973).

D. M. MacKay, *Human Science and Human Dignity* (Hodder, 1979).

J. A. Middleton and B. J. Walsh, *Truth is Stranger than it Used to Be* (SPCK, 1995).

J. R. W. Stott, *Your Mind Matters* (IVP, 1972).

D. Wells, *God in the Wasteland* (IVP, 1994).

D. Wells, *Losing our Virtue* (IVP, 1998).

11. Humanity in grace

There is nothing in humanity which can extend its story beyond creation and fall. 'Dead in transgressions and sins' (Eph. 2:1), we can no more prolong our autobiography than effect our own resurrection.

JESUS CHRIST, THE GOD-MAN

The extension of our story beyond our fallenness is wholly due to the miracle of God's grace. By the incarnation God united himself to human existence and moved in space and time as our human partner. Paul described Jesus as the last or second Adam (Rom. 5:12f.; 1 Cor. 15:22, 47f.), through whom the situation of Eden is recovered; here again is one who stands before God in full humanity without sin, true humanity, as we were intended to be.

Although the Bible does not present a full biography of Jesus, there is sufficient in the gospels for us to see the perfection of Jesus' humanity expressed in all five aspects of anthropology noted in the previous two chapters.

In relation to God

Jesus lived in unbroken communion with the Father, in fullest obedience to his will (Mt. 26:39, 42; Mk. 1:11; Lk. 9:35; Jn. 4:34; 8:29). Here a human being truly realized a life to the glory of God (Jn. 12:28; 17:4). Clearly, certain dimensions present in Jesus' case were not present in Adam even before the fall, since Jesus was simultaneously both human *and* the eternal second person of the Trinity. However, by virtue of the reality of his incarnation, he truly stood in Adam's place and hence as the normative human being, humankind with God.

In relation to his neighbour

Jesus perfectly embodied the commandment to love one's neighbour (Mt. 9:36; Jn. 13:1, 34; 15:12–16). As the 'man for others' he did not keep himself to himself but gave himself fully away to his fellow men and women. Nowhere is the perfection of his self-giving more manifest than in his death (Mk. 10:45; Rom. 5:8; Gal. 2:20; 1 Jn. 3:16).

In relation to himself

References to our Lord's inner life are limited, but they are sufficient to show that in his case, although he experienced the reality of temptation (Mt. 4:1–11; Mk. 8:33) and, in relation to the Father's call to sacrifice himself, an agonizing struggle to submit (Lk. 22:42–44), the inward tensions, disorientations and conflicts brought about through fallenness and guilt did not arise (Mt. 22:46; Mk. 3:4f.; Jn. 19:8–11). He stands before us as someone unified in his awareness of himself in relation to the Father, and in his unqualified commitment to fulfilling the Father's will and establishing his kingdom. Here is a human being realizing to the full his inherent potential before God (Mt. 11:28f.).

In relation to the created order

Though again the evidence is sparse, Jesus manifested true sensitivity to the creaturely order around him, recognizing it as the work of God (Mt. 6:26–30). Jesus also expressed that dominion over the created order which humankind was given at the first (Mt. 13:3–9; Lk. 5:4f.; 15:3–6).

In relation to time

Jesus was free from the sin which brings death in its train. He is master of death (Lk. 7:11–16; 8:49–56; Jn. 11); yet in the end he himself submits to it, not because of any claim which it had upon him, but in order to grapple with it and overcome it for us. That he remained master and was not finally subject to death is demonstrated unequivocally in his triumphant resurrection (Mt. 28; Jn. 5:21–29; 20; 2 Tim. 1:10; Heb. 2:14f.).

THE CHRISTIAN, THE NEW CREATION IN CHRIST[1]

This concluding aspect of biblical anthropology is best expounded under the two terms, regeneration and sanctification. *Regeneration* is that work of the Holy Spirit which enables fallen sinners to turn around, believe in Jesus Christ as their redeemer, and rise from spiritual death to a new life (*cf.* Jn. 1:13; 3:1–8; 1 Pet. 1:3, 23; Tit. 3:5), united with Christ in death, resurrection

---

1. These themes are dealt with more fully in Part 5.

and exalted life (Rom. 6:1–11; Eph. 2:5f.). From this perspective the full wonder and significance of Christ's perfect humanity can be grasped; for believers, through union with Christ, share in the fruits of that perfected humanity at every level of being.

From God's side this union with Christ is accomplished in the moment of regeneration; from ours it begins in an act of conscious repentance from sin and faith in Christ. It is followed by a period during which the benefits of this faith-union with Christ are progressively realized, a process commonly termed *sanctification*. Thus the new person, under grace, is one who has been regenerated and is now in process of being sanctified; this affects every area of our being.

In relation to God
The barrier of sin is removed through faith in Christ. We are reconciled to God, whose holy wrath is put away (Rom. 5:9f.); justified before God, whose holy law is totally satisfied by Christ (Rom. 3:24f.; Gal. 3:13); redeemed from slavery to sin and evil (Eph. 1:7); and enlightened to divine truth by the Holy Spirit (1 Cor. 2:10f.). Christians are adopted into the very family of God, sharing the life of God and spontaneously addressing him as their heavenly Father (Lk. 11:2), using the very word, *Abba*, used by Jesus (Rom. 8:15).

In relation to our neighbour
Union with Christ means union with his people, the body of Christ (Rom. 12:4f.; 1 Cor. 12:13). Just as Jesus the Messiah fulfilled his mission in loving solidarity with the messianic people as represented by his disciples, so the humanity he imparts to us is a *fellow* humanity which increasingly reaches out and embraces those who are truly 'in Christ' with us. Christians, like their Lord, are 'people for others' whose true being is expressed in humble service of our neighbour, and all that that implies at every level.

In relation to ourselves
Further, we recover a true awareness of ourselves in relation to God and an increasing deliverance from mistaken views of ourselves. With a new realism and a new humility we see ourselves for what we are, and find new freedom from self-preoccupation as we are set in relation to the whole purpose

of God. With this should go increasing self-respect, for despite the depravity which is uncovered to us, we recognize ourselves as God's creatures and children, the objects of his overwhelming love. We recognize also our innate created abilities and spiritual gifts; as these are dedicated to God and actively employed, there develops increasing, true self-fulfilment.

In relation to the created order

We acquire a new respect and sense of responsibility for the created world and its species. Obviously the degree of this will be affected by cultural, educational and temperamental factors, but every Christian will be led in some measure towards the kind of relationship which Adam and Eve knew in Eden as the lords and stewards of nature.

In relation to time

Regeneration takes us through a crisis which Scripture refers to as being made partner with Christ in his death at the cross (Gal. 2:20; Col. 2:12). The new person therefore has already passed beyond the grave. Although in a physical, temporal sense we shall still undergo bodily dissolution, death in its terror and judgment as the wages of sin lies for ever behind us. This truth is significantly reflected in the references to God's gift of 'eternal life' (Jn. 3:16, 36; *etc.*), which does not simply mean life in heaven, but a new kind of life which begins now and goes on endlessly into the beyond.

For Christians time is no longer an enemy, slipping remorselessly through their fingers, propelling them hourly to their inevitable end. They have time, not to waste but to use in the service to which Christ directs them. This final dimension of the new being takes us over the boundary of mortal existence to the fourth main division of biblical anthropology, humanity in glory.

12. Humanity in glory

This will be dealt with much more fully in Part 7. Here we simply note that this is the fulfilment of the renewal and restoration of God's people begun by grace in this age; humanity shall rise once again to the heights from which it has fallen. Scripture refers to this in terms of our being fully remade in the image of Christ (Rom. 8:29; 1 Cor. 15:49b; Col. 3:10). Thus the image of God in which we were originally made is the image in which we shall stand before God in the new age to be inaugurated at the return of Christ (2 Pet. 3:13; Rev. 22:1–5).

Hence the five dimensions distinguished throughout this Part as a framework for exposition will all be perfected. In glory we shall be perfectly related to God (Rev. 21:3; 22:4); to our neighbour (Eph. 4:13; Rev. 21:10); to ourselves (Rev. 21:4); to our environment (Rom. 8:21–23; Rev. 22:1f.) and to time (1 Pet. 1:3f.; Rev. 21:4).

Scriptures

Jesus Christ, the God-man: Mt. 1:23; 9:36; 10:27; 11:28f.; Lk. 5:4f.; 9:35; 12:24–28; Jn. 1:14; 4:34; 5:30; 6:38; 10:11, 18; 15:12–16; 1 Cor. 15:47f.; Eph. 5:25; 1 Tim. 3:16; Heb. 2:14; 10:7.
The Christian, the new creation: Jn. 1:12; 3:1–8; Rom. 6:1f.; 8:15; 1 Cor. 13; Gal. 2:20; 5:22; Col. 3:1f.; 1 Thes. 4:9; 2 Tim. 2:11; 1 Pet. 1:3–5.
Humanity in glory: Is. 2:1–4; 11:1–9; Mt. 22:30; Jn. 11:24; Rom. 8:18–30; 1 Cor. 15:35–57; 2 Cor. 5:1–10; Phil. 3:20; 1 Jn. 3:1f.; Rev. 21–22.

Questions

1. What do you understand by the reference to Christ as 'the second Adam'? Explore the implications of this title.
2. Marshal the biblical evidence which supports the Christian claim that Jesus was the perfect and normative human being.
3. At which points does Christ's perfect humanity most sharply challenge present experience and attitudes (a) in your local church/Christian group, (b) in your own life?
4. Consider ways in which the future glorification of humankind should affect our present attitudes.
5. Explore the implications of the Bible's teaching about humankind for (a) Christian social and political attitudes, (b) racial discrimination, (c) economic development in the Third World, (d) the women's movement, (e) abortion, euthanasia and organ transplants, (f) the campaign for the conservation of the environment and the protection of endangered species.

Bibliography

C. S. Lewis, *Mere Christianity* (Fontana, 1955).
D. M. Lloyd-Jones, *Life in the Spirit* (Banner of Truth, 1974).
R. Macaulay and J. Barrs, *Christianity with a Human Face* (IVP, 1979).
O. O'Donovan, *Resurrection and Moral Order* (2nd edn, Apollos, 1994).
C. Sherlock, *The Doctrine of Humanity* (IVP, 1996).
J. R. W. Stott, *The Contemporary Christian* (IVP, 1992).
J. R. W. Stott, *Issues Facing Christians Today* (Marshall, Morgan and Scott, 1984).

Application

ESSENTIAL HUMAN NATURE

Dependence

Creation asserts our utter dependence upon God. All that we are and have is from him; our every breath is quite literally his gift. Our proper response is therefore true humility before him, both explicitly in our acts of worship and implicitly in the whole spirit of our living.

Affirmation

Since humankind and the world are God's creation, Christians accept and affirm created reality in all of its forms, including (a) *themselves*. At times in Scripture God actually shows a certain 'impatience' with those who fail to do this (*cf*. Ex. 4:10–14; 1 Sa. 15:17; Je. 1:6f.). God affirms us as his creatures and in Christ as his very children; he calls us to echo that affirmation. Jesus, similarly, saw his disciples in terms of future potential (Mt. 4:19; 16:17f.; Acts 9:5f., 15).

This self-affirmation includes the unique, distinctive features of our personality, the essential 'me' which has its own irreplaceable significance in relation to God and his purposes (*cf*. 1 Cor. 12:14–26). It also includes our body which is from God and hence in no way to be despised (1 Cor. 6:13f.; Eph. 5:29; 1 Tim. 4:8); overwork and overstrain, neglect of hygiene or exercise, needless physical risks, all deny the sacredness of the body which God has created and made the shrine of his Spirit. It includes too our sexuality with its desire and drives. While vigilance and self-discipline are always necessary (Mk. 9:43f.; 1 Cor. 7:1–6), the essential God-givenness and therefore goodness of our sexual instincts must be maintained. True, Scripture recognizes that the full expression of these instincts in monogamous, heterosexual marriage is not for all; some are called to celibacy and are promised grace for the special disciplines and opportunities of that calling (Mt. 19:11f.; 1 Cor. 7:7, 32–35).

Christians accept and affirm (b) their *sociality* (Gn. 2:18f.; Mt. 22:39). This means taking family life from God and fully recognizing its responsibilities. Scripture sharply rebukes those who neglect this duty (1 Tim. 5:8), though the demands of the kingdom remain ultimate (Lk. 14:25f.). This responsibility applies to sons and daughters, parents and marriage partners (Jn. 19:26f.; Eph. 5:21 – 6:4), as frequently illustrated in biblical biography. Life in society is also to be taken from God. Monasticism denies created existence, and minimizes the opportunity to love our neighbour; responsible citizenship and its equivalent in university, college, factory, office and neighbourhood give practical expression to a belief in this biblical doctrine. Social life is also to be affirmed in other cultural areas: literature, music and other art forms, sport and so on. While we must allow for personal tastes, and exercise discrimination when we encounter the effects of the fall, the biblical principle holds: 'Everything God created is good ... if it is received with thanksgiving ... God richly provides us with everything for our enjoyment' (1 Tim. 4:4; 6:17).

The humanity which Jesus manifested and sanctified for us confirms this. The friend of embezzlers and prostitutes, welcomed into social gatherings (Lk. 15:1f.; 5:27–32; 7:36–50; Jn. 2:1–11), was not so named simply because of his teaching; though even that contains a genuine strain of humour (Mt. 23:24; Lk. 7:31–34). There is a dimension of warm, outgoing, cheerful humanity which is proper to Christian life in the world and which is not incompatible with deep sensitivity to suffering or the depravity of the human heart. Co-creation in God's image is also an argument for that love of neighbour which expresses itself in genuine, involved concern for social well-being at all levels.

The doctrine of creation also leads us to accept and affirm (c) *the world of 'nature'* as from God, to accept God's mandate to exercise responsible stewardship and to stand against all forms of unnecessary environmental pollution and destruction (Gn. 1:26 – 2:20).

Confrontation
The fact that our God is creator of all things means that no part of our life, or indeed of the life of the entire cosmos, is outside his concern or a stranger to his presence. Christians should therefore bring to life in all its aspects a proper seriousness and sense of responsibility, since God is the one with whom we have

to do at every point, in work, home, society, church, leisure or whatever.

Purpose

God created all things for a purpose. We are therefore constituted as purposive beings, designed to seek in all things God's glory, our neighbour's good and our own self-realization under God.

HUMANITY IN SIN

Our view of the world (i.e. organized human society)

The fact that all are fallen delivers Christians from unrealistic optimism. They recognize the inadequacy of all efforts at human moral betterment which appeal merely to our ability to raise ourselves to self-mastery and achieve true community. It is no surprise when schemes of social betterment fail, when 'great men' or 'great women' show their feet of clay; even in Christian circles we must resist the temptation to idealize unduly our leaders and other greatly used servants of God.

The fallenness of the world also means that the world has become the domain of a usurping power of darkness. Though broken by Christ's victory, this satanic authority retains a stubborn hold wherever the gospel is not received. The fall has therefore rendered the world a place of conflict and warfare for all who identify with Jesus Christ; hence the Christian's affirmation of the world which we referred to above must always be discerning and open-eyed. The world is not neutral territory for the Christian, though that is no reason to flee from it. The Christian who reckons with the fall will study Scripture to learn about the spiritual enemy, how he is manifest in the world, the kind of attacks he launches on God's children and God's work, and how to wield the weapons of God in the spiritual warfare (2 Cor. 10:3–5; Eph. 6:10–18).

Recognizing the fallenness of the world and the plight of their contemporaries, Christians will long to make known in the world the one message which can save and liberate them, the good news of Jesus Christ. Motivation for evangelism is a richer thing than simple compassion, but it includes this element (Mt. 9:36). Knowing that men and women are in the final analysis morally and spiritually helpless, we beseech God in mercy and grace to awaken this generation to their need, so that turning to him they may experience his everlasting mercy and salvation.

Our view of ourselves

The doctrine of human fallenness should produce a spirit of humility and penitence, for we see ourselves as those who in their folly and rebellion against God could be saved in no other way than by the cross. Although we are forgiven our guilt before God, we retain a fallen nature. All sin stands against God, and his full purpose for us cannot be fulfilled until all sin is eradicated from our lives. So in every Christian there is work of moral renewal to be done, a whole, lifelong course of character rebuilding. We are therefore called to self-examination in the light of God's Word to identify our sins, that we may repent and turn from them. We should be practically and biblically realistic in this, recognizing how deeply sin has been rooted in us and how extensive the work of renewal must be, and not become discouraged if the work of grace in us appears slow and fragmentary.

In this renewal we can expect God to use the circumstances of our lives, even painful, trying eventualities such as disappointments, frustrations, physical and emotional sickness or the like. That does not mean of course that we ought not to seek relief from them; on the contrary; but when they come upon us unbidden or even as a result of our own folly and disobedience, we can often discern God's hand disciplining us 'for our good, that we may share in his holiness' (Heb. 12:10).

All this is only the negative side of the work of God in us. There is also the positive side, the experience of the blessings of Christian life through the Holy Spirit and our manifestation in measure of the Spirit's fruit (Gal. 5:22).

HUMANITY IN GRACE

Worship

The story of humankind would contain no sequel were we left to ourselves. There are men and women under grace only because there is a living God of grace. When we realize that, we cannot but praise and worship him.

Hope

Despite the setbacks to their Christian growth, the assaults of the evil one and periodic times of dryness, the people of grace will never utterly despair, for 'he who began a good work in you will carry it on to completion' (Phil. 1:6). They will look again and again to Christ and see there what they too are on the way to becoming: perfectly related to God, their neighbour, their selves, the world, and time. 'The great stay of the believer is not the grace of God within him; that is a well whose streams sometimes run dry; but it is the grace of God without him, the grace that is in Jesus Christ, which is an ever-flowing fountain, to which the believer can never come amiss' (Boston). As we look to Christ in hope we learn to see the commands of Scripture as glorious promises; 'You shall ...' means that one day you *will*. In other words we recognize the precepts as promises in bud.

Christians' hopefulness is also expressed in their attitude to non-Christians; for if God has changed our lives by his sovereign grace, there is hope for anyone.

Fellowship

God's work of grace goes on within the living fellowship of God's people where the limitations and weaknesses of each individual are complemented and the people of God grow up together towards maturity in Christ (Eph. 4:12–16). Our concern for renewal and growth in ourselves will be expressed corporately in a deepening commitment to the local church fellowship to which we belong.

HUMANITY IN GLORY

Here Christian hope finds full expression. One day humankind will be fully renewed and stand before God as Adam and Eve stood before the fall. Many Christians have been brainwashed by modern criticism of religion and the materialistic tone of our culture into virtually discounting the prospect of heaven, until they are actually faced with death and the beyond. The NT writers were not inhibited in this way, nor were the Christians of earlier ages; Calvin saw meditation on the future life as one of the primary marks of a Christian. Only in deliberately adopting this eternal perspective shall we see human existence in this world in true proportion, and death as the gate through which we shall pass to the everlasting life of the new age. Further, the perfect moral character which will be ours in that coming world is itself a major incentive to press on in the work of sanctification.

Above all, this perspective will awaken us to new depths of praise, giving God glory for all he has accomplished in lifting fallen humanity from the depths of its corruption and raising us to stand before God as those over whom he can again pronounce the words spoken of Adam at the first: 'very good' (Gn. 1:31; Is. 42:1; Mt. 17:5; Lk. 3:22; Rev. 21:1–4).

PART 4
The person and work of Christ

13. The humanity of Jesus Christ

There is ample material in the gospels to establish the true humanity of Jesus. Indeed this is one of the few points on which virtually all students of the gospels are today in agreement.

The gospels commence by setting Jesus in the stream of a human genealogy (Mt. 1:1–16; Lk. 3:23–38). Irrespective of the means of his conception, his birth was a normal human one (Mt. 1:25; Lk. 2:7; Gal. 4:4). He was a developing foetus in the womb of Mary and came into the world through a human birth canal at the climax of a normal period of gestation and labour. His life ran, like ours, 'from womb to tomb' (Kierkegaard). Jesus' birth was followed by years of apparently normal growth and development (Lk. 2:40–52; Heb. 5:8) within a home and family (Mk. 6:1–6).

The Jesus of the gospels was subject to normal physical limitations: weariness (Jn. 4:6), hunger (Mt. 21:18), thirst (Mt. 11:19). In his final hours he endured intense agony of soul and body before his eventual physical death (Mk. 14:33–36; Lk. 22:63; 23:33).

He experienced the full range of human emotions: for example, joy (Lk. 10:21), sorrow (Mt. 26:37), love (Jn. 11:5), compassion (Mt. 9:36), astonishment (Lk. 7:9), anger (Mk. 3:5). 'Those who imagine the Son of God was exempt from human passions do not truly and seriously acknowledge him to be a man' (Calvin). An examination of the words used in the Greek NT reveals the depths and intensity of his human emotions, *e.g.* 'convulsed with uncontrollable grief' (Lk. 19:41); 'a consternation that is appalled dismay' (Mt. 27:46, *cf.* Jn. 12:27); 'hot indignation which ... consumes him like fire' (Jn. 2:17).[1]

HIS RELIGIOUS LIFE

Reference to Jesus' religious life may appear strange since he himself is the object of our worship. However, the terms of incarnation clearly involved Jesus in religious activity.

Jesus engaged in public worship (Lk. 4:16), and he clearly studied, meditated upon and expounded Scripture (Mt. 4:4f.; 19:4; Lk. 2:46; 24:27). Quite apart from his inner, continuous communion with the Father, Jesus frequently engaged in audible prayer (Lk. 3:21) and sometimes continued in prayer through a whole night (Lk. 6:12). John's gospel in particular bears witness to Jesus' life of utter submission to, and total dependence upon, the Father who had sent him (Jn. 4:34; 6:38; 12:49; *etc.*). Although his relationship to the Father clearly differed from ours (Lk. 10:21f.; Jn. 20:17), it is still appropriate to call Jesus 'the pioneer of our faith' (Heb. 12:2, RSV).

HIS LIMITED KNOWLEDGE

This is a difficult area to define with certainty, for clearly Jesus' knowledge was never simply equivalent to our fallen and limited awareness. Thus he knew an individual's undisclosed past (Jn. 1:47; 4:29), and the thoughts of enemies (Lk. 6:8) and friends (Lk. 9:47). Furthermore, he understood the OT in an unprecedented manner (Mt. 22:29; 26:54, 56; Lk. 4:1f.; 24:27, 44f.). We need, however, to set alongside this such passages as Mark 5:30f.; 6:38; 9:21; Luke 2:46, where Jesus appears to ask questions simply to dispel his ignorance. In particular he confessed ignorance of the 'day or hour' of his return (Mk. 13:32). Ignorance, however, does not equal error. Significantly, this verse is immediately preceded by an astonishing claim for the infallibility of his teaching: 'Heaven and earth will pass away, but my words will never pass away' (Mk. 13:31).

The distinction between ignorance and error is crucial.

1. B. B. Warfield, 'The Emotional Life of our Lord', *The Person and Work of Christ* (PRPC, 1950).

Human thought, experience and perception form one unbroken continuum. It is impossible therefore to think of Jesus as mistaken at some fundamental point in his convictions, or deliberately teaching as truth the erroneous views of his age, and yet cling to the notion that he can act none the less as our morally impeccable representative and sin-bearer.[2]. The Scripture presents a careful balance here; a unique and unclouded awareness of the Father and his will (Lk. 2:49) co-exists with a search for further understanding (Lk. 2:46).

TEMPTATION

Jesus' humanity is further confirmed by his being tempted to sin (Mt. 4:1–11; 27:42; Mk. 1:24; 8:33; Lk. 11:15–20). The testimony of the gospels is gathered up in Hebrews, 'tempted in every way, just as we are – yet without sin' (Heb. 4:15).

A frequent objection is that Jesus' temptations were not real, either because he was not a sinner and therefore sin and the devil had no leverage, or because as *God*-become-human he could not conceivably have sinned. The assertion of the 'charade' character of the temptations simply does not square with the language of Scripture concerning them; further, Adam before the fall is a clear case of sinless human nature subject to very real temptation (Gn. 3:1f.). There is of course a sense in which it would have been unthinkable for Jesus as incarnate Godhead to succumb to temptation; but that in no way excludes or diminishes the reality of his confrontation with Satan's assaults on his obedience to the Father's will.

When one army assaults another, it may not possess an infiltrated battalion behind enemy lines, ready to disrupt the enemy at the crucial moment. This does *not* necessarily imply, however, that the attack will be less severe or less likely to succeed; a purely external attack may be effective when one with internal help may fail. The determining factor in each case will be the total strength of the attack. Applied to Jesus, the fact that temptation lacked an internal support force 'behind the lines' (which it certainly has in our case) does *not* necessarily imply that he did not face an equivalent or even much greater weight of assault. Paul's reference to God's restraining the power of temptation so that we are not tempted 'beyond what [we] can

---

2. *Cf.* Part 1, 'Jesus' view of the Old Testament'.

bear' but have 'a way out' (1 Cor. 10:13) is surely to the point here: temptation which we meet is filtered through God's protecting hand. In Jesus' case the filter was removed. Who among *us* can speak of forty days and nights of unbroken temptation (Mt. 4:1f.), or of sweating blood in our struggle to do God's will in face of temptation (Lk. 22:44)? Only one who resisted temptation totally could experience its total power. Jesus did not share original sin and remained impeccable throughout his life, but as truly human he endured the weight and pull of temptation to a degree we shall never experience.

POST-RESURRECTION

The period between Jesus' resurrection and ascension belongs more obviously to the evidences for his deity. His dealings with Mary (Jn. 20:11f.), Thomas (Jn. 20:24f.) and Peter (Jn. 21:15f.), however, express the deepest human sensitivity and sympathy, as if the suffering of the cross had bound Jesus even closer to his human companions.

The evidence thus far has been confined in the main to the four gospels. The rest of the NT carries further impressive witness to Jesus' true humanity (Acts 2:22; 13:38; 17:31; Rom. 8:3; Phil. 2:8; Col. 1:22; 1 Tim. 2:5; Heb. 2:14; 1 Pet. 4:1). The biblical teaching is clear: 'Whatever else he may be he is a man' (Hoskyns and Davey).

Scriptures

Mt. 1:1–16, 25; 4:1–10; 9:36; 11:19; 21:18; 27:43, 46; Mk. 3:5; 6:1–3; 9:21; 10:21; 13:32; Lk. 2:7, 40–52; 4:16f.; 7:9; 19:41; 22:41–44; 24:41f.; Jn. 1:14; 4:6; 6:38; 7:16; 12:27f.; 15:14f.; 19:28, 34; Acts 2:22; 13:38; 17:31; Rom. 8:3; Gal. 4:4; Phil. 2:8; Col. 1:22; 1 Tim. 2:5; 3:16; Heb. 2:14; 5:7f.; 12:2; 1 Pet. 2:21–24; 4:1.

Questions

1. Summarize the New Testament evidence for Christ's true humanity. Which aspects appear to you the most convincing and why?
2. How would you respond to the accusation that Jesus' (a) temptations, (b) confession of ignorance, were unreal or else irreconcilable with his deity?
3. Consider the theological implications of the true humanity of Christ for (a) the Christian doctrine of humanity, (b) the Christian doctrine of redemption.
4. How would you seek to use the fact of Christ's true humanity to help someone who was experiencing (a) acute temptation, (b) a sense of having been forsaken by God, (c) intense physical suffering?

Bibliography
R. T. France, *The Man they Crucified* (IVP, 1975).
G. W. Grogan, *What the Bible Says about Jesus* (Kingsway, 1979).
D. Macleod, *The Person of Christ*, (IVP, 1998).
J. R. W. Stott, *Christ the Controversialist* (Tyndale Press, 1970).
B. B. Warfield, *The Person and Work of Christ* (PRPC, 1950).

14. The deity of Jesus Christ

Here we arrive at the staggering truth which lies at the heart of the Christian religion, that Jesus Christ while truly human was also true God. This is one of Christianity's distinctives. Jews and Muslims also acknowledge one supreme God, and revere the patriarchs and prophets of the OT, but in the claims made for Jesus Christianity stands alone.

Although in the final analysis a true confession of the deity of Christ is possible only through the supernatural ministry of the Holy Spirit in the heart ('No-one can say "Jesus is Lord" except by the Holy Spirit'; 1 Cor. 12:3; *cf*. Mt. 16:17; Lk. 10:22), the Spirit uses Scripture to reveal this truth to us. Accordingly we turn first to its plain statements.

DIRECT STATEMENTS OF DEITY

The texts which assert the deity of Christ are predictably among the most debated in the entire NT. In several the grammatical evidence calls for hesitation before interpreting them as assertions of Christ's Godhood. But in at least nine passages the clear weight of relevant evidence supports our reading them as straightforward assertions of the deity of Christ:

'Christ, who is God over all, forever praised!' (Rom. 9:5).

'About the Son he [God] says, "Your throne, O God, will last for ever and ever"' (Heb. 1:8).

'In the beginning was the Word, and the Word was with God, and the Word was God' (Jn. 1:1–2).

'No-one has ever seen God, but God the only Son, who is at the Father's side, has made him known' (Jn. 1:18).

'The glorious appearing of our great God and Saviour, Jesus Christ' (Tit. 2:13).

'Thomas answered, "My Lord and my God!"' (Jn. 20:28).
'The righteousness of God and Saviour Jesus Christ' (2 Pet. 1:1).
'The church of God, which he bought with his own blood' (Acts
　　20:28).
'. . . Jesus Christ. He is the true God and eternal life (1 Jn. 5:20).
The NT contains numerous other verses which possibly, though
not definitely, imply the deity of Christ (*e.g.* Mt. 1:23; Jn. 17:3;
Col. 2:2; 2 Thes. 1:12; 1 Tim. 1:17; Jas. 1:1; 1 Jn. 5:20). The nine
texts quoted above are sufficient to establish the biblical position
beyond doubt; there is, however, much more material.

JESUS' IDENTITY WITH YAHWEH/JEHOVAH

The NT attributes to Jesus many of the perfections of Yahweh
(or, Jehovah), the creator/redeemer God of the OT. There are
seven main points of identity.

God's name

When the OT was translated into Greek in the 2nd and 3rd
centuries BC (the Septuagint), the sacred name of God, *YHWH*,
usually rendered Yahweh or Jehovah, was translated by the
Greek word *Kyrios* (*Lord*); there are approaching 7,000 instances
of this. This sacred and exalted title was attributed directly to
Jesus (Rom. 10:9; 1 Cor. 12:3; Phil. 2:11; *etc.*, *cf.* also *Lord of
lords*, 1 Tim. 6:15; Rev. 17:14; 19:16). Indeed the confession *Jesus
is Lord* is probably the earliest confession of faith (Rom. 10:9; 1
Cor. 12:3; 2 Cor. 4:5). On several occasions NT writers apply
OT passages concerning Yahweh directly to Jesus (Acts 2:34f.;
Rom. 8:34; Heb. 10:12f.; 1 Pet. 3:22 apply Ps. 110:1. Rom. 10:13
applies Joel 2:32. Phil. 2:9–11 applies Is. 45:23. Jn. 12:41 applies
Is. 6:10. Eph. 4:8 applies Ps. 68:18). These passages clearly
identify Jesus with Yahweh.

　　Another link is provided by self-designations of God appropriated by Jesus or referred to him. Supremely significant is the
I AM (Ex. 3:14; *cf.* Jn. 8:58; 6:35; 8:12, 24; 11:25; 14:6; 18:5f.; Mk.
14:62). Others are *bridegroom* (Is. 62:5; Je. 2:2; Ezk. 16:8, *cf.* Mk.
2:19f.; Jn. 3:29; 2 Cor. 11:2; Rev. 19:7); *shepherd* (Pss. 23:1; 80:1;
Is. 40:11; Ezk. 34:15; *cf.* Jn. 10:11–16; Heb. 13:10; 1 Pet. 2:25; 5:4);
the first and the last (Is. 44:6; 48:12; *cf.* Rev. 2:8; 22:13).

God's glory

God's glory is the visible manifestation of his majesty (Ex.

24:15–18; 40:34f.; Lv. 9:6, 23f.; 2 Ch. 7:1–3; Is. 6:1–4; Ezk. 1:28). In Judaism it served as a reverential substitute for the sacred name itself. God's glory is incommunicable (Is. 42:8; 48:11), yet the NT speaks of Isaiah 6:1f. as the manifestation of Jesus' glory (Jn. 12:41), and of Jesus as the manifestation of the glory of God (1 Cor. 2:8; 2 Cor. 4:4; Heb. 1:3; Jas. 2:1; *cf.* Jn. 17:5).

God's worship

To offer worship to any other being than the LORD God (Yahweh) was for the Jew unthinkably offensive, the most fundamental of all sins (Ex. 20:3–6; Dt. 6:4f., 13–15). Yet the earliest disciples, all of them Jews, directed worship to Jesus. It is this fact which, despite their comparative infrequency, makes the NT ascriptions of deity to Christ so overwhelmingly impressive.

Doxologies are ascribed to Christ (Rom. 9:5; 2 Tim. 4:18; 2 Pet. 3:18; Rev. 1:5f.); two are addressed to both Father and Son (Rev. 5:13; 7:10). Prayers are addressed to Christ (Acts 7:59f.; 9:13f.; 1 Cor. 16:22; Rev. 22:20). OT worship passages are transferred from Yahweh to Christ (Is. 8:13f. in Rom. 9:33; 1 Pet. 2:7f.; 3:15; the Septuagint version of Dt. 32:43 in Heb. 1:6). Worship is used in connection with Christ: in the Septuagint the common translation of *šāḥâ* (worship, bow down) is *proskyneia*. In Jesus' teaching it describes the attitude we should adopt to God alone (Mt. 4:10). The evangelists, however, use the word to describe people's attitude to Jesus (Mt. 2:2, 8, 11; 14:33; Mk. 5:6; Jn. 9:38). Hence the reaction of the disciples to the risen Christ is typical: 'they worshipped him' (Mt. 28:17; Lk. 24:52), a response echoed by the angelic company of heaven: 'Worthy is the Lamb, who was slain, to receive ... honour and glory and praise!' (Rev. 5:12), an unambiguous assertion of deity.

God's creation

That Yahweh created all things and is therefore Lord of all was axiomatic for OT faith (Gn. 1:1f.; Pss. 33:6–9; 148:5f.; Is. 42:5; 48:13; 51:9–16). Yet the NT freely applies this divine function to Jesus. God's creative work had four aspects: (a) God brought the world into being at the first; (b) he preserves and sustains all things; (c) he is leading the created universe to its end or goal; (d) he will bring about the new creation. All four aspects are referred to Jesus. Through him all things came to be (Jn. 1:1, 3; Heb. 1:3; *cf.* Col. 1:16; 1 Jn. 1:1) he is the sustainer and upholder of all things (Mt. 28:18; 1 Cor. 8:6; Col. 1:17; Heb. 1:3); he is the one in whom the universe is destined to be brought to its goal (Rom. 11:36; Eph. 1:9f.; Col. 1:16), and the 'new creation' is nothing other than the realization of the purpose of God in Jesus Christ (Is. 65:17; 66:22, 'Behold, I [Yahweh] will create new heavens and a new earth', *cf.* Jn. 3:5; 20:22; 2 Cor. 5:17; Phil. 3:20; Col. 3:10; 2 Pet. 3; Rev. 21 – 22).

God's salvation

Yahweh is a saviour God, another bedrock of OT conviction. In contrast with other gods, he alone has power to save; 'I, even I am the LORD, and apart from me there is no saviour' (Is. 43:11; *cf.* 45:21; Je. 3:23; 11:12). His deliverance came frequently by way of human 'saviours' (Jos. 10:6; Jdg. 2:16, 18; 6:14f.), but the forgiving of sins and the raising from death to eternal life are prerogatives of God alone. Yet the NT attributes these to Jesus. At birth he was hailed as the one who 'will save his people from their sins' (Mt. 1:21). He claimed the power to grant forgiveness (Mk. 2:7–10; Lk. 7:48) and is seen as the saviour of sinners (Jn. 3:17; Acts 4:12; 5:31; 15:11; Gal. 1:4; Eph. 5:23; Heb. 7:25; Rev. 1:5). He raised the dead (Mk. 5:35–43; Lk. 7:11–17, 22; Jn. 11) and through him eternal life is given now to all who believe in him (Mk. 10:21; Jn. 3:16; 5:24; 1 Jn. 5:11f.) and will be fully experienced by them in the future (Mk. 10:30; 1 Cor. 15:22f., 54; 1 Thes. 1:10; 2 Tim. 1:10).

God's judgment

For the OT Yahweh alone is judge. His holiness and majesty are essentially expressed in his righteous judgments (Dt. 32:4; Ps. 99; Is. 5:16). Certain forms of divine judgment were realized through human agents (Dt. 1:16f.; Is. 10:5; 45:1), but final judgment was God's prerogative (Dn. 7:9f.; Ec. 12:14; Joel 2:31). Once again these uniquely divine functions are both claimed by Jesus and freely attributed to him (Mt. 25:31–46; Mk. 8:38; Jn. 5:22–30; Acts 17:31; 2 Cor. 5:10; 2 Thes. 1:7–10; Rev. 14:14–20). At the Last Day Jesus will submit 'the secrets of men' (Rom. 2:16) to definitive, divine judgment.

God's witness

One final link between Jesus and Yahweh may be noted. In the OT God commissions his people: '"You are my witnesses" declares the LORD' (Is. 43:10); yet in Acts 1:8 Jesus sends out his apostles with identical words, 'You will be my witnesses.'

While we have clearly seen that the NT writers on occasion state straightforwardly that Jesus is God, their mainly Jewish cast of mind expresses the conviction most naturally in terms of Jesus doing what only God could properly do. Their attribution of deity to Jesus Christ is therefore stated less frequently in metaphysical equations ('Jesus is God') than in assertions that he participates in the strictly incommunicable attributes and functions of God. Thus the staggering truth is unfolded: Jesus, the man who walked the streets of Nazareth, sweated in Gethsemane and died on the cross at Calvary, is to be identified with Yahweh, the creator-redeemer God.

Trinitarian references

The deity of Christ is confirmed by passages which identify him with the Father and the Spirit in the Godhead (Mt. 28:19; Jn. 14:15–23; 1 Cor. 12:4–6; 2 Cor. 13:14; Eph. 1:3–14; 2:18, 22; 3:14–17; 4:4–6; Rev. 1:4f.).

OTHER GOSPEL EVIDENCE

The resurrection

The resurrection is central to the entire biblical revelation and there are innumerable references to it throughout the NT. To deny it is to empty faith of all content and value (1 Cor. 15:14). Because of this the resurrection has undergone a barrage of sustained criticism.

Criticism of the gospel texts

This has concentrated on two lines of attack: (a) alleged discrepancies in the narratives of the resurrection appearances of Jesus; (b) the claim that the 'empty tomb' narrative was added later to the original tradition about the appearances of Jesus. The narratives of the appearances, however, are quite capable of accommodating one another,[1] and the claim that the empty tomb was not part of the apostles' original testimony is arbitrary and unproven. From the appearances of the risen Jesus the apostles

1. *Cf.* E. F. Kevan, 'Note on the Resurrection Appearances of our Lord' in *New Bible Commentary*, first edition, ed. F. Davidson (IVF, 1953), p. 864.

would obviously have drawn implications for the corpse, which his followers had seen on the cross and laid in the tomb (Mk. 15:47). Besides, the empty tomb is clearly implied in the earliest statement of the Christian gospel (Acts 2:22–32; 1 Cor. 15:3f.). The apostles could simply not have carried conviction for their resurrection-centred faith in Jerusalem (Acts 5:28), within a mile of Jesus' tomb, without its emptiness being a major consideration for them and their hearers, to say nothing of their opponents. Further, the narratives themselves combine the two elements of empty tomb and appearances without embarrassment or incongruity (Mt. 28:1–9; Jn. 20:1–18).

Theological criticism

On the basis of a philosophical distinction between fact and meaning, some have argued that the crucial NT factor is the Easter faith of the disciples: their conviction that Christ had conquered their foes and raised them to a new life of hope and meaning. Whether an actual resurrection from the tomb lay behind this faith is secondary, they say, and impossible finally to determine. Some simply assert that the resurrection is quite impossible in view of the universal fact of death. The distinction between fact and meaning, however, belongs to the philosophy of Kant (1724–1804) and was reflected in the 19th-century positivist view of history which many of the critics in question have imbibed. Today it is acknowledged that the two cannot be held apart in this way, and in any case the distinction is clearly inadequate to account for the rise of faith in the resurrection. It involves believing that the tradition of the Easter *fact* derived from the Easter *faith* of the disciples, and not *vice versa*. The circumstances in which Jesus died render this interpretation utterly fanciful.

Historical evidence

Three strands of evidence stubbornly refuse to go away, *i.e.* any sceptical interpretation of them is much harder to sustain than the NT explanation that Jesus was raised from death. These are that the tomb was empty, that Jesus was seen alive, and that the disciples were transformed. It was this third fact (based on the other two) which launched the church upon the world where, for all its weaknesses, it still stands and bears witness to Christ.

In this sense the evidence for the resurrection of Jesus is as irrefutable as the faith which underlies the production of this book or as the bricks and mortar of the nearest church building. Without the resurrection there simply would have been no Christian community to uphold and proclaim the gospel over twenty centuries. Bearing in mind the circumstances in which Jesus died, the resurrection remains the only credible explanation of the church's birth in that vitality and conviction which we can still investigate and experience from its literary legacy, the NT Scriptures. 'The existence of the Christian Church, the existence of the New Testament: these incomparable phenomena in human history are left without adequate or convincing explanation if the resurrection of Jesus be denied' (Denney, *Jesus and the Gospel*, p. 112).

The resurrection and Jesus' deity

It has been claimed that the resurrection, even if true, does not prove Jesus' deity since Jesus raised other people from death without their being acclaimed divine. This, however, completely fails to note (a) that these 'resurrections' were performed on the authority of Jesus, which is laden with significance – people who can resuscitate corpses are not exactly thick on the ground in any known society! (b) that in Jesus' resurrection we are not concerned with mere restoration of physical life. He did not confront the disciples after Easter as a temporarily resuscitated corpse; what spontaneously drew forth their adoration and worship was nothing less than the vanquishing of death by one who had grappled with the dread enemy and trodden it underfoot (Rom. 6:9; 2 Tim. 1:10).

In the OT the giving of life is God's prerogative (Gn. 2:7; 1 Sa. 2:6). Jesus claimed to be the life-giver (Jn. 5:21; 11:25) and proved it by rising from death (1 Cor. 15:45). Considered in isolation the resurrection might fall short of proof of deity, but in the total context of Jesus' claims and ministry it is difficult to see how we can interpret it except as an overwhelming vindication of his divine claims. Paul says as much, bearing in mind the link between *Lord* and *Yahweh* in the OT: he 'was declared with power to be the Son of God by his resurrection from the dead: Jesus Christ our Lord' (Rom. 1:4).

The ascension

The ascension of Jesus (Mt. 28:16f.; Lk. 24:50f.; Acts 1:1–11) has been criticized as the expression of an outdated mythological worldview, the 'three-decker universe'. In fact, the ascension can be properly grasped only in the whole context of Christ's redemptive ministry. Following his resurrection, Jesus appeared among his disciples during a period of forty days to complete his teaching of them and to bring them utter assurance of his conquest of death and the coming of God's kingdom through him. This exceptional situation had to come to an end and required some climactic appearance which would express this. When we recall the significance of the cloud in the OT (Ex. 40:34; 1 Ki. 8:10f.; *cf.* Lk. 9:34f.) as a manifestation of God's glory and presence, and the risen Lord's concern to convince the disciples that he now reigned over the universe (Mt. 28:18; Acts 2:33), we have the necessary rationale for the ascension as a real event in space and time. The apostles saw the Lord gathered up into a cloud and disappear from view. As the NT epistles constantly reiterate, Jesus' ascension represents a very significant confirmation of his divine nature; for it means nothing less than his sharing in the glory of Godhead and exercising the rule of God in heaven and earth.

His self-consciousness and claims

Jesus' self-consciousness is without historical parallel and represents a very weighty piece of evidence concerning his unique nature. It is expressed in particular in his relationship to his Father. At twelve years of age he revealed a remarkable sense of oneness with and responsibility to the Father (Lk. 2:42–50). He made frequent reference to this special relationship (*e.g.* Jn. 4:34; 5:17–24; 10:30), distinguishing clearly between his own sense of divine sonship and that shared by others (Mt. 11:27; Mk. 12:6f.). This unique relationship is expressed in his prayers; with the sole exception of the cry of dereliction on the cross, he addresses God in a unique and characteristic way, 'Abba', the child's intimate name for its father: 'my own dear father'. There is no parallel in the entire OT, or in the wealth of 1st-century Jewish prayers and liturgies. At this point Jesus stands quite alone. Nor is this uniqueness dispelled by the early Christians' use of the term (Rom. 8:15). Their right to use this intimate term arises only because the unique Sonship of Jesus is by God's grace shared with them by 'the Spirit of the Son' (Gal. 4:6).

Jesus was also conscious of pre-existence, of having lived with the Father before his incarnate life on earth (Jn. 3:31; 8:58). He even received worship (Lk. 5:8; Jn. 20:28), in sharp contrast with Paul in similar circumstances (Acts 14:11–15).

Jesus saw himself as the fulfilment of the entire redemptive expectation of the OT (Mk. 1:14f.; 12:35; Lk. 11:31f.). The titles of Jesus in the gospels bring this into clear focus. We now study the four most prominent, which in varying degree also express Jesus' identity with God.

Messiah (Gk. Christos)

As the English 'Christ' this has become the most common designation of our Lord. It literally means 'anointed one' (Heb. *māšîaḥ*). In the OT it referred particularly to the king (1 Sa. 9:16; 24:6), but can also be used of prophets (1 Ki. 19:16), priests (Lv. 8:12), and even a heathen king (Is. 45:1).

With the Jewish exile in Babylon the promises to the king (Pss. 72; 89:3f.) begin to be seen in terms of a new and future kingship, exercised by a coming descendant of David (Ezk. 37:24f.). This hope developed between OT and NT times into a general expectation, painted in strongly nationalistic colours, of a political Messiah-king.

Some have queried whether Jesus believed himself to be Messiah, owing to his reluctance to use the title, particularly in the earlier part of his ministry. This is largely accounted for by the radical misunderstanding of messiahship in his day, by both Jews (Jn. 6:14f.) and Gentiles (Mk. 10:42f). There are clear evidences that he was conscious of being Messiah, notably his recognition that his person and mission were crucial for the dawn of the kingdom (Mt. 12:28; Mk. 1:15; Lk. 17:21). There are also clear claims to the title: the triumphal entry (Mk. 11:1–10) and his testimony during his trial (Mk. 14:61f.). Further, he accepted the title from his close disciples (Mk. 8:29). Certainly the later NT does not hesitate to use the title (1 Cor. 1:1ff.; Heb. 3:6; 1 Pet. 4:1). Jesus is God's anointed who inherits the promise to David (Lk. 1:32) and through him will come the glorious promised day of God's kingly rule.

Son of Man

This is Jesus' preferred self-designation. It comes primarily from

Daniel 7:13f., where the Son of Man, a heavenly figure, comes at the close of history as the lord and judge of all and inherits the kingdoms of the world. While its use may not always carry the same weight, many references clearly have great significance (Mt. 9:6, 12:40; 16:27; 26:24; Mk. 8:31; Lk. 19:10; Jn. 3:14). Mark 14:62 is important, for here Jesus reaches beyond the messianic title proposed to him and claims to fulfil the role of the heavenly Son of Man of Daniel 7. For Jesus, the Son of Man is particularly bound up with judgment (Mt. 25:31–46; Jn. 5:27). This meaning for 'Son of Man' should make clear that it is unhelpful to think of the 'Son of God' title as referring to Jesus' deity, and the Son of Man as referring to his humanity. The latter is an exalted title with clear overtones of deity.

Paul's concept of Christ as the last Adam (Rom. 5:14; 1 Cor. 15:45f.; Phil. 2:5f.), may reflect an identification in 1st-century Judaism of the Son of Man and Adam, the original man.

Son of God

In the Greek-speaking culture of NT times this title was used of rulers, emperors and miracle workers. In the OT it has three uses. The people of Israel are addressed in this way (Ex. 4:22; Ho. 11:1), it is referred to kings (2 Sa. 7:14) and to Messiah in the kingly psalms (Ps. 2:7). The NT also links it to Messiah (Mt. 16:16; Mk. 14:61). Common to all these strands are the election and the obedience which it requires in response (Mal. 1:6).

It is associated with Jesus at his baptism (Mt. 3:17) and temptation (Mt. 4:3, 6). His claim to the title relates generally not to miracle working but to obedience to his allotted task, particularly his suffering (Mt. 16:16; Mk. 15:39). It certainly implies oneness with God; the Jews understood his use of it as a blasphemous claim to deity (Jn. 10:33, 36). The early church referred frequently to Jesus by this title (Acts 9:20; Rom. 1:4; Heb. 1:1f.; 1 Jn. 4:15), which expresses both his life of obedience and his unique relationship to the Father, with distinct overtones of his deity as the eternal Son of God.

Lord (Gk. Kyrios)

This title occurs in NT times in the general sense of 'master' or 'owner' and is also a general designation for gods (1 Cor. 8:5). Used of the emperor it referred to both political power and divinity. Jewish Rabbis were sometimes addressed thus as a mark of high respect (Mt. 7:21); but the principal use of 'Lord' (Heb. *'aḏôn*) was in place of God's name which was thought too sacred to mention. Thus the Greek equivalent of Lord (*Kyrios*) was used to translate YHWH in the Septuagint, and, after Easter, was ascribed to Christ exalted and reigning (Acts 2:36).

Jesus is now Lord over the universe (Rom. 10:9), 'Lord of lords' (1 Tim. 6:15); in this sense the title is similar to 'king'. The NT also makes frequent use of Psalm 110:1 with its reference to 'the Lord' (Acts 2:34f.; Rom. 8:34; Col. 3:1; Heb. 1:13; 1 Pet. 3:22); here it is a mighty and exalted title, affirming the deity of Christ (Is. 45:21–23, *cf*. Phil. 2:9–11; Joel 2:32, *cf*. Acts 2:21, 36).

Indirect claims

Jesus' call to follow him, in its sheer radicalness, echoes the call of God in the OT (Dt. 1:36; Jos. 14:8f.; Mk. 1:17, 20). It is not merely a call to follow his teaching, but in essence demands utter self-giving to his own person (Mt. 10:38; Lk. 14:26). Nor can one miss his deliberate centring of himself at the heart of God's dealings with humankind; the entire purpose of God for the race hinges on his person and mission. As we respond to Jesus so shall we be judged at the last day (Mt. 25:31–46; Jn. 5:25–29).

William Temple's observation is fully justified: 'The only Jesus for whose existence we have evidence at all is a gigantic figure making stupendous claims.' These claims and the revolutionary self-consciousness behind them, when set alongside the moral impact he made on his contemporaries, present a dimension of Jesus' person which has never been adequately accounted for in purely human terms.

Miracles

During the course of his life, our Lord wielded impressive power over disease, nature and even death. Not surprisingly this has regularly been challenged. The modern scientific worldview has made the miracles an embarrassment to many. They are often dismissed out of hand and put down to the creative imagination of the gospel writers or the early church, or a few are salvaged which might have a naturalistic explanation (*e.g.* a psycho-somatic factor in some of the healing miracles). Such an approach is, in the strict sense, *non*-scientific, for it is clearly based on unproven assumptions about what is possible. On the Christian presupposition of the omnipotent creator God, miracles are not only possible but inherently probable. The NT, however, does not encourage a faith based simply on miraculous signs (Mt. 16:1–4; Jn. 6:30f.). The miracles may be adduced as supporting evidence of Jesus' deity, but are best understood as signs of the arrival and character of the kingdom of God through Jesus (Mt. 11:4–6; Lk. 4:18f.; 11:20).

The virgin birth

Jesus' birth from a virgin is clearly taught (Mt. 1:18; Lk. 1:35). Mark and John have no reference to it because their accounts of Jesus' career begin with his public ministry, though John's prologue pushes the beginnings back into Jesus' pre-existence (Jn. 1:1f.). Paul may reflect a knowledge of it (Gal. 4:4), and certainly nothing in the NT in any way denies it. Matthew characteristically finds reference to it in the OT (Is. 7:14). Debate continues about the precise meaning of the Hebrew world *'almâ*, used by Isaiah, but it has certainly *not* been shown that its meaning cannot include 'virgin'; Matthew's interpretation gives us clear authority for this traditional translation. The textual evidence in support of the birth narratives in Matthew and Luke is as solid as for any other major section of the gospels, and it is impossible to read them except as intended historical narrative.

Some critics dismiss the virgin birth, arguing that it is a docetic doctrine (*i.e.* it denies Jesus' true humanity); that, however, appears an unnecessary conclusion. Provided we assert that from the moment of his inception the eternal Son was truly united to a full human nature, no denial of his humanity need be implied.

On the other hand there is a danger of building too much on the virgin birth. All it implies is that Jesus' human nature was not derived as is ours from a human father. The Scriptures, however, nowhere cast God the Father in the role of the male progenitor supplying the male chromosomes for the developing foetus. A moment's reflection shows the questionableness of this position, for a being so produced would certainly not be a true God-man, but a half-human hybrid. A similar view of Jesus arose in the 5th century and was declared heretical (*cf.* below on Eutychianism). It also opens the door to follow the early father Irenaeus in drawing an unwarranted parallel between Eve and Mary, taking us to the threshold of viewing Mary as a co-redemptrix; biblically sensitive ears can hear this only as a blasphemous denial of the sole sufficiency of the mediation of Christ. It has also led in

Catholic thought to an unbalanced exaltation of virginity.

The mystery of the union in one authentic person of the eternal nature of the Son of God and a true human nature with its limitations and needs is not significantly lessened by the virgin birth. Since God chose this way, we may reverently conclude that any other would have been less serviceable to him. What, then, is its significance?

1. It proclaimed the unique character of the babe to be born. In Scripture special children often have special births (Gn. 21:1–7; Lk. 1:5–23).

2. It demonstrates the operation of the supernatural in the incarnation. For this reason biological objections are entirely beside the point. On the presupposition of an omnipotent God, the virginal conception was wholly possible.

3. The coming of the Spirit upon Mary declared that in Christ God entered completely and fully into our human experience from the very moment of conception.

4. It wholly agrees with Paul's teaching (Rom. 5:12f.; 1 Cor. 15:22) that Christ is the second Adam in whom there takes place a new beginning to the moral history of the human race. There is no suggestion that original sin was avoided by the absence of sexual intercourse, as though sin were a genetical contagion, which in any case would have been as surely inherited from Mary as from Joseph; such a view logically requires the impeccability of Mary on the principle that a sinless child requires a sinless mother. Roman Catholicism has not hesitated to assert and authorize this wholly unscriptural dogma, the immaculate conception of the Virgin Mary. Rather, the virgin birth proclaims God's sovereign disruption of the age-long bondage and corruption brought about through the race's involvement in the fall of its representative head, Adam.

5. It is consistent with our Lord's pre-existence. In our case the act of conception is the coming into existence of a new person; in his case the eternal Word pre-existed conception. This is expressed in the biblical statements that 'the Holy Spirit will come upon' and 'overshadow' Mary (Lk. 1:35).

6. It provides an analogy of redemption elsewhere described as a 'new birth' (Jn. 1:12; 3:3ff.; 1 Pet. 2:2; Tit. 3:5). The setting aside of Joseph expresses in vivid fashion the helplessness, and in this sense the judgment, of humankind in face of God's work of redemption.

The corporate Christ

In the immediate post-Easter period the NT writers, particularly Paul, refer to Christ in more than personal terms. Christians are 'in Christ' (Rom. 8:1; 16:7; 1 Cor. 15:22; 2 Cor. 5:17); the church is 'the body of Christ' (Rom. 12:4f.; 1 Cor. 12:12; Eph. 3:6), and the 'temple of Christ' (Eph. 2:21; 1 Pet. 2:4f.); Christ's death is 'for his people' (Rom. 8:32; 1 Pet. 2:21; 1 Jn. 3:16); or 'for their sins' (Gal. 1:4; 1 Pet. 3:18). These earliest witnesses knew, of course, that Jesus had lived among them in Palestine as a distinct, complete individual human being. Yet these corporate terms 'reflect an experience of Christ which implies such dimensions as any theist would ascribe to God himself' (Moule).

THE CONCLUSION OF THIS TESTIMONY

The evidence we have examined points overwhelmingly to Jesus Christ as the eternal Son of God become incarnate for the redemption of sinners. He is the second person of the Trinity, God manifest in the flesh.

Quite apart from those incontrovertible evidences, the deity of Jesus Christ is the essential presupposition of the finality of Christian revelation and the validity of Christian redemption. If Jesus is not God himself come to us, then the revelation he brings is not that of Godhead; it is therefore not final revelation and may be superseded. The denial of Jesus' deity fells the entire Christian truth-claim at a stroke and we are back where we were before the gospel came to us, groping in the darkness of our own unenlightened reason.

If Jesus is not God himself come to us, the redemption he brings is powerless to forgive and save. It is God we have wronged and only God can redeem. If Jesus is not God, he is quite simply not party to our relationship with God; then his death and atonement are finally irrelevant to our moral status before God, our feelings of peace and forgiveness through him are just feelings and no more, and we are committed again to the endless and utterly impossible task of justifying ourselves before God.

Thankfully we can let these two particular nightmares pass from our minds. We can wake up again to reality: Jesus is God, and so final truth is revealed in him and final redemption is brought through him.

Scriptures

Jesus Christ is God: Mt. 28:19; Jn. 1:1f., 18; 20:28; Acts 20:28; Rom. 9:5; 1 Cor. 12:4–6; 2 Cor. 13:14; Eph. 1:1–15; 2:18, 20–22; 4:4–6; Col. 1:15–19; 2:9; 2 Thes. 1:12; Tit. 2:13; Heb. 1:8; Jas. 1:1; 2 Pet. 1:1; 1 Jn. 5:20; Rev. 5:13.

Jesus and Yahweh: Mt. 24:30f.; Mk. 2:1–12, 19f., 8:38; 14:62; Jn. 1:1–3; 5:22–30; 6:35; 8:12, 24, 58; 10:9, 11f.; 11:25; 12:41; 14:6; 15:1; 17:5; 18:5f.; Acts 1:8; 2:34f.; 7:59f.; 9:13f.; 17:31; Rom. 8:34; 9:5; 10:9; 1 Cor. 2:8; 12:3; 16:22; 2 Cor. 4:4f.; Eph. 1:9f., 20; 4:8; Phil. 2:9–11; Col. 1:16; 3:1; 1 Thes. 3:11f.; 2 Thes. 3:5; Heb. 1:1–13; 13:20f.; Jas. 2:1; 1 Pet. 2:7f.; 3:15, 22; 2 Pet. 3:18; Rev. 1:5f.; 2:8; 5:12, 21.

Other New Testament evidence: Mt. 3:17; 7:21f.; 9:2; 11:2–6, 27; 16:16; 25:31–46; Mk. 1:17; 4:41; 10:21; 12:6f.; 13:32; 16:1–8; Lk. 1:35; 5:8, 21; 7:14f., 47; 11:20; 24:1–52; Jn. 3:31; 5:17–24; 8:46; 10:29–38; 11; 13:13; 14:6; Acts 2:24–33; 8:36–38; Rom. 1:3f.; 8:1, 34; 16:7; 1 Cor. 15:1–20, 45; 2 Cor. 5:15; Gal. 2:20; 3:28; Eph. 1:10–23; 3:8f.; Col. 3:1; Heb. 1:1f.; 3:6; 4:14; 1 Pet. 1:19; 2:21f.; 3:18, 22; 1 Jn. 3:5; 4:15; Rev. 17:14; 19:16.

Questions

1. Outline your response to the statement 'The NT nowhere states that Jesus is God.' (It would be worthwhile to memorize the main NT passages where his deity is asserted.)
2. Marshal the main biblical evidence for the identification of Jesus Christ with Yahweh.
3. What are the implications for Jesus' person of (a) his claims, (b) the virgin birth, (c) his resurrection?
4. Why is it important to insist on the bodily resurrection of Christ?
5. Explore the implications of Jesus' deity for (a) the human search for truth, (b) the search for salvation.

Bibliography

Art. 'Christology' in *NDT*.
J. N. D. Anderson, *The Evidence for the Resurrection* (IVP, 1950).
M. Harris, *Jesus as God* (Baker, 1992).
G. E. Ladd, *I Believe in the Resurrection* (Hodder, 1975).
D. Macleod, *The Person of Christ* (IVP, 1998).
I. H. Marshall, *The Origins of New Testament Christology* (IVP, 1976).
L. Morris, *The Lord from Heaven* (IVP, 1958).
C. F. D. Moule, *The Origins of Christology* (CUP, 1977).
J. Owen, *The Glory of Christ* (*Works*, 1) (Banner of Truth, 1965).
G. Vos, *The Self-Disclosure of Jesus* (Eerdmans, 1954).

15. The one person

The biblical evidence leads us to two fundamental statements concerning the person of the Lord Jesus Christ: he is truly human; he is true God. How these two realities combine in one authentic person, Jesus Christ, will always remain mysterious;

that in itself, however, ought not to foreclose the attempt to examine the incarnation at greater depth. If we neglect this task, others will attempt it in ways which lead to error and confusion. In the doctrine of Christ's person, as surely as in all other areas of Christian doctrine, careless shepherds invite predatory wolves (Jn. 10:11–13). So we now consider the most important issues in this area, known technically as Christology.

THE EARLY DEBATES

While the theological discussions before AD 500 are historically remote, they remain important because in the course of them most of the principal Christological options made their appearance. The discussions which culminated in the formula agreed at Chalcedon in 451 represent the framework for all subsequent reflection. In the first generations believers were probably content with an uncomplicated faith. Pliny's letter to the Emperor Trajan at the beginning of the 2nd century described Christians as 'reciting a hymn to Christ as to a God'. There were, however, early heterodox views.

Ebionism
This offshoot of Jewish Christianity solved the problem of the relationship of humanity and divinity in Christ by effectively removing the divinity. Jesus was simply the human, though divinely appointed, Messiah who was destined to return at the end of the age to reign on the earth by God's sovereign power. In effect this left the gulf between God and humankind unbridged.

Docetism
This movement dates from apostolic times. In contrast to Ebionism, it solved the problem by excising the humanity of Christ. Jesus only *seemed* human (Gk. *doceō* = seem). Its roots lie in Graeco-oriental convictions that matter is inherently evil and that God cannot be the subject of feelings or other human experiences. Docetism was unacceptable because it cut the bridge between God and humanity at the other end; God did not really come to *us*, hence no effective sacrifice was made for our sins.

Gnosticism
Precise dating of this is still disputed, though the assumption that it was essentially pre-Christian has been shown to be mistaken.

The thought-world of gnosticism is chock-full of bizarre specu-
lations, and it is unclear how far it was a unified system of
thought. Christ is seen by some gnostic writers as descended
from the heavenly stratosphere or 'fullness' (Gk. *plērōma*); he
united himself for a time with a historic person, Jesus, whose
body was formed of a psychic substance, the two elements being
loosely linked in him. Gnosticism clearly reflected a strong
docetic tendency. It effectively cut the bridge at both ends;
neither true God nor true human being, Christ was unfitted to
be the mediator.

Arianism

These earliest debates did not substantially effect the church as a
whole. The same could not be said of subsequent discussions,
particularly those which revolved around the views of Arius
(246–336), a presbyter of Alexandria who had been influenced
by the great teacher, Origen. Arius came to hold that 'the Son
was created'. He had imbibed Plato's division between the
tangible world of sense experience and the intangible world of
ideas. God, the absolutely unique and unoriginated source of all
things, belonged to the second of these worlds, so was radically
separated from the created world. Once this framework is
accepted, there is obviously great difficulty in fitting the Son
(*Logos*, the Word, Jn. 1:1) into the picture. Arius concluded that
the *Logos* must belong to the creaturely side of being; hence he
is not eternal, but is himself a created being: 'there was a time
when he [Christ] was not'. Christ is the most exalted of all
creatures, certainly, but ultimately only that.

The debate was strenuously pursued through much of the 4th
century. After the Emperor Constantine professed Christian
faith in AD 312, imperial politics became a significant factor in the
ebb and flow of the controversy, which even in its theological
terms was often confused. Constantine, concerned for the unity
of the church, called a Council at Nicea in 325 to resolve the
issue, but only at the Council at Constantinople in 381 was the
debate significantly resolved.

The opposition to Arius was led by Athanasius (296–373)
who, reared in the episcopal school in Alexandria, had maintained contact with the biblical and Hebrew tradition. He had
been deeply moved by the Christian martyrdoms that took place
in his youth under the Emperor Diocletian. Rejecting the

absolute dualism of his opponent, he sought to understand Jesus Christ from within the biblical witness to him. It is difficult to overestimate the heroic, and at times almost single-handed, stand of Athanasius. With great clear-sightedness he recognized that anything less than a fully divine Saviour would be insufficient to meet our need; therefore he clung tenaciously to the position that Christ was 'of one substance' (*homoousios*) with the Father, the position affirmed at Nicea and Constantinople.

Arian-type Christologies are far from dead. Jehovah's Witnesses, Christadelphians and many others deny the true deity of Jesus Christ, often in sophisticated philosophical and theological terms. This unbiblical heresy must be as decisively rejected in every form today as it was in the 4th century, for it denies the gospel and robs our Lord Jesus Christ of his own proper glory and majesty.

Although Nicea and Constantinople settled the point that Christ was not a created being and clarified his relationship to the Father, they did not resolve other related questions. The next period focused attention on the person of Jesus himself, asking how the divine and human elements were combined in his person. Three views were championed, which had in turn to be rejected.

Apollinarianism

Apollinarius (310–390), an over-enthusiastic supporter of Athanasius, held that in Jesus the eternal Word (*Logos*) took the place of the human soul. At the incarnation God the Son took up residence in a human body, so that Christ did not possess a full human nature. The position, obviously docetic in tendency, was rejected since it in effect denies that God truly became human.

Nestorianism

Nestorius was appointed Archbishop of Constantinople in AD 428. In the interests of preserving the full humanity of the mediator, Nestorianism taught the separation of the two natures in Christ to the extent of rendering questionable his authentic personal unity; this rendered the incarnation invalid and imperilled salvation. Many scholars today believe that Nestorius himself did not hold many of the views attributed to him by his 'orthodox' opponents. Removed from office in 431, he spent the remainder of his life in the most energetic missionary labours.

Eutychianism

Eutyches, an outspoken opponent of Nestorianism, championed the unity of Christ's person and claimed that, while there were two natures before the incarnation, there was only one composite nature after it. This implies that Jesus is a third sort of being, neither true human nor true God, and hence unable to act as mediator. Eutyches was condemned at the Synod of Constantinople in 448, but reinstated somewhat dubiously at Ephesus in 449.

Clearly, matters could not continue in this manner and a major council was summoned at *Chalcedon* in 451 to resolve the debates once and for all. The statement of the Council of Chalcedon, which was deeply influenced by the more pragmatic theology of the West, failed to please all the parties, but has been the basis for orthodox formulations of the person of Christ ever since. Its central clause affirms: '.... we should confess that our Lord Jesus Christ is one and the same Son ... perfect in Godhead ... perfect in manhood ... of one substance (*homoousios*) with the Father in Godhead, *homoousios* with us in manhood ... made known in two natures (*physeis*), without confusion, without change, without division, without separation ... the property of each nature being preserved and concurring in one person (*prosōpon*) and one subsistence (*hypostasis*).'

OTHER IMPORTANT CONCEPTS

The hypostatic union

This is shorthand for what the incarnation involved: the union in one person (Gk. *hypostasis*) of a full human nature and a full divine nature. At Chalcedon the church expressed the terms of this in careful balance: the two natures are united in this hypostatic (*i.e.* 'personal') union 'without confusion, without change, without division, without separation'.

Anhypostasia and enhypostasia

This terminology was coined in the 6th century by Leontius during discussions of the identity of the personal centre, the self-conscious 'I', of Jesus Christ. If this self-conscious 'I' was the divine Word, the human nature assumed lacked a human self-consciousness; this looked dangerously like the Apollinarian denial of Christ's true humanity and hence of his fitness to act as our redeemer. The contrary theory, of a full human self-consciousness in Christ independent of and alongside the Logos, threatened the integrity of the incarnation as an act by which the pre-existent Son of God became human, and also gave rise to another person alongside and independent of the Logos, *i.e.* Jesus of Nazareth, who is then not the eternal Son of God and can neither reveal God nor bring God's salvation to us.

Leontius proposed that, negatively, the human self-conscious 'I' had no existence of its own; it existed only within the hypostatic union with the Logos (Gk. *an* = without, hence *anhypostasia*).

Positively, he proposed that it is present and real only *in* (Gk. *en*) the divine 'I' (hence *enhypostasia*). This permits the assertion of full humanity but retains the biblical recognition that the essential self-hood of the God-man is that of the eternal Son and Word of God who effectually reveals God and brings divine salvation to humankind.

Communion of the properties

This ancient formula asserts that, while the two natures in the hypostatic union each retained its essential properties, there was a genuine communion between the two natures, so that the properties of each were genuinely communicated to the other. It attempts to avoid artificially attributing certain of Jesus' actions to his divine nature (raising the dead, multiplying the loaves and fish) and others to his human nature (weariness, ignorance of the time of his return).

The 'Calvinist extra'

So named because it was championed by the Reformed party in 16th-century debates, this formula asserts that neither during the course of his earthly ministry nor subsequently while retaining his human nature as the ascended Lord did the eternal Word divest himself of the functions and attributes of deity. He continued to uphold all things (Col. 1:17; Heb. 1:3) and remained head over the angels (Mt. 26:53). If carried too far, this idea can develop into a Nestorian division of Christ's person. Both the 'communion of the properties' and the 'Calvinist extra' appear necessary to do justice to the biblical evidence.

Two-state Christology

The Reformation brought a new sense of the living reality of Christ encountered in history in the gospel of his grace. This led the Reformers to enrich the Chalcedonian definition, which they heartily endorsed, with a complementary, two-state Christology. Here the person of Christ is approached in terms of a dynamic movement of the one person from a state of humiliation in his flesh culminating in his death on the cross, to a state of exaltation in his resurrection and ascension (Acts 2:22–36; 2 Cor. 8:9; Phil. 2:5–11). This approach combines helpfully with the Chalcedonian formula, the latter being like a horizontal cross-section of the person of Christ, while the two-state approach resembles a vertical section.

Kenosis

This Christological theory develops the two-state Christology by arguing that in his career as a human being the eternal Word divested himself of many essential divine attributes (often specified as omnipotence, omniscience and omnipresence). It appealed for biblical support to Philippians 2:7 and the assertion that Christ 'emptied himself' (RV, Gk. *ekenōsen*). It sought thus to preserve the full humanity of Christ, including a frank admission of his human limitations, alongside the traditional confession of his deity. In modified forms it argued that the divine attributes were simply 'rendered latent' or 'exercised only intermittently', or even that the kenosis related to the consciousness of Christ rather than to his being.

Certainly some form of condescension was involved for the eternal Word in accepting union with the human nature assumed in Mary's womb. It remains doubtful, however, whether kenosis is a particularly helpful way of expressing this. The biblical support is decidedly insecure, since Philippians 2:7 refers to surrendering not divine powers and attributes but divine glory and dignity. 'He made himself insignificant' is the real sense.

At a theological level kenosis appears to move in the wrong direction. Its basic equation is: incarnation = God minus. The biblical equation is rather: incarnation = God plus. In becoming incarnate the divine Word did not relinquish his deity; he added to it, if one may so speak, by taking a full human nature into hypostatic union with the Word. Further, if the incarnate Son lacked any essential divine attribute, he immediately fails us at three quite fundamental points: revelation (being less than God he cannot truly reveal God), redemption (being less than God he can no longer reconcile us to God) and intercession (if union with human nature necessarily diminishes the divine nature, the ascended Lord could not 'take to heaven a human brow'; his high-priestly intercession is immediately invalidated). Finally, Archbishop William Temple asked: 'What was happening to the rest of the universe during the period of our Lord's earthly life?' If the second person of the Trinity was wholly enclosed in the babe of Bethlehem, who was performing the role of the upholding Word in the universe? Appeal to the notion of the co-inherence of the persons of the Trinity does not help, since it is precisely a separation of the persons which the kenotic theory requires.

MODERN INTERPRETATION

Functional versus ontological Christologies

Today a number of writers wish to replace 'ontological Christology' (Christ's person interpreted in terms of his *being and natures*, usually = the Chalcedon formula) by 'functional Christology' (Christ's person interpreted in terms of his *active role* within God's purpose). The distinction between the two is valid enough, so long as we do not suggest that these are alternatives, rather than complementary. The ontological cannot be given up without reducing our Lord's person and hence his ability to mediate, and the notion finds no encouragement from Scripture. A statement such as 'The Word became flesh' (Jn. 1:14) answers questions about the being and nature of the mediator (*cf.* Jn. 1:1–18; 2 Cor. 8:9; Phil. 2:5–11; Col. 1:15–20; Heb. 1:1–3).

Further, the Bible's view of reality, its distinction between different kinds of being with fixed natures (God, humankind, angels, *etc.*) and the universal categories at the heart of its interpretation of redemption ('in Adam', 'in Christ') provide this framework of substances and entities; the ontological is simply not dispensable. Chalcedon itself is not in the Bible; in principle, then, it is open to revision and replacement. Something akin seems inevitable, however, the moment we ask questions about the biblical presentation of Christ. Christology must be both ontological and functional.

The incarnation as 'myth'

During the 1970s, debate was sparked when a few Christological writers argued that to speak of Jesus as God incarnate is a mythical, or poetical, way of expressing his significance for us: he was simply someone 'approved by God', open to God in a special sense and uniquely conscious of the divine reality. In essence this view revives a line of thought stemming from Ebionism in the immediate post-biblical period. It solves the Christological problem by excising the divine and reducing Jesus to simple humanity – a very special human being, no doubt, but merely human none the less.

This modern restatement is no more palatable or persuasive than its historical ancestors. The attempt to find a merely human 'original Jesus' behind the exalted figure of the NT has, in all conscience, been made often enough in the past, with signal failure. Far from being an addition to an original understanding of Jesus, belief in his deity undergirded the church's response from the beginning. Besides, the substantial biblical evidence for Christ's deity, expounded earlier, stands unshaken.

This human Christology means (a) the denial of the Christian God: Jesus is not divine, therefore God is not triune, at least in any manner we can know; (b) the elimination of Christian worship – no prayer and praise to or through Jesus; (c) the overthrow of Christian conviction – no final revelation in Christ – leaving us agnostic about God and in the end about everything; (d) the invalidation of Christian redemption, for since Christ is not God incarnate he is irrelevant to our relationship to God; (e) most serious of all, the denigration of the honour and glory of God in Christ. No Christian to whom God's glory is dear will find any inclination to countenance such views.

FURTHER COMMENT

One pointer to further understanding of the incarnation may be indicated in John's gospel.[1] Fundamental to its presentation of Christ is his utter dependence on the Father (4:34; 6:38, 44; 7:16; 8:27, 50, 54; 10:18). The eternal Word of God shares the divine nature in fullest measure, and, as the eternal Son, is eternally

---

1. *Cf.* J. N. D. Anderson, *The Mystery of the Incarnation* (Hodder, 1978), ch. 6; J. I. Packer, 'Jesus Christ the Lord', in *Obeying Christ in a Changing World*, 1, *The Lord Christ* (Fountain Books, 1977).

going forth from the Father. This mysterious divine generation he expresses by living under the conditions of divine-humanity in utter, adoring dependence on the Father. In every moment and detail all the prerogatives and perfections of deity are his to command, yet he submits to the Father's pleasure in all things: knowledge, speech, action, conflict, suffering.

In the last analysis the incarnation, being in a class of one, can scarcely be interpreted on the analogy of human experience. True, human analogies have some validity since Christ was God become human, and humankind was made in God's image; but they have necessary limits since we simply do not know what it means to be divine-human. Beyond a certain point the person of Jesus can be understood only in terms of his own self-testimony, which means in terms of the God-breathed witness of Scripture. 'Great is the mystery of our religion: He was manifested in the flesh' (1 Tim. 3:16, RSV). The apostle's caution neither invalidates reverent attempts to explore the mystery, especially in the interests of refuting error, nor implies uncertainty about the fundamental reality of Jesus Christ as true God and true human being; but it recalls the limits to our understanding of these realities and reminds us that the person of our Lord reveals its deepest secrets to those who approach like the Christmas shepherds, in humble faith and adoring worship.

Scriptures
Jn. 1:1–18; 10:30–38; Acts 2:22–35; Rom. 1:4; 2 Cor. 8:9; Phil. 2:5–11; Col. 1:15–20; 2:9; 1 Tim. 3:16; Heb. 1:1–3; 1 Jn. 1:1f.

Questions
1. State the major heresies concerning the person of Christ. Can you identify contemporary expressions of these errors?
2. 'No Christology can ever go back on Chalcedon.' Discuss.
3. What is meant by 'kenosis'? To what extent does the concept help or hinder in understanding Christ's person?
4. Consider the importance of a correct Christology for (a) our view of God, (b) the gospel of redemption, (c) our view of humankind, (d) our approach to Scripture.

Bibliography
Arts. 'Incarnation' in *IBD* and 'Christology' in *NDT*.
J. N. D. Anderson, *The Mystery of the Incarnation* (Hodder, 1978).
M. Green (ed.), *The Truth of God Incarnate* (Hodder, 1977).
D. Macleod, *The Person of Christ* (IVP, 1998).
I. H. Marshall, *The Origins of New Testament Christology* (IVP, 1976).

E. L. Mascall, *Theology and the Gospel of Christ* (SPCK, 1977).
C. F. D. Moule, *The Origin of Christology* (CUP, 1977).

16. The work of Christ: biblical teaching

The phrase 'work of Christ' covers all that Christ did to bring salvation to the world. A closely allied term is *atonement*, which is one of the few Anglo-Saxon words in the theological vocabulary. Referring to the reconciliation of humanity and God, it points to the means whereby the estrangement between the two is overcome and God and humanity made at one. Because this section ranges rather more widely than examining what happened at the cross, the term 'work of Christ' is probably to be preferred as an overall title.

ATONEMENT IN THE OLD TESTAMENT

Although it is admitted that we meet the same God in both Testaments, many suspect that while NT religion is grace (we are accepted on the basis of our response to what God did for us in Christ), OT religion is law (our acceptance with God depends on our moral obedience). We need to begin, therefore, with the unambiguous assertion that in the OT salvation is as assuredly by the free grace and mercy of God as in the NT. The basis of Israel's relationship with God and of her hope of salvation lay in God's electing grace (Gn. 12:1–7; Ex. 3:6–10; Dt. 6:21–23; Is. 41.8f.), realized through the covenant with Abraham and his descendants (Gn. 15:18; Ex. 6:6–8; Ps. 105:8–15, 42–45; Is. 51:2–6; Ezk. 37:35f.; Lk. 1:32f., 54f.; Acts 13:17–23). This grace called for a response of faith or trust (Gn. 22:17f.; Ps. 33:16–20; Is. 31:1). On this covenant basis, the law came into effect as God's demand that his people live in accordance with his holy character (Ex. 20:1–2).

This understanding of the law, however, was only partially grasped. Rabbinic sources make clear that, formally speaking, fulfilling the law was viewed as the way of remaining within the covenant community rather than the road into it. But the degree to which that was popularly grasped is uncertain. There were a number of strains within the religion of Judaism around the NT period, some of which were accurately reflected in the polemic against legalism and self-righteousness which Jesus delivered (Mt. 6:5f.; Lk. 18:9–14; Mt. 23:1–15), and which Paul reiterated in his day (Rom. 3:19–22; Gal. 2:15f.; 3:10–14). This legalism, which taught that our observance of the law earned our right standing with God, was OT religion gone wrong, *not* the religion of the OT itself. There salvation and atonement are rooted not in the law but (as in the NT) in God's grace.

Similar accord with NT atonement teaching is expressed in the Jewish sacrificial system. The sacrifices were of several classes. Gift offerings expressed homage and thanksgiving (Dt. 33:10; Jdg. 6:21); burnt offerings most commonly concerned the community as a whole (Ex. 29:38–42; Nu. 28f.). Of particular significance for atonement were the sin and guilt offerings. These dealt with unintentional offences against God for which the worshipper sought pardon (Lv. 4 – 5). The most important were made on the annual Day of Atonement (Yom Kippur) when the high priest, on this occasion only, entered the Holy Place behind the veil with a blood sacrifice to make atonement for all the sins incurred by the people of Israel in the course of their worship (Lv. 16). The crucial aspect of the whole system was the shedding of blood in the death of a substitutionary victim.

These sacrifices inculcated an awareness of God's holiness and taught that breaches of God's will (infringements of his law) necessitated the death of a ritually clean substitute to secure reconciliation with God. When offered in obedient faith, regardless of any possible accrual of merit and with trust in God's mercy alone, the sacrifices brought appropriation of the covenant blessings. Here again, the OT clearly recognizes that the sacrifices *in themselves* were quite unable to atone for sin (Ho. 6:6; Mi. 6:6–8). Psalm 51 is particularly eloquent in this respect; moral guilt cannot be blotted out by sacrifices (v. 16) but only by God's free grace (v. 1) in response to the heart repentance of the psalmist (v. 17). The point is made very clear in the NT commentary on the OT sacrifices, in Hebrews 9:9f.

The ultimate reference point of divine grace is also identical in the two Testaments, the person and work of Christ. While for us today the virtue of Calvary is projected forward, in the case of the OT saints it is projected backwards (Mt. 8:16f.; Lk. 2:38; Jn. 3:14f.; 8:56; Rom. 4:1–25; 10:11–13; 1 Cor. 5:7; Heb. 9:15;

10:12–14; 1 Pet. 1:18f.). For them as for us atonement, ultimately considered, is by the blood of Christ.

JESUS THE MESSIAH

'Messiah', we saw, means God's anointed. In Israel three offices were established to which people were appointed by anointing with oil: kings (1 Sa. 16), priests (Lv. 8) and prophets (in this case spiritually, perhaps, rather than literally, Is. 61:1). Generations of theologians have spoken of Jesus' 'three-fold office', meaning that he was anointed by God (Acts 10:38; Heb. 1:9) in order to fulfil, perfectly and normatively, the triple office of priest, prophet and king for the people of God. The use of the singular (*office*) is important. We are concerned with what are simply three distinguishable facets of one indissoluble reality, the work of Jesus Christ the mediator.

The prophetic office

The prophet is one who speaks for another (Ex. 7:1f.; Dt. 18:18f.). His office presupposes people's ignorance and blindness with respect to God's will and purpose, which the prophet as spokesman of the Almighty seeks to dispel. Prophethood was classically expressed in the person of Moses and the later OT figures like Isaiah, Amos, Hosea and Jeremiah. The OT messianic anticipation includes this prophetic role: 'The LORD your God will raise up for you a prophet like me . . . You must listen to him' (Dt. 18:15). The early church saw this fulfilled in Jesus (Acts 3:22f.; 7:37).

It was as prophet that Jesus was first acclaimed by his contemporaries (Mt. 21:46; Mk. 8:28; Lk. 7:16; Jn. 9:17). He himself accepted the title (Mk. 6:4; Lk. 13:33), though with reservation (Mt. 11:9–11), and in the traditional sense it was clearly not adequate to Jesus' claims for himself (Mk. 9:1–8; Jn. 10:30; 14:6). He stands within the long line of prophetic heroes who bore the Word of God, and yet he towers above them for he also *is* the Word he bears (Jn. 1:1–14). This fundamental link between the work of Christ and his person is explicit in John 1:14, 'the Word became flesh.' In Jesus, the prophetic Word of God finds its ultimate expression as a truth not only of his teaching but of his very being. The later NT amplifies this dimension; Jesus is the incarnate wisdom of God (1 Cor. 1:30), the one 'in whom are hidden all the treasures of wisdom and knowledge' (Col. 2:3).

Christ's prophetic function therefore consists in his bringing to ignorant, sin-darkened humanity the very truth of God. In revealing God himself to us (Jn. 14:9) he is the supreme Teacher whose word bears authority and to whom we must submit in all things (Mt. 7:24–29; Mk. 1:22f.; Jn. 13:13f.). He both proclaims and incarnates God's demands on us, as well as the divine grace by which alone we can enter the kingdom of the God of truth (Mk. 1:14; Jn. 1:17; 10:9).

The priestly office

The presupposition of priesthood is our sinful estrangement from God. The priest is God's appointed mediator through whom the estrangement is overcome (Heb. 5:1). This crucial strand of OT religion (Ex. 28 – 29) was particularly embodied in the high priest whose functions included the annual Day of Atonement offering in the Holy Place in the temple (Lv. 16; Heb. 9:1–8). The work of Jesus Christ is interpreted in terms of his fulfilling the priestly office primarily in the letter to the Hebrews, which links him to the OT high priest at two points.

First, his *identity*: the 'high priest is selected from among men . . . to represent them' (5:1). As true man Christ was qualified to act on our behalf in relation to God (2:7–17; 4:15; 5:1–3; 10:5–9). This solidarity with our humanity, foundational to his priestly mediation, is further pictured in the OT idea of the *gō'ēl*, or kinsman-redeemer. In certain circumstances a blood relation could act as *gō'ēl* on behalf of a relation to deliver him or her from a particular distress (Lv. 25:48f.); the action of Boaz with respect to Ruth (Ru. 4:1–13) is the classic OT example. This title is also applied to God (Ex. 6:6; Is. 41:14). In Christ God has acted as our kinsman-redeemer by taking our flesh (Jn. 1:14) and acting on our behalf to save us from the curse and dominion of sin.

Second, his *self-offering*: 'Every high priest is appointed to offer both gifts and sacrifices' (8:3). Christ was not only the offering priest but also the sacrificial victim; in unspeakable love and grace he entered the Holy Place and offered *himself* on the alter of the cross (Heb. 1:3; 9:12–14; 10:10–22; 13:12). That Jesus understood his own mission in priestly terms is clear from his free use of sacrificial language (Mk. 10:45; Lk. 22:20; Jn. 10:11, 15; 15:13).

His allusions to Isaiah's Suffering Servant reinforce the idea.

The Servant passages (Is. 42:1–4; 49:1–7; 50:4–11; 52:13 – 53:12) were variously interpreted at the time of Jesus, but there was almost no inclination to interpret them messianically, for they were apparently irreconcilable with the messianic-kingly motif. Jesus' link with the Servant was established by the Father at his baptism (Mk. 1:11, *cf.* Is. 42:1) and there are frequent references in the gospels (Mt. 8:16f.; 12:18–21; Jn. 1:29), echoed in other NT books (Acts 3:13; 8:32f.; 1 Pet. 2:21f.). There may be yet another hint of Jesus' appropriation of the priestly office in Mark 14:62 where he applied Psalm 110:1 to himself and hence by implication Psalm 110:4.

The priestly office covers the whole saving work of Christ in his death. In order to unfold its full significance we need to expound the three major NT metaphors used to interpret Christ's death.

The penal metaphor: justification

Hebrew thought concerning righteousness has an invariable legal (forensic) atmosphere. The righteous person is the one 'whose sin the LORD does not count against him' (Ps. 32:2). But we are all in a state of guilt, having breached the moral law of God (Ps. 14:1–3), and are under its curse or condemnation (Dt. 27:26; Ps. 1:5f.). Nor is there any way out in terms of God's simply relaxing his law and ignoring human law-breaking. The law[1] is not some arbitrary series of demands which God chooses to lay upon the human conscience; at its heart it is nothing less than the demand of the character of God that we should conform to God's being and side with him against all that threatens and opposes God (Lv. 11:44f.; Is. 1:4). It is the law of God, 'holy, righteous and good' (Rom. 7:12, 22).

Any infringement of the moral law, therefore, amounts to a direct assault upon God. The moment we commit it, it becomes an integral part of that whole resistance movement which, in affirming his Godhead, he is bound to take account of and to oppose.

God's 'taking account of' sin draws attention to the *guilt*

---

1. By 'law' here is meant the fundamental OT moral prescriptions summarized in the decalogue (Ex. 20:1–17; Dt. 5:1–21). OT ceremonial laws have been superseded in the sense that Christ has fulfilled them; OT social legislation ceased to be normative in the sense that the church has replaced the theocracy of Israel. Principles underlying both ceremonial and social laws have continuing relevance and application.

which inevitably accompanies all our sinning. The moment we commit sin, it enters the unalterable past. To be a sinner means to be a person with a past; the copy-book is marked and stained. We cannot begin again because the sin of yesterday remains to our account, inexorably confronting God, opposing his majesty and Godhead. 'We have a strange illusion that mere time cancels sin. I have heard others, and I have heard myself, recounting cruelties and falsehoods committed in boyhood as if they were no concern of the present speaker's, and even with laughter. But mere time does nothing either to the fact or to the guilt of sin' (C. S. Lewis). The past remains; time does not heal this particular breach; it cannot.

What then can be done? In one sense, nothing. In face of our guilt, we are helpless and can but await the coming judgment which is the inevitable consequence of sin in God's world.

At this very point, in face of our helplessness, Scripture directs us to the wonder of God's grace in Christ, the work of Christ. As a human being he was 'born under law' (Gal. 4:4) and fully obeyed all of God's commands (Jn. 4:34; 8:29), even 'to death' (Phil. 2:8). In his death he bore the 'curse of the law by becoming a curse for us' (Gal. 3:13). Thus in the death of Christ the sins of his people were judged (Rom. 3:23–26) and 'forgotten' (Heb. 8:12), and 'the result of [his] act of righteousness was justification that brings life for all' (Rom. 5:18). The judgment and curse of our disobedience passed to Christ at the cross and he bore it there for us, being 'made sin', treated and punished as a sinner, 'so that in him we might become the righteousness of God' (2 Cor. 5:21).

This act whereby God remits the sins of guilty men and women, accounting them righteous on the basis of Christ's representative obedience and redemptive death, is called in Scripture *justification* (Lk. 18:14; Rom. 3:24; 4:25; 1 Cor. 6:11; Tit. 3:7). It is in no way a reward for our own righteous efforts nor in any respect a matter of our co-operating with God to make any moral contribution to our justification. Justification is an act of sheer unmerited mercy on God's part.

The glorious positive side of justification (Rom. 4:1–12; Phil. 3:9) should be noted since it is frequently given inadequate stress. Our justification is not simply a matter of God's overlooking our guilt; our need can be met only if righteousness, full and entire holiness of character, is credited to us. This is the amazing gift of grace. Christ's law-keeping and perfect righteousness are made ours by faith in him (1 Cor. 1:30; Phil. 3:9). It is not simply that our abysmal failure in life's moral examination is overlooked; we pass with 100%, First Class Honours! Well may Athanasius speak of 'the amazing exchange' whereby, as Calvin puts it, 'the Son of God though spotlessly pure took upon himself the ignominy and shame of our sin and in return clothed us with his purity'.

In justifying sinners in Christ, God acts justly, for he does not overlook sin thereby or condone it (Rom. 3:25f.). He truly judges and punishes it on the cross, and thereby affirms his eternal, holy antagonism to it. Correspondingly there is no lowering of standard as far as sinners are concerned; God receives them only on the grounds of the perfect righteousness of Christ, which is credited to them through their faith-union with him. To be justified means that we are accepted before God without fear; that we can truly come before him and can experience being embraced by him and affirmed as his own dear children. To be justified therefore means that we can sing with Charles Wesley:

> *No condemnation now I dread;*
> *Jesus, and all in him, is mine!*
> *Alive in him, my living head,*
> *And clothed in righteousness divine,*
> *Bold I approach the eternal throne,*
> *And claim the crown, through Christ my own.*

Recent studies of the idea have drawn attention to the communal dimension of justification. Paul's concern in Galatians in particular is with the question: who are the true children of Abraham? And hence who are the true people of God? His answer is that membership belongs to all who believe in the gospel of Jesus, *i.e.* all who have been justified (Gal. 2:15–21; 3:6–14). Thus justification needs to be lifted out of the merely individual and personal. It is nothing less than the gateway to belonging within the new covenant people of God, where 'there is neither Jew nor Greek, slave nor free, male nor female' (Gal. 3:27).

To summarize, the Bible teaches that the heart of Christ's work consists in his having on our behalf and in our place borne the punishment due to us on account of our sin and brought us pardon and reconciliation with God in righteousness. This is often referred to as 'penal substitution' and has been the centre of evangelical teaching and preaching on the atonement since the Reformation. It is frequently assailed by critics who argue: (a) the use of legal terminology, God as a judge inflicting punishment, human beings as criminals, *etc.*, seriously depersonalizes our relationship to God; (b) the God of this theory who demands punishment is not the forgiving God of love who pardons freely; (c) the whole idea of substitution is unjust, even immoral in this context, since it means that the innocent is punished and the guilty go free; or, alternatively, God's justice appears more easily satisfied than ours, since in human thought justice is not done until the guilty pay the penalty themselves.

Penal substitution can, however, be readily defended against all three criticisms. First and generally, we recall that it is clearly taught in God's Word; this is no human construction but part of what God himself teaches us about the cross. More particularly, against the charge of depersonalization, it is evident that the Bible does not contrast the personal and the legal in this manner. The biblical writers clearly loved legal metaphors and appeal to legal processes again and again to explain God's dealings with humanity. 'To deny that the New Testament makes use of legal imagery to describe Christ's work for us is to refuse to face reality' (L. Morris). Underlying this line of criticism is almost invariably a failure to interpret law in a biblical way, *i.e.* as the unchanging character of God impinging upon human existence.

As for the second charge, objecting to the notion of God's requiring punishment, the alternative proposed, the God who simply overlooks sin, is really a figment of the human imagination, nowhere found in Scripture. He is certainly not the God of the OT and therefore not the God in whom Jesus believed. Nor is he the God whom Jesus himself revealed, as is clear from his frequent and solemn warnings of the dangers of impenitence (Mt. 11:20–24; Lk. 13:1–5; 16:19–31) and the place which his impending death held in his understanding of his mission (Mk. 8:31; 10:45; 14:34; Jn. 10:11; 12:24).

As far as the third charge of injustice is concerned, there is the obvious point that penal substitution involves the Trinity and the incarnation, *i.e.* the unity of Father and Son in Godhead, and Christ and ourselves in humanity; hence there is a fundamental propriety in Christ's entering into our guilt under the Father's wrath.

More substantially, J. I. Packer has pointed out[2] that it is a mistake to press biblical categories such as penal substitution beyond their limits. They are essentially thought-models given us by God to instruct us concerning himself and his activities. Because they are God-given they should command our total trust, and indeed it is only by submitting our minds to them and tenaciously retaining them that we can be assured of arriving as near as we may to the truth about the atonement.

When seen in this way penal substitution can be fully defended (assuming we can demonstrate its biblical basis) without our having to justify it at every point by appeal to common-law practice or to general norms of personal relationships. While we do not lightly set aside our general moral instinct, since God is creator as well as redeemer, equally we cannot make our fallen norms the final determination and judge of God's action. In fact, of course, there is the most profound justice expressed in God's pardoning condemned and helpless sinners through the cross – the justice of God's redemptive love (Rom. 3:21–26).

The cultic metaphor: reconciliation/propitiation

In a measure this locks into the previous metaphor, further expounding the means of our justification. One result of our disobedience to God's law lies in our unfitness for God's presence and exposure to his holy wrath; the way back to Eden is barred by a flaming sword (Gn. 3:24). Humankind, estranged from God, is now his enemy. Again we see in stark terms the utter helplessness of humankind in sin. In this context Scripture directs us again to the wonder of God's love in Christ.

Reconciliation means the abolition of enmity between two parties who have quarrelled. It is used of Christian salvation in several important NT passages (Rom. 5:10f.; 2 Cor. 5:18–20; Eph. 2:16; Col. 1:20). An allied notion is 'making peace' (Rom. 5:1; Col. 1:20). For humankind is indeed the enemy of God (so Rom. 5:10; Col. 1:21; Jas. 4:4), and not simply just short of being God's friend. Reconciliation is effected by removing the cause of the quarrel (in this case our sin) which God has done in Christ,

---

2. 'What did the Cross Achieve?', *Tyndale Bulletin* 25, 1974.

in particular by his death. Christ is therefore 'our peace' (Eph. 2:14); we are reconciled 'through the death of his Son' (Rom. 5:10), 'through his blood, shed on the cross' (Col. 1:20).

The Bible's teaching is seriously misrepresented when reconciliation is confined to our side of the relationship, as though it were simply our attitude that needs changing. While it can be badly distorted, the wrath of God is a solemn biblical reality (Ex. 22:24; Ps. 78:31; Ho. 5:10; Lk. 3:7; Jn. 3:36). To suggest, as some do, that the cross simply demonstrates the love of a God who is already reconciled to us, ignores God's wrath and misses the real purpose of the cross. Indeed the cross demonstrates God's love only because of this deeper theological meaning: it is love dealing sacrificially with the implications of our sin (Jn. 3:16; 1 Jn. 4:9f.). Only such an understanding does justice to the NT view of the cross as a decisive act of redemption by which alone we are delivered from divine wrath. We must therefore speak of a 'change from wrath to grace in the historical sphere' (Berkouwer).

The means of this reconciliation is spelled out more precisely by a closely related term, *propitiation* (Rom. 3:25; Heb. 9:5; 1 Jn. 2:2; 4:10). It refers to the removal of wrath by the offering of a gift. Christ's, however, was no impersonal or abitrary offering; nor was he a third party introduced from outside humanity's relationship to God: 'God was reconciling the world to himself in Christ' (2 Cor. 5:19). Christ is none other than God himself taking upon his own holy and eternal heart the implications of his own wrath. Obviously there is impenetrable mystery here, but all the terms of this equation are clearly present in the NT interpretation of the work of Christ, and in the notion of propitiation in particular.

In order to avoid any suggestion of 'placating an angry deity', some writers opt for the term 'expiation' as an alternative to propitiation. This latter implies 'removal of guilt', without any particular explanation of how this is effected. It is difficult to see how this leads either to greater clarity or to a more biblical understanding. The guilt concerned cannot be reduced to subjective guilt feelings; God objectively resists us in our sin. The removal of that personal divine antipathy is what is involved in our reconciliation and which constitutes it. But that in turn implies some sense of God's treating the sinner differently, his wrath giving place to grace, on the basis of Christ's self-offering.

That is precisely what propitiation indicates.

The real reason expiation was preferred by some was uncertainty about the fact of God's wrath. If expiation is tied to a denial of wrath, then its unbiblical character stands exposed; if it is not so tied, it is difficult to see why it is to be preferred to propitiation.

Sacrifice belongs in this context (1 Cor. 5:7; Eph. 5:2; Heb. 7:27; 8:3; 9:23–28; 10:10–26; 13:10–13). The NT draws on various aspects of the OT sacrificial system to expound the meaning of Christ's death: he is the lamb slain (Jn. 1:29f.; 1 Pet. 1:18f.); the passover lamb (1 Cor. 5:6–8, *cf.* Ex. 12:1–12); the sin offering (Rom. 8:3, *cf.* Lv. 5:6f.); the Day of Atonement offerings (Heb. 9:1, *cf.* Lv. 16); the fulfilment of the covenant sacrifices (Mk. 14:24, *cf.* Ex. 24:8). The basic theme of the OT sacrificial system was propitiation: God's wrath was averted as a price was paid for the people's guilt and sin.

Another fundamental element of Christ's work which comes into focus in this picture is *substitution*. There is no evading this when the OT context is kept in view. The death of the ritually clean animal (which is what blood shedding refers to) was essentially substitutionary; the sacrificial animal died in the place of the guilty offerer (Lv. 1 – 5; 16). Substitution also lies at the heart of the ministry of the Servant (Is. 53:4–6, 10–12). Likewise, when Christ shed his blood on the cross, it was a substitutionary death, 'for us', in our place, that we might escape the death our sin had brought on us (Mk. 10:45; Jn. 11:50f.; Rom. 5:8; 1 Cor. 15:3; Gal. 3:13; 1 Tim. 2:6; Tit. 2:14; 1 Pet. 2:21, 24; 3:18).

It is sometimes urged that substitution should be dropped in favour of the term *representation*, in order to convey better the relationship between Christ and sinners in his work of atonement. The word is acceptable enough, particularly to express our union with him in his death and resurrection (Rom. 6:1f.; Gal. 2:20; Col. 2:12; 3:1f.; 2 Tim. 2:11); it also covers the thought of Christ as the last Adam (Rom. 5:12f.; 1 Cor. 15:22f.). As far as atonement is concerned, however, it cannot tell the whole story, for it implies that the representative is provided and put forward by those he represents. At that point the word is fundamentally misleading; we do not put Christ forward on our behalf. We are helpless and condemned, 'separated from Christ . . . and without God in the world' (Eph. 2:12); his is wholly a work of grace. He acts for us in the radical sense of going on our behalf where we cannot, doing in our place what we cannot do. *Substitution* is the obvious, indeed only, way of expressing that essential factor at the heart of the atonement.

The dramatic metaphor: redemption

Redemption is a term with two levels of meaning. It is used as a general synonym for the work of salvation, often coupled with creation (Ps. 19:1, 14; Is. 43:14f.; Heb. 9:12). It also has a more precise meaning, relating to our enslavement to sin (Jn. 8:34; Rom. 7:14; 2 Pet. 2:19) and the devil (Eph. 2:2; 1 Jn. 5:19). In his grace God brings redemption to us in our helpless condition.

Redemption carries the idea of deliverance by the payment of a price (Ps. 49:7; Is. 43:3; Mk. 10:45; 1 Pet. 1:18f.). There are several OT examples. Exodus 21:30 speaks of ransoming a man's life by paying a sum of money. The central act of redemption in the OT was Israel's deliverance from Egypt (Ex. 6:6; 13:13f.). Here the ransom price was the death of the animals sacrificed by Israel. In the NT, bondage to sin and evil is focused in the saying of Jesus: 'everyone who sins is a slave to sin' (Jn. 8:34). The ransom price is Christ's own death: 'we have redemption through his blood' (Eph. 1:7), 'the redemption that came by Christ Jesus . . . a sacrifice of atonement, through faith in his blood' (Rom. 3:24f.). This latter passage welds into a perfect unity the three figures of justification, propitiation and redemption.

Hesitation has been expressed over the ransom price. Why should God have to pay a price? And to whom? Some avoid these difficulties by reducing redemption to a synonym for deliverance, but this is inadequate and misleading. The redemption which the Bible expounds as an aspect of our salvation was accomplished by Christ's self-offering at Calvary. The point of the ransom price idea is that salvation is costly. God cannot deliver humankind by an arbitrary act of power; there is a price to pay and that is nothing less than the life of Christ, the God-man.

The kingly office

This office is rooted in the OT prophecies of the perpetual throne and kingdom of David (2 Sa. 7:12f.; Ps. 89:3f.). Thus Messiah is anticipated in regal terms (Is. 9:6f.; Je. 30:8f.; Ezk. 37:21f.; Zc. 9:9). The presupposition of kingship is our weak and rebellious submission to sin and darkness, which leaves us helpless under the reign of sin and its allies, demonic powers, death and judgment (Lk. 4:6; Rom. 5:17f.; 7:14–24; Eph. 2:1ff.; 1 Jn. 5:19).

At his birth Jesus is welcomed as the one who fulfils this OT hope (Mt. 1:1; 2:2; Lk. 1:31). He is the King come to restore the fortunes of God's people and to exercise God's rule on earth. The title has very close links with 'Lord'. Again, Jesus hesitated to take up the title, for fear of misunderstanding on the part of those around him (Jn. 6:14f.; Acts 1:6). It is, however, implicit in the central category of his preaching, the kingdom of God, which was at hand (Mk. 1:15), because he, its instrument and embodiment, was at hand (Mk. 12:34; Lk. 17:21). His triumphal entry ('Blessed is the King', Lk. 19:38) and his trial (Mk. 14:61f.; Jn. 18:33–37; 19:14–22) are clear witness to his fulfilment of this messianic role, and the later NT echoes this (Acts 17:7; 1 Tim. 6:15; Rev. 17:14).

His kingship is significantly linked with Calvary, for there he grappled with the enslaving powers of darkness (Jn. 12:31; Col. 2:14f.; Heb. 2:14f.). His resurrection sealed his triumph, 'declared with power to be the Son of God' (Rom. 1:4), King and Lord over all things (Mt. 28:18; Acts 2:33f.; 7:55f.; Rev. 1:5). This office in Scripture is bound up with three particular moments in Jesus' mission: his resurrection, his ascension and his glorious return. These together form the climax of his work.

The resurrection

We have already commented upon the resurrection in terms of the light it casts upon our Lord's person. Here we examine its implications for his work.

It fulfils his priestly work. Christ's priestly mediation consisted in going to the cross to bear God's penal judgments and holy wrath in order to bring us righteousness, reconciliation with God and freedom from sin's power. In the resurrection God the Father in effect pronounced his divine 'Amen' on the priestly work of his Son (2 Cor. 1:20). He openly declared it effective; real atonement has been attained and hence righteousness, reconciliation and freedom are truly brought to sinners (Rom. 4:25). Further, in the risen Christ we see our flesh-and-blood humanity preserved and affirmed before God on the further side of condemnation, wrath and all the assaults of evil. Here is humankind beyond the reach of judgment. Thus in face of all the assaults of our conscience or of the devil we can rely with defiance: 'Who will bring any charge against those whom God has chosen? It is God who justifies. Who is he that condemns? Christ Jesus, who died – more than that, *who was raised to life*' (Rom. 8:33f.).

It manifests his kingly work. In the cross Jesus confronted the age-long enemies of our sorry race: sin, death and the powers of darkness. His resurrection proclaims his victory over all three. He has conquered sin (Heb. 9:28) and the principalities and powers of darkness (Eph. 1:20f.), and even destroyed death itself (2 Tim. 1:10). The risen Jesus is the evidence of God's victory in him over all challenges to his lordship and rule and therefore demonstrates the establishment of the kingdom of God.

It embodies the promise of his future reign. When the disciples met the risen Jesus they were quite literally gazing on the end of the world: God's final triumph in the creation of a righteous new heaven and earth (Is. 65:17–25; 2 Pet. 3:13; Rev. 21 – 22). Paul links the Easter triumph of Christ to his final triumph and his coming, visible reign over all things at 'the end' (1 Cor. 15:20–25). The risen Jesus is the 'first-fruits' of the coming harvest of the dead at his return in glory (see Part 7).

The ascension
Christ's kingly office is manifested in his ascension to the right hand of God.

It proclaims Christ's triumph. He is 'at God's right hand with angels, authorities and powers in submission to him' (1 Pet. 3:22). He is 'crowned with glory and honour' (Heb. 2:9) and 'exalted to the highest place' (Phil. 2:9). 'He led captives in his train' (Eph. 4:8). The ascension confers on Jesus Christ the sovereign rule over the cosmos which the OT ascribes to the LORD (Pss. 8; 115; Is. 40:28). The man of Nazareth is now Lord over all things (1 Cor. 12:3; Eph. 1:22f.). His reign is not confined to the sphere of the church, nor is it suspended until his return at the end. The NT is absolutely unambiguous that Jesus Christ is *now* Lord and King over all.

It establishes the conditions under which the church is called to serve. We live, work, pray, believe, witness, serve, worship, obey and die under a Lord who is now exalted as head in earth and heaven. This was the secret of the early Christians' unquenchable zeal and buoyant optimism in the face of persecution and violent opposition. Here is the church's secret of peace in a world of turmoil, its resources for effective ministry and service to a fallen world: Jesus its head is exalted over all and sends his blessed Spirit to the church, as the life-flow from the exalted head to the earth-bound members of the body, communicating thereby the power of his victory (see Part 5).

This is also the great encouragement of the church in terms of Christ's high-priestly ministry. Christ carried his humanity into the presence of God when he ascended. He is therefore able to identify empathetically with us and to minister his grace to his people in the variety of their human suffering and need (Heb. 4:14–16). This ministry is also one of intercession (Rom. 8:34; Heb. 7:25), in which he appears in the presence of God as our heavenly advocate (1 Jn. 2:1).

It guarantees Christ's future final rule in glory. His ascension is his taking of authority in the universe. Nothing exists which can hold back the completion of his triumph. Hence 'God has appointed a day' (Acts 17:31, *cf.* Mk. 13:32); Christ is destined to reign 'until he has put all his enemies under his feet' (1 Cor. 15:25).

The return of Christ

This aspect of our Lord's kingly office constitutes Part 7. Some reference is necessary here to complete the present exposition. Any account of the work of Christ which neglects the future dimension can make no claim to adequacy. Christ's future reign in glory is the perspective from which everything else must be viewed, when he shall gather up all things under himself, and reign openly over a fully redeemed cosmos (Rom. 8:21–23).

Here is the supreme expression of Christ's kingly office, for at his glorious return he will be *manifested* as King and head over all, King of kings and Lord of lords (Phil. 2:9–11; Rev. 19:11–21; 21:22–27).

Scriptures

Atonement in the Old Testament: Gn. 11:31 – 12:7; 15:17f.; Ex. 3:6–10; 12:1–27; Lv. 16; Ps. 51; Is. 52:13 – 53:12; Je. 31:31f.; Ezk. 37:26; Mi. 6:6–8.
Christ the prophet: Dt. 18:15–18; Is. 61:1f.; Mt. 7:29; 11:9f.; Mk. 1:14; 6:4; Lk. 7:16; 13:33; Jn. 1:1–14; 7:15–18; 13:13f.; Acts 3:22f.; 7:37; 1 Cor. 1:30; Col. 2:3.
Christ the priest: Ps. 110:4; Mt. 8:16f.; 12:18–21; Lk. 4:18; Rom. 8:32; Heb. 4:14 – 5:10; 7:23–28; 9:11–14; 23–26; 10:11–18.
Justification: Ps. 32:2; Lk. 18:9–14; Rom. 3:21 – 4:25; 1 Cor. 1:30; 6:11; 2 Cor. 5:21; Gal. 2:15 – 3:29; Phil. 3:9; Tit. 3:7.

Propitiation: Jn. 1:29f.; 3:16, 36; Rom. 1:16–18; 3:25; 5:1, 8–11; 8:3; 15:3; 2 Cor. 5:18–20; Gal. 3:13; Eph. 2:14, 16; 5:2; Col. 1:19ff.; 1 Pet. 3:18; 1 Jn. 2:2; 4:9f.; Rev. 5:6–12.

Redemption: Ex. 6:6; 13:13f.; Jb. 19:25; Ps. 49:7f.; Mk. 10:45; Lk. 1:68; Jn. 8:34–36; Rom. 3:24–26; 6:17f.; 1 Cor. 1:30; 6:19f.; Eph. 1:7; Col. 1:14; 1 Pet. 1:18f.; Rev. 5:9.

Christ the king: 2 Sa. 7:12f.; Pss. 2; 89:3f.; Is. 9:6f.; Ezk. 37:21f.; Zc. 9:9; Mt. 2:2; 28:18; Lk. 1:32f.; 17:21; 19:38; Jn. 6:14f.; 12:31; 18:33–37; 19:14–22; Acts 2:33f.; Rom. 1:4; 1 Cor. 15:24f.; Eph. 1:20–22; Phil. 2:9f.; Col. 2:10; Rev. 17:14.

Questions

1. What are the points of continuity and discontinuity between OT and NT atonement teaching?
2. What is meant by Christ's prophetic office? 'I am the truth'; 'in [Christ] are hidden all the treasures of wisdom and knowledge': explore the implications of these biblical statements for (a) Christian discipleship, (b) Christian doctrine, (c) human investigation in the arts and sciences, (d) forms of political and social organization, (e) human culture, (f) the home and family life.
3. Why is Christ our 'Great High Priest'? What are the implications for (a) cleansing from sin, (b) a guilty conscience, (c) temptation and other trials, (d) Christian worship, (e) Christian fellowship? Find and study passages on each in the letter to the Hebrews.
4. State as precisely as you can the meaning of justification, supporting your definition from Scripture. Why can God not just 'overlook' our sin?
5. What is meant by the 'imputed righteousness of Christ', and what are its implications for the Christian's attitude to failure?
6. How may 'penal substitution' be defended against the suggestion that it is unjust?
7. What is meant by propitiation? Support your answer from biblical texts. Is 'expiation' a viable alternative term?
8. Examine the place of (a) substitution, (b) ransom price, in the atonement. Support your conclusion with biblical texts.
9. What is meant by Christ's kingly office? How does (a) the resurrection, (b) the ascension, relate to the understanding of the atonement? Examine the implications for (a) the church and its mission, (b) Christian living and evangelism, (c) Christian involvement in society, (d) Christian hope.
10. What are the points of contact between the incarnation and the atonement?

Bibliography

Art. 'Atonement' in *NDT*.

F. F. Bruce, *What the Bible Says About the Work of Christ* (Kingsway, 1979).

John Calvin, *Institutes of the Christian Religion*, 2, 15–16.

R. E. Davies, 'Christ in our Place', *Tyndale Bulletin* 21 (1970).

J. Denney, *The Death of Christ* (Tyndale Press, 1951).

M. Green, *The Meaning of Salvation* (Hodder, 1965).

C. Kruse, *Paul, the Law and Justification* (Apollos, 1996).

R. Letham, *The Work of Christ* (IVP, 1993).

D. M. Lloyd-Jones, *Romans 3:20 – 4:25 – Atonement and Justification* (Banner of Truth, 1970).

L. Morris, *The Apostolic Preaching of the Cross* (Tyndale Press, 1955).

J. R. W. Stott, *The Cross of Christ* (IVP, 1986).

17. The work of Christ: historical perspectives

We can do no more than outline several of the more important views of *how* Christ has effected his people's redemption. These can be categorized in terms of stress on the objective attainment of redemption by Christ and, by contrast, of stress on our subjective response to what Christ has done.

OBJECTIVE INTERPRETATIONS

Anselm (1033–1109) and the satisfaction theory

Anselm set out to show that God could not simply overlook sin; it had robbed God of his honour, leaving him the alternatives of punishment (which would frustrate his purposes) or receiving adequate satisfaction for the dishonour done to him. In the latter case, however, we can never provide the needed satisfaction; even were we to live perfectly from now until death, our previous dishonour of God would remain. Yet humankind must make the satisfaction, having committed the offence. Hence only God is able to provide it, only a human can properly make it. The solution lies with one who is both divine and human. Owing to his perfect life, Christ had no need to die; his death is therefore an act of infinite merit which becomes available for us as the means of his making satisfaction for our sin. Anselm is not particularly forthcoming on how this merit is appropriated by us.

There are certain artificial features to the theory such as the quantifying of merit, or the notion of God's facing a dilemma. Punishment as an alternative to satisfaction, instead of being the essential means of satisfaction, the inadequate reference to divine love as the ground and motive of the atonement, and the lack of any doctrine of faith-union with Christ as the means of appropriation, are other weaknesses. It has very significant strengths, however, which prompted Denney to call Anselm's *Cur Deus Homo* 'the finest book on the atonement ever written'; there is the rooting of atonement in the moral character of God, the profound sense of the majesty and lordship of God as determining his dealings with his creatures, the terrible seriousness of even a single sin, and the recognition of the cruciality of the cross for humankind's redemption.

Luther (1483–1546) and the penal view

Martin Luther is rightly one of the most honoured names in the church's history. His whole life demonstrated the paramount need for a true doctrine of the atonement and the disasters which overtake the church when it has lost touch with the biblical gospel. As an Augustinian monk Luther wrestled for years with the problem of his personal salvation, striving assiduously to merit it by various penances, prayers, sacraments and good works which the Catholic church prescribed. Only as he wrestled with Scripture and with Paul's teaching on righteousness by faith in Christ (justification, Rom. 1:17) did light break through, bringing him peace. His great slogans – by faith alone, by grace alone, by Scripture alone – brought direct confrontation with the church authorities, so that a protest against the scandalous indulgence trade turned into a full-scale controversy about the gospel itself; Christendom was divided and there emerged the great historic Protestant churches which restored the biblical gospel of grace.

In the next generation Calvin built on Luther's heroic stand and expounded Reformation theology in more systematic terms. The Reformation viewed sin as a contravention of the moral law which is ultimately correlative with the eternal character of God; the atonement is an act of redeeming love whereby God takes on himself in Christ the penalty and judgment of our sin, so obtaining for us pardon from all guilt and the free gift of righteousness before God through faith in Christ our sin-bearer. Anselm's alternatives of punishment or satisfaction are thus drawn together in an atonement by penal satisfaction.

The Reformers also sought to counter the danger of over-objectivizing Christ's work. Luther, for example, insisted that while 'faith alone justifies, it is never alone' but is always followed by the works of love. Calvin gave this a fuller theological basis by his teaching on faith as 'faith-union' with Christ (see Part 5). Our righteousness is wholly and solely that of Christ, imputed to us; we contribute nothing. But believers in Christ are united to him, so that justification is indissolubly linked to sanctification: God's people are morally renewed through their faith-union with Christ.

SUBJECTIVE INTERPRETATIONS

These views pay scant attention to Christ's work as dealing with our guilt through the cross, concentrating rather on its impact on us. Since they explicitly or implicitly deny Christ's objective work, it is scarcely proper to call them truly Christian views. But they must be noted, for they still circulate, sometimes united to some form of the classic view (*cf.* below). This approach is generally traced to Abelard.

Abelard (1079–1142) and the moral-influence view

For Peter Abelard, God who is all love has no need for the sacrifice of Christ. Sin is not an objective barrier between humanity and God, but a subjective state of mind which is overcome by the love awoken in the sinner's heart by the death of Christ. 'Redemption is that greatest love kindled in us by Christ's passion.' This awakened love redeems us by enabling us to live in free obedience to God out of love for him. Despite its value in reminding us that gratitude is a proper response to the mighty atoning act of God in Christ, as a theory of atonement it is seriously inadequate. It says nothing about the basis upon which sinners may be reconciled to God, while God's holiness and majesty and the seriousness of sin before him are virtually ignored and replaced by a somewhat sentimental conception of his all-pervasive love.

Schleiermacher (1768–1834) and the mystical view

Whereas Abelard was concerned with a moral response to Christ, Schleiermacher in his 'gospel for modern man' focused on the communication to us of a mystical sense of oneness with God. Schleiermacher saw Jesus as the archetypal human, the spiritual head of the race, the perfect human whose uniqueness and perfection consisted in his unbroken sense of union with God. Atonement consists in his communicating to sinners an inner experience of God-consciousness like his own. 'The redeemer assumes believers into the power of his God-consciousness, and this is his redemptive activity.' This, too, completely fails to reckon with the seriousness of sin and the guilt before God which it involves. It does no justice to the clear witness of Scripture to Jesus, not merely as perfect human, but as God incarnate, and thereby undercuts his role as mediator.

Inevitably, it bypasses the entire biblical witness to Christ's death as the act which redeemed sinners once for all. Like the moral influence view, it is not really a theory of atonement at all but an attempt to account for certain psychological elements in human experience of Christ.

MODERN INTERPRETATIONS

Aulén (1879–1978) and the classic view

In Gustav Aulén's book, *Christus Victor*, the essence of Christ's work is his triumph over sin and the devil. Christ comes as humankind's champion to deliver us from bondage by his Easter victory. In one sense, this is simply unpacking the biblical idea of redemption. Aulén's book is distinctive because it makes this the central category of the atonement, and attempts to show that it has been central to thinking about atonement throughout the church's history; hence its name, the 'classic' view.

Part of its appeal lies in its simplicity and its dynamic quality, compared with somewhat abstract, judicial approaches. Its appreciation of the reality of humankind's bondage to sin and the demonic powers also strikes a chord in the contemporary consciousness. Further, it certainly cannot be dismissed as unbiblical; redemption from the bondage of sin and of demonic powers is a major biblical metaphor of atonement. Its inadequacy lies in its claim to exclusiveness. Sin is not only enslavement; it is also the disobedience which renders us unrighteous and under condemnation, and the moral uncleanness which brings us under divine wrath. In other words, our problem includes *past guilt*: 'The problem of the past finds no answer in the classic motif of atonement' (Berkouwer).

The political interpretation

In recent years considerable interest has been stirred, especially in the Third World, in interpreting the work of Christ and Christian discipleship in essentially socio-political terms. This sprang partly from the radical theology of the early 1960s. A sharp reaction to the notion of a God 'out there', objective to the world and known through revelation, ushered in a God 'down here', immersed in the human process and encountered in the stuff of everyday existence. More immediately the movement was fathered by developments in the World Council of

Churches, whose growing concern to interpret the church's mission in socio-political terms crystallized at Uppsala in 1968. Here the goal of mission was stated as 'humanization' rather than evangelization; with modifications, that remains the Council's position. A primary source, however, is simply the social and cultural realities, particularly in the Third World, the entrenched poverty, injustice and economic dependence, and the apparent failure of the churches to confront these problems.

A key to this theological approach is the Marxist term, *praxis*, which asserts the inseparability of theory and practice. Theological statements are inescapably ideological, reflecting a theologian's socio-political commitment. Theology must begin, therefore, with the sociological reality, the present socio-political involvement of the church and the Christian theologian, interpreted with the tools of the social sciences; out of this analysis of praxis there develops a new standard for understanding Scripture and the church's tradition.

The second ingredient is the idea of the kingdom of God, understood as the ideal social and political order which is the promised goal of God's purposes in the world. This coming order is both the judgment of all present unjust regimes and social forms and the inspiration for all efforts to reshape human life.

What of the work of Christ? This is interpreted along the lines of the 'classic' view of the atonement. Christ embodies God's purpose for the world, and in his life and death confronts the forces of evil in the universe, thereby giving promise of the new coming order. The forces which he 'overcomes' are not so much personal sin and evil as 'the world' understood as political and social structures, in particular the forces of reaction, injustice, oppression, inequality, prejudice, *etc.*

Political theology, and more particularly liberation theology (a related but essentially Third World movement) has continued to evolve. As far as liberation theology is concerned, its expression has continued to lie primarily within Latin American Catholicism. After an initial phase of confrontation with the Roman curia there has developed a more mutually tolerant stance, possibly connected to the fact that leadership in the movement has increasingly passed from scholars in the colleges to the Ecclesial Base Communities, small groups of grass-roots lay people.

On the positive side, this interpretation of Christ's work should alert us to the real danger that economic and political commitments might condition the way we hear the gospel and respond to God's Word. Without question, the church and individual Christians have often failed, or frankly refused, to turn the critical judgment of Scripture and the law of its holy God on the political and economic basis of their own society. These theologians, therefore, can be heard as an echo of James, calling the church to express its faith in 'works' relevant to today's world and today's neighbour (Jas. 2). Nevertheless, one cannot help asking whether many of these political and liberation theologians themselves fall into this very danger of enculturing the gospel by their uncritical acceptance of Marxist categories for restating the Christian message.

Again on the positive side, while we need to avoid a simplistic identification of the 'poor' in Scripture with the oppressed proletariat of Marxist philosophy, God has a particular concern for the poor and oppressed, as Scripture constantly repeats (1 Sa. 2:8; Pss. 35:10; 113:7; 140:12; Is. 10:2; 41:17; Am. 5:12; Zc. 7:9f.; Mt. 11:5; Lk. 1:46–55; 6:20; Gal. 2:10; Jas. 2:3ff.). We must therefore be very sensitive, as God clearly is, to the cry of the wretched and downtrodden. Further, the increasing polarization of rich and poor in the world, and the simple recognition that the majority of Christians and unevangelized people around the world are among the poor, lay heavy responsibility on any theology which presumes to have any impact in the new millennium to show deep sensitivity to issues of poverty and injustice.

However, major questions remain. In our understanding of truth we do *not* begin with human experience in any shape or form, but with God as he is self-revealed in his Word incarnate and written; we know nothing truly about humankind except what God himself tells us. When this basic principle is abandoned, inevitably, as the Christian centuries eloquently testify, we lose our understanding of our own nature, and are thrown back on our own biased, fallen insights.

In its view of humankind's need, political theology is particularly inadequate. The human predicament cannot be reduced to social and political alienation, even assuming we can be certain of their root cause and of correct social and political means of dealing with them — which is itself not infrequently a deceptively subjective issue. Our deepest need is infinitely more serious than economic and political deprivation. As Jesus himself taught, the nadir of human need concerns not the body but the soul (Lk. 12:4f.): the wrath of God against our sinning. Political theology does not touch this dimension. In so far as it makes reference to our deliverance from sin at all, it commonly assumes the truth of universalism: all are already saved from sin, so that the question of our eternal standing with God can be put to one side, leaving us free to concentrate on salvation in this-worldly, socio-political terms. That assumption is tragically mistaken, but such an unbiblical viewpoint is not altogether surprising when the Bible is relegated to a secondary role.

While the kingdom of God is linked with the socially deprived in some of Jesus' sayings (Mt. 11:5; Lk. 6:20), he clearly did not interpret it in overtly socio-political terms. The Zealot movement sought the violent overthrow of the oppressor society, Rome; that path Jesus plainly disavowed. He interpreted the kingdom in essentially moral-spiritual terms, stressing faith and forgiveness and repentance towards God (Mt. 6:12ff.; 9:2ff., 22; 11:20; 15:28; Lk. 7:47f.; 13:3; 18:42). This is confirmed by the significance his impending death held for him and the categories in which he interpreted it (ransom, new covenant, self-sacrifice for God's flock, *etc.*), and also by his link between the kingdom and the Holy Spirit (Mt. 12:28; Jn. 3:3–8). This trend continues in the apostolic teaching. The kingdom is entered through the Holy Spirit in the context of personal faith in Christ (Rom. 14:17; Gal. 5:21f.; Col. 1:13). There is no kingdom other than that entered by personal submission to Christ the King (Acts 8:12; 20:20–25; 28:23; 1 Cor. 6:9–11; 15:24; Eph. 5:5; 2 Pet. 1:11; Rev. 1:9; 11:15).

God's particular concern for the poor and his judgment of the oppressor are biblical emphases. We must, however, be careful not to exaggerate these and thereby threaten one of the supreme glories of the gospel, its universal appeal. God's grace is offered to all, irrespective of their moral history, economic status or political commitment. Although the manifestation of human depravity may be greater in some social groups than in others, so making the ethical implications of belief in the gospel correspondingly more radical, we dare not obscure the fact that God also loves the oppressors, that Christ died also for the rich, and conversely, that the poor and oppressed will also face God's future judgment if they remain impenitent.

Finally the absence of a clear stress in these theologies on the need for regeneration means that their promise of liberation must remain sharply qualified, even at the social level. While no opportunity for improving social conditions should ever be neglected, in the final analysis nothing but regeneration by the Holy Spirit in the context of personal faith in the gospel of Christ can break the entrenched power of sin and selfishness in the human heart, and produce the men and women who can be the raw material for a truly liberated society.

PLURALISM

One of the clearest marks of the religious instinct at the present time is religious pluralism. This is the view that there is no single religious way which can claim an exclusive possession of the truth. Whereas in an earlier time the attempt was sometimes made to try to combine all the major world religions into a single faith (known as syncretism), pluralism recognizes the integrity of each and asks that all be recognized in their own terms.

The attractiveness of pluralism has been promoted by the resurgence of the old world faiths in our time as part of the general global disaffection with materialism. It has also been stimulated by the global migration of peoples, which has brought previously 'foreign' religions and their devoted adherents into the neighbourhoods of many western communities. The primary influence in the spread of pluralism, however, has undoubtedly been the way it responds to the temper of our time (see 'Postmodernism', pp. 142–144). Today's climate is profoundly tolerant and inclusive. Truth lies in the assertion of all views rather than being the possession of any one. To claim exclusiveness, particularly in the religious sphere where all our ideas are, it is claimed, necessarily fragmentary, is accordingly viewed as virtually amounting to intolerant bigotry.

How should the Christian respond? Is Jesus the only way to God? Is there no truth in other religious paths?

We begin with the person of Jesus himself. Basic to the NT presentation of him is the uncompromising and mind-blowing claim that in him God, the Creator and upholder of all that is, entered our world in person (see above on 'The deity of Jesus Christ', pp. 165ff.). Jesus was not just a special holy man, a great religious teacher, a spiritual master or miracle-worker, or even the greatest of all of these categories. He was nothing less than

Emmanuel, God himself with us. Necessarily, therefore, if this is true (and the entire NT message is predicated upon its truth), Jesus stands apart. To bracket Jesus with Muhammad, or Buddha, or Krishna, or any other religious leader, is to fail to understand him, and indeed to detract from his proper glory. At this point Christians have no choice; to concede the premise of pluralism is in fact to deny their Lord.

But there is a second point of distinctiveness, in terms of Christ's work. Jesus comes among us not only to reveal the heart of God, which he does, but to bring humanity back to God. For biblical faith the human condition is a deeply serious one. We have rebelled against our Creator and separated ourselves from him and become the objects of his just wrath. No amount of religious practice or devotion at whatever shrine and from within whatever religious tradition (including Christianity) can in itself atone for our sins and restore us to a right relationship with God. We are helpless: we cannot save ourselves. In infinite mercy, Jesus, as God incarnate, takes up our need himself. At the cross he assumed responsibility for the whole extent and implications of our sin. He died for us. By that act of atonement he has made it possible for sinners to be forgiven and restored in relationship with God as his own children. Of necessity, since he alone could make the sacrifice for our sins, and since his sacrifice is the only way sinners can be pardoned and reconciled, Jesus is the only way to a saving relationship with God. As he himself claimed, 'I am the way . . . no-one comes to the Father except through me' (Jn. 14:6). Peter affirms likewise: 'Salvation is found in no-one else [than Jesus Christ], for there is no other name under heaven given to men by which we must be saved' (Acts 4:12).

Finally, Jesus rose from the dead. He is alive. By faith we know him now in a living, ongoing relationship. A Christian is simply a person who is in a personal relationship with Jesus Christ. This means that, in the continuing humanity of Jesus, God shares our life. Unlike the other religious founders and teachers, Jesus is still here, alive and among us.

Thus at three points – the manger in Bethlehem as he is born among us, the cross of Calvary as he dies for us, and the empty tomb in Jerusalem where he rises again – Jesus stands apart. He is unique. He alone is God; he alone brings God to us and us to God.

To unpack the NT teaching in this manner, however, does not

imply that all other religious paths are devoid of truth, or that God cannot work within them. God is 'not far' from all his creatures; he sustains them all in life (Acts 17:27–28; Heb. 1:3; Col. 1:17). By virtue of creation all people are his 'offspring' who 'have their being in him' (Acts 17:27–28).

We cannot forget, of course, that there is a deeply entrenched instinct in the human heart to set up an idol in place of the living God, and to resist his judgment and his grace by trying to justify ourselves before him. Religion (including Christianity where it is devoid of a living faith in Christ) is a prime means of attempting this evasion. These other religious roads do not escape the twin dangers of idolatry and self-righteousness. But God, with whom 'nothing is impossible' (Lk. 1:37), and who 'does not show favouritism' (Acts 10:34), and who 'wants all men to be saved and to come to a knowledge of the truth' (1 Tim. 2:4), is able to work within the hearts of those who follow these other paths, as he did in the heart of the Roman centurion Cornelius in Acts 10, to lead them to hear the good news of Jesus Christ, and to find salvation through calling upon him.

Questions

1. Discuss the relative place of subjective and objective theories of the atonement. Why is the objective indispensable?
2. 'Truth, but not the whole truth.' Is that a fair estimate of the 'classic' theory of the atonement?
3. Assess the pros and cons of political and liberation theologies of the work of Christ.
4. In what senses is Jesus 'the only way to God'?
5. What are the indispensable features for 'a theory of atonement for today'?

Bibliography

Art. 'Atonement' in *NDT*.
Anselm, *Cur Deus Homo*.
G. Aulén, *Christus Victor* (SPCK, 1970).
G. C. Berkouwer, *The Work of Christ* (Eerdmans, 1965).
J. Denney, *The Christian Doctrine of Reconciliation* (Hodder, 1918).
J. A. Kirk, *Theology Encounters Revolution* (IVP, 1980).
R. Letham, *The Work of Christ* (IVP, 1993).
D. F. Wells, *The Search for Salvation* (IVP, 1978).

Application

THE PERSON OF CHRIST

The fact of God incarnate carries the profoundest application to our entire attitude to life in this world. More particularly it means:

Affirmation

'The Word became flesh' (Jn. 1:14). God has come right to us in Jesus and taken our flesh and blood, our space and time into union with himself. By this fact the importance of the world and human life which follows from God's being creator (Part 2) receives massive endorsement. Despite the usurping powers of darkness, the terrestrial order remains in God's hands and is not so alien to him that he cannot assume a real place within it. By the coming of Jesus, therefore, God sanctifies our life in the flesh. His interest and concern cannot be confined to the inward and spiritual, since the outward and material is also taken into union with him in Christ. By incarnation he lays his hand on the whole of our life. 'There is not a single inch over which Jesus Christ does not say: that is mine' (A. Kuyper). Thus home, employment, friendships, vocation, college, life in society, culture, leisure, everything that goes to make up the content of our days, is claimed by him and can be dedicated to him.

Condescension

'He made himself nothing' (Phil. 2:7). In the incarnation God himself has condescended to minister to his creatures' need (Jn. 13:1–16); a servant God! This staggering event has far-reaching and deeply challenging implications for Christ's disciples: a fundamental humility of heart which renounces selfish ambition and vain conceit, a genuine and compassionate concern for others' interests, considering them better than ourselves (Phil. 2:1–5) – nothing less than a reflection in us of the mind of Jesus.

Concentration

'I have set you an example' (Jn. 13:15). Our Lord's entire life as depicted in the gospels represents one long application, for he is both our redeemer and our example. We are to be like him in his single-minded concern for the Father's glory (Jn. 8:49f.), his life of communion with his Father (Mk. 1:35), his unbroken obedience (Jn. 8:29), his concern for human need (Mt. 9:36), his commitment to mission (Mk. 1:38). Our personal study and meditation on the Scriptures should regularly include a passage from the gospels so that we are daily and deliberately concentrating our gaze upon him. 'Let us fix our eyes on Jesus ... Consider him' (Heb. 12:2f.).

THE DEATH OF CHRIST

Here is the heart and centre of all Christian faith and understanding, preaching and living, serving and dying. It should draw from us:

Wonder

'The Son of God, who loved me and gave himself for me' (Gal. 2:20). The cross is more than a theory of atonement to be mastered with the mind, though the more our understanding of the cross accords with the biblical teaching, the greater will be our sense of wonder in contemplating it. Through the centuries nothing in all of human experience has so affected people's hearts and minds and so moved them to wonder, love and praise as the deed on Calvary; and that is as it should be, for there is quite literally nothing to compare with it. Here above all is a place for silence, for laying our hand to our mouths, for putting our shoes from our feet.

> *Then let us sit beneath his cross,*
> *And gladly catch the healing stream,*
> *All things for him account but loss,*
> *And give up all our hearts to him;*
> *Of nothing think or speak beside,*
> *'My Lord, my Love, is crucified.'*

Challenge

'Christ died for our sins' (1 Cor. 15:3). The biblical gospel of atonement for sin through the death of Christ has been expounded above. We cannot avoid in application asking, has Christ's death brought atonement to *me*? Have I seen my sin and guilt laid on Christ at Calvary, judged and punished there in him? Have I called on him to save me and found grace to trust in his finished work of the cross for forgiveness, peace and righteousness? And if not, may we come now to him and ask him to save us. 'Come to me all you who are weary and burdened ...'; 'whoever comes to me I will never drive away' (Mt. 11:28; Jn. 6:37).

Thanksgiving

'To him who loves us and has freed us from our sins by his blood ... be glory for ever and ever' (Rev. 1:5f.). If we have experienced salvation through the cross, then our deepest beings should cry out in thanksgiving and praise, recognizing that our forgiveness and justification and all the blessings which flow from it derive wholly from God's eternal grace to us in Christ, in particular from the love which led him at the last to Calvary. 'Worthy is the Lamb, who was slain!' (Rev. 5:12).

Confidence

'Therefore ... since we have confidence to enter the Most Holy Place by the blood of Jesus ... let us draw near' (Heb. 10:19, 22). The bearing of all our sin by our Lord Jesus, his atoning sacrifice in all its completeness and sufficiency, means that the barrier of sin between ourselves and God is for ever, like the curtain of separation in the temple (Mk. 15:28), torn asunder and removed. We can therefore draw near to the living God in all his blazing holiness and awesome majesty and say '*Abba*, Father', and know ourselves embraced, welcomed, and affirmed. We are 'accepted in the beloved one', we are eternally at home in the heart of God.

Consecration

'In view of God's mercy, offer your bodies as living sacrifices' (Rom. 12:1). In the light of God's self-giving for us in the cross, we are stripped of every claim to ourselves. Indeed, to the extent that we resist God's will and refuse to consecrate ourselves to him, we are simply expressing our failure to grasp what the cross meant.

> *Were the whole realm of nature mine,*
> *That were an offering far too small;*
> *Love so amazing, so divine,*
> *Demands my soul, my life, my all.*

Mission

'Christ's love compels us ... we implore you on Christ's behalf: Be reconciled to God' (2 Cor. 5:14, 20). To have come to the cross ourselves and experienced there the miracle of free justification, propitiation and redemption is to be under obligation to share the message of the cross with our fellow sinners, in the confidence that the strong grace which has saved us is sufficient to save all who trust it, however great their need or deep their sin. This last application will affect our whole lifestyle, our conversation, the use of our time, the stewardship of our money, the theme and extent of our prayers, as well as our involvement with the evangelistic witness of our local church or Christian group, even the form and location of our life's vocation.

THE RESURRECTION OF CHRIST

Jesus risen from the dead means for the Christian, among so many things:

Joy

'Even though you do not see him now, you believe in him and are filled with an inexpressible and glorious joy' (1 Pet. 1:8). To know that he is there with us, loving us with his own deep, boundless love, is the joy of all joys to the Christian heart.

Peace

He 'was raised to life for our justification' (Rom. 4:25). Jesus risen is the pledge that his atoning sacrifice has truly benefited us: our sin is gone and we are accepted before God in him.

Worship

'Declared to be the Son of God by his resurrection from the dead' (Rom. 1:4). The resurrection further confirms the eternal Godhead of Jesus Christ and therefore the propriety of our worship of him. Like the first disciples we meet the risen Jesus with the confession 'My Lord and my God!' (Jn. 20:28). 'They worshipped him' (Lk. 24:52).

Hope

'Christ has indeed been raised from the dead, the firstfruits of those who have fallen asleep' (1 Cor. 15:20). Death is defeated. Jesus is the firstfruits of the coming harvest of the dead, the firstborn of the sons and daughters of the resurrection. Because he has risen we too will live beyond the grave in God's new order. The resurrection thrusts back the horizons of our existence to the limits of eternity, and this has innumerable implications at every level of our lives. We need not grasp at life here, but are freed to invest it in the service of others; for all this is but preliminary to the everlasting life which awaits us beyond death and is indeed already ours in him.

Victory

'All authority in heaven and on earth has been given to me' (Mt. 28:18). The victory over sin and evil has been truly won. The forces of darkness and despair have done their worst and fallen under Christ's conquering feet. Despite all the contrary evidence sin's 'doom is writ', for God's rule and kingdom belong to our blessed Saviour.

THE ASCENSION OF CHRIST

The ascension was a very significant reality for the first Christian disciples but has lost much of its importance for modern Christians. It is replete with implications for our Christian living.

Security in an insecure world

'All authority has been given to me.' The ascension proclaims the reign of Christ. Wherever we are and whatever our circumstances, he is King and Lord over them. The world is even now within his authority. Nothing can affect or afflict us but by his permission.

Comfort in our suffering

'We have a great high priest who has gone through the heavens' (Heb. 4:14). Christ has carried his humanity into the transcendent being of the Godhead. There is now a human being in the Godhead: ascension means that God has for ever a human heart. This truth is graphically expressed in the vision of the wounded Lamb on the throne (Rev: 5:6). His scars in heaven are signs not of failure to overcome his physical brokenness, but of his compassionate identification with us in all our struggles and sorrows.

Mission in Christ's name

'All authority has been given to me. Therefore go.' The ascended Lord sends out the church to preach the gospel to every creature, to teach, to heal and to minister to every human need in Christ's name. This is not in order to make Jesus king in the world, but because the world's King has sent us.

Resources for all our Christian living and serving

'The promised Holy Spirit [he] has poured out' (Acts 2:33). Jesus exalted in glory sends the Holy Spirit to the church; so, the Spirit binds the body of Christ on earth to its exalted head and through him the victorious life of the head flows into the members. The ascended Jesus gives the gifts of the Spirit (Eph. 4:8–12) and anoints the witnesses of Jesus with power and authority (Acts 1:8). The ascension puts at the church's disposal nothing less than the power which resurrected Jesus and set him at the right hand of God in glory (Eph. 1:19f.).

Promise of Christ's coming reign

'He must reign until he has put all his enemies under his feet' (1 Cor. 15:26). The resurrection and the ascension point irresistibly forward to the return of Christ in glory, when he will come to judge everyone and establish God's eternal kingdom in the new heaven and earth in which righteousness will dwell. To know and worship and serve Christ here is to live in the anticipation of his glorious appearance and everlasting rule in glory. This may appear a somewhat ethereal concept, but, rightly applied, it will shed light over every single activity of our lives.

PART 5
The person and work of the Holy Spirit

18. The person of the Spirit

OLD TESTAMENT TEACHING

The Hebrew for 'Spirit', *rûaḥ*, also means 'wind' or 'breath' (Ps. 148:8; Ezk. 1:4). The 'Spirit of the Lord', however, is always the personal agency of God, denoting God in his activity in the world (Gn. 2:7; Jdg. 11:29; Ps. 139:7). The OT looks forward to a new era, the age of the Spirit of God (Is. 11:2; 44:3; Ezk. 36:27f.; Joel 2:28f.).

NEW TESTAMENT TEACHING

The Greek term for Spirit, *pneuma*, also covers 'wind' and 'breath' (Jn. 3:8; Rev. 11:11). In the NT, with the dawning of the messianic age, the Spirit comes into clearer focus and is prominent in the events relating to the birth of Christ (Mt. 1:18; Lk. 1:35, 41, 67f.; 2:27f.). At Jesus' baptism he appears 'in the form of a dove' (Mt. 3:16) and is associated at a number of points with his mission (Mt. 4:1; 12:28; Lk. 4:14, 18; Heb. 9:14).

In his farewell message to his disciples Jesus refers to the Spirit as the 'Counsellor' (Jn. 14:16, 26; 15:26; 16:7). The Greek word, anglicized as *paraclete*, basically means an advocate who takes up one's case or an ally fighting on one's side: someone who strengthens and encourages. The new age, established through the death and resurrection of Jesus, brought the promised outpouring of the Spirit (Acts 2:1), creating the church and empowering it in its mission to the world. The Christian life in this period between the two comings of Christ is a life in the Spirit (Rom. 5:5; 8:1–17; 1 Cor. 12–14; Gal. 5:16–26).

A personal being

The Holy Spirit is not 'it', an impersonal force or power, but a divine person. Although the Greek noun for 'spirit' is neuter, the Greek NT always calls the Holy Spirit 'he', never 'it' (Jn. 16:13).

The term *paraclete* is essentially personal, referring to a personal agent (Jn. 14:16, *etc.*, *cf.* 1 Jn. 2:1). In Jn. 14:15 Jesus speaks of the Spirit as '*another* paraclete' in addition to himself; it is difficult to see how this parallel can meaningfully be drawn without investing the Spirit with fully personal qualities. Similarly Paul speaks of 'grieving' the Holy Spirit (Eph. 4:30); one can resist a power, but grieve only a person.

A divine being

Scripture witnesses unambiguously to the deity of the Holy Spirit. He is a member of the Godhead, the ever blessed object of our worship, love and praise, who shares the same divine nature as the Father and the Son (Mt. 28:18f.; 2 Cor. 13:14; Eph. 4:4–6).

The Spirit is the 'Spirit of the Lord' (YHWH/*kyrios*) (Jdg. 3:10; 2 Cor. 3:17). Frequently he is referred to as God in his creative and redemptive action (Jb. 33:4; Ps. 51:10f.; Ezk. 37:14; 2 Cor. 3:3). Jesus speaks of the sin against the Holy Spirit as greater than that against the Son of Man (Mt. 12:28–32). Since the Son of Man, Jesus, is divine, this is further testimony to the divinity of the Spirit. Again, since only through God himself can God be known, the Spirit must be divine for he is the one through whom God is revealed to us (1 Cor. 2:10f.; 1 Jn. 5:7–9). Finally, the Trinitarian passages remove any lingering doubt (Mt. 28:19; Jn. 14:15–24; 2 Cor. 13:14; Eph. 1:13f.; 2:18; 2 Thes. 2:13f.; 1 Pet. 1:2f.). In these passages the Spirit stands before us in indissoluble unity of essential Godhead with Father and Son.

Scriptures

Jdg. 3:10; 11:29; Jb. 33:4; Pss. 63:4; 139:7; Is. 11:2; 59:21; 61:1; Ezk. 37:1–4; Hg. 2:4f.; Zc. 7:12; Mt. 3:16; 12:28–32; 28:19; Lk. 1:35; 4:18; Jn. 3:8; 14:16, 26; 15:26;

16:7–15; Acts 13:2; Rom. 8:9f.; 1 Cor. 6:11; 12:3; 2 Cor. 3:3, 17; 13:14; Eph. 1:13f.; 2:18; 4:4–6, 30.

Questions
1. State the biblical evidence for the deity of the Holy Spirit.
2. Explore the implications of the Spirit's Godhood for (a) the authority of the Bible, (b) the person of Jesus Christ who gives the Spirit, (c) the authenticity of Christian experience.

Bibliography
Art. 'Holy Spirit' in *NDT*.
G. D. Fee, *God's Overpowering Presence* (Paternoster, 1996).
G. D. Fee, *Paul, the Spirit and the People of God* (Hodder, 1997).
S. Ferguson, *The Holy Spirit* (IVP, 1996).
M. Green, *I Believe in the Holy Spirit* (Hodder, 1975).
J. Owen, *Works*, 3 (Banner of Truth, 1966).
J. I. Packer, *Keep in Step with the Spirit* (IVP, 1984).

19. The Spirit of promise

THE SPIRIT BEFORE CHRIST'S COMING
The Spirit's work in this period can be gathered round three main themes.

Life
The Spirit is commonly referred to in relation to the creation of the cosmos. Genesis 1:2 can be rendered, 'the Spirit of God brooded over the waters', like a bird hovering over its young (*cf.* Ps. 104:30; Is. 40:12f.). His bringing life out of nothing at the beginning is an important foreshadowing of his NT work of giving life to the people of God, regeneration. The Spirit also gives life to humankind (Jb. 27:3; 33:4; Ps. 104:29f.); hence just as we depend utterly on the constant 'upholding' of the Word (Col. 1:17; Heb. 1:3), so we depend on the continuous life-giving energy of the Spirit.

Knowledge
The Spirit illuminates the mind with the knowledge of God and his truth (Dt. 34:9; Ps. 143:10), particularly in prophetic insight (1 Sa. 10:10), but also in a general capacity for understanding (Gn. 41:38f.). A primary form of this is the production of OT Scripture; he inspired specially chosen, prepared witnesses

whose writings express God's Word (2 Pet. 1:21). This foreshadows his ministry in the NT (Jn. 16:12f.; 1 Cor. 2:9–13; 2 Pet. 3:15f.).

Promise

The link between the Spirit and the promised messianic age is two-fold. First, the Messiah who is to come is himself anointed by the Spirit (Is. 11:2; 42:1; 61:1f.; *cf.* Lk. 4:16–20); second, in the messianic age God's Spirit will be poured out in a special manner and degree (Ezk. 36:27f.; Joel 2:28f.).

THE SPIRIT AND CHRIST

The relationship between Jesus and the Spirit establishes the theological foundation for the Spirit's ministry and is absolutely crucial for a proper view of the work of the Spirit. We can distinguish two aspects of the Spirit's relation to Jesus Christ.

The Spirit received by Christ

The reception of the Spirit by Christ is seen particularly clearly at his baptism, where the 'Holy Spirit descended on him in bodily form like a dove' (Lk. 3:22). The Spirit's role began with Jesus' conception and birth (Lk. 1:35) and continued in his ministry (Mt. 4:1; 12:28). While this in no way diminishes Jesus' deity, we who share humanity with him may see here some indication of that dependence on the Spirit in terms of which we are called to obey and serve God.

The Spirit given by Christ

John the Baptist prophesied that Jesus' ministry would involve his baptizing 'with the Holy Spirit and with fire' (Mt. 3:11). Acts 1:5 (*cf.* 2:33) relates this to the climax of Jesus' ministry in his death and resurrection. This link is explicit in John 7:39: 'the Spirit had not been given, since Jesus had not yet been glorified' (referring to his triumph in death, resurrection and ascension, *cf.* Jn. 13:31; 20:22). This brings us to the key to understanding the ministry of the Holy Spirit in the NT: *the profound connection between the ministry of the Spirit and the glorification of Jesus.*

We recall that the OT associated the coming new age with a new and glorious dispensation of the Holy Spirit. The new age of the kingdom of God was brought in by Jesus and established by his death, resurrection and ascension. Hence the pouring forth of the Spirit at Pentecost was simply the coming into human history of the kingdom of God inaugurated through Jesus' triumph. This is why Jesus states that unless he 'goes away' the Spirit will not come (Jn. 16:7). The point is not that the two persons of the Godhead cannot be co-present, but what Jesus meant by 'going away'; it is only on the basis of his 'going away to the Father' (Jn. 14:5, 12) in death, resurrection and ascension that the Spirit could come upon the disciples, be their paraclete, and bear his witness to the world through them. In other words, *the dispensation of the Spirit in the church and in the world which found glorious initial expression at Pentecost depends utterly on the triumph of Jesus* (Jn. 7:39).

Luke confirms this by deliberately commencing his story of the church's birth and beginnings under the impact of the outpouring of the Spirit (Acts 2:1ff.) with an account of the *ascension* of Jesus (Acts 1:9–11), despite already having recounted the ascension at the conclusion of his 'first treatise', his gospel (Lk. 24:50f.). 'What does this mean?' asked the crowd at Pentecost (Acts 2:12). Peter made two points. First, the outpouring of the Spirit is the coming of the new age of the kingdom: 'This is what was spoken by the prophet...' (2:16–21). Second, it is the result of the exaltation of Jesus Christ; 'This Jesus ... exalted to the right hand of God ... has poured out what you now see and hear' (2:32f., *cf.* 22–36). Paul likewise sets the gifts of the Spirit for the upbuilding of the church in the context of Christ's ascension (Eph. 4:8–10). The gifts of the Spirit are the spoils of the victorious Christ, the fruits of his triumph.

The Holy Spirit is therefore *none other than that member of the eternal Godhead who brings to bear in the life of God's people the fruits of the victory won by Christ in his life, death and glorification.* The ministry of the Spirit is in this sense a 'spilling over' from the throne of God of the blessing wrought by Christ for sinners.

This understanding carries important implications. For one thing it underlines the folly of any attempt to separate the work of the Spirit from the work of Christ. Manifestations of the Spirit, or the pursuit of them, when not related to an overriding concern for the glory of God in Jesus Christ, entirely lack the authorization of the Holy Spirit-inspired Scriptures; they can only harm and counter the great Christian tasks of glorifying God in preaching the gospel and building the church. 'To him

226 The person and work of the Holy Spirit

who sits on the throne and to the Lamb be praise and honour and glory' is the authentic exclamation of the Spirit-filled disciple (Rev. 1:10; 5:13).

Conversely, recognizing the indissoluble link between the ministry of the Spirit and the glorification of Jesus ought to deliver us from fear concerning the ministry of the Holy Spirit. The Spirit is not a 'ghost', an eerie or arbitrary agency. He is 'the Spirit of Jesus' (Acts 16:7) who comes to minister Christ to the Christian community. Alarm at an *authentic* ministry of the Spirit needs the reassurance the disciples received when they saw Jesus walking on the sea of Galilee and cried out for fear it was a ghost: 'Take courage! It is I. Don't be afraid' (Mt. 14:26f.). This also provides a standard with which to test claims to authentic ministries of the Spirit: if they are irreconcilable with the Jesus we meet in the gospels, with his warm compassion and sane humanity, then they can be dismissed. The Spirit is Jesus, in the sense that he seeks to bring Christ to us and bring us into an even fuller appropriation of Christ's redemption blessings.

Scriptures
Old Testament: Gn. 1:2; 2:7; Ex. 31:1–5; 35:31; Nu. 11:17f.; Jdg. 13:25; 1 Sa. 10:10; 1 Ch. 28:12; Jb. 33:4; Ps. 104:30; Is. 11:2; 40:13; 42:1; 44:3f.; 61:1f.; Ezk. 2:2; 36:27f.; Joel 2:28f.; Mi. 3:8.
The Spirit and Christ: Mt. 1:18, 20; 3:11; 4:1; 12:28; Lk. 1:35; 3:16, 22; 4:14, 18; Jn. 3:34; 7:39; 14:5, 17; 16:7; Acts 1:5; 2:32f.; Eph. 4:7–16.

Questions
1. Identify the essential elements of the Spirit's work in the OT. Show how these are developed in the NT.
2. 'The Son is at once the bearer and dispenser of the Spirit.' Does this statement correctly reflect the NT evidence?
3. What implications may be drawn from the fact that the Spirit ministered to Jesus at certain points in his ministry?
4. Examine the biblical passages dealing with the relationship between the work of the Spirit and the work of the Son. What implications does this carry for our experience of the Spirit today?

Bibliography
H. Berkhof, *The Doctrine of the Holy Spirit* (John Knox, 1964).
S. B. Ferguson, *The Holy Spirit* (IVP, 1996).
M. Green, *I Believe in the Holy Spirit* (Hodder, 1975).
T. A. Smail, *Reflected Glory* (Hodder, 1975).

20. The Spirit and Christian beginnings

Christian conversion and growth could have been considered in Part 4 under the title 'The Application of the Work of Christ'. That context would underline the crucial relationship between the work of the second and third Persons in the Godhead; but it might risk obscuring God's genuine self-giving to us in the third Person of the Godhead.

It might also have appeared under Part 6, the doctrine of the church. This would have offset the view that reduces the church to peripheral significance – a help to the Christian, no doubt, and hence worth supporting, but in no way intrinsic to the Christian's existence. Such a view would have surprised the NT writers whose instruction on Christian living is usually contained in letters written to corporate groups, *i.e.* churches.

Dealing with Christian experience in this Part, however, establishes the fundamental truth that all valid Christian experience is the action of the Spirit of God upon and through us. The exposition, however, includes the link between the Spirit's work and Christ's work on the one hand, and the Spirit's work and the church on the other.

THE FOUNDATION: THE GRACE OF GOD

The supreme underlying reality in all Christian experience of the Spirit is God's sovereign grace (Ex. 34:6; Eph. 1:7f.). Grace (Lat. *gratia*; Gk. *charis*; Heb. *ḥēn*) means the free display of favour, particularly by a superior to an inferior. Referred to God, it is that free decision of God, apart from all constraint and in no way compelled by our merit, to have mercy upon his sinful creatures, saving his people from all the effects of their sin, through Jesus Christ (Acts 15:11; Eph. 2:8; Tit. 2:11). The *freedom* of divine grace needs to be underlined. God acts to save because he chooses to; it is a work of God over and above all the requirements of creatorhood; as with Israel, so with the church, it was in no way because of what we were or ever will be (Dt. 7:7f.). God loves and saves his people because he loves and wills to save them. There can be no 'explanation' beyond that.

God's grace is also *sovereign* (Acts 18:27; Rom. 11:5f.; 1 Cor.

15:10). Because it is *God* who purposes to save his people, he will certainly carry that resolve into realization. No power, demonic or human, is able to thwart his purpose. Let God be God! The various facets of Christian experience of the Spirit expounded below are simply distinguishable facets of this foundational reality, the sovereign grace of God in its operation to save sinners.

THE ESSENCE: UNION WITH CHRIST BY THE SPIRIT

The heart of Christian experience of the Holy Spirit lies in his bringing us into a living relationship to Jesus Christ so that we share in his redemption and all its blessings. All Christian experience can be focused in this one gift of God to us through his Spirit, our union with Christ.

The biblical basis of union with Christ lies in the NT's view of faith. Faith is faith 'in' Jesus Christ (Acts 16:30f.; Rom. 3:22; Phil. 3:9f.). The Greek prepositions used with 'believe' (*eis, en, epi*) carry the idea of believing 'into' or 'on' Christ. Faith therefore involves a living relationship to its object; to be a Christian believer means to be united to Christ.

The background to the notion of 'faith-union with Christ' is the OT concept of the solidarity between the Messiah and the messianic people. A Messiah separated from his people was unthinkable; he represented God to his people (Is. 11:9) and the people to God (Je. 30:21). Two of the principal messianic figures, Son of Man and Servant of the LORD, hover accordingly between the individual and the corporate (Dn. 7:13, *cf.* 15ff.; Is. 42:1, *cf.* 41:8f.).

Further, to be united to Christ means being united to him in the whole sweep of his redemptive mission (*cf.* Phil. 2:5–11). The Christian has died *with Christ* (Rom. 6:1–11; Gal. 2:20), has been resurrected *with Christ* (Eph. 2:5f.; Col. 3:1f.), has ascended *with Christ* to share now his reign in the heavenly places (Rom. 5:17; Eph. 2:6), and is destined to share Christ's coming glory *with him* (Phil. 3:20f.; 1 Jn. 3:2). The work of the Spirit in regenerating the believer is therefore a work in which the Spirit unites us to Christ. 'The Holy Spirit is the bond by which Christ effectively unites us to himself' (Calvin). The principal elements of this union are our election, calling, regeneration, repentance, faith, justification and adoption.

Election

This refers to that work of God's grace whereby he chooses individuals and groups for a purpose or destiny in accordance with his will. It occurs in the OT first with reference to Abraham (Gn. 11:31–12:7) and then with reference to his seed, the people of Israel (Ex. 3:6–10). It is also referred to the Messiah (Is. 42:1f.; 53:10f.). In the NT Jesus is in a special sense the object of election (Lk. 9:35; 1 Pet. 2:4f.).

The church is referred to as the elect (Mt. 22:14; Mk. 13:20; Lk. 18:7; 1 Pet. 2:9). This has been the occasion of considerable debate and uncertainty. This is greatly to be regretted, as election properly understood is *good* news. God has claimed us from all eternity! His grace has triumphed over all the opposition of our sin and rebellion, and over all the accusations of the evil one. We are his forever; God is for us; he always has been, he always will be. He has chosen us as his own. Praise be to his name!

Difficulties surrounding this great biblical and Christian doctrine can be confronted by noting the following truths concerning election.

It is a *revealed* truth, disclosed in Scripture. It is therefore to be received humbly from God and tenaciously believed along with all other revealed truths.

It is a *Christian* truth to be met only from within the experience of regeneration by God's grace. It is not an explicit part of the gospel which the Christian presents to the unbeliever. It ought not to inhibit the universal appeal of Christian evangelism (Mt. 28:18f.; Acts 1:8).

It is a *trinitarian* truth. Election is not only related to the Father. Jesus Christ elects (Jn. 15:16) and the ministry of the Holy Spirit is also referred to in the context of election (1 Pet. 1:2).

It is a *Christological* truth. In the NT the eternal purpose of God centres in the person and work of the second Person of the Trinity; Scripture does not present it as an arbitrary decision of the Father taken in eternity in total isolation from the ministry and will of the Son. There is an indissoluble link and identity between Father and Son. People are 'chosen in Christ' (Eph. 1:4); the elect are saved only through Christ's work of atonement (Rom. 8:29f.; Eph. 1:7f.). All the blessings of the elect come through Christ (Eph. 1:3), *i.e.* through their union with him. Any attempt to separate finally the Father from the Son and

Spirit in election, or to move the centre of attention in the Christian doctrine of salvation from the person and work of Christ, is unbiblical and therefore harmful.

It is a *complementary* truth. Election must be held in relation to, or in tension with, the Bible's clear insistence on human responsibility in face of God's summons in the gospel (Mt. 23:37; Heb. 12:25). To stress only one of these clear strands of Scripture and effectively ignore the other is to put asunder what God has joined together.

It is a *divine* truth. The relationship between human freedom and divine election can never be fully grasped by the human intellect. Both aspects are taught in Scripture and both are to be believed. If we acknowledge that mystery is inevitable in any attempt to describe God himself, then we should neither be surprised nor stumble at the presence of mystery where this transcendent God relates himself to us.

It is a *practical* truth. Like all Bible truths, election is given for the good and growth of the people of God. Danger will always exist in handling this doctrine where people fail to observe the Bible's practical context, which can be focused in three words:

1. *Doxology.* Discussion of this matter has too often overlooked the fact that Paul's fullest treatment of election is a piece of doxological writing. Ephesians 1:1–14 is one unbroken outburst of praise. Paul is not standing at his desk engaged in dialectical argumentation; rather he is on his knees, lost in adoring worship. If we are honest, one of the major objections which we have to election is that it takes the basis of our salvation out of our hands, for it implies that even our response to God is made possible by his grace. Our salvation is all gift. To see this is to be released as never before to worship, adore and praise.

2. *Security.* In Romans 8 Paul points to another implication, the utter security election brings to the child of God in face of every threat, moral (v. 33), physical (v. 35) or spiritual (v. 38; *cf.* Jn. 10:28).

3. *Holiness.* Israel's election involved strenuous and demanding service (Lv. 18:4f.; 19:2f.; 20:22f.; Ezk. 20:5–7). God's election is never thought of as the passport to self-excusing moral laxity ('What does it matter? I'll be saved in the end anyway'). Paul shrinks back horrified from any suggestion of 'taking advantage of grace' (Rom. 6); rather, election finds its goal in our being 'holy and blameless in his sight' (Eph. 1:4). The historical

evidence from nations such as the Netherlands and Scotland, where belief in election has been a significant factor in the shaping of national character, refutes the idea that this conviction undermines moral motivation; quite the reverse.

Related issues

1. *Foreknowledge.* One way of relieving the tension between sovereign divine election and human freedom is to argue that election is simply a matter of foreknowledge. The all-knowing God, seeing how individuals will respond to the gospel, 'elects' those who he foreknows will freely respond. Despite its appeal to Romans 8:29, this view effectively empties election of real significance, since it thereby ceases to be the triumphant *action of God*. It also founders on the meaning of 'knowledge'. In Scripture knowledge, particularly with reference to God, means more than an intellectual awareness; behind the Greek of Romans 8:29 is the Hebrew *yāda‘*, which means 'know' in the sense of entering into relationship with (Gn. 4:1; Am. 3:2). God's foreknowing is not merely passive; it is a synonym for his active election, rather than an explanation of it.

2. *Reprobation.* This is the view that God has not only elected certain individuals to salvation, but has also elected certain individuals to damnation. Calvin, not surprisingly, referred to this as 'an awesome decree'. While logically the election of some implies the rejection of others, Scripture is clearly reluctant to set these two ideas in strict balance. The passage most commonly appealed to (Rom. 9:14–24) needs to be read in its context: it refers to the special case of Israel, *not* to humankind in general. 1 Peter 2:8 and Jude 4 are clearer references to reprobation, but these verses also maintain human responsibility ('they disobey', 1 Pet. 2:8; 'godless men, who change the grace of our God into a licence for immorality and deny Jesus Christ', Jude 4). Even over people's decision to reject him, God remains Lord. Scripture, however, remains unwilling to carry election to its logical counterpart in a full doctrine of reprobation.

Calling

This refers to that work of God by his Spirit in which he summons men and women to come to him and receive his mercy in Jesus Christ. The thought of God 'calling' is common in Scripture (Gn. 3:9; Ex. 3:4; 1 Sa. 3:4; Is. 43:1; Je. 7:13; Jn. 10:3). In particular, God calls through the proclamation of the gospel, whether in formal 'preaching' or through some other means (Eph. 1:11–13; 2 Thes. 2:13f.). God's sovereign grace does not operate in an impersonal or arbitrary manner but always through personal, purposeful means. He personally addresses his creatures, graciously and patiently calling them to turn to him and trust in his mercy in Christ.

It belongs to the mystery of human unbelief that not all who hear God's call through the gospel respond to it. Accordingly, we can draw a distinction between God's *general* call, by which he summons all who hear the gospel to come to him (Mt. 9:13), and God's *effective* call, in which God's summons leads to a response of repentance and faith in Christ (Rom. 1:6; 8:28, 30; 1 Pet. 1:15). This distinction can be clearly observed in Jesus' teaching (Mt. 22:14).

Regeneration

Regeneration literally means 'born over again', or 'rebirth'. The OT referred to a future work of the Spirit by which he would reside 'within' the people of God, bringing them new life and enabling them to fulfil God's will (Ezk. 36:25f., *cf.* Je. 31:33). In the NT Jesus speaks to Nicodemus of regeneration by the Spirit as the only means of entry to the kingdom of God (Jn. 3:1–8). Other biblical terminology closely echoes these references: 'born of God' (1 Jn. 2:29; 3:9; 4:7; 5:4, 18; Jn. 1:13), 'born again by the Word' (1 Pet. 1:23, *cf.* Jas. 1:18), 'new creation' (2 Cor. 5:17; Gal. 6:15), 'created' by God (Eph. 2:10; 4:24).

Regeneration marks the moment and the means of our coming into union with Christ. It is an instantaneous change from spiritual death to spiritual life, a spiritual resurrection (Eph. 2:1, 5), the once-for-all event at the beginning of the Christian life, parallel to physical birth. It differs from conversion, with which it is closely associated, in emphasizing God's action in giving new life; conversion is the human act of turning from sin to righteousness, which accompanies regeneration. Through regeneration the believer receives a new spiritual nature which will express itself in new concerns and interests. The regenerate are primarily concerned with 'the things of God', his Word, his people, his service, his glory, above all God himself. They will also experience new powers to resist sin and obey and serve God.

It is a mistake to assume that regeneration must necessarily have certain conscious emotional accompaniments. Our awareness of change in outlook, desires, attitudes may be gradual and scarcely perceptible. Those reared in Christian homes and taught the gospel from infancy may be drawn to Christ and reach adult life with a clear faith in Christ but with no specific, single crisis to which they can point as the moment of their new birth. Christian 'testimonies' can be unhelpful here if they imply that every person must be able to point to a specific time and place as the moment of regeneration. Such is commonly the case, but it need not be so. Indeed, some who experience an emotional and 'spiritual' crisis subsequently give evidence of almost certainly never having been regenerated at all. This point was helpfully made by C. H. Spurgeon, who remarked that our ignorance of the precise time of our birth is no evidence that we are not alive! The proof of regeneration by the Spirit is the believer's own inward persuasion that Christ is indeed Lord and Saviour and the evidences of the Spirit's life in and through us.

Repentance

This literally means a 'change of one's mind'. In biblical contexts it refers to a changed mind concerning sin and evil. It is seen in the Bible as a fundamental element in human response to God and commonly linked with faith; we turn *from* sin *to* Christ (Mk. 1:15; Acts 2:38; 20:21). Conversion, literally 'change of direction', is closely related.

God's call to repentance is a reminder of the fundamentally moral character of the gospel and the new life which issues from a response to it. The gospel is essentially concerned with human sin and God's remedy for it. Repentance is an element in all genuine response to the gospel. Conversely the absence of any changed attitude to sin is evidence that a person is not truly regenerate (1 Jn. 3:9).

Like faith, repentance is not confined to the earliest moments of Christian experience. Christians are called to life-long repentance, an ever-repeated turning away from sin as it is revealed to us. This spirit of repentance or brokenness before God, the daily dying to self and sin, is a mark not of spiritual adolescence but of closeness to God and genuine maturity.

Faith

Faith is fundamental to all genuine Christian experience. Without faith it is 'impossible to please God' (Heb. 11:6). It may be provisionally defined as 'trust in the truth of Jesus Christ crucified and risen'.

Faith is *trust*. It involves active personal commitment to God in Christ and not simply an awareness of God's reality. In this latter sense the devil and the demons are 'believers' (Jas. 2:19). The devil is no atheist, or agnostic; he is agonizingly aware of the reality of God and of his redemption in Christ. But he is in no sense committed to God; he does not have faith.

Faith is trust in *truth*. It rests on an objective reality; it is the correlative of the truth of God's revelation in Christ and the gospel. As Luther stated, vindicating his dogmatic disputes in defence of the gospel, 'there is no Christianity where there are no assertions ...' Amending or reducing the content of the gospel in the interests of effective communication to modern people is therefore a perilous undertaking which is finally self-destructive, since it inevitably weakens faith or even renders it impossible by removing the basis upon which faith rests.

Faith is trust in the truth of *Jesus Christ, crucified and risen*. The objective content on which it reposes is the Christ of the gospel, who was 'delivered over to death for our sins and was raised for our justification' (Rom. 4:25; *cf.* Jn. 1:12; 3:16; Acts 16:30f.; Rom. 10:9). Faith in Christ means commitment to him as the one who died and rose for us personally. It means being united to Christ.

Justification

Justification is that work of God's grace whereby sinners through their faith-union with Christ are accounted righteous before God on the grounds of Christ's obedience and death (see also Part 4). It is crucial to recognize that justification refers to the *status* of righteousness which God grants the believer and not primarily to actual intrinsic righteousness. It is this fact which is the basis of the Christian's peace, security and joy. Sinners as we are, we are accepted – *not* on the ground of our feeble efforts to obey God adequately, but on his crediting us with the perfect righteousness of Christ.

Does this, then, mean that *how* a justified believer lives is irrelevant? This has been long discussed; indeed, the NT appears at first reading to speak with two voices: 'You see that a man is justified by works and not by faith alone' (Jas. 2:24, RSV); 'we hold that a man is justified by faith apart from works of the law' (Rom. 3:28, RSV). The apparent contradiction between James and Paul dissolves when we note their different use of terminology and the different errors they address.

Faith in James' discussion is equivalent to the intellectual acceptance of monotheism (2:14), the kind of faith which demons possess and which we distinguished above from the full NT meaning of faith, personal trust in Christ. Works for James means to 'keep the royal law found in Scripture, "Love your neighbour as yourself"' (Jas. 2:8). Paul uses the term to refer to works of the law done specifically to *earn* salvation apart from Christ. Thus Romans 3:28 speaks of living faith and self-justifying works, while James 2:24 speaks of merely nominal faith and spontaneous, God-honouring works. Righteousness for James means a person's actual moral character, while in Paul it usually occurs in the context of justification, meaning a 'given', credited righteousness. When Paul thinks of future judgment, he too introduces the issue of conduct (Rom. 2:6; 2 Cor. 5:10). He is as concerned as James for 'faith expressing itself through love' (Gal. 5:6) and utterly repugns moral laxity among the justified (Rom. 6:1f.).

Paul was grappling with the Jewish confidence in meritorious good works as the ground of salvation, against which he proclaimed salvation by grace through faith alone. James faced a different problem, a dead orthodoxy which 'believed' but saw no moral implications from this. He wished to stir his readers by the reminder that a faith which does not change our daily life is spurious and dead. Thus for both James and Paul faith and works are both essential to genuine response to God. Good 'works' have a place, not as the basis of justification, but as its inevitable outcome.

It is crucial to understand justification as 'in Christ' (Gal. 2:17), *i.e.* as part of what God imparts to us when we believe in Christ and are thus united to him (see above on 'Union with Christ'). Faith means that 'Jesus and all in him is mine', to quote Wesley. But 'all in him' means not only all of his righteousness, but by implication all the other believers who are also united with him by faith. In other words, justification is finally a corporate and ecclesial reality. It affirms our participation in the body of Christ, the covenant people of God.

Adoption

Adoption refers to that work of God's grace by which he receives us as his very own children through Christ and in our union with him. The practice of legal adoption was widespread in the ancient world. There are examples of it in the OT (Ex. 2:10; 1 Ki. 11:20; Est. 2:7) and the idea is present in the description of Israel as God's son (Ex. 4:22; Ho. 11:1). In the first century under Roman law an adult wanting an heir could adopt a male, commonly of adolescent or maturer years, a custom readily transferable to the Christian's new relationship to God. Paul makes particular use of it (Rom. 8:14–17; Gal. 4:1–7; Eph. 1:5; *cf.* 1 Jn. 3:1f.).

When we recall what we were in our sins, the thought of adoption speaks most powerfully of the magnitude of God's mercy to us. That we should be pardoned all our sin is wonder enough; but that the pardoned rebels should become God's very sons and daughters, installed within the intimacy of his own family circle, is surely wonder beyond wonder.

Adoption implies that the Christian life is, first, life with God as Father (Rom. 8:15; Gal. 4:6). Both these verses speak of our using the word *Abba* in address to God. This is the very word which Jesus had made his own in his prayers and which means 'my own dear Father.'

Secondly, it is also life with others. 'Adoption' teaches us to see our fellow Christians as brothers and sisters in the family of God. Here is possibly the deepest word we can speak about our Christian relationships; we belong together in God's one great family drawn from all nations and generations.

Thirdly, adoption means life with Christ as our elder brother (Rom. 8:14, 29; Heb. 2:10f.). In the Roman world, the adopted son was granted full legal status in the family alongside any other natural sons. He could even be nominated by the father as legal heir over the claims of his natural children. What a wonder this is! We are given full status within the family of God along with the 'natural' Son of the Father, the Lord Jesus Christ.

Finally, adoption expresses the certainty of our hope (Rom. 8:14; Gal. 4:6). We are heirs of God, co-heirs with Christ. In his free grace the Father gives us the right to a share in his coming glory in Christ.

Scriptures

The grace of God: Gn. 6:8; 12:1ff.; 15:1–5; Ex. 34:6; Dt. 7:7f.; Ne. 9:31; Ps. 145:8; Jn. 1:14–17; Acts 15:11; 18:27; Rom. 3:24; 5:15–21; 11:5f.; 2 Cor. 8:9; Eph. 1:7f.; 2:8; Tit. 2:11.

Union with Christ: Dn. 7:13–18; Jn. 15:1–16; Rom. 5:12–6:14; Gal. 2:20; Eph. 2:5–10; Col. 3:1–4; 2 Tim. 2:11–13.

Election: Gn. 11:31–12:7; 1 Ch. 16:13; Is. 42:1; Mt. 3:17; 22:14; 24:22, 24, 31; Lk. 9:35; 18:7; Jn. 15:16, 19; Acts 2:23; 4:28; 9:15; 13:48; Rom. 8:29f., 33; 9:11; 11:5, 7, 28; 1 Cor. 1:27f.; Eph. 1:5, 11; Col. 3:12; 2 Tim. 2:9f.; Tit. 1:1; Jas. 2:5; 1 Pet. 1:2; 2:4; 6, 9; 2 Pet. 1:10; Rev. 17:14.

Calling: Gn. 3:9; Ex. 3:4; 1 Sa. 3:4; Is. 49:1; Joel 2:32; Mt. 9:13; Mk. 1:20; Jn. 10:3; Acts 2:39; Rom. 1:6f.; 4:17; 8:28–30; 9:11, 24f.; 1 Cor. 1:2, 24, 26; Gal. 1:15; 1 Thes. 2:12; 2 Thes. 1:11; 2:13f.; 2 Tim. 1:9; Heb. 3:1; 1 Pet. 1:15; 2 Pet. 1:10.

Regeneration: Je. 31:33; Ezk. 36:25f.; 37:1–14; Jn. 1:12f.; 3:1–8; Rom. 8:9; 1 Cor. 12:13; 2 Cor. 5:17; Gal. 6:15; Tit. 3:5; Jas. 1:18; 1 Pet. 1:23; 1 Jn. 5:4, 18.

Repentance: Jb. 42:6; Ezk. 14:6; 18:30; Joel 2:12ff.; Mt. 3:2; 11:20f.; 12:41; Mk. 1:15; 6:12; Lk. 15:17–19; Acts 2:38; 3:19; 8:22; 17:30; 26:20; 2 Cor. 7:10; Rev. 2:5; 16:9.

Faith: Gn. 15:6; Ex. 14:31; 2 Ch. 20:20; Ps. 116:10; Pr. 3:5f.; Is. 7:9; Hab. 2:4; Mt. 8:13; 9:22; 21:21f.; Mk. 9:23f.; Lk. 8:48, 50; 22:32; Jn. 1:12; 3:15–18, 36; 11:25f.; 14:1; Acts 3:16; 8:37; 10:43; 15:9; 16:31; Rom. 1:16f.; 5:1; 10:9f.; 1 Cor. 1:21; 15:14; Gal. 2:20f.; 3:22–29; Eph. 1:13; 2:8; 3:17; Phil. 3:9; Col. 2:12; 2 Thes. 2:13; 2 Tim. 4:7; Heb. 10:39–11:39; 1 Jn. 5:1–4, 10; Jude 3.

Justification: Jb. 25:4; Ps. 143:2; Hab. 2:4; Lk. 18:14; Acts 13:39; Rom. 3:21–4:25; 8:30, 33; 1 Cor. 6:11; Gal. 2:15–3:29; 1 Tim. 3:16; Jas. 2:14–26.

Adoption: Ex. 4:23; Is. 1:2; Je. 3:19; Ho. 11:1; Mt. 5:9; Lk. 6:35; 20:36; Jn. 1:12; Rom. 8:14–17, 21; 9:4, 8; Gal. 3:26; 4:1–7; 5:6; Eph. 1:5; 5:1; Heb. 2:10–14; 1 Jn. 3:1f., 10.

Questions

1. What does Scripture mean by 'grace'? Discuss the view that it is the primary term in the Christian's vocabulary.
2. What do you understand by 'union with Christ'? Explore its implications for (a) Christian salvation, (b) Christian service, (c) Christian fellowship, (d) Christian discipleship.
3. What is 'divine election'? What light is thrown on it by the election of Israel? Assess biblically the claims made for (a) foreknowledge as the basis of election, (b) reprobation. What are the implications of election for (a) the Christian's assurance of salvation, (b) Christian worship, (c) Christian hope for the future?
4. Does the Bible make a distinction between God's general and effective calling?
5. What does regeneration mean? Must it be consciously experienced? What implications does it carry for our understanding of the work of the Spirit in general and in particular for our evangelism?
6. What are the respective places of faith and works in relation to our justification and to the Christian gospel?
7. What is meant by adoption? What are its implications for (a) the Christian's thanksgiving, (b) the Christian's self-image, (c) Christian fellowship, (d) the Christian's prospects beyond death?
8. Explain as simply and fully as you can what is meant by 'believing in

Christ'. What does repentance mean and what place does it have (a) in the gospel, (b) for Christian living (*cf.* Rev. 2:5, 16; 3:3, 19)?

Bibliography

Arts. 'Grace', 'Election', 'Regeneration', 'Calling', 'Repentance', 'Faith', 'Justi-fication', 'Adoption' in *IBD* and *NDT*.

G. C. Berkouwer, *Divine Election* (Eerdmans, 1960).

G. C. Berkouwer, *Faith and Justification* (Eerdmans, 1954).

H. Burkardt, *The Biblical Doctrine of Regeneration* (Paternoster, 1980).

J. Calvin, *Institutes of the Christian Religion*, 3.

S. B. Ferguson, *The Christian Life* (Hodder, 1981).

S. B. Ferguson, *The Holy Spirit* (IVP, 1996).

D. M. Lloyd-Jones, *Romans 8:5–17 – The Sons of God* (Banner of Truth, 1974).

M. Luther, *Commentary on Galatians* (James Clarke, 1953).

J. Murray, *Redemption Accomplished and Applied* (Banner of Truth, 1961).

J. I. Packer, *Keep in Step with the Spirit* (IVP, 1984).

21. The Spirit and Christian growth

HOPE

In our earlier section we identified the essence of the Holy Spirit's work in us as lying in his uniting us with Christ (pp. 228–236). We also noted that this union with Christ involves our sharing with him in the whole movement of his redemptive action: life, death, resurrection, ascension and heavenly reign (Rom. 6:1f.; Eph. 2:6; Col. 3:1f.). One of the glorious fruits of this amazing reality is Christian hope. This follows inevitably from the fact that our participation in Christ includes his resurrection and exaltation. The presence of the Spirit is therefore marked by the presence of hope (*cf.* 1 Cor. 13:13; Gal. 5:5; Eph. 1:18 with 1:13f.; 4:4). Hope, the assured and joyful anticipation of the future triumph of God's purposes and the glorious coming of our Lord Jesus, is a shining mark of the religion of the NT (*cf.* Rom. 5:2; Col. 1:4; 1:27; Tit. 2:13; 3:7; 1 Pet. 1:3f.). Paul speaks of it vividly as a 'helmet, the hope of salvation', which is accordingly a basic, crowning feature of Christian discipleship (1 Thes. 5:8). Despite the 'painful trial' which was regularly their lot as they lived out their faith in an increasingly hostile environment, they were sustained in an irrepressible hope and joy by the reality of their risen Lord and the assurance of their future, heavenly life with him (1 Pet. 4:12; 1:3–9).

The link between the Holy Spirit's indwelling presence in our lives and our future hope is secured also from the perspective of the Spirit himself (see below, 'The Holy Spirit and the End'). The Holy Spirit is the life of the kingdom of God already present (Peter's point at Pentecost, *cf.* Acts 2:16–21). But the fullness of the kingdom will be experienced in the future when the Lord returns. The Spirit is therefore the 'first instalment' or 'downpayment' (Eph. 1:14; 2 Cor. 1:22; 5:5) of the full inheritance. He is quite literally 'glory begun below'. Not surprisingly, therefore, he imparts to the disciples, as a basic fruit of his presence, an assurance of the 'hope of glory'.

ASSURANCE

The hopeful confidence with respect to the future which we have just identified with respect to God's total purpose is also experienced by the Christian at the personal level as the assurance of salvation. This is another fruit of the Holy Spirit's presence in our lives: 'this is how we know that he lives in us: we know it by the Spirit he gave us' (1 Jn. 3:24). In similar vein Paul refers to the Holy Spirit as a 'seal' (2 Cor. 1:22; Eph. 1:13; 4:30), a word in the first-century world for something which guaranteed security, such as a locking device (Mt. 27:66; Rev. 20:3). It had the allied meaning of a mark of ownership. Something of this is expressed in the Spirit's coming on Jesus at his baptism, when the Father affirmed Jesus as his own Son (Mt. 3:16f.). It is applied to Christian experience in verses concerning the Spirit's witness within the believer (Rom. 8:16; Gal. 4:6; 1 Jn. 3:24; 4:13; 5:10).

Subjectively, this experience of assurance consists in an inward peace of conscience concerning our standing with God, the firm persuasion that Christ's merits atone for our sins and that we have been brought into light, freedom and sonship in Christ. This subjective persuasion has an objective point of reference, the 'inward witness of the Spirit' (*cf.* Part 1), which is a persuasion concerning the truth and divinity of the written Scriptures centred in the gospel of Christ. In practice either of these persuasions can vary, indeed they can vary relative to each other. It is possible to be persuaded of the truth and validity of the Word of God and the gospel it enshrines, while doubting whether it really includes us; conversely, we can be sure of our standing in Christ, while questioning God's Word in some particular respects. Neither condition represents God's full intention for his children. True assurance persuades at both objective and subjective levels.

What ought we to do if doubts about our standing in Christ should ever come to us? First, these doubts do not mean we are unregenerate; the devil is 'the accuser of our brothers' (Rev. 12:10). 'I believe; help my unbelief!' is a cry of the believer (Mk. 9:24, RSV).

Secondly, we should read the Word of God and listen to it being expounded. The Spirit used Scripture to bring us assurance of salvation initially; that continues to be his way. Calvin's maxim is sound: 'To be assured of our salvation we must begin with the Word.'

Third, we should look for evidences of the work of God in our lives. This can be precarious since only God can judge truly (1 Cor. 4:3f.), but 1 John gives identifiable marks of grace. One of these is our attitude to sin; true children of God, though they regularly fall into sin, cannot continue carelessly in sin (3:9). Hence a real concern to be free of sin is a mark of grace. Another mark is our attitude to God's children. The true Christian will love God's people. 'We know that we have passed from death to life, because we love our brothers' (3:14). A third evidence is our approach to God's truth. 'Everyone who believes that Jesus is the Christ is born of God' (5:1). Commitment to the truth of Christ as God manifested in the flesh is a further sign of our regeneration.

Fourth, we should observe the role of the gospel sacraments in deepening and confirming faith.

Some claim that assurance of salvation is not possible before God's final judgment, that indeed it represents an act of presumption; others say that assurance is confined to a privileged minority. Scripture, however, clearly holds out to every Christian the privilege of knowing that they are God's children. It is obviously implied by our adoption, for what father would willingly leave his children in perpetual uncertainty about their relationship to him or about their status within the family? Our heavenly Father is pleased to give us through his Spirit a firm assurance that he has received us.

SANCTIFICATION

Having brought us to birth 'in Christ', the Spirit continues to work upon us to conform us more and more to the image of the

Christ with whom he has united us. This process of moral renewal and transformation is commonly referred to as sanctification.

The meaning of sanctification

The root idea of 'sanctify' is to 'set apart' or 'consecrate'. This root meaning is really akin to 'justify', since it refers to a once-for-all reality: our being set apart by God for his own possession (Acts 26:18; 1 Pet. 1:2). But it has a second meaning in Scripture which now prevails in theological usage: the attainment of intrinsic holiness of character (Lv. 11:44f.; 1 Thes. 4:3; 5:23; *cf.* 2 Cor. 3:17f.). Scripture's lack of a single term to refer to the growth in holiness of God's people, and its use of a term rooted in the once-for-all status we receive in faith-union with Christ, underline the impossibility of separating the crisis of renewal from subsequent moral transformation. In theological terms, justification (a once-for-all act affording the Christian righteous standing before God) cannot be separated from sanctification (the life-long process of moral transformation into more of Christ's image).

Sanctification by the Spirit

The crucial role of the Spirit is underlined in the language used of the Christian life: 'live in accordance with the Spirit' (Rom. 8:5; *cf.* Gal. 5:16); 'the kingdom of God is ... righteousness, peace and joy in the Holy Spirit' (Rom. 14:17, *cf.* Acts 9:31). In the moral transformation of the believer he produces 'the fruit of the Spirit ... love, joy, peace, patience, kindness, goodness, faithfulness, gentleness and self-control' (Gal. 5:22f.). Particular place is given in the NT to the fruit of *love* (Mt. 25:31–46; Lk. 7:47; Jn. 13:34f.; 17:21; Rom. 5:5; 1 Thes. 4:9; 1 Jn. 3:11–18). It is supremely set forth in 1 Corinthians 13, where Paul describes the various ingredients of Spirit-born love in the Christian community. It is truly 'the greatest' (1 Cor. 13:13).

Sanctification in Christ

The Spirit's ministry in sanctification must be understood from the perspective of the fundamental, indissoluble relationship between Christ and the Spirit. It is a common error to present the Christian life as a two-stage process whereby the beginning (justification) is concerned with Christ, and the continuation (sanctification) is concerned with the Holy Spirit. Rather, sanctification is as much a work of Christ as is justification (Eph. 5:26f.).

The heart of sanctification: union with Christ

Sanctification is essentially that process whereby the Spirit makes increasingly real in our lives our union with Christ in his death and resurrection. There are two far-reaching implications.

First, the Christian life is a matter of becoming in intrinsic character what we already are in Christ. 'Become what you are' is the sum of the call to holy living (Eph. 5:8). Faith means union with Christ by the Holy Spirit in the whole sweep of his redemption, and that means that *all* Christians, however new or immature their faith, have died with Christ, been raised with Christ, are ascended in Christ and will share Christ's glory. 'I have been crucified with Christ and I no longer live, but Christ lives in me' (Gal. 2:20). That is simply a definition of a Christian. The implications of these amazing truths are, of course, appropriated by Christians to an infinite variety of degree. Even the saintliest realize them only in a measure, but they remain true for all. The Christian life in this sense is grace from beginning (when we first believe in Christ) to end (when he shares his glory with us). God has united us with his Son; it is ours to believe and receive and to live thankfully in the light of it, and in this the Holy Spirit is our helper as he brings more and more of Christ's triumph to realization in our lives (2 Cor. 3:18).

Secondly, the Christian life is inescapably corporate. Teaching on Christian holiness has frequently concentrated almost exclusively on the 'holy man' or the 'holy woman', to the neglect of the biblical concern for 'the holy people' or the 'holy church'. The ideal of the 'omnicompetent Christian individual', able to meet every spiritual challenge and live a life of unbroken victory over sin and the devil, has undoubtedly produced remarkable examples of Christian character; but, as every Christian counsellor knows, this emphasis has driven many to a lonely struggle ending in despair and disillusionment, or, worse, in the hypocrisy of a double-standard life.

This whole approach needs re-examination. The bulk of NT teaching on the Christian life, including the major sections on holiness, occur in letters addressed to corporate groups, to churches. All the major exhortations to holy living are plural –

'we', 'you' (Rom. 6:1–23; Gal. 5:13–6:10; Eph. 4:17–6:18) – including exhortations to 'put on the full armour of God' (Eph. 6:11–18; Col. 3:1–17; 1 Thes. 4:1–12; 1 Pet. 1:13–2:12; *cf.* Mt. 5–7). Similarly, all the NT promises of victory are corporate (1 Cor. 15:57; 1 Jn. 5:4; Rev. 15:2). In other words, the apostles envisaged the Christian life and Christian sanctification in the context of a loving, caring fellowship. Individual weaknesses, character defects, personality problems, which we all have, are complemented, supported, healed and compensated for by the other members of the body of Christ. This must not be misunderstood, for God *does* deal with us directly as individuals: *each* Christian is summoned to costly, personal repentance from sin, and to the highest standards of holiness. This recognition of the corporate aspect is no road to moral compromise; rather, it is a road to Christian sanity, realism and wholeness.

The future perspective of sanctification

The 'has come'/'still to come' tension of the kingdom of God (see Part 7) is mirrored in the life of Christians. We are already within the kingdom of God through our union with Christ (Col. 1:13) and now 'sit in heavenly places' in Christ by the Spirit. But we still experience the old era of decay and corruption, of sin and physical death. The NT expresses this tension in a number of ways. The 'old man' or 'old self', *i.e.* what we once were 'in Adam' under condemnation, has been crucified with Christ (Rom. 6:6; Col. 3:9); none the less we have to mortify our fallen human nature with its evil desires and propensities (Rom. 8:12f.; Gal. 5:16f.; Col. 3:5f.). Again, the devil has been overthrown and defeated in Christ (Jn. 12:31; Col. 2:15), yet the Christian is called to warfare against the devil (Eph. 6:12f.; 1 Pet. 5:8f.).

Similarly, while at times the realities of faith stand out sharp and certain, and our commitment is correspondingly clear and wholehearted, at other times we are called on to hold fast our convictions though everything seems to stand against them, and to battle on against world, flesh and devil even though the heavenly powers appear conspicuously absent. This believing 'in spite of' belongs to the reality of our situation before the fullness of the kingdom.

Christians know that this present state of affairs will not continue indefinitely. He who has begun his good work in us has sworn to carry it to its completion at the coming Day of Christ

(Phil. 1:6). We are destined to be 'like him' (1 Jn. 3:2).

> *Sin, my worst enemy before,*
> *Shall vex my eyes and ears no more;*
> *My inward foes shall all be slain,*
> *Nor Satan break my peace again.*
>
> (Isaac Watts)

What a prospect! And it is certain as the dawn. This very prospect is a most potent incentive to press on with the work of sanctification in the grace and power of the Spirit, until that coming day when the people of God will be presented spotless to their heavenly Bridegroom (Eph. 5:26f.; Rev. 21:1f.).

Questions about sanctification
Crisis or process?

Does sanctification take place gradually or in a definable crisis experience: a 'second blessing', 'baptism', 'fullness', 'perfect love', 'clean heart', 'full assurance', or whatever?

Union with Christ by the Spirit, and the Christian life as an appropriation of what we already have through that union, support a processive understanding of sanctification. This finds confirmation in other NT statements. 'I die every day' (1 Cor. 15:31); 'we always carry around in our body the death of Jesus' (2 Cor. 4:10); 'being renewed' (Col. 3:10); 'being transformed into his likeness with ever-increasing glory' (2 Cor. 3:18); 'grow up into him' (Eph. 4:15); 'as you used to offer . . . your body . . . to ever-increasing wickedness, so now offer [it] in slavery to righteousness leading to holiness' (Rom. 6:19).

This need not rule out crises in experience. Manifestly God has periodically dealt with his people in such a way over the centuries. The Spirit is free and sovereign. He may at times bring the implications of our union with Christ home to us in a critical manner which significantly affects our subsequent Christian experience. In interpreting such crises it is worth noting four points.

1. The crisis experience *may* be the reverse of specific resistance to God's will. To use a medical analogy, our condition may have called for radical surgery rather than more conservative treatment.

2. An experience may be given to prepare us for a major trial of faith in the future.

3. It may have reference to a new field of Christian ministry or responsibility (Acts 18:9f.; 23:11). This latter class, special blessing in relation to special service, is related to sanctification only in a secondary way. Many a Christian leader has had to learn the hard way that special enduements of the Spirit for special public ministry do not absolve us from the discipline of daily Christian living.

4. God does not necessarily set aside our 'natural' personality in his sanctifying work. The Redeemer is also the Creator. Some Christians by their very temperament will be more likely than others to experience crises in their sanctification.

The great danger is to presume that such experiences are for all Christians, or for specific Christians known to us. The basic biblical teaching is rather that the people of God grow in holiness by the ongoing, daily ministry of the Spirit which enables us more and more to live the reality of our union with Christ in his death, resurrection and ascension.

Rest or struggle?

Are Christians called on to struggle to conform to the moral standards set out in Scripture, or are we called essentially to an attitude of faith in Christ and what he has done, a 'resting' in Christ as our sanctification?

The NT incorporates both elements. Resting in Christ as our sanctification finds support in verses which encourage us to look to him in faith, yield ourselves to him and 'abide' in him (Jn. 15:1–10; Rom. 6:13; 1 Cor. 1:30; Gal. 2:20). Alongside this, Scripture sets the need to be 'up and doing' in the work of sanctification, putting to death the old nature with its desires and putting on the new nature in Christ (Rom. 8:12f.; 12:1–21; 1 Cor. 6:12–20; Gal. 5:13–26; Col. 3:1–7). Exhortations to holiness are never confined to vague appeals for surrender to the Lord or for entire submission to the direction of the Spirit; they spell out in detail the pattern of the holy life and urge us to make strenuous efforts to conform to it.

The NT also underlines our spiritual warfare against the powers of evil. Certainly we must 'stand firm' (Eph. 6:14) in Christ and his victory over the devil; but we must also 'put on the full armour of God' and wield the sword of the Spirit. Hence, sanctification is *both* resting in Christ in faith *and* wrestling to be conformed to his image.

Complete or partial? .

Some claim to have attained a state in which they no longer commit sin, and urge that this is possible for all Christians as they look continuously to Christ. Besides the difficulty of squaring such claims with the plain teaching of 1 John 1:8, 10, proponents of such views are found on examination to define sin in a rather limited sense: deliberate disobedience of God's will or something similar. Scripture, however, must define sin, and it is concerned about thoughts and attitudes as well as words and deeds, duties omitted as well as misdeeds committed. Sinlessness in biblical terms means to love God and every human being in every conscious moment with our whole heart, mind, will and strength, *i.e.* complete identity of character with Jesus Christ. In these biblical terms, sinless perfection is obviously impossible; in fact, those who have conformed most clearly to Christ in their character exhibit a common sense of personal unworthiness and weakness (Is. 6:5f.; Dn. 9:4–19; Eph. 3:8; 1 Tim. 1:15). Not only is it unbiblical and impossible; it can induce pride and mislead and disturb the faith of others.

The terminology of sanctification

Much of the discussion about sanctification centres round the meanings given to one or two key notions.

Filling with the Spirit

This term has its biblical base in Ephesians 5:18 where all Christians are called upon to be filled with the Spirit, and in passages in the Acts where Christians are described as 'filled with the Spirit' (Acts 2:4; 4:31; 6:5; 7:55; 9:17; 11:24; 13:9). 'Fill' is plainly a metaphor and it fundamentally misleads if pressed literally, as though the human objects of the Spirit's ministry were reduced to impersonal receptacles, and the blessed Spirit himself to a spiritual substance. Someone 'full of glee' simply means a person whose most obvious aspect is good humour and mirth. The glee is not required to attain some critical level, along with specific accompaniments (rolling on the floor?) before we apply the phrase. It simply means that glee is one's dominant characteristic. Likewise, to be filled with the Spirit implies that the Spirit is the dominant influence in our behaviour.

Is it a critical once-for-all experience? This is resolved by the obvious fact that the same people are described in the Acts as 'filled with the Spirit' on several occasions (see the verses cited above). In keeping with this the verb in Ephesians 5:18 is in the continuous tense: 'go on being filled with the Spirit', *not* 'have a critical experience of the Spirit'.

In the light of this biblical teaching, 'filling' with the Spirit means our coming under the influence of the Lord who is the Spirit, in such a manner and to such a degree that he becomes a dominant reality in our lives, enabling us on occasion to act in ways which particularly demonstrate his presence and, more generally, to live so that God is glorified through us (Eph. 5:19f.). It is a condition which all Christians ought to seek continually. Needless to say, since the Spirit who 'fills' the believer is the same Holy Spirit whose work we have expounded above, the marks of his 'filling' will be our likeness to Christ.

Baptism in/with the Spirit

This phrase caused considerable discussion in the twentieth century. Christians in the mainline Pentecostal churches commonly use it to refer to a second experience of the Spirit, subsequent to conversion and accompanied by speaking in tongues. In the middle of the century the charismatic movement (see below) brought the discussion to the centre of attention.

The verbal form, 'baptize(d) with the Holy Spirit', occurs seven times in the Bible. Six refer to John the Baptist's contrast between his preparatory heralding ministry, baptizing 'with water', and Jesus' coming messianic ministry, baptizing 'with the Holy Spirit' (Mt. 3:11; Mk. 1:8; Lk. 3:16; Jn. 1:33; Acts 1:5; 11:16). It also occurs when Paul expounds the essential unity of the experience of the Spirit in all of God's people: 'we were all baptised by one Spirit into one body' (1 Cor. 12:13).

An examination of these references and of the whole NT idea of baptism yields the conclusion that 'baptism in the Spirit' refers to an aspect of Christian initiation. In other words, in Scripture 'baptism in the Spirit' belongs to that complex of ideas which refer to Christian beginnings: repentance and faith, justification, conversion, regeneration, water baptism, ingrafting into Christ, adoption into God's family. It highlights what regeneration implies, entry into the promised messianic kingdom through immersion into the life of the Holy Spirit, who is the life of the kingdom. 'Baptism in the Spirit' is therefore one of the ways the NT speaks about 'becoming a Christian'; hence every true believer in Christ has been baptized in the Spirit, just as they have been regenerated, ingrafted into Christ, justified before God, *etc.* To use the phrase for a *subsequent* experience of the Spirit's power and blessing, no matter how overwhelming, strictly goes beyond the biblical usage and is liable therefore in the long run to be unhelpful and misleading.

What then are we to say about subsequent experiences of the Spirit if we cannot call them 'baptism in the Spirit'? Several possibilities have been suggested.

1. Deny the validity of the experience. While the dangers of spurious experience and misrepresentation certainly arise, this course hardly commends itself, particularly where there is evidence of a new spiritual reality and effectiveness as a result of the experience.

2. Follow the traditional Pentecostal line and continue to call these experiences 'baptism in the Spirit', despite the departure from NT usage. This alternative is complicated by the fact that there *are* those whose 'initiation' experience was so inadequate that the 'subsequent' experience has all the marks of an actual conversion, in fact their 'baptism in(to) the Spirit'. However, where there has certainly been a genuine experience of the Spirit at a previous point, which was plainly the genesis of Christian life, it is unscriptural and therefore unhelpful to name any subsequent experience 'baptism in the Spirit'.

3. See the later experience as the experiential realization in a new and fuller degree of what was given in essence at conversion. By this approach, the experience is interpreted as the Spirit into whom we were baptized in regeneration coming upon us with a fuller, even critically new, outpouring of his life. This experience is not a 'baptism' into the Spirit but a subsequent realization of his reality.

This subsequent experience ought not to be interpreted too rigidly, as is made clear from the difficulties which arise when trying to fit the experiences of the Spirit in Acts into too tidy a framework. In terms of correct terminology for subsequent experience, the notion 'fullness' of the Spirit has much to commend it in preference to 'baptism' (see the Acts verses cited on p. 246). In the NT period this biblical term covered the considerable variety of the Spirit's comings upon Christian disciples subsequent to their initiation into the new age through the regenerating power of the Spirit.

Hesitations concerning some 'second-blessing' terminology, however, must not be allowed to impoverish us spiritually. We must desire as much of the fullness and power of the blessed Spirit of God as our Father may be pleased to give us (Mt. 5:6; Lk. 11:13; 1 Cor. 12:31).

The corporate aspect of the Holy Spirit's work is again fundamental. The Spirit who fills and empowers is the Spirit who unites us to Christ and hence to his whole body. Experiences and ministries of the Spirit are never for the selfish indulgence of the individual. They are for the good and growth of the church, and ultimately for the glory of Christ through his people (Acts 2:1f., *cf*. 42–47; 4:31–35; Eph. 4:11–16).

PERSEVERANCE

If we are enabled to believe and the work of Christ is thus applied effectively to us, can we thereafter forfeit our salvation? This too has aroused considerable debate.

The idea that, once imparted, salvation cannot be lost is known as the perseverance of the saints. It has been consistently maintained in Reformed theology and there is clear support for it in Scripture. Christ tells his disciples, 'they shall never perish; no-one can snatch them out of my hand' (Jn. 10:28, *cf*. 6:37, 40); Paul asserts: 'those he justified, he also glorified . . . nor anything else in all creation will be able to separate us from the love of God that is in Christ Jesus our Lord' (Rom. 8:30, 39); 'he who began a good work in you will carry it on to completion' (Phil. 1:6); Peter assures his readers that 'through faith [we] are shielded by God's power until the coming of the salvation . . . in the last time' (1 Pet. 1:5). This is the final implication of the truth already underlined, that salvation is a work of God's sovereign grace. If our coming to God was his work rather than ours, our continuing with him is his work also.

Perseverance is also clearly implied in other doctrines already discussed. If we have been incorporated into Christ in his whole saving action, then we shall also share in his coming triumph. Paul uses this very argument. Since we died with Christ, inevitably we shall 'appear with him in glory' and we should be living now in accordance with this destiny (Col. 3:1–5). Perseverance is also a corollary of election, since our belonging to God from eternity implies our being his for the eternal future. Justification too implies the assurance of being declared righteous at the final judgment (Rom. 5:1f.; Tit. 3:7).

One strand of biblical teaching seems to open the door to the possibility of those who once believed being eventually lost. The letter to the Hebrews warns Christians against false presumption and the terrible implications of renouncing their faith in Christ (2:3f.; 4:1f.; 6:1–9; 10:1f.), as does Jesus himself (Mt. 24:13; Jn. 15:6; Rev. 2:5).

Such warnings and the doctrine of perseverance are not irreconcilable. Scripture states clearly that all who are drawn to Christ and come to faith in him are eternally delivered from sin and its condemnation, but never presents this as a ground for moral carelessness. People who are truly born again of the Holy Spirit will give evidence of it by striving to live a holy life, even though the attainment is often painfully slow – as biblical biography makes abundantly clear. Anyone who returns wholeheartedly to sin, renounces former Christian ways, manifests no remorse in so doing and continues in this apostasy to the end of life was, despite initial appearances, never truly 'born of God'. 'Say not that thou hast Royal blood in thy veins unless thou canst give proof of thy pedigree by daring to be holy' (Gurnall).

Sensitive souls need reassuring at this point. The Christian is certainly not without sin. Indeed, the very anxiety that makes a person search his or her life for tokens of moral renewal is itself evidence of regeneration. Further, backsliding is a real, if regrettable, fact of Christian living. Sometimes true Christians fall back a long way. However, they never completely lose their spiritual awareness and even in their backsliding retain some degree of desire to return to the Lord. Apostates who show they were never true disciples lose all moral and spiritual concern and reject even the idea that Christ's death puts away sins (Heb. 10:26–29).

Passages cited as evidence that true Christians might be lost either refer to cases where there was no genuine faith initially (1 Jn. 2:19) or else are simply reminders of the moral seriousness of the Christian life. The balance of Scripture, however, must be maintained. Christian salvation involves deliverance from the wrath to come. Christians can be assured that they will be preserved for the eternal kingdom of God, not because of what they are capable of themselves but because they are in the hands of the sovereign God of grace who has brought them life from the grave, holds them now in face of all the assaults of world, flesh and devil and can be trusted to continue this ministry of grace to all eternity.

MEANS AND END

The Holy Spirit and the Word of God

To complete this exposition of the Spirit and Christian growth, we note again his inspiration and illumination of the Scriptures (Jn. 14:26; 15:26; 16:13f.; Eph. 1:17; Heb. 3:7; 1 Pet. 1:11; 2 Pet. 1:21f.; 1 Jn. 2:20, 27). The bond between the Spirit and the Word is one of the keys to understanding his entire ministry in the church. In guiding, inspiring, sanctifying and upbuilding God's people, his supreme instrument is Scripture (2 Tim. 3:16f.). Conversely, any claim to the Spirit's presence, leading or blessing which bypasses the Word, or minimizes its authority, is clearly alien to the Spirit who led and empowered Jesus and the apostles, and hence foreign to all true, God-honouring faith (*cf.* Part 1, pp. 39ff.).

The Holy Spirit and the End

Several OT passages associate the ministry of the Holy Spirit with the new age (Ezk. 39:29; Joel 2:28f.). The Spirit's present ministry among the people of God is the unambiguous evidence that the new age of the kingdom has broken into human history. Through the Spirit we anticipate the realities which will obtain when the new era is fully manifest.

Paul uses two terms to express this future dimension of the ministry of the Spirit. The Spirit is the *aparchē*, 'firstfruits' (Rom. 8:23). In the OT this was a sacrifice offered to the Lord (Nu. 28:26–31) to demonstrate the people's thankfulness that God had given them a harvest. Paul uses the term to refer to his first converts in a particular area (*cf.* Rom. 16:5; 1 Cor. 16:15). It is used also of the risen Christ, the 'firstfruits' of the great coming harvest of the resurrection of the dead (1 Cor. 15:23). Its use with respect to the Spirit closely parallels this last passage. In the Holy Spirit we taste 'the powers of the coming age' (Heb. 6:5), we are those 'on whom the fulfilment of the ages has come' (1 Cor. 10:11).

The Spirit is also the *arrabōn* (2 Cor. 1:22; 5:5; Eph. 1:14), a word common in the first-century business world. When a contract was entered into or a deal completed, one paid an *arrabōn*, the 'deposit', which guaranteed the full payment to follow. Our present experience of the Spirit is the first instalment and guarantee of the future life of glory. In modern Greek *arrabōn* means an engagement ring, the token of a relationship now entered upon which promises a fuller union yet to be.

Scriptures

Assurance: Rom. 6:21; 8:14–17, 28–39; 14:5; 2 Cor. 1:22; Gal. 4:4–7; Eph. 1:13; 4:30; Col. 2:2; 1 Thes. 1:5; 2 Tim. 1:12; Heb. 6:18–20; 10:22; 1 Jn. 3:24; 4:13; 5:7, 9.
Sanctification: Ex. 19:6; Lv. 11:44f.; Dt. 7:6; Is. 62:12; Mt. 5–7; Jn. 15:1–10; 17:17; Acts 20:28–32; 26:18; Rom. 6:1–23; 8:12f.; 12:1–21; 15:16; 1 Cor. 6:11–20; 15:31; 2 Cor. 3:17f.; 7:1; Gal. 5:13–6:10; Eph. 4:17–6:18; Col. 1:22; 3:1–17; 1 Thes. 4:1–12; 2 Tim. 1:9; 2:21; Heb. 12:10, 14; 1 Pet. 1:13–2:17; 2 Pet. 3:11; 1 Jn. 2:6, 24–28; 3:6.
Perseverance: Jn. 6:37, 40; 10:27; Rom. 8:30–39; 11:29; Phil. 1:6; 2 Thes. 3:3; 2 Tim. 4:18; 1 Pet. 1:5.
The Spirit and the Word: Ezk. 2:1f.; Jn. 14:26; 16:13f.; 1 Cor. 2:4–16; 2 Thes. 2:13; 2 Tim. 3:16; Heb. 3:7; 2 Pet. 1:20f.
The Spirit and the End: Is. 11:2; 44:3; Je. 31:31f.; Ezk. 39:29; Joel 2:28f.; Rom. 8:23; 1 Cor. 10:11; 15:23; 2 Cor. 1:22; 5:5; Eph. 1:13f.; 4:30; Heb. 6:5.

Questions

1. What does 'sanctification' mean in both Scripture and common usage? In what ways is sanctification distinguished from justification?
2. What significance does our union with Christ have for sanctification? How would you try to interpret a 'crisis' experience of the Holy Spirit? What are the problems associated with the 'second-blessing' approach to sanctification?
3. According to Scripture, does sanctification in any sense depend on our efforts?
4. What do you understand from scriptural teaching by (a) 'baptism in the Spirit', (b) the 'fullness of the Spirit'?
5. What would you consider the essential marks of increasing sanctification in *all* Christian lives? Apart from these common elements, how might one expect increasing sanctification to be particularly expressed by a Christian (a) homemaker and mother, (b) student, (c) painter and decorator, (d) teacher, (e) factory employee, (f) civil servant?
6. Can we enjoy a firm certainty that we truly are Christians? Support your answer from Scripture.
7. Consider the role of the Spirit with reference to Scripture. What is the Bible's function in living the Christian life?
8. Can a truly regenerate Christian be finally lost? How do you interpret the 'warning passages' in Hebrews?

Bibliography

Arts. 'Sanctification' in *IBD* and 'Assurance', 'Justification', 'Perseverance', in *NDT*.
G. C. Berkouwer, *Faith and Sanctification* (Eerdmans, 1952).
G. C. Berkouwer, *Faith and Perseverance* (Eerdmans, 1958).
J. Bridges, *The Practice of Godliness* (NavPress, 1987).

Jonathan Edwards, *The Religious Affections* (Banner of Truth, 1961).
S. B. Ferguson, *Add to Your Faith* (Pickering and Inglis, 1980).
S. B. Ferguson, *The Holy Spirit* (IVP, 1996).
M. Green, *I Believe in the Holy Spirit* (Hodder, 1975).
D. M. Lloyd-Jones, *Romans 5 – Assurance* (Banner of Truth, 1971).
D. M. Lloyd-Jones, *Romans 6 – The New Man* (Banner of Truth, 1972).
D. M. Lloyd-Jones, *Romans 8:17–39 – The Final Perseverance of the Saints* (Banner of Truth, 1975).
R. Lovelace, *The Dynamics of Spiritual Life* (Paternoster, 1979).
J. Owen, *Works*, 4 and 5 (Banner of Truth, 1967).
J. I. Packer, *Keep in Step with the Spirit* (IVP, 1984).
J. I. Packer, *Knowing God* (Hodder, 1973).
D. Peterson, *Possessed by God* (Apollos, 1995).
J. C. Ryle, *Holiness* (James Clarke, 1952).
T. A. Smail, *Reflected Glory* (Hodder, 1975).
J. R. W. Stott, *Baptism and Fullness* (IVP, 1975).
D. Watson, *One in the Spirit* (Hodder, 1973).
John Wesley, *A Plain Account of Christian Perfection* (Epworth, 1958).

22. Historical perspective: the Holy Spirit today

The last half century has witnessed a great resurgence of interest in the Holy Spirit, centring on the 'charismatic movement'. As a significant factor within traditional churches the movement dates from the activities of the Full Gospel Business Men's Fellowship in the 1950s. Stressing individual 'baptism in the Holy Spirit' and the more spectacular gifts of the Spirit, particularly speaking in tongues, within a few years it affected Christians in all major denominations in the USA, then in Europe and around the world. From an early stage it penetrated Roman Catholicism, and some think the charismatic movement offers a more promising road for ecumenical rapprochement than the traditional, often relatively fruitless, route of theological dialogue.

After the early preoccupation with individual blessing, tongues and the like, in the second, arguably maturer, phase the movement's primary concerns were to recover practical Christian community and the meaning of the church as the body of Christ. In what may be discerned as a third phase, attention has moved to a quest for the ecclesiastical structures which will best serve the movement. This has had the effect of bringing into the open two distinct wings: one dedicated to renewal within the great historical denominations, the other separating from these and forming house churches and *ad hoc* groups.

During the 1990s the charismatic movement experienced what is generally referred to as a 'Third Wave' (the first two waves being the rise of Pentecostalism at the beginning of the twentieth century, and the emergence of the charismatic movement as described above). Stemming from the ministry of Rev. John Wimber and Fuller Theological Seminary in California, this Third Wave has seen particular stress on 'signs and wonders', the belief that God continues to authenticate the gospel in our time by supernatural phenomena such as miraculous healings, power encounters, 'slayings in the Spirit' and the like. A legacy was the founding of the Vineyard movement, a loosely federated body of charismatic churches in many parts of the world. An extended series of meetings in Toronto, Canada, during the mid-1990s was also influential in a further spread of this emphasis.

In some cases the movement has led to sharp division within churches, and sometimes to imbalance and excess. In others, contact with it has brought evident quickening of spiritual life. Some major Christian groups, particularly in North America, continue to view it with disfavour, possibly due in part to the extremism of much traditional Pentecostalism there. In common with the whole church today, the charismatic movement faces the challenge of translating the renewed awareness of the reality and the life of the Spirit into a revitalizing of the mission of the church, both in bringing men and women to Christ in significant numbers from every segment of society, and in effectively applying the gospel to social and cultural spheres.

While thanking God for the movement's achievements and rejoicing in all the other evidences of the Spirit's work across the world, many Christians continue to long and pray for worldwide revival. It is always dangerous, of course, to stereotype the Holy Spirit; but God has been pleased periodically since the first century to pour out his Spirit on his people in such abundance that not only has the church itself begun to live at something approaching the level of Pentecost, but the whole surrounding community has been profoundly awakened to the reality of God and the urgent need to get right with him.[1] Revivals of this sort

---

1. Revival in this classic sense must be distinguished from its popular use, particularly in the USA, to refer to local evangelistic campaigns.

were experienced during the twentieth century in various regions, notably East Africa, China and South-East Asia. Can anything less than this enable the church to face the enormous challenge of the new millennium and truly fulfil its calling to glorify its Lord?

> *O Breath of Life, come sweeping through us*
> *Revive thy church with life and power;*
> *O Breath of Life, come, cleanse, renew us,*
> *And fit thy church to meet this hour.*

Application

GOD AND HIS SERVICE

Our experience of God

The fact of the work of the Spirit confronts us with the wonder that God gives *himself* to us in our very experience. It is not only that God works for and upon us in his creation and redemption, but he actually works *in* us so that our very bodies become the shrine of God the Spirit, God himself in our being. Although identifying and interpreting this reality is not always straight-forward – one of the reasons for constant study and submission to the Scriptures – we do not stop short of this claim: *God himself is experienced by his creatures* (1 Cor. 6:19; Eph. 2:22).

Our worship of God

The fact that God in his sovereign mercy has condescended to give himself in his very being in the Spirit to our feeble, broken and sinful lives is supreme cause for worship and thanksgiving. All that God has done, is doing and will do through our union with Christ in terms of our election, calling, regeneration, repentance, faith, justification, adoption, assurance, sanctification and perseverance is reason to adore, bless and worship him. 'To him who loves us and has freed us from our sins by his blood, and has made us to be a kingdom and priests to serve his God and Father – to him be glory and power for ever and ever!' (Rev. 1:5f.). In our worship it is the same blessed Spirit who delights ever and again to blow on the dying embers of our sense of thanksgiving and worship, fanning them into a flame of praise and glory to our God (Phil. 3:3).

Our service of God
The Spirit equips us to serve God by imparting his gifts, directing our ministry and anointing us with power. Our horizons as far as God's service is concerned ought not to be measured therefore by our limited human capacities but by the abundant measure of the Spirit's provision (Rom. 15:18f.; 2 Cor. 3:5f.; Eph. 1:19–21).

THE WORLD AND ITS RESPONSIBILITIES

Regeneration from beyond the world
The Christian does not belong to this present age under the dominion of sin and darkness but has been born again by the Spirit to citizenship in the new, coming order of the kingdom. Therefore, we do not look to the world to nourish our spirits or to provide our deepest satisfaction. We are moving on a different level and find our ultimate fulfilment within a different order, in the life of God through the Holy Spirit (Pss. 16:11; 84:1f.; Rom. 8:5ff.; Heb. 11).

Relationship to the world
Although our deepest fulfilment lies beyond the world, the Spirit's ministry of regeneration and sanctification impinges very clearly on the creaturely order and on our experience in the world. The same Spirit who was poured out in supernatural power at Pentecost, thereby bringing the church to birth, was involved with the Father and Son at the beginning in bringing the material world to birth. The same Spirit who inspires and empowers God's people is also in some way present as an immanent reality in the life of all people (Jb. 33:4; Ps. 104:29f.). If these two dimensions of the one Spirit's work are sharply separated a dangerous imbalance is created which effectively shuts out the Spirit from creaturely realities and confines his activity to the manifestly supernatural.

This can be illustrated in two areas. On the question of divine guidance, Christians who have a full biblical doctrine of the Spirit will believe that the same Spirit of God will guide them through a careful assessment of the factors involved and their own 'natural' aptitudes and personality as well as by more dramatic circumstantial factors. Similarly in the area of physical healing they will recognize that it is the one Holy Spirit who heals the sick whether by modern medical means, the body's own inherent resources of recovery, or by the exercise of a special gift of healing in conjunction with the prayers of God's people.

At a practical level, this imbalance is best prevented by reminding ourselves that a major work of the Spirit is his inspiration and illumination of Holy Scripture. He always works in conjunction with the Word and hence our experience of the Spirit needs the continual check, balance and direction of the whole written Word of God.

Responsibility for the world

The Spirit is the divine witness in the world to God, his law and his redemption in Christ. He is the 'advocate' who authenticates the church's witness. Christians led by the Spirit will accordingly be marked by a sense of responsibility for the world in its unbelief and ignorance of God and will seek to bear witness to the gospel; significantly, the major biblical account of the ministry of the Spirit in the church (Acts) centres on the spread of the gospel through the world. The presence of the Spirit in a life or a church will always bring a concern for God's glory in the saving of lost men and women, what our predecessors called a 'passion for souls'. When experiences of the Spirit, whether individual or in a church, produce a preoccupation with the emotional and sensational, on biblical grounds we should ask whether the 'spirit' concerned is really the Spirit of Jesus whom we meet at work in the NT. A sense of responsibility for the world is an invariable mark of the presence of the Spirit, who is promised to give us courage and wisdom, to authenticate our testimony and to bring lost men and women to living faith (Acts 1:8; 4:31; 14:27).

OURSELVES AND OUR PROSPECTS

Corporateness

The Spirit who unites us to Christ unites us in that act to all God's people; our sanctification through the Spirit's renewing influence is set firmly in the context of the fellowship of God's people, particularly in the local church to which he calls us. The Spirit knows nothing of one-man-band Christians and ministries. We need to beware of claims to the Spirit's leading which have no explicit 'check' at the corporate level. Rather, among the most enriching dimensions of his work are those relationships of love and sharing which he gives us within the life of the family of God.

Character
The Spirit is holy, separate from all sin and evil. His presence in our lives will therefore always be manifest in moral terms, drawing us away from evil and sin into righteousness and holiness. We need to reckon with this in our thinking about our Christian lives; he is grieved by our sinning, he wills our holiness. The ministry of the Spirit is therefore misrepresented if thought of only in terms of certain experiences of God. Such he gives, if and as he wills, but they are only part of his work and must be integrated with his continuous ongoing ministry of conforming us to the image of Christ.

Consummation
The Spirit is the life of the new, coming age imparted to us under the conditions of the present, fallen order. His presence is always promissory: he directs us forward in hope to the coming consummation when Christ will return in glory. The Christian indwelt by the Spirit will therefore strain forward in growing anticipation of the fullness of the Spirit's life and blessing which will be the glad experience of the people of God on that day.

PART 6
The church

23. The identity of the church

Biblical religion is inescapably corporate. Even before the fall Adam was not fulfilled without a human partner (Gn. 2:18). Corporateness in God's creative purpose is echoed in his unfolding redemptive purpose. His covenants with Noah (Gn. 9:8) and Abraham (Gn. 12:1–3; 15:1–5; 28:14) clearly reach beyond the individual to embrace immediate descendants and even 'all peoples on earth'.

The OT is the story of a *people* and all the variety of God's dealings with them. True, great individuals stand out, and personal relationship with God in his grace is fundamental (Dt. 24:16; Pss. 23:1; 51:10–12; Ezk. 18), but the context remains essentially corporate. The believing community is the soil in which personal faith sprouts and is nourished. Thus the messianic hope has a corporate dimension in the OT, where the Son of Man and suffering servant are both individual and corporate figures (Dn. 7:13f., 27; Is. 42:1; 44:1). In the light of NT fulfilment we see that the primary thrust of these passages is individual: they refer to the Lord Jesus Christ. But equally clearly a Messiah isolated from the messianic people was unthinkable.

The NT continues this sense of corporateness. Jesus comes for the salvation of a people (Mt. 1:21). He gathers a group of twelve disciples, corresponding in number to the tribes of Israel; clearly they are in his mind the nucleus of the new Israel, the new people of God whom he will bind to God in the new covenant through his redemptive mission. Jesus explicitly refers to the 'church' which will arise beyond the climax of his ministry (Mt. 16:18; 18:17), and his final commission clearly envisages a continuing community of faith and witness (Mt. 28:19f.).

Pentecost itself was essentially corporate (Acts 2:1f.). From that point the disciples' experience develops in corporate terms (Acts 2:44–47; 4:32–35; 5:12–16; 6:1–7). As the gospel spread to the Gentile world, the disciples grouped in churches in the different centres of population (Acts 11:26; 13:1; 14:23). James expresses the apostolic understanding of the purpose of God as 'taking from the Gentiles a people for himself' (Acts 15:14).

Scripture then knows nothing of solitary religion. Individuals cannot be reconciled to God without being reconciled to the people of God among whom their experience of God's grace immediately sets them. Thus soteriology (the doctrine of *salvation*) is indissolubly bound up with ecclesiology (the doctrine of the *church*).

BIBLICAL IMAGES OF THE CHURCH

The people of God

God's relationship with his people is the central theme of the OT, expressed in the repeated declaration, 'I will be your God, and you will be my people' (Ex. 6:7; 19:5; Lv. 26:12; Je. 30:22; Ezk. 36:28; Ho. 2:23). This relationship began in the covenant made with Noah (Gn. 6:18f.) and then with Abraham and his descendants (Gn. 12:1f.; 15:1–19; 17:3–14). This latter was reaffirmed at a national level in the time of Moses (Ex. 6:6f.; 19–24) and of David (Ps. 89:3f.; 2 Sa. 7:12–17). Covenant does not mean a two-sided contract by which God was obligated by his people; it was always a covenant of *grace*, an agreement in which God was the initiating and determining party. Israel was guaranteed God's presence and blessing in the context of her obedience to God.

The notion of the people of God continues in the NT church, 'the Israel of God' (Gal. 6:16). Peter makes particular use of it (1 Pet. 2:9, *cf*. Tit. 2:14) and the Bible closes with the triumphant affirmation that 'the dwelling of God is with men, and he will live with them. They will be his people' (Rev. 21:3).

The covenant basis of the relationship also continues in the NT. The church inherits the promises to Israel on the basis of the *new* covenant made through the sacrifice of the Messiah, Jesus (Mt. 26:28; Lk. 22:20; Heb. 9:15; *cf.* Je. 31:31).

Something of the essential character of the 'people of God' is indicated by the two OT words used for them. The first, *qāhāl*, means a gathering in response to God's call (Ex. 35:1; Nu. 16:26; Dt. 9:10); this word was translated as *ekklēsia* (church) in the Greek version of the OT and is therefore the key to 'church' in the NT. The second, *'ēdâ*, means the national religious community one joined by birth (Ex. 12:3; Nu. 16:9; 31:12). The early Christians saw their historic precedent in the dynamic notion of *qāhāl*, the people of God assembled in response to the direct calling of God.

In Jesus, the call of God which constituted God's people in the past (Gn. 12:1f.; Ex. 3:1f.; Ho. 11:1f.) rang out again (Mt. 11:28f.; Mk. 1:14–20; Jn. 7:37f.). After his ascension, it continues to be heard in the call of the gospel (Acts 2:39; 2 Thes. 2:14). It is in responding to God's call through the gospel that we enter the church, the covenant people of God.

This biblical background implies that the 'church' is essentially the living community of those who have responded to the call of God, and therefore *not* the formal ecclesiastical structure immediately brought to mind today by the word 'church'. This latter may inevitably go with the *ekklēsia*, but it is not its essence.

Ekklēsia is used in the NT both of particular local groups (Acts 8:1; Rom. 16:16; 2 Thes. 1:4) and of the worldwide, age-long company of God's people (Mt. 16:18; 1 Cor. 15:9; Eph. 5:25f.). The relation between a local company of Christians and the whole of God's people is subtle and has no human parallel, for the local group is not simply one relatively incomplete part of the greater whole. The NT teaches rather that the local church, while indissolubly united to the whole people of God, is none the less a complete church. All the promises of God obtain for it, and Christ, the head and lord of the church, is as fully present there as in any extended entity (Mt. 18:20).

The body of Christ

This image of which Paul in particular is fond focuses more sharply what the people of God have in common. The 'call' which constitutes them is the call to believe in Christ Jesus (the 'word' which has 'become flesh') and therefore to be incorporated into him, made a member of his body. The concept is clearly figurative (*cf.* Jn. 15:5: 'I am the vine; you are the branches'). The relationship of the church to Christ is, however, very close indeed; it is a form of organic union by which we are made one in life and being with him (Col. 3:4).

Sometimes Christ is himself pictured as the whole body, while we are members 'within' him (Rom. 12:5; 1 Cor. 10:16; 12:27). Paul also handles the image in a slightly different way, presenting Christ as the head of the body (Eph. 5:23; Col. 1:18; 2:19). This is not an essential change, for Christ remains Lord of the whole body which in its entirety is his.

This image also stresses the reciprocal relationship between Christ and his people. Christ reigns at the right hand of God *for the church* (Eph. 1:22f.). His being the head implies that all our life and nourishment flow from him; we live out of him, from him, through him and unto him.

The bride of Christ

This vivid image has its roots in the OT where God speaks of Israel as his bride (Is. 54:5–8; 62:5; Je. 2:2). Tragically Israel proved unfaithful (Je. 3; Ezk. 16). Jesus took up this metaphor, referring to himself as the bridegroom whose presence among the wedding guests made fasting inappropriate (Mk. 2:18–20). Christ embodies God's husband-love for the church, expressed supremely in his self-sacrifice for her so that the church might be presented to her heavenly bridegroom 'as a radiant church, without stain or wrinkle or any other blemish, but holy and blameless' (Eph. 5:27). So John foresees the church's destiny: 'the wedding of the Lamb has come, and the bride has made herself ready'; the climax of his prophecy reveals 'the Holy City, the new Jerusalem, coming down out of heaven from God, prepared as a bride beautifully dressed for her husband' (Rev. 19:7; 21:2).

This image underlines that God's relationship to his people is one of unqualified love. He has chosen and redeemed us because his desire is towards us; we are the objects of his eternal love. This metaphor also confronts us with our responsibility to be single-minded in our devotion to God and to recognize the gravity of giving our affection and loyalty to other things, not least our own ambitions and interests. God's love is so deep that it cannot tolerate rival affections.

The building of God

This metaphor is rooted in the OT references to God's presence among his people (Ex. 25:8; Ps. 132:13f.; Is. 12:6) in the tabernacle housing the ark of the covenant (Ex. 25:8–22; 1 Sa. 4:21f.) and later in the temple built by Solomon (2 Ch. 7:1–3). It was clearly recognized, however, that no localized sanctuary could suffice for the God whose presence fills earth and heaven (2 Ch. 6:18; Ps. 139:7–12).

Solomon's temple was destroyed by the Babylonian invaders in 587 BC. A second temple, built by the returning exiles (Ezr. 3), stood nearly 500 years and was succeeded by Herod's temple, completed a few years before the birth of Jesus. Our Lord implied that the temple was no longer the place of God's abode: 'Destroy this temple, and I will raise it again in three days' (Jn. 2:19), his ultimate reference being to the temple of his body (Jn. 2:21). He also asserted that the overriding consideration in approaching God is not geographical location but the heart attitude and disposition (Jn. 4:23). Jesus' words about the temple proved prophetic; it was destroyed by the Romans in AD 70 (*cf.* Mk. 13:1–2).

The thought that God dwells among his people continues, however, for the body of Jesus offered up on the cross enabled the coming of the Holy Spirit; thus the church was created as the body of Christ, the new temple of God's presence. Christ is himself the foundation stone (1 Cor. 3:11; Eph. 2:20) on whom the people of God are built as 'God's temple' (1 Cor. 3:16), 'a dwelling in which God lives by his Spirit' (Eph. 2:22). The completion of this remains in the future, at the Lord's return: 'Now the dwelling of God is with men, and he will live with them. They will be his people, and God himself will be with them and be their God' (Rev. 21:3).

This image of the church in its developed NT sense points away from stone buildings, which makes all the more regrettable the common identification of the church with a building, however sacred its associations or sublime its architecture. It underlines the essentially spiritual character of the church as a creation of the Holy Spirit and Christ's central place as foundation and cornerstone; and stresses the fundamental mutuality of the Christian life in which experience and service of God are realized and expressed through our identification with each other as living stones in the one temple of God (1 Pet. 2:5).

The kingdom of God

This basic biblical idea is discussed more fully in Part 7. Its roots are again found in the OT. God's rule is rejected and ignored in the world. Even in Israel, although God chose them as 'his dominion' (Ps. 114:2), is his will resisted, his law breached and neglected. Out of this arises the prophetic hope of a coming Day in which God will affirm his royal authority and establish his rule or 'kingdom' among human beings. Jesus proclaimed the arrival of that era. Through his ministry with its Easter climax God's rule was indeed established, though its full expression awaits his glorious return. Meanwhile, God's rule is established in those who are 'rescued . . . from the dominion of darkness and brought . . . into the kingdom of the Son he loves' (Col. 1:13) and exercised by Christ through his Spirit (Rom. 14:17).

While it is wrong to equate the kingdom with the church, when the church truly submits to Christ by obeying his word she becomes the instrument of God's rule. Further, although the church awaits the full coming of the kingdom, she is able by the ministry of the Spirit to embody in a real measure the life of the kingdom in her experience of mutual love and service. In the community of the Spirit, where the vast diversities of human experience are overcome and the diverse members discover a unique unity in the family of God, the kingdom is truly pre-visioned and anticipated.

More generally, this image expresses the essentially servant character of the church and her need to bring her life in all its aspects constantly under the rule of God through his Word.

The family of God

This image was foreshadowed in the OT where Israel was called God's son (Ho. 11:1), referring forward to Jesus (Mt. 2:15), God's Son in the ultimate sense.

In the NT, the full terms of this image become apparent. In Christ we are born again into the family of God, adopted as his children, and God's Spirit is sent into our hearts so that we may call him Father (Rom. 8:14–17). The church is therefore the family or household of God (Eph. 2:19; 1 Tim. 3:15). This image reminds us of our high privilege: raised by his grace to the glorious status of sons and daughters of God. It speaks too of the character of our mutual relationships, as members of one family, and challenges us to trust our heavenly Father to meet all our needs (Mt. 6:25–34).

The flock of God
Israel was God's flock (Pss. 80:1; 95:7). When the leaders or 'shepherds' of Israel failed to tend the flock, God asserted his concern: 'I myself will tend my sheep' (Ezk. 34:15). Jesus makes this shepherding ministry his own (Jn. 10:1–30). He is the Chief Shepherd of God's flock (1 Pet. 5:4; 2:25; Heb. 13:20), giving his life for them (Jn. 10:11). He now sends his servants to be 'under-shepherds' to God's flock (Jn. 21:17; Acts 20:28f.; 1 Pet. 5:1–3). This image underlines the utter dependence of the church on its head and Lord, the compassion and love which the Lord expressed towards us, and his commitment to guide, protect and nourish his people (Jn. 10:2–15).

The vineyard of God
Israel is a vine which God brought out of Egypt and planted in Canaan; 'it took root and filled the land' (Ps. 80:8f.). But when God came to gather the fruit, the 'good grapes' of obedience and righteousness, it yielded only the bitter fruit of injustice and oppression (Is. 5:1f., 7); so God made it a wasteland (v. 6). In one of his parables Jesus applied this to the transference of God's redeeming purpose to the Gentiles, adding that the owner's son, killed by the tenants, would be the agent of this change (Mk. 12:1–12). He himself is the true vine whose branches are fruitful as they abide in him (Jn. 15:1–8). This image speaks of God's care of the church, the church's total dependence on its Lord for its life and existence, and his concern for its purity and fruitfulness in the world.

CHARACTERISTICS OF THE TRUE CHURCH
Where can the true church be found today and what are its essential features? First we must distinguish the various meanings of the word 'church':

1. The total people of God spread through all the ages, the total company of the elect. The Reformers spoke of this as the invisible church.

2. The local company of Christians visibly gathered for worship and ministry; this meaning covers the vast majority of NT references to the church (*ekklēsia*).

3. All the people of God in the world at any one time, perhaps best referred to as the universal church. This occurs only occasionally in the NT (1 Cor. 10:32; Gal. 1:13).

4. 'The church within the church'. We noted earlier the OT distinction between the *'ēdâ* (the entire visible congregation) and the *qāhāl* (those within it who respond to God's call). Jesus taught that the kingdom corresponds to this pattern: mixed with the wheat are the weeds (Mt. 13:24–30, 36–43). Within the company identified with Christ are the people of God, the real 'church'. Thus there is no pure church; within any congregation there are likely to be enquirers who have made no profession of faith and some whose profession will at the last day be proved unreal (Mt. 7:21–23).

Granted, then, that no pure or perfect church is possible this side of glory, where can we discover the true people of God visibly gathered? Traditionally, four marks of the authentic church have been recognized.

One
The unity of the church derives from its being grounded in the one God (Eph. 4:1–6). All who truly belong to the church are one people and hence the true church will be distinguished by its unity.

This unity, however, need not imply total uniformity. In the NT church there was a variety of ministries (1 Cor. 12:4–6) and of viewpoints on matters of secondary importance (Rom. 14:1–15:13). While there was uniformity in basic theological convictions (1 Cor. 15:11, NEB; Jude 3), the common faith was given different emphases according to the differing needs the apostles addressed (Rom. 3:20, *cf.* Jas. 2:24; Phil. 2:5–7, *cf.* Col. 2:9f.).

There was also variety in forms of worship. The kind of service held at Corinth (1 Cor. 14:26ff.) would not have been common in the Palestinian churches, where worship developed on the Judaistic synagogue model and had a more formal pattern centred on the exposition of the written word. This synagogue model accounts for the churches being seen in the earliest period as a branch of Judaism; James 2:2 actually uses the word 'synagogue' for Christians meeting. There are also discernible elements of more than one form of church government (see below).

The true unity in the Holy Spirit of all regenerate people is a fact, irrespective of outward denominational disunity. The call for unity in the NT is therefore a summons to 'keep' the fundamental oneness of life which the one Spirit has imparted through regeneration (Eph. 4:3). The Reformers made this point by distinguishing between the invisible church (all the elect who are truly one in Christ) and the visible church (a mixed company of the regenerate and unregenerate). The unity of the invisible church is an accomplished fact, given with salvation.

The Roman Catholic Church has used this mark polemically to claim that its unity, compared with the fragmentation of Protestantism, is evidence of its being the true church. This, however, overlooks three points. (a) Rome itself separated from the Orthodox church in 1054, and had never been universally regarded as the sole true church in earlier centuries; *e.g.* the Celtic church flourished in Britain and Patrick founded the Irish church long before Roman missionaries arrived at Canterbury. (b) The marks must be held together. Historical succession or outward unity is valueless if not associated with 'apostolicity' (see below), *i.e.* loyalty to the apostolic gospel. (c) While Protestantism has at times been unnecessarily divisive, it can be argued that through her deviation from biblical doctrine Catholicism has been a primary cause of schism throughout the centuries.

While Scripture encourages the fullest possible expression of unity among God's people, it also makes clear that division is fully in accord with God's will when the essentials of apostolic Christianity are at stake. Such was Paul's disagreement with the Judaizers (Gal. 1:6–12) and Jesus' difference with the Pharisees (Mk. 7:1–13). It is significant that when Jude intended to write about 'the salvation we share' he found it necessary to urge his readers to 'contend for the faith that was once entrusted to the saints' (Jude 3). For the NT, unity is based on conscious commitment to the revealed truths of apostolic Christianity.

The NT addressed its teaching on unity to specific Christian groups, with immediate implications for their visible relationships (Eph. 2:15; 4:4; Col. 3:15). Jesus prayed for a unity which would help the world to come to faith (Jn. 17:23); while the parallel between this unity and that of himself and his Father

(17:11, 22) confirms the essentially spiritual character of scriptural unity, it surely includes visible identity of life and purpose, as Jesus' whole mission expressed a visible, demonstrable oneness with the Father's will. In other words there is need to search for a fuller visible unity than is presently experienced among those who confess the apostolic gospel.

This is particularly relevant where two or more bodies who confess essential biblical faith are operating in the same area, such as a university campus. The deepest challenge of this teaching, however, is at the level of relationships in a local church. In that setting the unity of life in Christ should express itself in genuine and tangible care for, and commitment to, one another. In default of this the claim to be an authentic Christian church is called in question (1 Cor. 3:3f.).

Holy

The people of God are a 'holy people' (1 Pet. 2:9). In the deepest sense the church *is* holy, in the same way that every individual Christian is holy by virtue of being united to Christ, separated to him and credited with his perfect righteousness (*cf.* Part 4, pp. 193–197). As the church stands before God 'in Christ' it is spotless and without moral blemish. The distinction between visible and invisible church applies here, since this 'imputed holiness' does not belong to those in a congregation who have no personal trust in Christ as saviour.

Union with Christ involves also a certain visible holiness of life. Hence a church's relationship with Christ the church's head will be expressed in the moral character and tone of their common life and relationships. A church which is a stranger to holiness is a stranger to Christ. When Christ addressed his churches he clearly expected just such a moral difference and was severe in his judgment when he found it lacking (Rev. 2–3).

Lest we become discouraged in applying this test, it is worth recalling that much of the life of the NT church was marked by error, division, moral failure and instability. Nevertheless some visible degree of holiness is an invariable mark of a true church of God.

Catholic

'Catholic' literally means 'referring to the whole'. In its earliest usage the term simply denoted the universal church in distinction from the local church; later it meant the church which confessed the orthodox faith in distinction from the heretics. With time the Roman church adopted the term to refer to its historically developed, geographically extended ecclesiastical establishment centred in the papacy. The sixteenth-century Reformers sought to recover the earlier meaning of catholicity as the acknowledging of the orthodox faith; in that sense, they argued, they and not Roman Catholicism were in fact the catholic church.

The key aspect of the early church's catholicity was its openness to all. In distinction from Judaism with its racial exclusivism, and gnosticism with its intellectual and cultic exclusivism, the church opened its arms to all who would hear its message and embrace its saviour, irrespective of colour, race, social status, intellectual capacity or moral history. It broke upon the world as a faith for all (Mt. 28:19; Rev. 7:9). The only basis for entry was personal trust in Jesus Christ as saviour and Lord, with baptism as the authorized rite of admission, expressing as it did the gospel of grace (Mt. 28:19; Acts 2:38, 41).

This is the fundamental level at which this 'mark' must be applied. Churches which erect other 'tests' should be viewed with suspicion. There is no place in a true church for racial, colour, social, intellectual or moral discrimination, provided that in the last-mentioned case there is evidence of true repentance. Denominational discrimination also needs careful scrutiny in cases where the fundamentals of the biblical message are clearly acknowledged.

Apostolic

The apostle is a witness to the ministry and resurrection of Jesus, and hence an authorized bearer of the gospel (Lk. 6:12f.; Acts 1:21f.; 1 Cor. 15:8–10). The apostles stand between Jesus and all subsequent generations of Christian faith; we reach him only by way of the apostles and their testimony to him incorporated in the NT. In this fundamental sense the whole church is 'built on the foundation of the apostles' (Eph. 2:20, *cf*. Mt. 16:18; Rev. 21:14). The apostolicity of the church therefore lies in its conformity to the apostolic faith 'once entrusted to the saints' (Jude 3, *cf*. Acts 2:42). The apostles still rule and order the church in so far as the church permits its life, understanding and preaching to be constantly reformed by the teaching of Holy Scripture.

Since 'apostle' literally means 'sent one', not surprisingly the NT on occasion refers to other apostles (Rom. 16:7). In this general sense, all who today are *sent* by the Lord as evangelists, preachers, church planters, *etc.* are in NT Greek terms *apostoloi*, 'sent ones'. This in no way implies, of course, that they have special status or authority rivalling that of the original company whose rule continues through the apostolic scriptures. To claim apostolic *office* today is a misunderstanding of biblical teaching and in practice offers a serious challenge to the authority and finality of the divine revelation of the NT.

It is also an error to understand apostolicity as a historic continuity of ministry running back to Christ and his apostles through a succession of bishops. This interpretation lacks any clear NT support. The whole notion of the grace of God communicated through a historical succession of officials runs counter to the character of the church in the biblical writings. Further, as a guarantee of the truth of the apostolic message, episcopal succession has signally failed. It was a church which stood squarely within this historic succession which required the sixteenth-century Reformation, not to mention other lesser reformations such as the eighteenth-century awakening under Whitefield and the Wesleys.

Roman Catholicism extends this interpretation of 'apostolic' to include the claim that the bishop of Rome is the historical successor of Peter and the special custodian of God's grace in the church. The claim is untenable. Peter's primacy among the apostles was no more than conspicuous leadership during the earliest Christian mission. He clearly receded into the background as the church moved out from Jerusalem, as Paul was commissioned to pioneer the mission beyond Palestine, and as John struggled to repair the churches from the ravages of false teachers. Crucially, Peter did not appear in the principal role at the Council of Jerusalem (Acts 15) and was clearly in Paul's shadow in the incident recorded in Galatians 2.

Catholicism further claims that this alleged supremacy of Peter was to be continued for the eternal salvation and continuing good of the church. None of the verses cited in scriptural support (Mt. 16:18f.; Jn. 21:15–17; Lk. 22:32) makes any reference to a successor to Peter. These two Roman claims run counter to plain NT evidence, and their third claim, that Peter's primacy continues in the bishop of Rome, is even less credible.

That Peter ended his life as a martyr in Rome is an early tradition which has a good measure of support; the historical difficulties, however, in showing that there has been an established succession of monarchical bishops of Rome from the first century onwards are insurmountable.

Apostolic succession is properly the succession of the apostolic gospel, when the original deposit of apostolic truth is passed from one generation to another: 'faithful men ... to teach others' (2 Tim. 2:2, RSV). A church is apostolic as it recognizes in practice the supreme authority of the apostolic scriptures.

The Reformers' marks

While the Reformers did not dismiss these four traditional marks, the controversies into which they were plunged focused their attention elsewhere. They identified two characteristics of the true visible church. 'Wherever we see the Word of God purely preached and heard and the sacraments administered according to Christ's institution, there it is not to be doubted a church of God exists' (Calvin).

'The Word being purely preached' drew into the open the primacy of the biblical gospel and it was precisely here that the real break with Catholicism had been made. Underlying this stress lay a conviction concerning the indissoluble bond between the written Word and the Spirit; to belong to the fellowship of the Spirit would necessarily express itself in submission to the Word which the Spirit had inspired. The Reformers knew no Spirit which did not lead to the Word; they knew of no love for God which was not bound to faith and truth. The other point at which they discerned the true church, the sacraments, was also polemical, since it was at the point of its sacramental teaching and practice that the Reformers saw Catholicism in clearest violation of biblical religion.

The existence of Christian groups (*e.g.* the Salvation Army and the Society of Friends) who have no sacraments makes us hesitate before declaring sacraments essential to a true church. Nevertheless our Lord clearly saw baptism bound up most closely with the church's message and human response to it (Mt. 28:19f.) and the sharing in the Supper as fundamental to its continuing life (Lk. 22:19; 1 Cor. 11:24f.).

One can generalize these marks by asserting that the ultimate mark for the Reformers was Christ himself. He is the centre of the Word and the heart of the sacraments.

Mission – a missing mark?

In Jesus' instruction about the life of the church (Jn. 13–16; Lk. 10:1–20; Acts 1:1–8) we see an element which is hardly explicit in the characteristics of the church identified thus far: mission, the responsibility to take the good news of Jesus to the ends of the earth.

It is surely significant that the NT history of the church, Acts, has as its key theme the successive expansion in the preaching of the gospel, Jerusalem, Judea, Samaria, and then the Gentile world (1:8, *cf.* 6:8f.; 7; 8; 10:34–48; 11:19–26; 13:1ff.). 'The church is mission' is no doubt an over-statement; but in its total service of the purpose and glory of God, mission is a fundamental biblical ingredient.

Hence, a church which neither preaches the gospel, nor experiences a burden for the moral and spiritual welfare of those around its doors, nor expresses concern for the poor and needy wherever they are found, has lost its title to authenticity and is a living denial of its Lord.

To summarize: a true church will be recognized by its unity in relationships, its holiness of life, its openness to all, its submission to the rule of the apostolic scriptures, its preaching of Christ in word and sacrament, and its commitment to mission.

Scriptures

Gn. 9:8f; 12:1–3; Ex. 6:6–8; Ps. 95:7; Is. 5:1–7; Mt. 16:18; 18:15–20; 28:18–20; Mk. 12:1–12; Lk. 24:47–49; Jn. 10:1–30; 17:17–23; Acts 1:8; 2:42–47; 4:23–37; 15:13–18; 20:28–32; 1 Cor. 11:23–26; 12:1–28; Eph. 2:17–22; 4:1–6; 5:22–27; 1 Pet. 2:4–10; Rev. 7:9–11; 21:1–22:5.

Questions

1. Examine the relationship between the individual and the community in the experience of salvation in (a) the OT, (b) the NT.
2. Explore the primary biblical images for the church, identifying what each has to teach about (a) God and his attitude to us, (b) the privileges of the church, (c) the responsibilities of the church, (d) the church's mission in the world.
3. Discuss the value and dangers of the distinction between the visible and invisible church.
4. Take the 'marks' of unity, holiness, catholicity and apostolicity and examine with respect to each (a) the biblical basis, (b) the application to your local

church or Christian group, (c) the application to the church worldwide.
5. How biblical and relevant are the Reformers' 'marks of the church'?
6. Do you agree with the claim that mission belongs to the essence of the
   church? Justify your answer from Scripture. If so, examine the implications
   for the present weekly programme of activities at your local church.

Bibliography

J. Balchin, *What the Bible says about the Church* (Kingsway, 1979).

G. C. Berkouwer, *The Church* (Eerdmans, 1976).

E. Clowney, *The Church* (IVP, 1995).

D. M. Lloyd-Jones, *The Basis of Christian Unity* (IVP, 1962).

J. R. W. Stott, *One People* (Falcon, 1969).

D. Watson, *I Believe in the Church* (Hodder, 1978).

24. The function of the church

In this section we move from what the church *is* to what the
church *does*. The tasks and responsibilities of the church are
determined by the nature of the church. Since the church is the
people of God, it finds its *raison d'être* not in itself but in serving
God's glory and honour (Rom. 11:36; 1 Cor. 8:6). But *how* does
the church serve God's glory?

WORSHIP

Worship (Gk. *latreia*) represents the most obvious way in which
the church fulfils its purpose of bringing honour to God.

Biblical examples

Worship is frequently reflected in Scripture, supremely in the
Psalms, the 'hymnbook of the Jewish church'.

In the NT, as well as the many expressions of the practice of
worship (Mt. 6:9; Mk. 14:12f.; Lk. 1:46–55, 68–79; 2:14, 29–32;
4:16; Acts 3:1f.; 4:24f.) and numerous doxologies (Rom.
11:33–36; 16:27; 1 Tim. 1:17; 6:15f.; Jude 24f.; Rev. 1:5f.), there
are lines from early Christian hymns (Eph. 5:14; Phil. 2:5–11;
Col. 1:15–20; 1 Tim. 3:16) and liturgical formulae (*Maranatha*,
meaning 'O Lord, come', 1 Cor. 16:22; *Amen*, a Hebrew term
meaning 'let it be so', Rom. 1:25; *Abba*, 'Father', Rom. 8:15).
Worship is also shown as fundamental in the heavenly order

(Rev. 4:8–11; 5:11–14; 7:9–12).

The church is a company of priests who bring to God 'a sacrifice of praise' (Heb. 13:15; 1 Pet. 2:5). This recognition of our responsibility to offer worship corresponds to the root meaning of *latreia*, which is 'service' or 'ministry'. We retain this meaning when referring to 'services' of worship, and it has deep implications for our approach to such gatherings. Too often Christians come to worship in a spirit of 'What will I get out of this?', whereas in fact the proper spirit is 'What can I give (to God) in this?'

The elements of worship

The offering of praise was fundamental. *The Word of God*, another basic element, came into Christian practice through the church's inheritance in the Jewish synagogue where the chief element was the reading and exposition of the law (Lk. 4:16–27; Acts 13:14f.). In early Christian worship Scripture was publicly read (Col. 4:16; 1 Thes. 5:27) and expounded (Acts 2:42f.; 6:2). It is important to identify with the Reformers' conviction that the preaching of the Word of God is not an addendum to worship or, worse, a merely human activity following the divine activity of the worship in praise and prayer. Rather the sermon is the climax to our worship as we hear the living voice of God and are moved to give ourselves to him in consecration and service. *The offering* was another element. There is rich Old Testament background here in the bringing of the tithes and offerings to God (Gn. 14:20; Lv. 27:30; 1 Ch. 29:6f.; Ezr. 1:6; Mal. 3:30). In the NT the main passage is 1 Cor. 16:1–4 (*cf.* Mt. 6:2–4; 2 Cor. 8–9). The *gospel sacraments* of baptism and the Lord's Supper represented another quite fundamental aspect (see below).

Features of worship

1. The living Christ is present in the midst. This has no parallel in other religions. We gather not to revere a memory but to celebrate a presence, to rejoice in the victory of our Lord and to meet him in the Spirit through the Word (Mt. 18:20; 28:20, which, while introduced in the context of the exercise of church discipline, has been understood by many believers over the years as expressing the essential reality of Christian worship. In effect it unpacks how our Lord understands 'church' in verse 17. *Cf.* also 1 Cor. 5:4).

2. The Holy Spirit empowers the worship (Jn. 4:24; Phil. 3:3). He creates reality (1 Cor. 12:3), checks unworthy instincts (1 Cor. 14:32f., 40), inspires prayer (Rom. 8:26f.), moves to praise (Eph. 5:18f.), leads into truth (1 Cor. 2:10–13), imparts his gifts (Rom. 12:4–8), and convicts unbelievers (Jn. 16:8; 1 Cor. 14:24f.).

3. A spirit of loving fellowship pervades the congregation. Early Christian worship was marked by deep mutual concern and genuine congregational participation (Acts 2:42–47; 4:32–35). This was expressed particularly in terms of a concern for mutual encouragement and upbuilding in Christ (Eph. 4:12–16).

The 'overflow' of worship

Worship, the adoring response to God, was not seen as confined to acts of corporate praise and ministry but was to be carried over as an attitude to the whole of life. Thus Paul can urge the Colossian slaves to obey and serve their masters diligently and wholeheartedly 'as working for the Lord' and with 'reverence for the Lord' (Col. 3:22f.). Worship is to be a whole lifestyle in which 'whatever you do, whether in word or deed, do it all in the name of the Lord Jesus, giving thanks to God the Father through him' (Col. 3:17).

FELLOWSHIP

Fellowship (Gk. *koinōnia*) and the church's glorifying God are closely linked: 'Accept one another, then, just as Christ accepted you, in order to bring praise to God' (Rom. 15:7). As Christians live together in true fellowship God is magnified. *Koinōnia* essentially means sharing together in something. Its emphasis is therefore somewhat different from the general use of 'fellowship' among us today, *i.e.* mutual association. The two meanings are not finally distinct, however, since common participation involves mutual association.

The fellowship of the people of God is grounded in a common participation in the life of God (1 Jn. 1:3, 7). It was a marked feature of the church from its beginnings (2 Thes. 1:3). NT fellowship, however, was not indiscriminate; it might be withdrawn in cases of extreme misconduct (1 Cor. 5:4f.; 2 Thes. 3:14) and did not extend to those who denied the 'apostles' doctrine' (Acts 2:42; Gal. 1:8f.). Its essential expression was *agapē*, self-giving love for the brethren (1 Cor. 13; 1 Jn. 3:16), which Jesus spoke of as the distinguishing mark of the new community (Jn. 13:34f.) and a means of bringing the world to faith in its message (Jn. 17:23).

Strikingly, this noun, *agapē*, had no general usage outside the Scriptures and among the churches. The common term for love, *erōs*, was felt to be inadequate to convey the essential feature of Christian love: love for the *un*worthy, the love encountered by the disciples in Jesus and experienced for one another through the Holy Spirit. This is why its definition in the NT explicitly refers to the cross: 'this is *agapē* ... that God ... sent his Son as an atoning sacrifice for our sins' (1 Jn. 4:10, *cf*. Rom. 15:7). *Agapē* means Calvary love, that stooping, forgiving, costly love which was the hallmark of early Christian community and is an essential feature of a God-honouring church in any generation. Love of this quality is not a human possibility, which is why the NT consistently speaks of it as a gift of the Holy Spirit (Rom. 5:5). It is, however, intensely practical (1 Jn. 3:17f., *cf*. Rom. 15:25f.; 2 Cor. 8–9).

These last references are to Paul's collection, levied among the Gentile churches for Christians in the Jewish/Palestinian churches suffering from the effects of famine. Not only did it express the fellowship between the two streams of early Christianity, it also cemented and deepened that fellowship.

NT fellowship also involved the practice of hospitality (Heb. 13:2; 1 Pet. 4:9); bearing one another's burdens (Gal. 6:2); mutual encouragement (Heb. 10:25) and prayer for one another (Phil. 1:9–11, 19). It found particular expression in the Lord's Supper (1 Cor. 10:16f.).

The early Christians' rich communal life was the major attraction of the Christian faith to the pagans of their day, and it is not difficult to establish the relevance of this to an age like ours where the discovery of 'fellowship' both locally and internationally is the price of our survival. The church surely has few things of greater immediate relevance to offer the world than the secret of genuine human relationship. The call to experience *agapē*, therefore, represents one of the deepest challenges which Christ issues to his church.

MINISTRY

The early church was committed to service (Gk. *diakonia*), a further means of bringing glory to God (1 Pet. 2:12). Unlike the Gentile world where greatness was equated with authority and the power to coerce, Jesus taught that greatness was to be found in humble service (Mk. 9:33–37; Lk. 22:24–27). This radically challenges our attitudes today as it did those of the disciples: service is not the pathway or preliminary to greatness as we commonly assume; rather, it *is* greatness. Behind this lies the ministry of Jesus himself, 'even the Son of Man did not come to be served, but to serve' (Mk. 10:45). The servant Messiah calls the church to identify with him in the servant community. This truth carries an enormous compensation; it means that fulfilment in life lies immediately to hand in humble service one of another.

The biblical teaching on the church's ministry (*diakonia*) has three further aspects.

The gifts of the Spirit

Along with the gift of new life in regeneration, the Spirit imparts to every believer a special gift or ministry. All the main NT passages dealing with this theme assert that a gift or gifts of the Spirit are the possession of *every* truly regenerate man or woman (Rom. 12:3ff.; 1 Cor. 12:7–1; Eph. 4:7, 16; 1 Pet. 4:10). The image of the body (Rom. 12:5) is eloquent: each member has a function in relation to the whole. The NT gives no hint that the receiving and exercising of this special ministry of the Spirit depends on some experience of the Spirit subsequent to regeneration. Thus each Christian is called to minister; to be a member of Christ is to be a minister of Christ (1 Cor. 12:7, 11).

Both OT and NT give examples of the gifts and ministries of the Spirit (Ex. 35:30–33; Jdg. 3:10; Rom. 12:3–8; 1 Cor. 12:4–11, 28; Eph. 4:11f.; 1 Pet. 4:10f.). The Spirit is free and sovereign in distributing gifts and ministries: 'There are different kinds of gifts . . . All these are the work of one and the same Spirit, and he gives them to each man, just as he determines' (1 Cor. 12:4, 11). We are responsible for identifying our gift and ministry and for exercising it for the good of our local church or group. The purpose of these gifts and ministries is twofold. Primarily they glorify the Lord Jesus Christ; as gifts of the ascended Lord, they demonstrate and vindicate his Easter victory (Eph. 4:8; Acts 2:32f.). They also serve to promote the growth of the body of Christ (Eph. 4:12).

Specialized ministry

This is one form of the Spirit's gift. The OT affords clear

precedent in the ministries of priests (Gn. 14:18; Ex. 28:1f.), prophets (Dt. 18:15f.; Is. 6:1ff.) and elders (Ex. 3:16; Dt. 19:12). Jesus continued this principle by calling the twelve disciples and the later NT reflects the same pattern in the appointment of elders (*presbyteroi*) or bishops (*episkopoi*), and deacons (*diakonoi*) (Acts 14:23; 1 Tim. 3:1–3; Tit. 1:5) and in the ministry of such as evangelists, pastors and teachers (Eph. 4:11).

These 'orders' of ministry do not imply a two-tier model of the Christian life. The distinction between specialized and lay ministry (Gk. *laos* = people) is essentially functional. 'Full-timers', whatever their title, are neither 'above', 'more important', nor 'nearer to God' than the lay members of their congregations.

Can the local community appoint a person to ministry without reference to the wider church? Opinions vary. Some hold that the local church is competent to act under Christ to appoint officers without reference to the rest of the church; others believe that ordination to ministry requires the authorization of the wider church.

The authority of these ministries also varies. In general we can note that the NT knows nothing of a sacerdotal priesthood which intervenes between God and human beings and mediates God's grace to sinners. It is highly significant that in the NT the word 'priest' is used in the singular only of Jesus. His unique sacerdotal priesthood effected at Calvary renders all other priestly mediators eternally obsolete; any attempt on the part of a human being to act as such is a blasphemous denial of Christ's once-for-all offering and challenges its efficacy. The plural concept 'the priesthood of all believers' refers to the general priestly functions of the whole people of God (Heb. 13:15f.; *cf.* Rom. 12:1f.; 1 Pet. 2:5, 9; Rev. 1:6).

The dangers of unduly elevating a human being, whether ordained or not, are best avoided by recognizing that Christian ministry is the ministry of Christ himself. The deepest word which can be spoken about Christian ministry in all its forms is that it is nothing other than the ministry of the risen Lord among and through his people (Rom. 15:18); this is also implicit in the very notion of the church as the body of Christ.

A notable feature of recent discussions about ordination is the question whether the gender of the ordinand is significant (see also pp. 123–125 on 'Man and woman'). The fact that women exercised ministry functions in the apostolic period seems clearly established from the NT. Paul talks approvingly of their contribution in a number of places (Rom. 16:1–2, 12; 1 Cor. 16:19; Phil. 4:2–3). He refers to women praying and prophesying in the church in Corinth (1 Cor. 5:5), and gives Timothy instruction concerning deaconesses (or female deacons) in 1 Tim. 3:11, NIV mg. Acts 21:9 refers without comment to Philip's daughters 'who prophesied'. Further, Jesus clearly affirmed women among the group around him, and they were accordingly among the disciple community upon whom the Spirit came at Pentecost (Acts 1:14; 2:1–4) and presumably part of the testifying company which amazed the onlookers by their many-tongued fluency (2:7f.). Not surprisingly, Peter cites Joel's prophecy in explanation, including its affirmation of the Spirit-enabled ministry of women alongside men (2:18). Moreover, the lists of ministry gifts in the NT make no reference to any gender exclusivity, but are referred to 'all' believers (see p. 277 above, 'The Gifts of the Spirit').

However, while the ministry, and specifically the *public* ministry of women, is established in the NT, should a gender factor be introduced at the point of ordained ministry? The degree of seriousness around this question obviously varies with the degree of distinctiveness churches attach to ordination. The matter is most acute in churches where the ordinand is thought in some real sense to represent Christ.

Exegetically Paul's apparent strictures against women's leadership weigh heavily with many (1 Cor. 11:3–16; 14:34–36; 1 Tim. 2:11–15). Note is also made of Jesus' twelve disciples being male, and the linkage of male leadership to the priority apparently established at creation (1 Tim. 2:13f.; 1 Cor. 11:12). Others, however, believe the Pauline passages are all capable of interpretation in terms of the specific pastoral situations addressed by the apostle, rather than as establishing universal norms for ministry. Paul's statement that in Christ there is 'neither male nor female' (Gal. 3:27) is seen as the essential NT view of gender distinction, not least in terms of ordained leadership, which is finally, as are all forms of ministry, a matter of God's call and the Spirit's gifting.

The reader is referred to the bibliography for further discussion.

Ministry beyond the church

The service the church offers is directed first to those within the community of faith (Gal. 6:10). It cannot stop there, for Jesus' deepest service was offered on behalf of those who were his enemies (Rom. 5:6–8). The church therefore must glorify God by being the salt and light of society (Mt. 5:16), not merely through evangelism but also by its efforts to influence society towards a form of life which is more just, pure, honest and compassionate, a closer reflection of God's own character and therefore more honouring to him, and also in the end a society which is happier and altogether more fulfilling for its members.

The primary means by which the church discharges this responsibility, apart from its direct evangelistic witness, is through creating men and women of strong, resolute Christian character whose daily presence influences the colour and tone of society. In addition there are occasions where the church feels it necessary to act corporately in response to social needs.

WITNESS

The call to witness (Gk. *martyria*) lay at the heart of Jesus' final instructions to the apostles (Acts 1:8) and at Pentecost they set about the task. Not that the Jerusalem church addressed itself immediately to worldwide evangelism; it took the martyrdom of Stephen and the ministry of Paul to confront the church with the full dimensions of its responsibility. But as the story unfolds in Acts, the programme of the Master is carried through: 'my witnesses in Jerusalem, in Judea, in Samaria, and to the ends of the earth' (Acts 1:8). The church of today stands in spiritual succession to the first generation of believers only as it commits itself to similar witness.

In the legal context *martyria* means making a defence; spoken testimony is the essence of its meaning. Notions of 'witnessing by life', 'letting my life tell', do not really convey what is intended. Of course, our lives must correspond to our profession, but the task committed to the church by Jesus involves verbal declaration, even if the full terms of Jesus' commission are wider than this (Mt. 28:19f.; Jn. 20:21ff.; Acts 10:42f.).

In witness, attention is to be directed to the objective work of God in Christ. Unfortunately, witnessing is sometimes equated with telling the story of how one personally came to faith. No doubt at points the account of God's dealings with us can usefully illustrate and authenticate the witness which we offer, but the heart of witnessing lies in directing people to Christ, seeking to confront them with his saving work.

In this work of worldwide 'witness' the NT church as the new Israel inherited the task which OT Israel had failed to carry through (Gn. 12:1–3; 18:18; Is. 49:6, *cf.* 43:10, 12; 44:8).

Too often the church, and perhaps its theologians in particular, have forgotten that the great theological writings of the NT were composed by missionaries and evangelists engaged in costly, sacrificial evangelistic and pastoral work. It is difficult to see how anyone can truly evaluate their thought, or interpret their teaching, who has not identified with their mission and felt something of their throbbing passion to carry the world to the feet of Christ.

There has been considerable discussion of the relationship between verbal proclamation and other forms of Christian ministry in the world, educational, medical or even socio-political. It is helpful to see witness in the terms expounded above, *i.e.* proclamation, but to recognize that it does not cover all the church is called to do in the world. This wider perspective can be called 'mission', interpreted as 'everything the church is sent into the world to do' (John Stott). Bearing witness is therefore not the whole of the church's task, though it remains central. The task of witnessing to the gospel in the whole world falls afresh on the church in each generation. It is an element of her purpose which she dare not relegate to a secondary level.

It is worth observing also that responsibility for witness, carrying forward the apostolic task, rests first of all on the apostolic community, the *church*. While the individual is respons-ible for witness among friends, work colleagues or neighbours, it is the church corporately which is commissioned in the first instance. Hence the first level of application is that of the local congregation. We discharge a basic part of our personal respons-ibility as Christ's witnesses in the world by throwing our effort, prayers and gifts behind the evangelistic programme of our local church or Christian group; this may be especially relevant to those who find personal witness particularly difficult.

Scriptures

Worship: Gn. 8:20; Ex. 15:1–18; 1 Sa. 2:1–10; 1 Ch. 29:10–13; Ne. 9:5f.; Pss. 148 – 150; Is. 6:1ff.; Am. 5:21–27; Mal. 3:10; Mt. 6:1–18; 18:20; Mk. 14:22–26; Jn.

4:24; Rom. 12:4–8; 1 Cor. 11:18–22; 16:1–4; Phil. 1:9–11; 3:3; 4:20; 1 Tim. 1:17; 3:16; 4:13; 6:15f.; Heb. 10:19–25; 13:15; Jas. 5:13; Jude 24f.; Rev. 1:5f.; 4:8–11; 5:11–14; 22:16.

Fellowship: Acts 2:42–47; Rom. 5:5; 12:13; 15:1, 5–7, 25f.; 1 Cor. 10:16; 13; 1 Thes. 3:6, 12f.; 2 Thes. 1:3; Heb. 13:2, 16; 1 Pet. 4:9; 1 Jn. 1:3, 7.

Ministry: Ex. 35:10–33; Dt. 18:15f.; 19:12; Jdg. 3:10; 1 Sa. 10:10; Ne. 8:7f.; Mk. 4:10f.; Lk. 6:12f.; 22:24–27; Jn. 13:14–16; 20:21; Acts 6:1–7; 11:30; 14:23; Eph. 4:11–16; 1 Tim. 3:1–13; 1 Pet. 5:1–5; Rev. 1:6.

Witness: Is. 43:10–13; Mt. 28:18f.; Acts 1:8; 4:20; 13:1–3; 2 Cor. 5:11–20; 1 Jn. 1:2.

Questions

1. What were the principles which underlay the worship of God's people in the OT? In which ways is worship under the new covenant (testament) different?
2. Discuss the roles of freedom and order/form in worship: what guidance does Scripture offer here?
3. What does fellowship (*koinōnia*) mean? Examine ways in which fellowship was expressed in the NT churches. What are today's equivalents?
4. Assess the significance for true fellowship of (a) 'apostles' doctrine' (Acts 2:42), (b) the Lord's Supper (1 Cor. 10:11), (c) the Spirit and his gifts (1 Cor. 12 – 13).
5. What is the significance of the Bible's teaching about spiritual gifts as far as ministry in the church is concerned?
6. List the New Testament requirements for specialized ministers in the church (*cf.* 1 Tim. 3:1–13; Tit. 1:9–15; Acts 6:3f.).
7. How does the church's witness serve God's glory?
8. What does 'mission' entail?
9. What are the main biblical bases for Christian social involvement?
10. What does Scripture teach about mission through (a) prayer, (b) financial gifts, (c) personal witness, (d) corporate church witness? Examine in each area the implications for your personal commitment to mission.

Bibliography

Arts. 'Worship', 'Fellowship', 'Ministry' in *NDT*.

J. Blauw, *The Missionary Nature of the Church* (Lutterworth, 1974).

D. Bridge and D. Phypers, *Spiritual Gifts and the Church* (IVP, 1973).

E. Clowney, *The Church* (IVP, 1995).

E. M. B. Green, *Called to Serve* (Hodder, 1964).

S. J. Grenz, *Women in the Church* (IVP USA, 1995).

W. Grudem (ed.), *Are Miraculous Gifts for Today?* (IVP, 1996).

J. B. Hurley, *Man and Woman in Biblical Perspective* (IVP, 1981).

R. P. Martin, *Worship in the Early Church* (Marshall, Morgan and Scott, 1964).

B. Milne, *We Belong Together* (IVP, 1978).

D. Peterson, *Engaging with God* (Apollos, 1992).

J. Piper, *Let the Nations Be Glad* (IVP, 1994).

J. R. W. Stott, *Baptism and Fullness* (IVP, 2nd edn, 1975).

J. R. W. Stott, *Our Guilty Silence* (Hodder, 1969).

J. R. W. Stott, *Christian Mission in the Modern World* (Falcon, 1975).

25. The life of the church

The church is an organism rather than an organization; it is a living, growing reality. This growth is both *extensive*, increasing its membership through evangelism, and *intensive*, deepening and maturing its life and faith. In this section we are concerned with growth in the second, *intensive* sense, but the two dimensions can never be separated. A healthy, growing church will be blessed both with conversions to Christ and increasing conformity with Christ. In order to promote the church's growth into the divine image God has provided certain means for achieving this. These are commonly referred to as 'the means of grace'.

THE WORD OF GOD

God's supreme instrument for renewing his people after the image of Christ is his Word (Jn. 17:17, *cf.* 2 Tim. 3:16f.), hence the centrality of the teaching of the Word in the work of the minister (2 Tim. 4:2) seen in Paul's own example (Acts 20:20f.). Just as the Spirit used the Word to bring us to faith in Christ (Eph. 1:13), so he uses it in our sanctification (Eph. 5:26f.).

Expository preaching
The public exposition of Scripture in the power of the Spirit has incalculable significance for the renewal and growth of the people of God. Indeed, the church cannot live above the level of its expository preaching, *i.e.* preaching which is concerned essentially to lay bare the teaching of the Bible and apply it relevantly.

Personal study of Scripture
To be a man or woman of God involves being a man or woman of the Word of God. The discipline of daily Bible study is therefore an obvious and God-owned means of spiritual growth.

As well as innumerable blessings there are also dangers in this practice: for example, an almost superstitious, 'horoscope' attitude can develop whereby the portion to be studied each day is detached from its biblical context and forced to yield some hidden, special message relevant to the reader's immediate situation. No doubt God does at times make his Word remarkably relevant to specific needs, but we need to keep before us that the whole Bible is God's Word to us all of the time; the truth which each passage and text has for us is its truth within its whole biblical and theological context (see Part 1, 'Hermeneutics'). Correct principles of interpretation are as pertinent for private as for public understanding of Scripture.

We also need to beware of developing a legalistic attitude whereby we presume to earn God's blessing because we have fulfilled our daily devotional obligations, or of becoming burdened with a sense of guilt and the feeling that 'today is bound to go wrong' if we miss our Bible study time. The sovereign God of glory does not depend on our feeble religious exercises for the operation of his purpose in our lives, or to protect and bless us in his grace.

These dangers, however, should in no way be permitted to outweigh the incalculable value of the life-long practice of daily study of God's Word.

Group study of Scripture
We find informal group Bible study in the NT (Acts 17:11). It has certainly been a factor in the church's renewal, particularly during periods when public preaching has been forbidden or has declined. It also has its dangers. It needs good leadership and the suppressing of the tendency to digress, to air personal opinions, or to exchange testimonies which have no clear anchor in the passage of Scripture being studied. If these dangers are recognized and avoided, group Bible study is without question a genuine means of grace.

THE SACRAMENTS
'Sacrament' (Lat. *sacramentum*) may be simply defined as 'an outward and visible sign of an inward and invisible grace' (Catechism of the Church of England). If we limit the term to those ordinances instituted by Christ, there are only two: baptism and the Supper ('the bath and the bread' as Luther denoted them). Some see this confirmed by the two OT ordinances, circumcision and the Passover. At the Council of Trent (1545–63) the Roman Catholic Church identified seven sacraments, on the basis of church tradition adding penance, priestly ordination, marriage, confirmation, and extreme unction ministered to the dying. There is no scriptural warrant for regarding these as sacraments.

The Salvation Army and the Society of Friends do not administer sacraments and stand as a witness against any attempt to overvalue the sacraments or to confine God's grace to them. Most Christians, however, agree that this is not sufficient ground for neglecting Christ's command to administer them. Some Mennonite churches and some other similar Christian groups practise an additional sacrament of 'foot-washing' on the basis of John 13:14f. While almost all interpreters see Jesus' command here implying only the need for an attitude of humble service to one another, footwashing has regularly produced in these groups a deep humility and depth of mutual commitment.

A sacrament has three principal elements:

1. *The visible sign* is represented by the water of baptism and the bread and wine of the Lord's Supper.

2. *The invisible grace* is that to which the sacrament points and, many would wish to add, of which it is a seal to believers. In the case of baptism, this is the 'washing of rebirth' (Tit. 3:5), forgiveness of sins (Acts 2:38), union with Christ in death and resurrection (Rom. 6:1ff.), and entry into the one body of Christ (1 Cor. 12:12f.). In the case of the Supper, it is the receiving of the benefits of Christ's sacrifice (1 Cor. 10:16), a spiritual 'feeding upon' Christ (1 Cor. 11:24f.), and communion with the people of God (1 Cor. 10:17).

3. *The sacramental relationship* between the visible sign and the invisible grace is understood in a variety of ways, from the one extreme in Roman Catholicism where 1 and 2 are identified, to the other, often associated with the name of the sixteenth-century Reformer, Zwingli, that sees the relationship between 1 and 2 as purely symbolic. The primary passages where Christ authorizes baptism and the Lord's Supper refer to 'teaching' (Mt. 28:20) and 'proclaiming' (1 Cor. 11:26). The sacraments are sacraments of the gospel, pointing us to Christ and his death and resurrection for sinners. When correcting the superstitious abuse of the sacraments in Roman Catholicism, the Reformers stressed the need to preach the Word whenever the sacraments are administered. They echoed Augustine's description of the sacraments as 'visible words of God'. This is an important principle, for only in the light of the Word do the sacraments find their proper confirmatory and supporting role pointing to Christ and confirming our faith in him.

Baptism

The OT refers to ritual and other washings, or acts of purification involving water, to express a cleansing from the pollution and guilt of sin (Ex. 19:14f.; Lv. 16:4, 24; *cf.* Ps. 51:2).

In the immediate context of Jesus' mission baptism was practised by John (Mk. 1:2–11; Jn. 19:34). John's baptism focused on two points. It was a baptism of repentance from sin (Mt. 3:2), and it anticipated the coming of the kingdom of God which was imminent and would involve severe judgment (Mt. 3:7–12).

Jesus was himself baptized by John. This prompts the question of why the sinless one should have submitted to a baptism of repentance, which was also a problem in John's mind (Mt. 3:14). Its explanation is two-fold. First, Jesus recognized that as the promised Messiah he was called to identify with the people he had come to deliver: 'it is proper for us to do this [by way of identification] to fulfil all righteousness' (Mt. 3:15). Secondly, Jesus consecrated himself publicly to the Father for the work of deliverance (Mt. 3:17) in a manner which explicitly recognized John as his God-ordained forerunner (Lk. 7:24ff.; Mal. 3:1).

Jesus authorized baptism on the part of the disciples at the beginning of his public preaching ministry when John was still active (Jn. 3:22; 4:1). Jesus also spoke of his mission as a baptism, a drowning under waters of great anguish (Lk. 12:50; Gk. *baptizō* = dip, or cause to perish as by drowning).

As the risen Lord, Jesus sent out the church to make disciples and to baptize all such in the triune name of Father, Son and Spirit (Mt. 28:19f.). The rest of the NT shows the church fulfilling this commission.

The meaning of baptism

Baptism is *a confession of faith in Christ* (Rom. 6:3–4; 1 Pet. 3:21; Acts 8:37), associated with public acknowledgment of Jesus Christ as Lord and Saviour (Acts 2:38; 10:48; 8:16).

Baptism is *an experience of communion with Christ* (Col. 2:12). The candidate is linked by faith with the Lord in whose name he or she is baptized, so as to enter in some sense into the very death and resurrection of Christ (Rom. 6:3–5). Hence for the NT baptism is the point at which ideally the sinner is gathered into union with Christ in the whole course of his redemptive action: life, death, resurrection, ascension, reign (Gal. 2:20; Eph. 2:5f.). This does not imply that salvation is conveyed in the act of baptism itself. It is faith alone which saves, or rather, Christ alone whom faith embraces; but, for the NT writers, baptism was the normal point at which faith came to public expression, laying hold of Christ and the blessings of his salvation: cleansing from sin, renewal in the Spirit, equipping for service, and entrance into the body of Christ (1 Cor. 12:12; 1 Pet. 3:21).

Baptism is *a consecration to living for Christ* (Rom. 6:4–22). Thus careless living is seen as a denial of baptism.

Baptism is *a promise of consummation through Christ* (Rom. 6:22). Like the Lord's Supper it points us both back to the great gospel events of the past, and forwards to our share in the future consummation of the kingdom, which we have already entered upon in our faith-union with Christ.

Baptism and church

In the NT period a Christian unattached to a church was unknown, since a person's very response to the gospel in baptism would have brought him or her into the fellowship of a local company of Christ's people. Our difficulties today in applying this teaching arise from separating baptism and conversion so that a considerable number of years frequently lie between the two, whichever may have come first. We are also hampered by 'church' having become a formal institutionalized structure rather than the living communion of men and women in Christ, which it was at the first.

Baptism and the Spirit

A number of Scriptures indicate a link between water and Spirit baptism (Gal. 3:26f.; 1 Cor. 12:12; Acts 2:38).

The proper objects of baptism

While much of the biblical teaching above would meet with the agreement of evangelical Christians across a wide spectrum of denominational affiliation, one basic point of division has still to be mentioned. Is baptism to be confined to those who profess personal faith in Christ, or are seeking to give expression to that faith; or may it also be administered to the children of believers? Since in the NT baptism was clearly administered to those professing personal faith, the issue becomes: what scriptural support is there for extending the rite also to infants? The following are among the commonest arguments.

1. It is claimed that the OT covenant had two sacraments, circumcision and Passover. Under the new covenant baptism replaces circumcision as the rite of initiation, and the Lord's Supper replaces the Passover as the rite of redemption/ communion. Circumcision was a family rite administered at eight days old to the male children born to the people of God (Gn. 17:12); hence baptism ought similarly to apply to the children of believers. The identification of the two is seen in Colossians 2:11f. and the identity of the two covenants as *both* covenants of grace and faith is expressed by Paul in Romans 3:21–4:24. It is in these terms that the promise of Acts 2:39 would have been understood. Such is the paedo- (*i.e.* infant) baptist case.

The issue then becomes: is this the correct exegesis of Colossians 2:11f., and can this conclusion really be drawn from what Paul is urging in Romans? The question is also asked whether this view can meet the fact that in the NT period the two rites of circumcision and baptism continued side by side. Jesus, his disciples, and the first generation of Jewish Christians all received *both*; hence clear evidence that the early church saw the one replacing the other is to that extent lacking.

2. A number of references are made to whole 'households' having been baptized (Acts 16:15, 31; 1 Cor. 1:16; 16:15f.). By implication, would these not have included infants? Objectors point to the references to faith in Acts 16:31, 34, that what we know of Lydia does not obviously cast her in the role of a young mother; and that the Corinthian household are spoken of in responsible terms (1 Cor. 16:15f.). Are these counter-points conclusive?

3. Paul speaks of the children of a believer being 'holy' (1 Cor. 7:14). No explicit reference is made to baptism, but he does seem to indicate a distinction between the children of believers and those of unbelievers. On the other side it is pointed out that the same term (Gk. *hagios, hagiazō*) is used earlier in the verse for the Christian partner's 'consecrating' effect on the unbelieving partner in a mixed marriage. Any conclusion drawn from the text with reference to believers' children would apparently need to apply equally to unbelieving marriage partners.

4. Support is urged for infant baptism because it exemplifies in a unique manner God's gracious willingness to save even

before the object of his mercy has had any opportunity to exercise faith. Opponents question whether this separation of grace and faith is in fact true to the NT doctrines, either of grace or of faith.

Ultimately disagreement about infant baptism appears to lie in the realm of the nature of the continuity and distinction between the old and new covenants. Thus, those who restrict baptism to believers need to ask if they really allow for proper continuity between the two covenants. If the continuity is far-reaching, the virtual silence of the NT on the question is as significant a factor in its favour as any clear teaching that it should be practised. Those who baptize the infant children of believers must ask if they allow for the elements of discontinuity between the two covenants. Is their new covenant really *new*, its newness focused on the inbreaking of the kingdom of God, centred in the coming of the Messiah with all its implications for the meaning of faith? If not, the lack of clear exegetical support for infant baptism in the NT constitutes a serious difficulty.

In all of this we dare not ignore the fact that God has signally blessed and honoured the ministry of his servants on both sides of this divide, whether paedobaptists like Luther and Wesley, or Baptists like Spurgeon and Billy Graham. One need but recall the mutual esteem between the Anglican John Newton and the Baptist William Carey to recognize the needlessness of bitter division over this issue.

The Lord's Supper

This second Christian sacrament, variously entitled Lord's Supper, eucharist, communion, breaking of bread, is rooted in the Last Supper, when 'on the night he was betrayed' (1 Cor. 11:23) Jesus instituted the supper as a continuing ordinance among his disciples. Examination of the relevant evidence appears to support the view that the Last Supper was the traditional Passover meal to which Jesus gave a new meaning. This identification aids our interpretation at several points.

'This is my body ... this cup is the new covenant ... do this in remembrance' (Lk. 22:19ff.). Jesus spoke in Aramaic and so what he said, in accordance with Aramatic usage, was 'this bread my body broken for you.' We ought not therefore to make too much of the verb 'is', for it would have been omitted and the meaning left to be inferred. Similar constructions must guide us in deciding what word to supply in translation. Galatians 4:24 is one such; literally 'these women the two covenants'. In this case the idea 'mean' or 'represent' would be demanded; it would make no sense to say the women *are* the covenants (*cf.* Gn. 40:12; Dn. 2:38; Gal. 4:25).

More important than these biblical parallels, however, is the Passover meal itself, and the way in which the first-century Jew understood its relationship to the events of the exodus which it depicted (Dt. 16:3). In the Passover meal it was believed that the past events were made to come alive again in the present, so that, as the *Mishnah* puts it, 'in every generation a man must so regard himself as if he came forth himself out of Egypt'. Thus the bread broken by Jesus in the supper and the cup which he took spoke of his body and blood offered up in sacrifice as the means of a new exodus (*cf.* Lk. 9:31) and the establishing of a new covenant. As the meal was repeated among his disciples it implied that they shared in the fundamental event by which the new covenant was established (the death of Christ) and so participated in its blessing.

Any thought of identifying the elements with the actual flesh and blood of Jesus, on the basis of a supposed original 'is' ('this *is* my body'), is quite unwarranted. The other extreme, however, by which the Supper is only a symbolic remembering, a sort of Christian poppy day, is also challenged by this evidence, which implies a genuine communion with the Lord in his death, not merely a mental recollection (*cf.* 1 Cor. 10:16ff.).

The old covenant between God and Israel had long since been vitiated by the disobedience and apostasy of the nation (Je. 3:20). Amid the ashes of the old order, Jeremiah dreamed of a new covenant which God would make, under which his law would be written 'on their hearts' and their sin put away (Je. 31:31–34). It is this new relationship, with its stress on inwardness, individual responsibility and full, final forgiveness which Jesus inaugurates in his sacrifice.

The 'cup' of the covenant has various associations in the OT. In general, it refers to our relationship with God. When this relationship is positive, Christians enjoy a full cup (Ps. 23:5). If we sin and turn from God, we receive a bitter cup (Ps. 75:8). The essence of the bitterness lies in our becoming subject to the divine wrath, and it is here we probably need to look to find the full meaning of the Supper reference. *This* was the cup Jesus asked to be freed from in Gethsemane (Lk. 22:42f.). The new covenant with all its blessing is not lightly or easily inaugurated. Only as the awful implications of our broken relationship with God are met, by the bearing of the divine wrath against sin, can the new covenant be actualized and redemption brought to sinful humankind.

Just as the Jews were continually to repeat the Passover meal, ever confessing anew their dependence on that historic act of redemption and appropriating its benefit (Ex. 12:14; 13:9), the church in the repeated celebration of the Lord's Supper bears testimony to the great historic act of redemption on which it stands (1 Cor. 11:24–26) and tastes again through faith the benefits of that holy sacrifice.

Each account of the Supper directs our thought forward to the end of the age. Matthew and Mark record Jesus' saying that he will not drink again of the fruit of vine until he drinks it new in the coming kingdom (Mt. 26:29; Mk. 14:25). Luke records Jesus' saying in the same context that the disciples will 'eat and drink at my table in my kingdom' (Lk. 22:29f.). Paul adds the word that the Supper is to be celebrated 'until he comes' (1 Cor. 11:26). Thus the Supper, in the thought of Jesus, ought to be celebrated in deliberate and conscious anticipation of the coming fullness of the kingdom of God. 'He added to "adieu" the note of "au revoir"' (R. P. Martin). Modern celebration of the Lord's Supper, particularly in Catholic and mainline Protestant traditions, has often signally lost this basic biblical dimension of joyful anticipation of the perfect communion which awaits us at the return of the Lord. Historically the Orthodox Churches have at times achieved a greater realization of this dimension, arising in part from their focus on the resurrection. The early Anabaptists also often attained this note of joyful anticipation through their stress on the Supper as an occasion of fellowship and celebration.

As alternatives to the Roman Catholic view, the Protestant Reformers formulated three distinguishable lines of interpretation which, broadly speaking, remain the major options in the Protestant understanding of the Supper today.

The Roman Catholic view

In the mass, the elements of bread and wine, when duly consecrated by an apostolically ordained priest, are changed into the body and blood of Christ. Admittedly, they retain their properties of taste and form, but are *in substance* nothing other than the true body and blood of Christ. This is known technically as 'transubstantiation'. In recognition of this, the priest elevates the 'host' (Lat. *hostia*, 'sacrificial victim') for worship by the congregation. Those who partake are spoken of as having fed upon Christ's very body and blood. The roots of this view lie with the pagan philosopher, Aristotle, and it operates in a framework of ideas patently foreign to a Jew such as our Lord. It also appears to obscure and even to challenge the crucial insistence that the only atoning sacrifice was made once for all time at Calvary (Heb. 7:27; 9:12; 10:10). Further, the claim that the priest offers Christ on the altar cannot but sound not too far from blasphemy to biblically sensitive ears.

A further unscriptural aspect of Roman Catholic practice is the 'communion in one kind', whereby only the bread or wafer is offered to the congregation; the wine is taken by the priest alone. Since Vatican II in the early 1960s, however, the wine is offered to the laity on special occasions.

The Lutheran view

Luther rejected 'transubstantiation' and argued instead that the body and blood of Christ are present 'in' and 'under' the elements of bread and wine. There is no change in the substance of the elements; but as the communicants physically partake of them they actually receive the glorified body of Christ which is everywhere present. Thus there is a true presence of Christ in the Supper, localized in the elements, which do not change their nature.

The Zwinglian view

This position is that the Supper is merely symbolic. It vividly reminds the communicant of what Christ has done for him or her on the cross, and calls for the rededication of life to God in the light of Calvary. Christ is present only in the sense and to the degree that he is always present to the believer through the indwelling Holy Spirit.

The Reformed view

Calvin argued that Christ is truly partaken of in the Supper when the communicant comes in true faith. While it is the whole Christ, flesh and spirit, who is partaken of, stress fell on the spiritual and mystical aspects of communion with Christ through the Holy Spirit. By the Spirit, the church is lifted up in the Supper to experience fellowship with her glorified head and Lord and enabled to feed on him for the nourishing of her faith.

To summarize

The Lord's Supper is one of the legacies bequeathed by Jesus to his church. It is his gift to us and should be cherished and celebrated in that light. Clearly, his giving it to us reflected his own sense of its importance for the life of his people through the ages. Despite the controversies which have sadly occurred, we need today to come to the Supper with thanksgiving and in the conviction that it has a great deal to contribute to our Christian growth. One helpful way of gathering up its significance is to see it in terms of the three tenses: past, present and future.

The past. The Lord's Supper points us back to the unspeakable love of God in Christ in the sacrifice of Jesus. Here we encounter the very heart of God, and are moved again by his 'amazing grace' to worship, wonder and adore.

The present. The Lord's Supper is a place of meeting with our risen Saviour. He affirms once again his love for us and the forgiveness he has purchased at such cost, quickens our responding love, and deepens our faith and commitment to him. He meets us too in the brothers and sisters who surround us at the table and whom we embrace again within the family of God.

The future. The Lord's Supper lifts us beyond the immediate horizons of space and time into the larger company of heaven, and rehearses the glorious 'marriage supper of the Lamb' when he shall come.

PRAYER

The OT has numerous examples of God blessing his people in response to their prayers (Gn. 18:16–33; Ex. 3:7–10; Nu. 21:4–9; 1 Ki. 18:20–46; Ne. 1:1–11). It is deeply instructive to note how prominent and regular an activity prayer was in the ministry of Jesus (Lk. 3:21; 5:16; 9:28f.; Heb. 5:7) and how closely the apostles, both corporately and individually, followed his example (Acts 1:14; 2:42; 4:4–6, 23–31; Eph. 1:16; Phm. 4). Jesus, however, did not leave it simply to example; he both instructed his disciples to be prayerful and taught them how to go about it (Mt. 5:44; 6:5–15; Lk. 11:1–13; 18:1–8).

Again there are echoing exhortations in the later apostolic writings (Eph. 6:18; Col. 4:2; 1 Thes. 5:17; 1 Tim. 2:1f.; Jas. 5:13–18). We do not pray, of course, simply because it does us good; balanced prayer embraces worship and thanksgiving to God and intercession for others as well as personal petition. Nevertheless we are clearly encouraged to come frequently to God and beseech his help and blessing in face of the challenge to live for him and serve him in the world.

Nor ought corporate prayer to be neglected. Special promise of blessing is associated with corporate intercession (Mt. 18:19f.), as the early church discovered (Acts 1:14; 2:42), to say nothing of the way in which regular times of prayer with fellow Christians can breathe new life and vigour into our own often weak and fitful intercessions and petitions. It is doubtful whether there has been any genuine revival in the church over the centuries which has not been preceded and accompanied by fervent personal and corporate prayer.

It is the promise of Scripture that God hears such prayer and is pleased to answer it. The answer may not always be quite in the terms we wish, but we may be confident that it will be in terms of our highest interest and the expression of his deep love for us. Further, although we do not seek it for this reason, there is a grace which time spent with God in prayer will bring to us. It is not something immediately perceptible or directly quantifiable, and it is surely for our good that it remains so, lest we seek God simply for what he gives us. However, Christian history certainly confirms that a life in which prayer is a regular and serious exercise is a life which will know much of the peace and power of God.

FELLOWSHIP

Fellowship with others in the body of Christ is a powerful means of grace to the people of God. God never intended the Christian life to be lived in isolation; indeed, it is folly to attempt it (Jn. 15:1–8; Eph. 4:1–16). Circumstances arise from time to time which deprive a Christian of this means of grace; we may be confident that the Lord will not leave any of his children in such a circumstance bereft of his comfort and presence (1 Ki. 19:1–18; Acts 23:11). But where fellowship is open to us it is courting spiritual disaster to hold ourselves aloof from it. It is surely significant in this connection that the bulk of the Bible's direct teaching on the Christian life is addressed to churches, *i.e.* to corporate groups of Christians. It is in that context, a caring, praying, supportive fellowship, that God intends the Christian life to be lived. In this connection we ought not simply to recognize the obligation of other Christians to provide this context for our own Christian life and growth, but also to play our full part in the support and growth of our fellow church members (1 Cor. 12:24f.; Gal. 6:2; 1 Thes. 5:14).

SUFFERING

The church is called to be conformed to its head and Lord, in particular in his suffering and rejection (Lk. 14:25–33; Jn. 12:23–25; Rom. 8:17; Rev. 1:9). Just as the cross was determinative of the life and mission of Jesus, so it is of the life and mission of his people. The church is the community of the cross (Mk. 8:3–38; Acts 14:22; 2 Tim. 3:12). Suffering is therefore a fundamental hallmark of living Christian testimony according to the NT. The Greek word for 'witness' is *martys*, from which we derive our English 'martyr'.

In fulfilling his purpose of conforming the church to the image of its Lord and releasing its witness ever more fully in the world, God uses suffering, both corporately and individually (Jb. 23:10; Ps. 119:67, 71; Jn. 15:2; Rom. 5:3; Heb. 12:4–13; 1 Pet. 1:6f.).

Scriptures

The Word of God: Dt. 29:29; 2 Ch. 34:14–33; Ne. 8:1–8; Pss. 1:1–3; 19:7–11; Mt. 4:1–10; Mk. 12:24; Acts 17:11; 20:27–32.

Baptism: Ex. 19:14f.; Lv. 16:4; Mt. 3:1–17; 28:19f.; Mk. 10:38f.; Jn. 3:22; 4:1; Acts 2:38, 42f.; 8:16, 36; 9:18; 10:47; 16:15; 1 Cor. 1:13–17; 10:2; 12:12; Gal. 3:27f.; 1 Pet. 3:21.

The Lord's Supper: Ex. 13:1–16; Je. 31:31–34; Mt. 26:17–30; Lk. 22:7–23; 1 Cor. 10:14–22; 11:17–34.

Prayer: Gn. 18:16–33; 32:9–32; Ex. 17:4–16; 33:12–23; Jos. 7:6–13; 2 Sa. 7:18–29; 1 Ki. 3:3–15; 18:20–39; 2 Ki. 19:14–37; 20:1–11; Ne. 1:1–11; Dn. 9:1–23; Mt. 9:38; 26:36–44; Mk. 1:35; 9:29; 11:22–25; Lk. 3:21; 5:16; 11:1–13; 18:1–8; Jn. 16:24; 17:1–26; Acts 1:14; 12:5, 9; Rom. 1:9; 8:26; 10:1; 12:12; Eph. 6:18; Col. 4:2; 1 Thes. 5:17; 1 Tim. 2:1f.; Heb. 5:7; Jas. 5:13–18.

Fellowship: Gn. 2:18; Ex. 17:8–16; 1 Sa. 23:16; Lk. 22:28; Jn. 15:1–8; Acts 2:42–47; 4:32–37; Rom. 1:12; 15:1–7; 1 Cor. 12:24ff.; 2 Cor. 7:6; Gal. 6:2; Phil. 2:4; 1 Thes. 5:11, 14; Heb. 3:13; 10:24f.; Jude 20.

Suffering: Jb. *passim*, 23:10; Pss. 66:10–12; 119:67, 71; Mk. 8:35–38; Lk. 14:25–35; Jn. 12:23–25; 15:2, 18f.; Acts 14:22; Rom. 5:3; 8:17; 2 Cor. 1:3–9; 4:10f.; 12:7–10; Gal. 6:14; Phil. 1:29; 3:10; 2 Tim. 3:12; Heb. 12:4–13; 1 Pet. 1:6f.; 4:13; Rev. 1:9.

Questions

1. What do you understand by 'the means of grace'? Show from Scripture the role they play in the growth of the people of God.
2. 'The church cannot rise higher than its expository preaching.' Discuss.
3. Examine the benefits and the problems associated with (a) personal Bible study, (b) group Bible study.
4. What is a 'sacrament'? Clarify the biblical basis for the view that there are two, and only two, sacraments.
5. What place should be found at the Lord's Supper for (a) the Word of God, (b) the fellowship of the whole congregation, (c) the recollection of Christ's suffering at Calvary, (d) the assurance of forgiveness to the penitent believer, (e) the expectation of the return of Christ in glory?
6. What can be learned about baptism from (a) the OT, (b) Jesus?
7. What are the main biblical arguments used in support of the baptism of infants? Do you find them persuasive? Explore the possibilities of genuine fellowship and co-operation among those who differ on this issue.
8. In what ways are (a) fellowship, (b) suffering, 'means of grace'? Illustrate their value from (a) biblical teaching and biography, (b) your own experience, (c) the experience of other Christians known to you.

Bibliography

Arts. 'Word of God', 'Sacrament', 'Baptism', 'Eucharist', 'Prayer', 'Fellowship', in *NDT*.

P. Adam, *Speaking God's Words* (IVP, 1996).

G. R. Beasley-Murray, *Baptism in the New Testament* (Paternoster, 1972).

G. C. Berkouwer, *The Sacraments* (Eerdmans, 1962).

H. Bonar, *When God's Children Suffer* (Evangelical Press, 1966).

D. Bridge and D. Phypers, *The Water that Divides* (IVP, 1977).

D. A. Carson, *A Call to Spiritual Reformation* (IVP, 1992).

M. Green, *Baptism* (Hodder, 1987).

O. Hallesby, *Prayer* (IVP, 1961).

E. F. Kevan, *The Lord's Supper* (Evangelical Press, 1966).

D. Kingdon, *Children of Abraham* (Carey Publications, 1973).

E. Kreider, *Given for You* (IVP, 1998).

G. Kuhrt, *Believing in Baptism* (Mowbray, 1987).

D. M. Lloyd-Jones, *Preaching and Preachers* (Hodder, 1971).

R. P. Martin, *Worship in the Early Church* (Marshall, Morgan and Scott, 1964).

B. Milne, *We Belong Together* (IVP, 1978).

J. Murray, *Christian Baptism* (PRPC, 1952).

J. C. Ryle, *Knots Untied* (James Clarke, 1964).

R. C. Sproul, *Knowing God's Word* (Scripture Union, 1980).

C. H. Spurgeon, *Lectures to My Students* (Baker, 1977).

A. M. Stibbs, *Sacrament, Sacrifice and Eucharist* (Tyndale Press, 1962).

J. R. W. Stott, *I Believe in Preaching* (Hodder, 1982).

26. The church in history

FORMS OF ORGANIZATION

We can distinguish four general patterns, though many groups do not fall precisely into any of these.

Episcopalian

This is government by bishops (*episkopoi*). It is the order pursued by Anglican, Lutheran, and, with modification, Methodist churches. A three-fold ministry is recognized, comprising bishops, priests (mainly local clergy who give leadership in the congregational and parochial setting) and deacons/deaconesses, who provide an auxiliary ministry in the church. In practice, the deacons are usually probationer priests. Only bishops may ordain others to ministry and they trace their succession back through the centuries. This system cannot claim to be biblical, if by that we mean incontrovertibly demanded by the NT. It is now generally accepted among scholars of all traditions that the Greek words *episkopos* (bishop) and *presbyteros* (elder) are equivalents in the NT (Acts 20:17, 28; Phil. 1:1; Tit. 1:5, 7). Hence, the NT understanding of 'bishops', in general, is not that encountered in Episcopalianism. They were officials of the local church, several commonly operating in a congregation on the pattern of the OT elders in the Jewish synagogue.

On the other hand, Episcopalians point to two other significant factors in support of their procedures. First, the presence in the early church of ministries which transcended those based in local congregations. The apostles are the supreme example of this; prophets also appear to have sometimes operated in this way. Timothy, Titus and James are seen as particular embodiments of this 'third dimension' of NT ministry, since they clearly were invested with responsibilities over a number of congregations. Secondly, there can be no doubt that the three-fold order of ministry goes back nearly to the apostolic era, and by the middle of the second century was the almost universal pattern for Christian ministry. As the church was confronted with heresy within its own ranks and persecution from without, it strengthened its official leadership, particularly the episcopate, to cope with these challenges. It is therefore a form of ministry which may claim to have proved of considerable value to the church over the centuries.

Presbyterian

Government by elders (*presbyteroi*) characterizes Reformed and Presbyterian churches throughout the world and, with certain episcopal modifications, Methodism. Usually the elders unite in a central body, such as a national assembly, and in local presbyteries with jurisdiction over smaller geographical territories. A form of Presbyterianism also operates where a local church is ruled by a group of appointed leaders, 'the oversight' or 'the elders' meeting' in some independent churches. This form claims direct biblical authorization from the NT pattern of appointing elders in local congregations. These officials appear in consultation with the apostles at the Council of Jerusalem in Acts 15. Among the elders in the local congregation, one may be set apart as a 'teaching elder' to minister the Word and sacraments in distinction from the other 'ruling' elders who share effective leadership with the teaching elder (1 Tim. 5:17). At a more general level, government is usually exercised by a system of church-appointed committees or courts with graded authority. Presbyterianism also recognizes the right of the whole congregation to have a say in the selection of ministers. Deacons act as a support ministry, concerned with practical day-to-day affairs of the church. As distinct from Episcopalianism, all ministers are formally of equal status.

Congregational (independent)

This is government by the whole local congregation, followed in Baptist, Congregational, Pentecostal (usually) and other independent churches. The local congregation is the fundamental unit: no individual official or church body may exercise rights over it. All matters of policy are submitted finally to the judgment of the whole congregation in which the minister, deacons and elders (if any) are on the same level as all the other members. Each local congregation is free to interpret the mind of Christ without interference from other congregations or bodies, though in practice most independent churches unite with others in matters of common concern. Ordination to ministry may be carried out without the involvement of other churches, though in practice that is rare; indeed, many 'congregationalists' see such wider representation as essential. Ministry is usually two-fold, ministers (pastors) and deacons, though in some cases the pastor shares the spiritual responsibility with a number of elders. Some 'congregational' churches, such as the Christian Brethren, have traditionally questioned the validity of appointing one particular individual to 'minister' in the local congregation, though this position is less regularly maintained today.

Adherents appeal to the significance of the local church in the NT. As we have seen, Scripture uses language concerning the nature of the church equally of the local and the 'total' church. Further, there is an absence of evidence in the NT of imposition upon the life of the local congregation by wider bodies or officials from beyond its ranks, with the obvious exception of the apostles or their personal delegates such as Titus and Timothy. Underlying this is the conviction that Christ's headship of the church implies his immediate presence among his people and his power to convey his will without the mediation of some other agent, whether personal or corporate.

In practice, Congregationalism recognizes the value of mutual fellowship and co-operation between churches, though not such as to qualify the ultimate freedom of the local body to act in accordance with the will of the Lord as it discerns it.

The house-church movement which has developed in many parts of the world, mainly in association with the charismatic renewal movement (see pp. 253–255), represents another contemporary form of Congregational organization. As with other Congregational groups, the links between churches vary all the way from a total independence, where no reference is made to any other Christian body, through to a strong denominational-type relationship with clearly drawn boundaries of accountability and association. Some of these groups give their leaders the title 'apostles', on the view that that title has a continuing validity today, either as part of God's restoring the church in its original NT reality, or simply as a means by which the living Spirit continues to lead his people into the truth and reality of God.

Roman Catholic

Catholicism is essentially a particular historical expression of episcopalianism. We have already noted departures from biblical norms in its understanding of the church. The unique feature of its organization is the primacy of the bishop of Rome, the pope; it also differs from the Reformed churches in its concept of a sacerdotal priesthood, found also in the Orthodox churches of the East and among some Anglicans.

From this brief summary it is evident that neither the Episcopalian, Presbyterian nor Congregational system may lay sole claim to the support of Scripture, though this would be denied by some within each tradition. This is not to suggest that biblical evidence be set aside and the issue determined on pragmatic grounds. But in order to identify with the body of Christ we need to throw in our lot with one of these groups and a degree of commitment to its forms is essential to give that adherence meaning. We must recognize, however, the limits as well as the extent of our convictions in matters which do not clearly contradict biblical teaching, and exercise that charity which is the hallmark of the people of God (Jn. 13:34f.).

HISTORICAL PERSPECTIVES

The early centuries

In the immediate post-apostolic period the church was conceived as the people of God, the new spiritual society of believers in Jesus to which admission was gained through baptism. They were a sort of third race, over against Jews and Gentiles, noted for their high moral standards and strong community life.

During the second century, discernible change occurred. The rise of heresy necessitated clear boundaries; the authorized apostolic traditions were protected by bishops, who were seen as the apostles' successors. This move encouraged centralized structures, and the essentially 'spiritual' character of the church gave place to the thought of the church as an external institution. This did not take place without resistance; Montanism (2nd century), Novatianism (3rd century) and Donatism (4th century) in different ways attempted to recover the earlier moral and spiritual purity.

The church hierarchy in general rejected these movements and the trend continued. Thus for Cyprian, writing about the middle of the third century, to withdraw from the visible church founded upon the episcopate was to forfeit salvation. Over a century later Augustine conceded that the church is the invisible company of the elect, the communion of saints, who have the Spirit and are characterized by true love. But he argued that the true 'church' lies within the Catholic church which wields apostolic authority through its historical episcopal succession; only within its pale can one be filled with divine love and receive the Holy Spirit through its sacraments. During the early centuries the church divided into East and West. While the roots of this split lie in the administrative and political division of the Roman empire, ecclesiastically it arose from failure to resolve the post-Chalcedonian debates about the person of Christ. The Eastern churches were more sympathetic to Nestorian (*cf.* p. 182) and monophysite[1] views; they also differed over the Holy Spirit, holding that the Spirit proceeds from the Father alone, while the West argued for a double procession of the Spirit from Father and Son. These eastern churches are known today as the Orthodox churches.

The Middle Ages
In the medieval period the church was the foundation of all else in society and accordingly did not require any theoretical justification. Two particular developments may be noted. First, the tradition that Peter was given primacy over the other apostles and that he had been the first bishop of Rome was supplemented by the claim that this supreme authority was transmitted to Peter's successors in the bishopric of Rome. The pope was acclaimed as the 'universal bishop' by the beginning of the seventh century. This development in the papacy was resisted in the East and caused further division between East and West.

Secondly, the visible Catholic church was more closely identified with the kingdom of God. This view, based on a misunderstanding of Augustine, was furthered by the circulation of two ninth-century forged documents claiming ancient authority for the notion. As a result there was increasing effort to bring cultural and political matters under the sway of the church.

The Reformation
In the early sixteenth century a dispute over indulgences (papal certificates guaranteeing absolution) soon became a question of

---

1. The view that there was only one nature in the incarnation.

the very nature of the church. Led by Martin Luther, the Reformers challenged the whole fabric of medieval Catholicism in the name of the gospel of salvation by grace alone. When the road of reform from within was blocked, they moved outside the Roman fold and set up new Reformed congregations, from which sprang the Protestant churches. The Reformation understanding of the church involved the virtual rewriting of the theological textbooks of earlier ages. The Reformation did not produce one common view but a single approach covering several relatively diverse interpretations.

Luther rejected the Roman claims for the infallibility of the church under the leadership of the pope, the sacerdotal priesthood and the automatic operation of the sacraments (the claim that they automatically convey grace, regardless of the faith, or lack of it, of the recipient). He restored the idea of the church as a spiritual communion of believers, all of whom are priests to God, but retained infant baptism. Calvin added an emphasis on discipline and on the educational function of the church, attempting in Geneva to reform the whole of society by the Word of God.

A third view of the church which came to light at the same time has arguably become the most influential of all. This was the view of the Anabaptists, so named because they insisted that baptism was for believers only and therefore re-(*ana-*)baptized those who had received baptism in infancy. Despite an extreme fringe which has unfortunately received the limelight in the history books, they were generally people of balanced views and impressive piety. They sought a more radical reformation than Luther and Calvin, a 'sectarian' church consisting only of those who professed faith and gave evidence of its reality. Church forms and hierarchies of ministry were minimized and immediate individual experience of the grace of God became central. They taught strict separation of church and state.

The modern period

From the Reformation have come the major branches of historic Protestantism which have grown alongside the continuing Roman tradition. A number of the many important factors in the recent period may be noted.

1. The identification of church and state has been steadily eroded. Correspondingly, religion has become increasingly a

matter of freely determined personal conviction, although in most western democracies one of the Reformed churches was given special rights and privileges as the 'national' church.

2. The worldwide missionary movement has carried the Christian gospel to the ends of the earth. From this visionary and deeply sacrificial endeavour has emerged the phenomenon of the international Christian community which is the church of Jesus Christ today.

3. Related at points to the above is the development of the international ecumenical movement, which led to the founding of the World Council of Churches in 1948. The movement, though disavowing the aim of worldwide unification of Christendom, has consistently promoted moves in this direction. During the 1960s and 1970s, in particular, its path became somewhat thorny due to the WCC championing some radical and heterodox theological positions. More recently it has tended to modify these stances and expressed a welcome renewed appreciation for the importance of mission in the life of the churches, though this latter has been muted somewhat by a greater deference to and dialogue with other world religions. The Orthodox churches have come to play a larger role in WCC affairs, and links with the Roman Catholic Church (not a full member of the WCC) have been deepened. Some evangelicals support it; others, though linked to it through their denominational ties, find little enthusiasm for it, not least because of its failure to stimulate zealous evangelistic and missionary endeavours. Still others, suspicious of its ultimate intentions and repelled by its theological looseness, keep well away. During the last period evangelicals have discovered their own sense of global solidarity, notably in the Lausanne movement launched at a large international gathering at Lausanne in 1974, and furthered by a subsequent global congress in Manila in 1994. It remains active in encouraging networking and consultation among evangelicals worldwide in promotion of the goal of world evangelization.

4. There are signs of change in the Roman Catholic Church. The three centuries following the Reformation and the Council of Trent (1545–1563) saw Catholicism pursue its own course and consciously reject Reformed ideas. A 'new Catholicism' has, however, emerged, particularly with the Second Vatican Council (1962–65) called by Pope John XXIII. The new openness to modern influences has continued in the years since Vatican II,

including an unparalleled degree of contact with Protestant spokespersons and churches. It has also come to play an increasing role in the world ecumenical movement despite not being a full member of the WCC. The papacy of John Paul II has seen a variety of tendencies at work. The Pope's basically conservative theological instincts have led to a refusal to give any ground to proponents of women's ordination, a reduced emphasis on Mary, a greater flexibility on birth control, and some concession on priestly celibacy. His own charismatic personality, his penchant for international pilgrimages, and his sensitivity to the influence of the media, have brought the church new visibility. Declining levels of recruitment to the priestly vocation is a continuing concern.

5. At the opposite end of the ecclesiastical spectrum, recent years have witnessed a highly significant mushrooming of new independent churches and Christian groups in all parts of the world. Many, though by no means all, are Pentecostal in their experience and forms of worship. They are strongly biblical and often show great zeal in evangelism, a spirit of sacrificial living, flexibility in structure, and a studied openness to what they believe to be God's direct leading. These churches and groups manifest a corresponding absence of vital commitment to Christian tradition or the forms of faith represented by the larger historic branches of the church. While these groups are most obvious in the West and the Third World, they have their counterparts in the former communist-bloc countries. Many Christians maintained a defiant and courageous witness behind the Iron and Bamboo curtains where years of communist domination brought remarkable church growth, often at great and continuing cost. Mention needs to be made of the heroic leadership role of the church in toppling several of the Marxist regimes in eastern Europe, and to the astonishing growth of the church in China largely through unofficial house-church fellowships. Although, by the nature of the case, the exact number of Christians in China today cannot be known, the growth of the church there since the Maoist expulsion of western missionaries in the early 1950s is arguably the greatest numerical expansion of Christianity since the first century.

6. Materialism, particularly in the western industrialized nations, has brought about a general secularization of life and a corresponding erosion of the deep Christian convictions of

earlier generations. The impact of this process continues to be felt, particularly among those who advocate 'liberal' forms of Christianity. Nor can one see any prospect of recovery in these quarters, with the disappearance of the accumulated capital of generations of biblical faith on which these brands of religion unconsciously draw. In today's world people who are not persuaded by the total claims of Jesus Christ are more likely to invest their lives in New Age religion, or a personal amalgam of different spiritual traditions or even a bizarre latter-day cult, than to opt for a watered-down, desupernaturalized version of the Christian faith. Happily, many Third World churches retain a vibrant faith more clearly continuous with the Christianity of earlier periods. There have also been some notable stirrings of hope among the older churches with the rediscovery, particularly by younger people, of the authority of the Bible and of Christianity as a living, present experience of God and a vital way of life in the world. While this evangelical renaissance is now of worldwide proportions, it is too early to say whether it is merely a reaction to materialism and the present world crises, or whether it heralds new and better days among the people of God. Beyond any doubt, the massive problems of modern global civilization make genuine revival imperative.

THE CHURCH'S FUTURE

As the creation of the Holy Spirit, the church looks constantly towards the future. The Spirit is the life of the new era of the fulfilled kingdom of God, and hence the foretaste of the coming glory. As such, he imparts to the people of God a longing for that fullness when the bride is to be united with her heavenly bridegroom (Eph. 5:25ff.; Rev. 21:1ff.)

We cannot, therefore, limit our thinking to the church we see now, which is often so unlike the heavenly bride it is called to be. We need to remember to dream of that coming glorious company with whom Christ is destined to share his eternal inheritance. No exposition of the biblical doctrine of the church can neglect this dimension, which will be dealt with at length in Part 7.

Scriptures

Nu. 11:16f.; Ezk. 34; Mt. 18:15–20; Lk. 5:1–12; 6:12–16; Acts 6:1–6; 15:1–29; 20:17, 28; 1 Cor. 1:2; 4:1; Eph. 4:1–16; Phil. 1:1; 1 Tim. 3:1–13; 5:1, 17f.; Tit. 1:3, 5–9; Heb. 13:17; 2 Jn. 1; Rev. 21:1–22:5.

Questions

1. State and assess the biblical support for the Episcopalian, Presbyterian, and Congregational forms of church organization. 'As far as church government is concerned the NT gives principles rather than a detailed pattern.' Discuss.
2. What are the benefits to be derived from the study of the history of the church over the centuries?
3. Identify signs of hope in the present development of (a) your local church or Christian group, (b) the national Christian scene, (c) the progress of Christianity worldwide.
4. What is the destiny of the church? What values derive from contemplating that prospect?

Bibliography

J. F. Balchin, *What the Bible Teaches about the Church* (Kingsway, 1979).
T. Bradshaw, *The Olive Branch* (Paternoster, 1990).
O. Chadwick, *The Reformation* (Penguin, 1964).
E. Clowney, *The Church* (IVP, 1995).
I. Murray (ed.) *The Reformation of the Church* (Banner of Truth, 1965).
M. Noll, *Turning-points* (IVP, 1998).
A. M. Renwick and A. M. Harman, *The Story of the Church* (IVP, 2nd edn, 1985).
M. A. Smith, *From Christ to Constantine* (IVP, 1971).
A. M. Stibbs, *God's Church* (IVP, 1959).
D. Watson, *I Believe in the Church* (Hodder, 1978).

Application

THE IMPORTANCE OF THE CHURCH

Union with Christ necessarily involves union with his people. The church is not simply a 'means of grace', useful to our growth; it is a necessary part of Christian experience, to be taken with utmost seriousness. In this sense every Christian is already within the church and it represents the essential context of their faith.

It was God's love and concern for the church that brought Christ to Calvary (Eph. 5:25). Hence the measure of our conformity with the mind of Christ will be the extent of our concern for the church, its calling and extension, its life and zeal, its understanding and conviction, its growth and unity, its purity and holiness, both globally and in our local setting.

THE FUNCTION OF THE CHURCH

Worship
The church is a worshipping community. We need to affirm our commitment to public worship and examine our attitudes to it. As NT priests it is our privilege and responsibility as we assemble week by week to bring to God an offering of praise (Heb. 13:15). How are we exercising this ministry of worship?

Fellowship
The church is a fellowship in the Spirit. We need to affirm our commitment to the fellowship of our local church or group and examine our attitudes to our fellow Christians. Are there feelings of malice, envy or pride of which we need to repent? There may also be criticism, slander or gossip to confess; possibly even an apology to make, or past hurts to forgive. Perhaps there is need for greater generosity in our sharing in hospitality, in time and friendship, or with our money or our prayers, or in other practical ways.

Ministry
The church is a servant community. We need to examine our attitudes and affirm our commitment to serve the church and the world in Christ's name. This will involve identifying the gift or gifts of God's Spirit which he wants us to use for the growth of our local church and being alert to opportunities for service in our immediate neighbourhood or place of work. For some, all this will deeply influence their choice of career, and also where it is pursued.

Witness
The church is a witnessing community. We need to affirm our commitment and examine our attitudes to being a witness for Christ in the world. This will involve honestly facing certain questions. Are my prayers regularly and fervently directed to the spread of the gospel through the world? Are they intelligently directed through wise use of widely available prayer information? Do I contribute regularly and sacrificially to the work of Christ throughout the world? Am I involved in the efforts of my local church to make Christ known in our neighbourhood? Am

I seeking in God's strength to be a faithful and effective witness to Christ among my neighbours, workmates, fellow students, or wherever the Lord has set me?

THE LIFE OF THE CHURCH

We need to examine our attitudes to and use of the means of grace. This will mean a commitment to read and study Scripture and to listen regularly to it being expounded, being baptized if we have not yet been so, and regularly sharing in the Lord's Supper. It will involve making time for prayer and waiting on God, a genuine commitment to the fellowship of our local church, and a willingness to take our share of suffering for the sake of the gospel and for our own and the church's growth.

REMEMBERING TO DREAM

The church as we see and experience it may be unattractive, whether on the national ecclesiastical scene or in our local Christian community. At times we may find it difficult to discern any recognizable likeness of Christ. But we must resist the temptation to despair or become disillusioned by the observable church. For all its present weakness, the church is destined to become glorious and beautiful. We need at times quite deliberately to look beyond immediate realities and remember to dream of the coming great church, Christ's perfected people, his spotless bride, who will be presented to her heavenly bridegroom at his appearing.

That very vision will strengthen our resolve to invest our time and resources, to direct our energies and our prayers, and to labour on through our years to help conform the present imperfect and broken body of Christ more fully to that maturity and splendour which she is destined to reflect in the presence of her returning Lord.

PART 7
The last things

27. The kingdom of God

The study of the last things is technically known as *eschatology*, from the Greek word for 'last'. It is perhaps the dominant term of current theology. It is a more complex subject than might be supposed, for the 'last things' are not simply the events at the end of history.

The primary category in biblical eschatology is the kingdom of God, a term frequently on the lips of Jesus (Mt. 12:28; Mk. 1:14; 9:1; Lk. 13:18–20; Jn. 3:3). The basic meaning is God's 'rule' or 'kingly power' (Lk. 19:12), *not* a geographical area. It is a dynamic notion; God's kingdom is his rule *in action* (Ps. 145:13; Dn. 2:44).

OLD TESTAMENT BACKGROUND

In the OT God is seen as sovereign over all things. 'The LORD reigns ... the great King above all gods' (Ps. 93:1; 95:3) is the presupposition of all OT religion (Ex. 15:18; Is. 43:15). But God's reign is resisted and opposed. The devil entices humankind into rebellion against God (Gn. 3), the nations live in idolatry and wickedness (2 Ki. 17:29) and Israel herself falls into spiritual decline and is defeated by her enemies. At the personal level every Israelite experiences the contradiction between God's will and his or her own moral attainment.

Out of this contradiction there arises the conviction that God will vindicate his kingship beyond question (Is. 2:1–5; Zp. 3:15;

Zc. 14:9f.) in the coming 'day of the LORD' (Am. 5:18f.; Mal. 4:1f.). It will be associated with Messiah (Is. 4:2; 9:6f.; 11:1f.). He will be a great ruler after the order of David (1 Ch. 17:11–14; Ps. 72) and through him the day of the LORD will come in judgment for the nations and in deliverance for Israel (Mal. 3:1ff.). Sometimes continuity with present earthly history is stressed (Is. 11); at other times this future act of God is seen as coming from beyond history (Dn. 7).

After the close of the OT this hope came to be expressed as the 'new age to come', as distinct from 'this present age'. By Jesus' day this was a familiar distinction (Mt. 12:32; Mk. 10:30), with the additional feature that 'the age to come' was now commonly referred to as 'the kingdom of God' (Mk. 10:23–30; Lk. 18:29f.).

JESUS AND THE KINGDOM

This background is crucial for understanding Jesus' central claim, that 'the kingdom of God is near' (Mk. 1:15; Mt. 12:28); the longed-for day of salvation predicted in the OT has now arrived.

Jesus' teaching about the kingdom has two aspects. Through his proclamation and ministry, climaxed in his death and resurrection, the reign of God is now a reality in human history. As men and women trust and follow him, they enter the promised kingdom (Lk. 17:20f.; 18:28–30). The future fulfilment of the promise of God's rule, however, reaches beyond Easter to his glorious appearing at the end of history (Lk. 21; 22:29f.).

These twin claims are the key to all Jesus' teaching on the kingdom of God: the kingdom has come, and yet it is still to come.

In Matthew's gospel, written particularly for Jews, 'kingdom of God' appears as 'kingdom of heaven'. Heaven was a common first-century synonym for God among pious Jews who regarded God's name as too sacred to pronounce. Jesus used both phrases. There is therefore no difference implied by 'kingdom of heaven'.

Another clearly related idea is 'eternal life', literally 'the life of the age to come'. This was a virtual equivalent to 'kingdom of God' among the Jews of Jesus' day (Mk. 10:17). It is, of course, eternal in duration, but the real point is its quality rather than its duration; it is the life of the kingdom of God predicted in the OT. This equivalent occurs particularly in Jesus' teaching as recorded by John (Jn. 3:16, 36; 4:14; 5:24; 10:28).

LATER NEW TESTAMENT TEACHING

With time the gospel spread to the Gentiles where the whole notion of kingship was likely to be misunderstood, as Jesus himself acknowledged (Mk. 10:42f.). Other concepts were therefore used to convey the Christian claim about Jesus which would be less open to misunderstanding. Examples are 'salvation' (Acts 16:30f.; Rom. 1:16f.) and incorporation 'in Christ' (Rom. 8:1; Phil. 3:9f.).

When the kingdom is referred to, it is usually in terms of its future fulfilment at the end (Acts 1:6; 1 Cor. 15:24, 50). When it is spoken of as already established, it is seen as the kingdom of *Christ* which is entered through the Holy Spirit (Col. 1:13, *cf.* Jn. 3:1–8). The profound OT sense of the sovereignty of God is thus transferred in the NT to the person of Christ who exercises the rule of God at the Father's right hand through the Holy Spirit (Acts 2:33). The kingdom is therefore now realized in human experience through the ministry of the Holy Spirit, who on the basis of the work of Christ brings the life of the future age of glory into present reality.

THE KINGDOM AND CHRISTIAN EXPERIENCE

The tension between these two dimensions is the context of the Christian life. On the one hand, the Christian is a new person, united with Christ in his death, resurrection and reign, and sharing the powers of the new age of the kingdom in the Holy Spirit; on the other hand, the old nature is still a painful and persistent reality, dragging Christians below the moral attainments to which their new life directs them.

Thus we rejoice in the coming of the kingdom, in the fact of eternal salvation, in the blessings of the new age in our union with Christ; and yet we long for our deliverance, the final coming of the kingdom, the completion of our salvation and the full emergence of the new person in Christ.

The temptation always exists to escape this tension. It can happen in two ways. One is when we so despair of life in the here and now that we cease to expect God to work in the present, whether in our own lives or in the lives of others; God, if he is around at all, will have to do it all in the future. The other is the attempt to realize the kingdom wholly in the present. This expresses itself in unrealistic and unbiblical claims for Christian

experience, whether in terms of moral perfection (entire sanctification, see p. 246) or perfect health, or even in terms of a Christian's alleged 'right' to wealth and prosperity.

Scriptures

Ex. 15:18; 1 Ch. 29:11; Pss. 2:6; 99:1; 145:11–13; Is. 9:6f.; Je. 23:5f.; Dn. 2:44;
7:9–14; Am. 5:18f.; Zc. 14:9; Mt. 6:10; 11:2–5; 12:28; 13:16f., 24–30; 16:28;
19:28f.; Mk. 1:15; 10:23–30; Lk. 17:20f.; Jn. 3:5; Acts 1:3; 14:22; 20:25; 28:23;
Rom. 14:17; 1 Cor. 4:20; 6:9; 15:24, 50; Col. 1:13; 1 Tim. 6:15; Rev. 1:5f.; 11:15.

Questions

1. What do you understand by 'the kingdom of God'? How does it relate to
   the OT? What are the main points in Jesus' teaching about it?
2. 'The kingdom of God is inaugurated, but not yet realized.' Discuss.
3. How is the kingdom of God connected with (a) eternal life, (b) salvation,
   (c) union with Christ, (d) the new birth, (e) the final glory of the church?
4. How does the Bible's teaching on the kingdom affect the Christian's
   response to human society and its needs?

Bibliography

Arts. 'Kingdom of God' in *IBD* and *NDT*.
G. R. Beasley-Murray, *Jesus and the Kingdom of God* (Paternoster, 1986).
G. E. Ladd, *The Presence of the Future* (Eerdmans, 1974).
H. Ridderbos, *The Coming of the Kingdom* (Paideia Press, 1978).
G. Vos, *The Teaching of Jesus Concerning the Kingdom of God and the Church*
   (PRPC, 1972).

28. The second advent of Christ

Here we encounter the heart of biblical teaching on the
'last things', the glorious appearing of the Lord. Jesus himself
sees the climax in these terms: 'At that time men will see the Son
of Man coming in clouds with great power and glory' (Mk.
13:26). Paul's summary of the Christian hope is similar: 'we
eagerly await a Saviour from there [heaven], the Lord Jesus
Christ' (Phil. 3:20).

NEW TESTAMENT TERMS

Parousia is the commonest term used in the Greek NT for the second advent (Mt. 24:3; 1 Cor. 15:23; 1 Thes. 2:19; 2 Thes. 2:1, 8). It means 'coming', 'arrival' or 'presence' and was used in the first century for the visit of an emperor or other distinguished person. It conveys the idea that the Lord's return will be a definite and decisive action on his part. He will come himself, as surely as he came in the incarnation. It will be the return of the King (Lk. 19:12).

Apokalypsis means 'revelation' (1 Cor. 1:7; 2 Thes. 1:7; 1 Pet. 1:7). The Lord's coming will reveal who he is and what the world is. It will be a time for things which are now hidden to come to light.

Epiphaneia means 'appearing' or 'manifestation' (2 Thes. 2:8; Tit. 2:13). It also carries the idea of drawing back a veil so that what is there already may be truly seen for what it is.

BIBLICAL PASSAGES

Numerous OT passages speak of the glories of the messianic kingdom in terms which were not fulfilled at Christ's first coming (2 Sa. 7:16; Pss. 2; 72; Is. 2:1–5; 9:6f.; 11:1–10; 40:3–5; 49:6; 61:2; Je. 33:15; Mi. 4:1–3). In addition Daniel 7:13f. refers directly to the coming of the Lord in glory (*cf.* Mk. 13:26; 14:62; 1 Thes. 4:17; Rev. 1:7, 13; 14:14).

There are more than 250 clear references to the return of the Lord in the NT (*e.g.* Mt. 24–25; Mk. 13; Lk. 21; Jn. 14:3; Acts 1:11; 3:20; 17:31; 1 Cor. 15:23ff.; 1 Thes. 4:13–5:11; Heb. 9:28; Jas. 5:7; 2 Pet. 3:8–13; 1 Jn. 3:2f.; Rev. 1:7; 22:20). These references show unambiguously that the return of the Lord is taught in all the main strands of the NT.

This makes abundantly clear that the second coming of Christ is not confined to a few obscure passages, nor does belief in it depend on highly imaginative interpretations of symbolic visions. It lies on the surface of the Bible for all to see. Denial of the second coming can be viewed therefore only as a fundamental rejection of biblical authority.

THE NATURE OF THE SECOND COMING

A full description of the Lord's return is impossible. In this event our glorified Lord will manifest himself in a manner which will be utterly climactic for existence as we know it. It will obviously therefore transcend all events in space and time hitherto experienced. Accordingly any account which claims to tell the whole story down to the minutest detail is self-defeating from the outset.

Jesus himself likened his coming to a flash of lightning (Mt. 24:27), which conveyed to first-century listeners its essentially mysterious character. The Lord's coming will inevitably go beyond all 'this-worldly' description and we are forced to resort to symbol in order to represent it. The biblical symbols, however, are God-given and so we can interpret them in the confidence that, while they cannot say everything, they can tell us what we need to know.

It will be a *glorious* coming, in 'power and great glory' (Mt. 24:30); 'every eye will see him' (Rev. 1:7). The first advent of our Lord took place in obscurity and weakness, seeming to cause hardly a ripple on the surface of human history. His second advent by contrast will be universally manifest. He will come 'with the clouds of heaven' (Dn. 7:13; *cf.* Mt. 24:30; Acts 1:9, 11; Rev. 1:7). The clouds signify God's glory and manifest presence among his people (Ex. 24:15–18; 2 Ch. 5:13f.). In this sense the Lord's return will be the final act of the unveiling of the divine presence, the culminating revelation of the majesty and transcendent glory of the triune God.

It will be a *decisive* coming: 'Then the end will come' (1 Cor. 15:24). History will come to a close: the curtain will fall on the stage of time – Christ will come! It will therefore be an event in the history of all people. It is not confined to the church or to Christians who will be alive on earth when it takes place. Whether or not they know or even care, the life of every man and woman is moving towards the advent of Christ. All are marching to meet the Lord.

It will be a *sudden* coming. Despite references to signs of the times, the Bible speaks clearly about the unexpectedness of the Lord's return (Mt. 24:37–44; 1 Thes. 5:1–6). We can gather it up in a saying of Jesus: 'the Son of Man will come at an hour when you do not expect him' (Mt. 24:44). Even our Lord himself confessed ignorance as to the time (Mk. 13:32). The Christian therefore must 'watch' (Mk. 13:37).

Any interpretation of Christianity which lacks this future hope is out of step with the biblical witness. One error is to interpret these references in terms of the first coming of Christ by which the kingdom of God was established. This cannot stand up in the light of the clear futurist reference of some of Jesus' own sayings (Mt. 13:24ff.; 19:28; Mk. 14:25), to say nothing of the unambiguous teaching of the rest of the NT. Equally erroneous is the allied notion that references to Jesus' future vindication mean God's 'coming' to men and women during Jesus' ministry and subsequently through the gospel. While Christ indeed 'comes' to people through the Word of God, this does not begin to exhaust the meaning of the texts in question.

THE PURPOSE OF THE SECOND COMING

To complete the work of redemption
By his coming Christ will complete the redemptive purposes of God across the ages. All God's enemies, sin, death and the devil, will be removed from God's world (1 Cor. 15:22–28, 42–57; Rev. 12:7–11; 20:1–10) and a new order established in which God's original purposes for humankind and creation will find final realization (2 Pet. 3:1–13; Rev. 22:1–15).

It is important to maintain the essential links between the second advent and the first. It is not that the first advent was inadequate and needs the second to do the job properly. Rather, the work of Christ in his second advent is to implement the conquest and victory won decisively in his first (Jn. 14:3; Rev. 5:5–14). This essential link between the past achievement of Jesus' mission and its future climax goes a long way to explaining why the expectation of an imminent return of Christ runs through the NT writings. The end has already arrived and is 'at hand'; in principle nothing remains to be accomplished to bring about its full triumph. No intervening events can affect the Easter victory of Christ and so we can live in constant anticipation of his appearing.

To resurrect the dead
'All who are in their graves will hear his voice and come out – those who have done good will rise to live, and those who have done evil will rise to be condemned' (Jn. 5:28f.). By the power of God operating through Christ at his coming all who have ever

lived are to be called back to a form of embodied life. This resurrection is with a view to judgment.

To judge all people

Christ 'will judge the living and the dead' (2 Tim. 4:1; *cf.* Acts 17:31). His coming for judgment is taught in both OT (Pss. 2:9; 110:5; Is. 61:2; Mal. 3:1–3) and NT (Mt. 16:27; Acts 10:42; Rom. 2:3–16; 1 Cor. 4:5; Jude 14f.). All must appear before him at his coming.

To deliver the church

Several passages imply that the persecution of God's people will be particularly intense at the time of the Lord's return (Dn. 7:21; Mt. 24:12, 21ff.). By his coming the Lord will deliver his people from their enemies and gather to himself all his elect from all the ages (1 Thes. 4:17; Rev. 6:9ff.).

THE TIME OF THE SECOND COMING

The disciples' question, 'What will be the sign of your coming and the end of the age?' (Mt. 24:3), is answered by Jesus at considerable length. Paul gives similar indications of the time of this great crisis of the ages (2 Thes. 2:1–12) and Revelation, developing OT imagery, particularly from Daniel, appears to unfold the developments leading up to the return of the Lord. On the basis of this material and other supporting evidence from prophetic sections such as Ezekiel 38, some Christian teachers have developed a plethora of 'signs of the times' which are presented as a blueprint of the political, moral and religious scene at the time of Jesus' return, including in some cases a detailed account of future international conflicts between specified national armies. Can all this be justified?

Jesus responds to the disciples' question by speaking of a period of time preceding his return characterized by four general features: religious apostasy (Mk. 13:5f.), persecution and the worldwide witness of the church (Mk. 13:9–11, 13, 19), wars and conflict between nations (Mk. 13:7f.) and disturbances in the natural order (Mk. 13:8, 24f.).

Paul appears to speak in similar terms in 2 Timothy 3. 'There will be terrible times in the last days' (v. 1), brought about by intense self-centredness with all its accompanying anti-social expressions in family and society (vv. 2–4). In religious life there will be outward form but no inner reality (v. 5). In 2 Thessalonians 2 he states clearly that before the Lord's coming there will come 'the rebellion' and the appearing of 'the man of lawlessness' (v. 3) who will so exalt himself as to claim deity (v. 4). He will be slain by Christ at his coming (v. 8).

What conclusions can be drawn from this teaching? Does being watchful (Mk. 13:37) mean that we must constantly check to see if these signs are fulfilled in our lifetime, and ought we, like some, to attempt some prediction of the precise time of Christ's return?

Certain factors indicate the need for caution:

1. There is need for caution over the phrase 'the last days'. In some passages (*e.g.* Acts 2:17; 1 Cor. 10:11; Heb. 6:5) it clearly refers to the entire period between the two comings of Jesus, when the kingdom of God has truly come but still awaits full manifestation. 2 Timothy 3 lists primary features of life in this whole period. What Jesus gives us are signs of the presence of the kingdom. In this sense the end is always near, because Jesus the King is near (Phil. 4:5; Rev. 22:20).

2. Jesus did not encourage a 'signs of the times' mentality. He stated that 'the kingdom of God does not come visibly' and he refused to perform signs or point to them in relation to his ministry and its authentication (Mt. 12:38f.; 16:4). Certainly on other occasions he spoke more positively of 'signs', as when rebuking the Pharisees for not reading them correctly (Mt. 16:3; Lk. 12:56), and John sees Jesus' miracles as signs of his unique person (Jn. 2:11, 23; 7:31; 12:37; 20:30f.). Jesus' negative attitude to the signs is explained by their moral and spiritual implications. The Pharisees and the other 'sign-seekers' had no genuine concern to recognize Jesus and to make the necessary moral response to his presence and mission. Interest in 'signs' and fulfilled prophecy can become detached from a concern for God's will, and can pander to unworthy aspects in our characters. It is salutary to remember that these very matters are a preoccupation of non-Christian cults such as Jehovah's Witnesses.

3. There are passages which make clear the unexpectedness of the Lord's return when it does take place. No study of the signs will remove the sense of surprise, even among those who are faithful (Mt. 24:44). The disciples too were ignorant of the time of the coming: 'You do not know on

what day your Lord will come' (Mt. 24:42). Indeed, we are *not* to know (Acts 1:7).

4. In Matthew 24:36 (Mk. 13:32) Jesus stated that even he, at that moment, did not know the time of his coming. This is the more surprising because it follows a statement in which he shows an almost unparalleled consciousness of his divinity (Mk. 13:31). If Jesus admits ignorance of the time of his return, then clearly no-one dare claim such a knowledge. A sincere confession of ignorance is therefore not simply allowable and prudent; it reflects the mind of Christ.

5. Peter points out that God's timescale is entirely different from ours: 'With the Lord a day is like a thousand years, and a thousand years are like a day' (2 Pet. 3:8). Both sides of this equation need to be noted. Time for God has both an intensity and a brevity beyond our appreciation. We should hesitate, therefore, before committing God to our human timetables.

6. Over the centuries many earnest Christians have believed that the signs were being fulfilled in their lifetime and the end was imminent. These include some of the wisest and godliest of the Lord's people in past ages; we must surely pause before we dogmatize about our own day. Nor can we ignore the pastoral dangers of over-preoccupation with this area. The conviction that the end of the world is at hand is widespread at the present time.

Do we conclude then that Jesus could conceivably return at any moment? Paul teaches that certain events within history will precede the return of Christ (2 Thes. 2:3ff.); it cannot 'just happen' at any moment. In general, evil will intensify in the period before the Lord comes. Even this is not so precise that we can identify it beyond question, as is shown by the history of failed attempts already noted.

What can be said then in summary? The really important factor is our moral attitudes: what we are, our desire to do the Lord's will and to encourage others to a similar obedience. We are not to attempt to map out the details of the events in the last days and to try to predict the date and time of the Lord's return; however, the other extreme of turning our back on the whole question of the 'signs' is also wrong. The correct attitude is one of watchfulness, recognizing that the conflict between good and evil will sharpen before the end, though even that will not altogether escape the ambiguity of history. The Lord is always standing ready to come. The precise time lies in the perfect timing of God.

RELATED ISSUES

A number of issues associated with the return of Christ continue to spur debate. It is important not to let them assume undue importance: they are distinctly secondary to the primary fact of Christ's appearing. Here we can only summarize them.

The antichrist

One of the main figures associated with the Lord's return is the antichrist. Biblical references to this occur most clearly in John's letters. John states that the antichrist is already present and at work; indeed, there are 'many antichrists', the appearance of whom is a clear sign that 'it is the last hour' (1 Jn. 2:18) (*i.e.* 'last days'). The antichrist is marked by his teaching; 'he denies the Father and the Son' (2:22); he refuses to 'acknowledge Jesus' (4:3) or to 'acknowledge Jesus Christ as coming in the flesh' (2 Jn. 7). Most interpreters refer Paul's teaching on 'the man of lawlessness' in 2 Thessalonians 2 to the same subject.

Another, more controversial element of biblical teaching about the antichrist occurs in Daniel and Revelation. Daniel 7:20f. refers to a horn 'that had eyes and a mouth that spoke boastfully [and] was waging war against the saints and defeating them, until the Ancient of Days came'. Revelation 13 is claimed to be a similar allusion, where a grotesque beast comes out of the sea (vv. 1–4), blasphemes God's name and is given universal authority (vv. 5–10). It has 'man's number', 666 (v. 18). It is overthrown by the word of God and the armies of heaven (19:19–21).

On the basis of these passages numerous attempts have been made over the years to identify this 'man of lawlessness' or 'antichrist'. In interpreting this biblical teaching, it is wise to recall that the clearest references to antichrist occur in John's writings. There antichrist is not confined to one unique figure, but is a spirit which attaches to a whole group of people whose presence is a feature of the whole of the 'last days'.

It is correct on the basis of 2 Thessalonians 2 to anticipate a final, climactic embodiment of the spirit of antichrist prior to the Lord's return. Whether we should spend time attempting to identify him is doubtful in view of the mistakes so regularly made in the past. How far the Daniel and Revelation references are relevant, and what exactly we should learn from them, are matters where dogmatism is out of place.

What then do we do with this idea? We use the principle of interpretation which states that the obscure should be interpreted in the light of the clear. What are clear are the references in John's letters. The idea of the antichrist then becomes a call to vigilance in the church today against all that would deny the truth of God and in particular the full deity and true humanity of his eternal Son.

Israel

The Bible clearly shows that God chose this nation to be the channel of his purposes in the world. 'Theirs is the adoption as sons; theirs the divine glory, the covenants, the receiving of the law, the temple worship and the promise as well as the patriarchs' (Rom. 9:4f.). To Israel came the world's Saviour, Jesus Christ. In this sense, 'salvation is from the Jews' (Jn. 4:22). In spite of all this, most Jews rejected God's calling by crucifying the Messiah. God's salvation turned outwards to the Gentiles, in what Paul calls the 'mystery hidden for ages' (Col. 1:26f.), that 'the Gentiles are heirs together with Israel, members together of one body, and sharers together in the promise in Christ Jesus' (Eph. 3:6).

Has God finished with Israel, then? Some believe so. Others, however, are not so convinced and see Israel as having a future role in God's purposes, particularly in the events which will immediately precede the return of Christ.

The latter see three twentieth-century political events as being of tremendous significance. The first was the Balfour Declaration of 1917 which pledged support for the creation of a national home of the Jewish people. The second was the founding of the state of Israel in 1948, allegedly in fulfilment of a number of OT predictions (Is. 11:11ff.; Am. 9:14f.; Zc. 8:1–8). The third was the capture of Jerusalem by the Jews in June 1967 during the Six-Day War, seen to relate to Jesus' words concerning the end of 'the times of the Gentiles' when Jerusalem will be 'trampled on' (Lk. 21:24). As a 'sign of the times' these three related developments take on tremendous significance, implying the nearness of the second advent.

But is this correct? Certainly many passages predicting the restoration of the Jews appear to refer to the immediate historical context in the OT, *i.e.* their return from exile in Babylon (Dt. 30:1–10; Ezk. 36:17–24; Ho. 11:10f.). These promises were made to a remnant of the whole nation who had faith in the LORD, a condition certainly not met in these three political events, but met by those who returned from Babylon (Ezr. 3:4f.; 7:10; Ne. 1:4–11). Similarly, Jesus' words in Luke 21:24 can simply imply that the Jews will be removed from their central place in the redeeming purposes of God until the end of the present age, the period during which the gospel is taken to the ends of the Gentile world. Yet some of the OT prophecies appear, on the surface at least, to cover more than the restoration from Babylon (Je. 29:1; Ezk. 36:24–28; Am. 9:15; Zc. 8:1–8), and Luke 21:24 is set in a reference to military occupation.

Discussion of the future of the Jews in God's purpose is largely bound up with the interpretation of several NT passages, of which Romans 11:26, 'all Israel will be saved', is supremely significant. Its meaning is explained in various ways.

1. The whole race of Jews will be saved in the end. This keeps Paul's meaning for 'Israel' consistent through the passage, but it directly contradicts Paul's argument in Romans 9–11, that Israel has been judged by God because she has failed to seek him on the basis of his grace. Salvation by national identity is precisely what Paul is concerned to deny here. A modification of this interpretation holds that before the Lord's return, through the mercy of God alone there will be a great worldwide turning of the Jews to their Messiah, which will in turn be the means of great worldwide blessing for the church and its mission (*cf.* 11:12–15).

2. It refers to all within Israel who believe. Paul is then stating that in the mercy of God there is a saved remnant among the Jews who have as a nation rejected Christ.

3. 'All Israel' is the wholeness of the one people of God, both Jews and Gentiles who believe in Christ. Thus 'Israel' here is a synonym for the church (*cf.* Gal. 6:16).

4. Finally, is Paul thinking of the future at all? The whole debate concerns his hopes and motives as a Christian evangelist, who yearns for the salvation of his people (9:1–3). Romans 11:26 expresses his hope with respect to his witness among them and his confidence in God's ability to restore his ancient people.

Extended evaluation would require a whole book, and interested readers are referred to the bibliography. Equating biblical references to Israel with the present secularized state of Israel appears distinctly questionable. The prospect of a significant future recognition of Christ by Jews is plausible on the basis of Romans 11:11–24. However, interpretations 2 and 3 above are certainly entirely possible.

The millennium

This is one of the most hotly debated issues in the whole field of eschatology. The word comes from Revelation 20:2, 7, where Christ is said to reign for one thousand (Lat. *mille*) years with 'those who had been beheaded because of their testimony for Jesus' (v. 4); during this period the devil is 'bound' (v. 2). After this period the devil is released as a preliminary to the final conflict and overthrow of the devil and all his allies (20:7–10). Millennialism, the belief in a literal thousand-year reign, is also known as 'chiliasm' from the Greek *chilias* (a thousand).

What are we to make of this biblical teaching? It cannot escape notice that the phrase occurs in only one chapter of the Bible, in a book of disputed interpretation full of symbolic numbers. The idea of a thousand-year reign of Christ on the earth at the end of the present age appears in the writings of some of the early fathers. It was revived by the Montanists in the second century and espoused by numbers of anabaptists during the Reformation. Other early Fathers, however, make no reference to it, even when discussing eschatological themes.

Augustine (354–430) was attracted to millenarian views in his earlier period, but came to interpret the passage in Revelation 20 as the entire period between the two comings of Christ; the 'binding' of Satan in this period was the authority vested in the church to 'bind' and 'loose' sins (Jn. 20:22).

Millennial notions were almost universally rejected by the major Reformers. Calvin speaks of them as 'too childish either to need or to be worth a refutation'. The position was reasserted in the nineteenth century, and today is held in various forms by considerable numbers of evangelical Christians in all parts of the world, particularly the USA.

We can distinguish three main schools of interpretation of the millennium.

Postmillennialism

This view sees the millennium as an earthly reign of a thousand years; the *parousia* takes place *after* (*post*) the millennium. The thousand-year period is a time of great prosperity in the preaching of the gospel, which spreads through the earth winning universal acknowledgment of Christ prior to his glorious appearing and the establishing of the eternal order. Some see this promised in Romans 11.

This view finds fewer advocates today than in the late nineteenth century when the worldwide missionary movement erupted (partly fathered by postmillennialism), and optimism marked western society. Today's pessimism and the general sense of crisis in human culture call for a greater faith in the universal recovery of the fortunes of the gospel than most feel prepared to exercise without a clearer biblical basis.

The biblical evidence cited in support includes Matthew 28:18–20, seen as a promise of the evangelization of the nations, and Jesus' declaration of the triumph of the church (Mt. 16:18). Other passages are cited (Mt. 13:31–35, 47f.; 24:14; Rom. 11:11–16; 1 Cor. 15:25), including references to Messiah's universal reign (Nu. 14:21; Pss. 2:8; 72; Is. 11:9; Zc. 9:10). It has to come to terms with the biblical testimony that the end of the age will be a time of intense persecution when the fortunes of the gospel appear to be at a low ebb (Mt. 24:6–14; Lk. 18:8; 2 Thes. 2:3–12; Rev. 13). It is also difficult to reconcile with Jesus' repeated warnings to be watchful in view of the unexpectedness of his return.

Premillennialism

This is the view that the return of Christ will take place *before* (*pre*) the millennial reign of Christ on earth. Christ's coming will be the decisive ending of human history under the curse of the fall; following his return the antichrist will be slain and the devil and all the forces of evil removed from the earth. After this there will be approximately one thousand years of peace and bliss on earth when Christ will rule his people, including many Jews converted by his return.

Though still present, evil will be largely restrained. Even nature will share in the blessedness of this era. Towards the end Satan will be freed and will gather his forces for a final conflict against the saints. He will be defeated by fire from heaven and then will come the general resurrection of the dead, the universal judgment and the inauguration of the eternal age in the new heaven and earth.

Biblical support for this view is drawn from passages which describe Messiah's kingdom in terms of an ideal earthly order (Is. 2:2–5; Mi. 4:1–3; Zc. 14:9, 16f.). It also appeals to references which present the coming age in material forms (Mt. 19:28; Acts 1:6f.) or allow a passage of time between Christ's return and the eternal age (1 Cor. 15:23–25; 1 Thes. 4:13ff.). The major support, however, is clearly Revelation 20.

The interpretation of Revelation 20, however, is not a straightforward matter. For example, who is involved in the millennial reign? Only the beheaded martyrs? The most natural reading of the Greek would support this position, though the claim that the martyrs represent the whole body of the saints cannot be ruled out entirely.

Another problem in referring the chapter to an earthly reign of Christ with his saints is whether this reign is exercised on earth at all. The whole book of Revelation dwells largely on realities 'behind the scenes', in the heavenly order (4:2; 11:19; 12:7ff.; *etc.*). Those who participate in the millennial reign are 'souls' (Rev. 20:4), a word which indicates a disembodied state. While these are not absolutely conclusive objections, it is very disturbing to find difficulties of this magnitude arising from the single passage on which the whole view is based.

Similar questions arise with the other premillennial 'prooftexts' (*e.g.* 1 Cor. 15:22–28; 1 Thes. 4:13ff.); the premillennial reading is not the most obvious sense of Paul's words. The fact that the events placed on either side of the millennium will in fact happen concurrently appears to be taught in other passages (*e.g.* Dn. 12:2; Mt. 13:37–43, 47–50; 24:29–31; 25:31–46; Acts 24:15; Rev. 20:11–15). The biggest problem with the position, however, is its requiring the continuation of sin and evil, indeed their final climactic manifestation, *after* Christ's return in glory. The thought of glorified saints returning to an earth where evil is still present is a similar difficulty.

On the other hand something like the premillennial scheme is the most obvious reading of the passage in Revelation 20. Further, the terms of the coming kingdom of God in the OT are at points frankly this-worldly (*cf.* Is. 11:1–10; 35:1–10; Mi. 4:1–3, *etc.*); and in Ezekiel 36–39 there is just possibly some witness to an eruption of evil *after* the restoration and establishment of God's eternal kingdom, though the claim to a temporal sequence here is very tenuous. Part of the antipathy to premillennialism, both in the early church and today, arises from its identification with extremist tendencies which have used the millennial idea to develop patently unbiblical viewpoints, in ethics and politics. The abuse of a position, however, must not become the reason for its rejection. Here, as always, the determinative issue must be, what does Scripture really teach?

Amillennialism

This view holds that the millennium is symbolic and that there is no millennium in the *literal* sense (Gk. *a*, without). This position seeks to follow the principle of interpretation which lets the obscure and symbolic be interpreted by the clear and didactic. Thus, since the consensus of NT teaching appears to view the second advent as one single, many-sided, act of God, amillennialism rejects the notion of one thousand intervening years when Christ will reign visibly upon earth. The reference in Revelation 20 is taken as a symbol of the rule of Christ, stressing its perfection and completeness.

Many amillennialists view the 'binding' of Satan as his being bound by Christ through his whole redeeming work (Mt. 12:29). The thousand-year reign is exercised not on earth, but in heaven with Christ, and refers to the gospel age between the two comings of Christ; Satan's power is limited through the work of Christ, who reigns in the heavenly realms. Others do not feel compelled to spell out a detailed interpretation of the passage. They see it as asserting symbolically, without chronological implications, Christ's lordship over evil; even the ·martyrs, helpless and defeated, do in fact conquer with him, as will be disclosed at the end of the age when Christ appears in glory.

The danger of this view is that it can readily lose *any* concern about the final events, and can lead also to over-spiritualization. God's kingdom becomes so heavenly and transcendent that it fails to impinge on present realities and ceases to be a word of grace and judgment amidst the concrete realities of the present world. Further, it has to face exegetical questions. Can Revelation 20 be interpreted satisfactorily in this symbolic manner? Are the promises to Israel essentially fulfilled by the restoration under Ezra and Nehemiah? What is the element of continuity in the biblical vision of the kingdom and its relationship to the present world order?

Christian hope is not exclusively spiritual. The biblical prospect is of a new heaven and *a new earth*. If we consider that exegetical and theological considerations rule out any thought of a thousand-year reign of Christ bracketed by two comings and two resurrections, we dare not jettison the 'spirit' of that vision: the total vindication of the Creator in the final revelation of the Redeemer. All God's original purposes for his creation must find fulfilment. It is significant that support for these respective versions of the Christian hope has varied according to the apparent advance or retreat of the Christian enterprise. While the state of the church's health ought never to be the determinative factor, it is an inescapable fact that this has regularly influenced the appeal of optimistic or pessimistic interpretations.

Further, in practice all three millennial positions have been, and continue to be, both a stimulus to the church's faith and endeavour *and* a hindrance to it. This last ought to help us keep these issues in their proper perspective. The centre of the Christian hope is Christ himself and his glorious appearing. Division of opinion on the millennium ought *never* to be permitted to divide those united in their expectation of, and love for, the Lord Jesus Christ.

Scriptures

Christ's return: Gn. 3:15; 2 Sa. 7:16; Ps. 2; Is. 2:1–5; 11:1–10; 53:10–12; 66:15–23; Mal. 4:1f.; Mt. 24–25; Lk. 21; Jn. 5:28f.; 14:3; Acts 1:7, 11; 2:17; 3:20; 17:31; Rom. 8:18–23; 1 Cor. 15:22–57; Phil. 3:20f.; 1 Thes. 4:13–5:11; 2 Thes. 1:7ff.; 2:3f., 7–12; Heb. 9:28; Jas. 5:7; 2 Pet. 3:8–13; 1 Jn. 3:2f.; Rev. 1:7; 22:8–21.

The antichrist: Dn. 7:20f.; 2 Thes. 2:1–11; 1 Jn. 2:18–22; 4:3; 2 Jn. 7; Rev. 13.

Israel: Dt. 30:1–10; Ezr. 6:16–22; Ne. 1:4–11; Je. 30:24–31:6; Ezk. 36:17–28; Am. 9:14f.; Zc. 8:1–8; Mt. 19:28; Lk. 21:24; Jn. 4:22; Rom. 4; 9:6–13; 11:17–26; Gal. 6:16; Eph. 2:14–22; 3:6.

The millennium: Rev. 20:2–10.

Questions

1. List the major passages in both OT and NT which refer to the return of Christ. Why is it mistaken to expect a detailed description of it? What will be its main general features?
2. How would you answer claims that biblical references to Christ's return concern (a) his first coming only, (b) his coming spiritually to people now through the preaching of the gospel?
3. What does Scripture teach about the time of Christ's return? What does this imply for our lives now?
4. What does the Bible teach about the role of (a) the antichrist, (b) Israel, in

relation to the end?
5. Which view of the millennium do you find most consistent with biblical teaching? What are its implications for (a) the life of the church, (b) your personal discipleship, (c) evangelism, (d) Christian concern for social issues?

Bibliography

Arts. 'Eschatology' in *IBD* and *NDT*.
G. C. Berkouwer, *The Return of Christ* (Eerdmans, 1972).
W. Hendriksen, *Israel in Prophecy* (Baker, 1968).
W. Hendriksen, *More than Conquerors* (Baker, 1981).
A. A. Hoekema, *The Bible and the Future* (Paternoster, 1978).
R. Kyle, *Awaiting the Millennium* (IVP, 1998).
G. E. Ladd, *The Blessed Hope* (Eerdmans, 1956).
G. E. Ladd, *Crucial Questions about the Kingdom of God* (Eerdmans, 1977).
B. Milne, *What the Bible Says about the End of the World* (Kingsway, 1979).
S. Motyer, *Israel in the Plan of God* (IVP, 1989).
S. Travis, *End of Story?* (IVP, 1997).

29. The final state

There remains a further group of truths, mostly concerned with the future of the individual.

DEATH

We are 'destined to die once' (Heb. 9:27). There can be few biblical statements less open to challenge. Throughout our lives, each of us is a 'being unto death' (Heidegger).

Sin and death

The Bible consistently links death to sin (Gn. 2:17; Ps. 90:7–11; Rom. 5:12; 6:23; 1 Cor. 15:21; Jas. 1:15). Death is not natural to humans but has arisen because of our rebellion against God; it is a form of God's judgment. For the Bible, however, while death may be inevitable, it is not terminal since we are by nature immortal beings (Heb. 9:27).

Resurrection or immortality?

The biblical conception of the believer's life beyond death is commonly expressed in the phrase 'the resurrection of the body' (1 Cor. 15:35–58), which reflects the Bible's witness to the essential unity of the human person (see Part 3). This contrasts with 'the immortality of the soul', the future state from the perspective of Platonic philosophy. The Christian is to anticipate life with a new resurrection body with which God is going to clothe his people at Christ's appearing (1 Cor. 15:42–44).

The Christian hope

Faith in Christ involves our sharing in his death and resurrection; the events of the first Easter become events in *our* lives too (Gal. 2:20; Col. 3:1). The Christian therefore has already passed through the valley of death with Christ and emerged to new, eternal life.

If the second coming is delayed, the believer will of course face 'death' in the sense that he will pass from immediate space-time existence. Although it is still an enemy (Rom. 8:34, 38; 1 Cor. 15:26), it is not death in the full and terrible sense in which Scripture frequently refers to it, death as the judgment of sin (Lk. 12:4f.; Heb. 2:14f.; 9:27). The Christian already shares in eternal life in union with Christ and moves forward irresistibly to the new heavens and earth. The biblical teaching, however, raises the question of how we understand the condition of believers in the 'intermediate state' between physical death and the Lord's return.

THE INTERMEDIATE STATE

The Bible's teaching
Abnormal
There is more than a hint in the OT that life beyond the grave is less substantial than that experienced by us here and now (*cf.* Jb. 7:9f.; 10:20f.; Pss. 6:5; 30:9). In that sense it is not the 'norm' as far as God's purpose for us is concerned.

Non-temporal?
One way out of the difficulty created by the thought of a disembodied existence is to argue that passing out of this life means passing out of the whole time order. Thus from the perspective of the experience of those who die, their next conscious moment is the Lord's coming and the resurrection. It is obviously unwise to dogmatize concerning what the experience of time could mean beyond death. There certainly appears an incongruity in seeing it as virtually identical with what we have known here. On the

other hand, such biblical testimony as we have points away from this solution (Lk. 9:30f.; 20:37f.; 23:43; Acts 7:55f.).

'Sleeping'

A biblical term for the state of the dead is 'sleep'. It is not difficult to see how the term could come to be used, since death certainly implies some of the characteristics of sleep; rest from labour, easing of responsibility, abstraction from immediate involvement in events, a different kind of awareness (Acts 7:60; 1 Cor. 15:51; 1 Thes. 4:14). However, it is worth noting that sleep could be a fairly significant occupation (Gn. 28:10–17; 41; Dn. 2; Mt. 1:20f.; 2:13).

Some go beyond this to argue that in Scripture this term implies that death induces a cessation of all consciousness until the Lord's return and resurrection. This, however, is difficult to reconcile with Scriptures referring to a conscious existence during the intervening period (Lk. 16:22ff.; 2 Cor. 5:8; Phil. 1:23). 'To depart and be with Christ' (Phil. 1:23) appears particularly to the point here, as do Jesus' reference to the faithful dead as 'living' to God (Lk. 20:37f.) and Revelation's numerous scenes of departed believers worshipping the Father and the Lamb.

'With Christ'

This is the most important description (Lk. 23:43). To be 'away from the body' (2 Cor. 5:8) is to be 'at home with the Lord'. To die is to depart to be 'with Christ', which is 'far better' (Phil. 1:23).

'Waiting'

For all that it is 'far better', it is not the full reality. How time is experienced by the dead, we cannot know. Scripture, however, depicts the martyrs beneath the altar of God as also awaiting the Lord's appearing and the new age: 'How long, Sovereign Lord?' they cry (Rev. 6:9f.). The tension which the church experiences, caught between the two ages, exists also in some way for the dead.

Other theories
'Purgatory'

The Roman Catholic idea of purgatory claims that, in the period between death and the fullness of the new age, the souls of believers are subjected to an experience of purification to fit them for the final vision of God.

There is no clear biblical evidence for such an idea. 1 Corinthians 3:15, which is often cited in this connection, concerns the judgment of a Christian's service and ministry. Other passages mentioned as supporting the notion of purgatory (Is. 4:4; Mal. 3:2f.; Mt. 12:32; 18:34) certainly do not teach such a view on any straightforward interpretation. Purgatory is also to be rejected because it is fundamentally at variance with the biblical doctrine of justification (*cf.* Part 4). To die in faith, even when that faith is exercised in one's final conscious moments (Lk. 23:43; Rom. 5:1; 8:1, 33f.), is to die justified, clothed in the perfect righteousness of Christ and assured of full acquittal at God's judgment seat.

A second chance

The idea of a 'second chance' to respond to the gospel during the intermediate state is often incorporated in some statements of universalism (see below). There is no biblical foundation for this view. We are 'destined to die once, and after that to face judgment' (Heb. 9:27). That is as unambiguous as Jesus' account of the rich man and Lazarus (Lk. 16:19–31).

THE RESURRECTION

According to the NT a major accompaniment of the Lord's return will be the resurrection of the dead. All who have lived upon earth will share in this mighty act of renewal.

It is sometimes alleged that the OT has no resurrection hope. Such a claim is unfounded, as Jesus showed (Mt. 22:29–32). While clarity of conviction about resurrection develops and deepens through the whole OT period, there is no mistaking its presence (Jb. 19:25–27; Pss. 49:15; 73:24ff.; Pr. 23:14; Is. 26:19; Ezk. 37:1–14; Dn. 12:2). The resurrection of the dead is taught explicitly in the NT (Mt. 22:29–32; Jn. 5:23–29; 6:39, 40, 44f.; 1 Cor. 15). It is the true completion of redemption (Rom. 8:23).

What will it be like? We can make two general points about it.

First, it will be different from our present experience. Life in the new heavens and earth will be free from the limitations brought about by the fall and sin. We shall be changed; flesh and blood as we know them here 'cannot inherit the kingdom of God' (1 Cor. 15:50f.). Taking Jesus' resurrection body as a model, we meet new and strange properties (Lk. 24:31, 36ff.; Jn. 20:19–29). It will be different as the rich stalk and ear of grain is different from the bare, gnarled little seed from which it grows (1 Cor. 15:35–38).

Second, the resurrection will retain some continuity with our present existence. Some have expressed uncertainty about this teaching, owing to the sheer magnitude of what is implied in face of physical dissolution and decomposition. We do well therefore to ponder the words of Jesus to sceptical hearts in his own day, 'You are wrong, because you know neither the Scriptures nor the power of God' (Mt. 22:29). If we recall that all that now exists in the universe was brought into being out of nothing by God's power, we are delivered from concern about the 'difficulty' of the resurrection for an omnipotent God.

JUDGMENT

In the OT God often appears as the Judge (Gn. 18:25; Dt. 1:17; Pss. 50:4; 75:7) taking vigorous action against evil. His mercy and wrath work themselves out in human history (Dt. 10:18; 28:15ff.; Ho. 1:10). As the OT draws to its close, the judgment of God becomes identified with the coming 'day of the LORD' which will accompany the manifesting of his kingdom (Am. 5:18ff.; Mal. 4).

The NT also sees God's judgment as intrinsic to his nature (1 Pet. 1:17). It is already at work in human life (Rom. 1:18–28) and is particularly associated with Christ, who exercises the Father's judgments (Jn. 5:30). The emphasis falls on the 'judgment to come', which will accompany the return of Christ (Mt. 25:31–46). All people will be judged (2 Tim. 4:1), including Christians (1 Cor. 3:12–15; 2 Cor. 5:10).

The basis of judgment will be a person's response to the revealed will of God. Account will be taken of different degrees of knowledge of God's will, and hence the ability to fulfil it (Mt. 11:21–24; Rom. 2:12–16). The judgment will be utterly just and completely convincing (Rom. 3:19). In the face of the frequent injustices of life in the present age, we can rest in the certainty that God knows all, that he is not mocked and that he has appointed a day in which he will judge the world in righteousness (Acts 17:31).

Properly understood, therefore, God's judgment is good news as well as bad. The negative certainly arises for those who have committed evil and refused to repent. But there is a glorious positive here as well, for God's judgment means nothing less than the establishing of his just and joyous reign, the putting right of all that has gone wrong, and the liberation of all things from the usurping reign of evil. It is this perspective that enables the psalmist to celebrate God's judgments: 'Let the heavens rejoice, let the earth be glad ... let the fields be jubilant ... the trees ... will sing for joy ... before the LORD, for he comes ... to judge the earth ... and the peoples in his truth' (Ps. 96:11–13). And at the personal level for all the crushed and oppressed, the abused and exploited, the cheated and the victimized, God's coming judgments mean nothing less than a glorious vindication and undreamed-of recompense, wholeness and peace (Gal. 6:7–9; Rom. 12:17–19; Rev. 21:1–4).

Faith or works?

While Scripture clearly relates our justification before God to our faith in Christ alone apart from our good works (Rom. 3:28), judgment is declared to be on the basis of human works (Rom. 2:6). The discrepancy is more apparent than real.

To be justified means to be discharged at God's judgment seat; Christ's perfect obedience in life and death is credited to Christians here and now, to stand to their account on the judgment day (Rom. 5:1). In other words, Christ's 'good works' are made over to our account. The biblical references which link judgment to our human 'works' do not call this fundamental truth into question.

The parable of the sheep and the goats (Mt. 25:31–46) is often cited in this connection. Some argue on the basis of this parable that people who may explicitly deny Christ will, because of their 'good works' (such as helping the needy, feeding the hungry, even fighting wars of liberation) be acquitted at the judgment because in these 'good works' they unwittingly ministered to Christ himself. This interpretation sets a single passage directly against the rest of Jesus' teaching and the Scriptures as a whole. It is perfectly possible to interpret this passage in harmony with other aspects of Jesus' teaching. The 'good works' which the 'righteous' perform are done to his 'brothers' (v. 40). They are acts of mercy towards the disciples of Jesus, a sign of living faith: 'We know that we have passed from death to life, because we love our brothers' (1 Jn. 3:14–17, *cf.* Mt. 10:42). (See also 'Judgment for Christians' below.)

Unbelief and judgment

It is sometimes urged that the only basis upon which a person may be exposed to the final condemnation of God is explicit rejection of the gospel of Christ. Various Scriptures (*e.g.* Jn. 3:18, 36; Rom. 10:9–12; Eph. 4:18) are claimed to represent unbelief as the ground of condemnation. In reply we note:

1. These passages prove only that faith in Christ is the one way of salvation. That is not the same as proving that conscious rejection of Christ is the only *ground* of condemnation.

2. The Bible represents people as already under condemnation before the gospel is preached to them. It is precisely this prior condemnation to which the gospel is God's gracious answer (Rom. 1:16–18).

3. If deliberate rejection of the gospel causes condemnation, and if (as statistics show) a majority of those who hear the gospel do not accept it, then on purely utilitarian grounds we should not preach the gospel at all. This ludicrous conclusion shows how mistaken is the original premise.

People who have not heard

The germ of truth in the position discussed above is that increased knowledge and increased opportunities imply increased responsibility. Scripture certainly recognizes that people do not enjoy equal opportunity to know God. This factor will be taken into account when God exercises his judgment (Mt. 11:20–24; Rom. 2:1–24; 2 Pet. 2:21). The principle 'from everyone who has been given much, much will be demanded' (Lk. 12:48) applies at this point. Those who have never heard the gospel will indeed be judged by the light they have. God, however, has not left himself without a witness (Acts 14:17). He has made himself known to all people through the world he has made (Rom. 1:19–32) and, more particularly, through his moral law, of which all have some awareness through conscience (Rom. 2:14–16).

Hence, we must conclude with the Bible that all have turned away from the light of God, whatever form that light assumed in their particular case. 'All have sinned' and come under condemnation (Rom. 3:9–23). Only in Jesus Christ is there hope of salvation (Jn. 14:6; Acts 4:12).

Judgment for Christians

Christians also will face a judgment (2 Cor. 5:10). This cannot imperil the Christian's eternal salvation, for 'there is now no condemnation for those who are in Christ Jesus' (Rom. 8:1). If we believe in the Lord Jesus, God's final verdict has already been pronounced on the basis of Christ's perfect righteousness credited to us. Our judgment will be in respect of our stewardship of the gifts, talents, opportunities and responsibilities given in this life. It will be a fatherly judgment (1 Pet. 1:17), having all of a father's understanding and compassion; yet it is clearly not to be disregarded or treated carelessly. This fatherly judgment will be exercised by the Lord at his coming.

Two important NT passages speak of believers receiving rewards in the afterlife. In 1 Corinthians 3:10–15 the value of a Christian's service is likened to the relative durability of various building materials. There will be some kind of assessment made at 'the Day' (v. 13), when the service of each will be tested 'by fire'. If our work survives this test we 'will receive a reward' (v. 14). We are not told what the reward will consist of, but we may fairly infer that the value will be relative to the durability of the work we have done.

Luke 19:11–26 must be interpreted with care, since parables in general are presented to make one central point and we must not press the secondary details. In this case the servants' work is brought under scrutiny and those whose work is attested receive relative rewards. The distinctions in the rewards are different degrees of responsibility after the king has returned.

Thus our stewardship of talents, gifts, opportunities, ministry, witness, service and the like will be subject to some kind of assessment before the Lord at his coming. In so far as we have proved 'good and faithful' servants, we will receive an appropriate 'reward' in terms of the satisfaction of seeing our work preserved for the eternal kingdom, and perhaps also in terms of additional degrees of responsibility in the heavenly age. The basis of all this, however, remains God's grace. Calvin expresses it aptly when he observes that the 'rewards' are not a matter of 'servant's wages', but 'son's inheritance'.

HELL

The Bible teaches clearly that there will be a division at the final judgment between those who are acquitted and those who are condemned (Dn. 12:2; Mt. 13:39–43; Jn. 5:28f.). The common biblical word for the destination of those who pass under God's judgment is hell. The terrible idea of eternal punishment is reflected clearly in a number of texts (Mt. 5:29f.; Mk. 9:43; Rev. 14:11). The Bible's teaching here is quite unambiguous and of awesome seriousness. Those who remain unrepentant when confronted by God's claim on them, who reject his will when it is made known to them, and who continue through their lives in the blasphemy and rebellion which sin implies, will face God's just wrath.

No doubt some of the language used to describe hell is necessarily symbolic, as is the language describing heaven. However, the fact that we are thrown back on symbols does not mean we can disregard or devalue them. They are God-given, and while they cannot tell us everything, they will not mislead us. There can be no evading the Bible's witness at this point. Hell is a reality of unspeakable solemnity (Jn. 3:18–20, 36).

We need, of course, a proper reserve in speaking of hell. Even here we must be guided by Jesus and the Bible. Jesus at times saw the need to speak with great starkness concerning the coming judgment (Mk. 9:43–49; Lk. 12:4f.). If we call him Lord of our lives, he must be Lord also of our understanding of the gospel and the way we expound it (Jn. 13:13). It simply will not do to claim loyalty to Jesus and yet set aside a very significant element of his teaching.

We need to beware, however, of attempting to take the final judgment into our own hands by apportioning people to hell or heaven. There is more than a hint in the Bible that there will be surprises on Judgment Day (Mt. 7:21–23; 25:37–46). On that day the mercy of God will reach as far as divine mercy can reach. If we are truly trusting in Christ, we need have no fear for ourselves. For the rest, we must leave matters in the hands of God and press on with the task of spreading throughout the world the one hope of sinners, the gospel of Christ.

Universalism

This view holds that in the end all people will be saved. God's mercy and the merit of Christ's sacrifice are so great that, it is urged, all will eventually be forgiven and enter the new heaven and earth. Biblical passages are cited to support this (*e.g.* Rom. 5:18; 2 Cor. 5:19; Eph. 1:10; 1 Tim. 2:4; 4:10). Universalism is widespread today.

As far as biblical teaching is concerned it simply will not do. It is abundantly clear that the distinction between Christian and non-Christian is radical in this life, and will continue so after death (Jn. 3:36). None of the universalists' 'proof texts' supports their case when closely examined. Four factors need to be kept in view.

First, when Scripture speaks of 'all' acknowledging Christ as Lord at the end, that does not mean they will do so willingly. No doctrine of universalism can be built on the fact that Christ is destined to be revealed as Lord over all at his coming.

Secondly, the gospel was preached in the first century against a background of groups who confined salvation to their particular racial group (the Jews), or their monastic communities (the Essenes), or to those who were initiated into their peculiar rites (the pagan mystery religions). Against these exclusive groups, the Christian gospel stands out in its universal *appeal*. 'Whoever will may come' (*cf.* Rev. 22:17).

Thirdly, it is perfectly clear that Paul, from whose letters almost all these texts are culled, was not a universalist (1 Cor. 1:18–24; Eph. 5:4–6; Phil. 1:28).

Fourthly, Jesus' teaching is most difficult to interpret in universalist terms. Indeed both his parables (Mt. 12:37–50; 22:11–14; 25:40–46) and his direct assertions provide more warnings about the reality of the final ruin of the impenitent than any other section of Scripture.

We take sin too lightly and are quick to find mitigating circumstances to excuse it. God, however, cannot. It resists his lordship in the universe, contradicts his loving purposes and strikes at his glory. Just how seriously he views sin can be seen in the terrors of Calvary.

It is sometimes argued that God's taking sin so seriously in the cross is not incompatible with universalism, for in dying Christ bore the condemnation due to all humanity. But this form of universalism faces the very difficulty referred to above; it is impossible to square its conclusion with the many clear biblical references to those who will be exposed to God's future judgments despite the cross. It also denies the essential link between salvation and personal faith (Jn. 3:36; Acts 16:30f.; Rom. 1:17; 5:1, 10:9f.).

This critique does not imply any obscuring of the ultimate, cosmic triumph of God's purpose, nor of the fullness and perfection of Christ's redemptive work. At the end *every* knee will bow (Phil. 2:10) and God will be 'all in all' (1 Cor. 15:28). Within that perfection will lie the doom of those who will bow the knee only by constraint, not in joyful, adoring surrender.

Conditional immortality

This view teaches that the unjustified will simply pass into oblivion, either at death or at Jesus' judgment seat. It argues that all people were created mortal; immortality is a gift of God in Christ to all those who believe in him. By their rejection of the gospel unbelievers forfeit the gift of immortality.

Annihilationism is a closely allied view, differing from conditional immortality in that while the latter teaches that immortality is a gift imparted to believers at the time of their regeneration, and hence not received by the impenitent, the former holds that all people were created immortal but that those who continue to sin are deprived of their immortality and hence pass into oblivion at death.

Historically, these positions have been regularly disavowed by conservative biblical teachers, finding primary support in sources such as Socinianism in the late sixteenth century and among Seventh-day Adventists and Jehovah's Witnesses in the modern period. Today, conditional immortality is viewed by some as a viable biblical understanding of the future state of the impenitent.

It has to be conceded, however, that the biblical texts in question are not easy to interpret in a way that supports this view. Jesus' recorded teaching in several places appears quite explicit as to the 'eternal' duration of the pains of the impenitent (*cf.* Mt. 25:41, 46; 18:9; *cf.* Mk. 9:44, 48 quoting Is. 66:24). Paul appears to hold the identical view in 2 Thessalonians 1:7–9, and Jude 7, 13 appears to teach similarly, as does the admittedly highly graphic language of Revelation 14:9–11 and 20:10. The thought that 'eternal' might carry only its literal sense of 'pertaining to the age to come' (*i.e.* the kingdom of God) without any overtones as to duration comes to difficulty on the fact that 'the age to come', as Jesus and the Jews conceived it, *was* to be unending, as well as the fact that it is the same term which is used for the duration of the bliss of the redeemed.

Proponents of the conditionalist view appeal to the thought that other terms referring to the fate of the impenitent, such as 'destruction', 'ruin' or 'perishing', can imply some eventual termination of life (Mt. 7:13; 10:28; Jn. 3:16; 10:28; Rom. 2:12; 1 Cor. 1:18; 15:18; 2 Cor. 2:15; 4:3; 1 Thes. 5:3; 2 Thes. 1:9; 2:10; 2 Pet. 3:9). *Cf.* also references to the 'second death' (Rev. 20:14–15; 21:8). It is also argued that the continuing anguish of the wicked is incompatible with God's nature as love and with his final triumph in eternity, as well as being (in anticipation) difficult from the perspective of the bliss to be enjoyed by the redeemed. These considerations, however, appear somewhat speculative.

There can be no question that the thought of *eternal* judgment is an awesome and overwhelming one, but in all of this we must not forget that we see 'but a poor reflection' (1 Cor. 13:12). What we have are God-given words and images to which we are to hold tenaciously and in the light of which we are to live, believing that he who gave them to us cannot lie. In submitting to his Word lies our own and others' peace.

THE LIFE TO COME

The ultimate goal of the people of God and the reality towards which all God's purposes are moving is called 'a new heaven and a new earth' (Is. 65:17; 66:22; 2 Pet. 3:13). While a 'poor reflection' (1 Cor. 13:12) is all that we can now, in principle, attain, we can venture certain assertions about the destiny of the people of God.

An embodied life

The 'new earth' will obviously be different from this world which 'in its present form is passing away' (1 Cor. 7:31). Indeed, 'heaven and earth', as we have known them, 'will pass away' according to Jesus (Mt. 24:35). Nevertheless, the fact that the present creation waits with us in hope of sharing in the coming glorious liberty of God's children (Rom. 8:19–25) implies some degree of continuity between the old earth and the new. Similarly, although we ourselves must eventually go down into the dust of death, our flesh will also rest in hope (Jb. 19:26). We shall rise from the dust of death in the new immortal resurrection bodies which God shall give us (1 Cor. 15:35–37). We therefore anticipate a life in which our self-conscious, embodied existence will continue, though obviously at a new level and with many new and enhanced powers.

A social life

All the Bible's pictures of the life of the heavenly world are corporate. It is seen as a perfect city (Heb. 13:14), as a victorious kingdom (Heb. 12:28), as a holy temple (Ezk. 40–48) and as a wedding feast (Rev. 19:7). The life to come is therefore wrongly conceived when it is presented as a personal, lonely pilgrimage to some exalted vision of God. It is rather the fulfilment of all God's purposes for his creatures, not least in mutual relationships. The new heaven and earth will hold out undreamed possibilities at the level of our social relationships. If so many of life's 'solid joys and lasting pleasures' here and now are mediated to us through our human partners and neighbours, how much more will that be so in the society of glory.

A responsible life

The biblical basis of this assertion is less clear, but one or two verses suggest that the life to come will involve remarkable new responsibilities. 'His servants will serve him' (Rev. 22:3). The parable in Luke 19:11–26 certainly conveys the thought of responsibility in this life being carried over into the new age, and Paul speaks of saints destined to judge the world and the angelic hosts (1 Cor. 6:2f.).

A perfect life

In the new age humankind will attain to the fullness of life for which we were originally destined. We shall find a perfection of relationship with God, with our neighbour, with our environment and with ourselves. We shall perfectly glorify our Maker and find total self-fulfilment (Gn. 1:28; Ps. 8:4–6).

An endless life

The change in the conditions of existence with the coming of the new age can scarcely mean that the time sequence will remain unaltered. We cannot possibly grasp what time may mean in the heavenly world. What an 'eternal' existence may be like, we can have little conception of now; but we believe that in so referring to it, we do not misrepresent it, and for the remainder we can rest in the love and boundlessness of God.

A God-centred life

This is the supreme feature of the life to come. All else we may say about it is secondary to, and arises out of, this. The manifestation of the triune God himself, the sense of being as never before in his presence, will characterize the new life above and beyond everything else. Thus the Lord himself is the temple in the new Jerusalem (Rev. 21:22). Scripture refers to this as seeing God. 'They will see his face' (Rev. 22:4, *cf.* Mt. 5:8); 'we shall see him as he is' (1 Jn. 3:2).

To see and know God is the essence of the heavenly life, the fount and source of all its bliss: 'You will fill me with joy in your presence, with eternal pleasures at your right hand' (Ps. 16:11). We may be confident that the crowning wonder of our experience in the heavenly realm will be the endless exploration of that unutterable beauty, majesty, love, holiness, power, joy and grace which is God himself.

Scriptures
The future of the individual: Gn. 2:17; 3:19; Jb. 19:25–27; Pss. 49:15; 73:24ff.; Pr. 23:14; Is. 26:19; Mt. 22:29–32; Mk. 8:38; Lk. 12:4f., 33; 16:19–31; 23:43; Jn. 6:39f.; 17:24; Rom. 6:23; 8:28–39; 1 Cor. 15:51–55; 2 Cor. 5:8–10; Phil. 1:23; 2 Tim. 2:11; Heb. 2:14f.; 9:27; Rev. 5:13.
Judgment: Gn. 18:25; Is. 30:18; Dn. 12:1–3; Zp. 1:14ff.; Mal. 2:17–3:5; 4:1ff.; Mt. 3:7, 11f.; 5:29f.; 11:20–24; 13:37–43; 16:27; 22:13; Lk. 13:1–5; 19:12–27; Jn. 3:19, 36; Rom. 1:18–28; 3:5ff., 19; 8:1; 14:10–22; Eph. 2:3; 1 Thes. 1:10; Heb. 12:23; Jas. 3:6; 2 Pet. 2:4, 9; 1 Jn. 4:17; Rev. 6:16f.; 20:11–15.
The life to come: Pss. 16:8ff.; 23:6; Zc. 14:5; Mt. 5:8; 6:19–21; 22:1–14; 25:34; Lk. 14:16–24; 19:11–26; Acts 2:26; Rom. 8:19–25; 1 Cor. 6:2f.; Heb. 11:10; 13:14; 2 Pet. 3:13; 1 Jn. 3:2; Rev. 19:7; 21–22.

Questions
1. Why is the resurrection of the body to be preferred to the immortality of the soul to describe the Christian's future hope?
2. What is the basis of the Christian's hope in the face of death? What would you say to someone recently bereaved of someone he or she loved dearly?
3. What does the Bible teach about the 'intermediate state'? Why are the theories of (a) purgatory, (b) 'a second chance' to be rejected?
4. How can the importance of 'works' in the final judgment be reconciled with the Bible's teaching on salvation through faith alone?
5. What does Scripture teach about hell? Is it compatible with God's eternal love?
6. Does the Bible support universalism or conditional immortality/

annihilationism?
7. What does the Bible teach about rewards in heaven?
8. What are the principal features of the life to come? What differences should belief in it make to (a) daily discipleship, (b) family relationships, (c) church relationships, (d) evangelism, (e) attitudes to society?

Bibliography

Arts. 'Heaven', 'Hell', 'Judgment' in *IBD* and *NDT*.
R. Baxter, *The Saints' Everlasting Rest* (Epworth Press, 1961).
G. C. Berkouwer, *The Return of Christ* (Eerdmans, 1972).
P. Cotterell, *What the Bible Says about Death* (Kingsway, 1979).
B. Milne, *What the Bible says about the End of the World* (Kingsway, 1979).
L. Morris, *The Biblical Doctrine of Judgment* (Tyndale Press, 1960).
J. A. Motyer, *After Death* (Hodder, 1965).
J. O. Sanders, *What of the Unevangelized?* (OMF, 1966).
S. Travis, *Christian Hope and the Future of Man* (IVP, 1980).
S. Travis, *End of Story?* (IVP, 1997).

30. The last things in Christian thought

THE EARLY CENTURIES

In the post-apostolic period the significance of eschatology was maintained to some extent by the regular persecution of Christians. As the centuries passed and the church became established, interest in the last things inevitably diminished. In general, the theological energies of the church in the first five centuries were directed elsewhere. There is evidence that much early thought was millenarian (chiliastic), expecting an earthly reign of Christ.

THE MIDDLE AGES

In the medieval period, the gradual change of focus from the future to the present found its ultimate development in the Catholic church, 'the city of God', which was identified with the kingdom of God. Much was made of the church's control over the eternal world and human destiny. The church claimed to dispense the 'treasury of merit', a kind of 'capital account' of spiritual merit which the saints of the church had built up by their righteous deeds. The notion of purgatory was a most significant development in this period and by the sixteenth century had led to a crass materialization and commercialization of the whole realm of future destiny. This probably more than anything else provoked Luther and the Protestant Reformation. The Middle Ages also witnessed periodic outcrops of millenarian speculation.

THE REFORMATION

The concern of the Reformation centred primarily on the meaning of salvation and how it may be appropriated. Eschatological concerns were therefore subsidiary. The last things were treated mainly as the final future step in individual and corporate salvation. During the Reformation certain groups among the anabaptists revived the millenarian eschatology.

THE NINETEENTH CENTURY

Rationalistic critique of biblical doctrine, superficial views of sin encouraged by the Enlightenment humanist tradition, reaction against over-zealous attempts to drive people into the kingdom of God by dwelling on the terrors of hell, and the complex problem of responsibility awakened by discussions of heredity and the unconscious mind, all combined to lower theological interest in eschatology during this period. Jesus was simply the supreme exemplar of the race, the great embodiment of humankind's moral destiny.

Among evangelicals, however, there was a great resurgence of interest in the last things. Millennial views were championed and the hope of the Lord's imminent return burned strongly. All this had considerable influence in promoting the great nineteenth-century missionary and evangelistic endeavours, as well as evangelical concern for social improvement.

TODAY

With the dawn of the twentieth century, the liberal Protestant picture of Jesus came under attack as it was shown that Jesus' teaching about the kingdom of God and his expectation of its arrival were not peripheral but belonged to the core of his thought and mission. This insight set the trend for subsequent theology. Today, eschatology has become dominant in a way which was utterly unthinkable in the nineteenth century.

There is a widespread consensus today that the kingdom proclaimed by Jesus has to be understood as *both* present *and* future: it *has come* and it is *still to come*. Diversity exists, however, as to the relative weight to give these two terms and how they relate to each other in the mind of Jesus, in the teaching of the early church, and for our experience today.

Among evangelical Christians, after a lull occasioned by the ending of the Cold War, there is a renewed stirring of expectation concerning Christ's imminent return, fuelled by the turn of the millennium. There is a continuing need, however, to avoid excessive literalism in handling biblical prophecy, for genuine charity in differing from others whose eschatological understanding does not accord with our own, and, perhaps supremely, for carrying the Bible's teaching concerning the last things to its moral implications in our present experience (see below).

Application

Our concern that Christian doctrines be ethically applied is nowhere more pertinent than in this final area. In contrast to the 'crystal-ball gazers' (both Christian and non-Christian), the Bible's teaching is always *moral*. It does not merely feed our curiosity, but summons us to commitment and obedience (Dt. 29:29). We can gather the implications of the Bible's teaching on the last things around eight words.

HOPE

The Lord's return is our 'blessed hope' (Tit. 2:13). This is highly relevant in view of the relative pessimism of our time. Although the period immediately surrounding the entry upon the new millennium is likely to be accompanied by expressions of visionary optimism and lavish celebrations of the achievements of our race over the past centuries, the reality to which the world will reawaken after the millennial party is over is that of a deeply uncertain future. The burgeoning population, limited resources, the appearance of new and deadly viruses, the relative accessibility of nuclear weaponry, and the serious and deepening ecological crisis all serve to undermine our long-term hope. It is surely salutary to note that today our wisest men and women are our most anxious.

In this age of comparative hopelessness, the Christian stands apart. Our hope does not arise, like the humanist's, from an idealistic view of human nature, or from the social scientist's belief in the alterability of human behaviour through the transformation of the social environment, or from the New Ager's belief in the emergence of a new universal consciousness. Rather, the Christian is a person of hope because of a belief in God, and in particular in a God who has created the world and brought forth human life within it for a purpose, which he will infallibly fulfill.

This world is not running amok destined for disaster. God is Lord of his world and he will not permit it to escape from his grasp. The Lord is coming. 'Blessed hope' indeed!

COMFORT

The Christian's convictions about the coming of the Lord have implications for our attitude to death (1 Thes. 4:13–18). We are not to 'grieve like the rest of men, who have no hope' (v. 13). Our destiny, whether we die before the Lord returns, or are among those alive on earth at the time of his coming, is to 'live together with him' (5:10). The truths of the last things are therefore a comfort to Christians in face of death and all it implies in the breaking of our dearest relationships.

HOLINESS

Three lines of argument lead from the fact of the last things to our moral character in the present.

First, the coming end of all things shows the essentially impermanent reality of this present world and the folly of living for this world as though it were the supreme reality (Heb. 11:13–16).

Secondly, the Christian and the church are destined for a holy and sinless eternity. We are called therefore to move in the direction of our destiny through daily repentance from sin and increasing conformity with the holy will of God (2 Pet. 3:13; 1 Jn. 3:2).

Thirdly, at his coming we must render account to him (2 Cor. 5:10). If we truly believe in and anticipate the Lord's coming we shall 'make every effort . . . to be holy' (Heb. 12:14).

ACTION

The notion that belief in the return of the Lord leads to irresponsibility and idleness gets no encouragement from the Bible (1 Thes. 5:14; 2 Thes. 3:6). The truths of the last things should lead to *activity*, not ease.

Spread the gospel

Some link evangelism and the coming of the Lord in terms of our duty to warn people and encourage them to turn to Christ to escape the coming judgment. Scripture, and Jesus in particular, does not altogether disavow sounding the warning note (Mt. 3:7–12; Lk. 13:1–5). However, the link is more clearly made at another point.

God's purpose in the period between the first and second comings of Christ is to take 'a people for himself' out of the world (Acts 15:14). Jesus links this purpose to the end of the age: 'this gospel of the kingdom will be preached throughout the whole world as a testimony to all nations, and then the end will come' (Mt. 24:14). Thus, God holds back the end until the gospel has been universally proclaimed and all his people are brought in. Therefore, while there can be no thought of our forcing God's hand, the coming of the Lord is bound up with the universal spread of the gospel. We ought therefore to be wholeheartedly committed to evangelism through the world and in every sector of society, in the conviction that evangelism, and the saving of men and women as a result of it, is one of those factors which God makes his instrument in bringing about his final triumph.

Build the church

One of the great NT pictures of the church is the bride of Christ (Eph. 5:21–23). At the Lord's return the church, comprising all the people of God from every age, will be presented to the Lord as a bride to her husband (Rev. 21:2). Accordingly, we should labour to build the church, to sanctify its life, to cleanse it from all that mars and spoils its testimony and its purity, so that when Christ comes it may be ready for him, 'blameless at the coming of our Lord' (1 Thes. 5:23).

Serve our neighbour

The truth of the last things also has important implications for our involvement in the problems of society. Scripture witnesses to a new world in which, even allowing for symbolic language, there will be a form of perfected human society. The great social values of peace, justice, equality, tolerance, understanding, sympathy, concern for the vulnerable and the weak, true love for the neighbour, the use of all the resources for the good of the whole, *etc.* will find their fulfilment and expression. Although this dream will not be realized before the Lord's coming, it is profoundly relevant in two ways.

First, it gives in general outline a blueprint for the form of human society which accords with the will of God and hence which accords with his honour. Every means therefore by which our present society is moved closer to that biblical ideal contributes to God's eternal glory and is thus of abiding value.

The coming perfect order is relevant in a second and allied sense: the Christian is never driven to final despair, even when faced with the appalling intensity and depth of the social and political problems which confront us. Every stand taken for social righteousness and every effort made towards social renewal is, despite appearances, aligned with the ultimate purpose and goal of history (Rev. 21:24).

PRAYER

If we believe in the Lord's coming and the end of the age, then we should pray for it. Jesus set a petition for the coming of the end right at the heart of his pattern prayer: 'Your kingdom come.' There are other examples in the NT (1 Cor. 16:22; Rom. 8:19; Rev. 22:20).

WATCHFULNESS

One of the clearest indications and implications of a belief in the last things is an attitude of watchfulness (Mt. 24:42; 25:13). People expecting the end will be sober and alert, not as absorbed in the affairs of this age as the people of Noah's day (Mt. 24:37–39). The Lord's coming will not take them by surprise. He may not come in our lifetime and we dare not claim that he must, but he certainly may and we are called to be ready.

LOVE

The coming of the Lord and the eternal kingdom means that the relationships which we share in the church are eternal. This is itself a major argument for love of our fellow Christians. If we are destined for this future glory in the unity of the one great, indestructible people of God, surely we can find it in our hearts to receive them now, and to love them as God pours out his spirit of love in our hearts (Rom. 5:5).

PRAISE

A final expression of our conviction concerning Christ's coming triumph is joyful praise and worship. It is significant in this respect that the heavenly host and the church triumphant are portrayed in Revelation as engaged in worship and praise in the light of the coming end (Rev. 5:12ff.; 7:10–12; 11:17f.; 15:3f.;. 19:1–5). 'To him who sits on the throne and to the Lamb be praise and honour and glory and power, for ever and ever!' (Rev. 5:13). To this every Christian heart can sound the 'Amen', anticipating the coming triumph of God.

Index